Yale Studies in Economics: 13

CENTRAL PLANNING

IN POLAND

by John Michael Montias

New Haven and London, Yale University Press

Copyright © 1962 by Yale University.
Second printing, December 1963.
Designed by John O. C. McCrillis.
Set in Baskerville type and
printed in the United States of America by
Murray Printing Company, Forge Village, Massachusetts.
All rights reserved. This book may not be
reproduced, in whole or in part, in any form
(except by reviewers for the public press),
without written permission from the publishers.
Library of Congress catalog card number: 62–8256

To My Wife

Marie Agnes Montias

Preface

This book, in keeping with the Polish fashion of long and exact titles, should have been called: "Theoretical and Practical Problems in the Application of Central Economic Planning to Peoples' Poland with Special Reference to Industry, 1945–1961." For there are many aspects of "Central Planning in Poland" that are hardly touched on in this study: the organization of agriculture, transportation, and construction, for example, receive only brief mention. (In the case of agriculture this neglect is in part justified by the modest role played by central controls in directing this sector.) The rationale for relegating the question of planning at the level of the enterprise to a modest part of one chapter is that I wished to focus on the centralized aspects of the formulation of the plans. This also explains the tangential discussion of planning at the regional and city level.

Some readers may also question my neglect of Marxist doctrine, especially in my theoretical introduction. But, in point of fact, I have tried conscientiously to render to Marx the little that belongs to Marx in the methodology of contemporary Polish planning. Such direct influence as he exercises in this sphere can be perceived mainly in the details of national-income analysis and in price formation. No less an authority than Oskar Lange has pointed out that the methods of centralized planning and management that usually prevail in the first period of planning under socialism (i.e. in Poland before 1956) "are not peculiar to socialism . . . they are rather techniques of war economy. The difficulties start when these methods of war economy are identified with the essence of socialism and considered as being essential to socialism." [1]

The main protagonist of this book is the Planning Commission in Warsaw. I have tried to discuss the problems its officials had to solve without more than a perfunctory examination of the goals they pursued. I was concerned mainly with the means they adopted for achieving the ends laid down by the Communist authorities—

1. O. Lange, "The Role of Planning in Socialist Economy," *Indian Economic Review* (August 1958), p. 3.

keeping in mind that some of the means, particularly the institutions set up in replica of Soviet models, were almost as sacred as the ends and could not be reformed without political consequences. Accordingly, I have ignored, except for a brief discussion of Polish views on the subject in Chapter Nine, the possibility or desirability of dismantling centralized controls and of imitating the operation of a market in a competitive economy, a version of socialism that was once advocated by Oskar Lange and Abba Lerner.

This praxiological approach to planning is familiar to specialists in Soviet-type economies, who are generally inclined to take "planners' preferences" as given. In my theoretical introduction, I have gone one step further and defined efficiency, not in the context of all the possible patterns of output open to the economy at a given time, but within the limits of the information made available to the Planning Commission. The principal question posed in Chapter One is whether the Commission can make efficient use of this information, however incomplete or, in the case of the production functions of producing plants, however inexact its information may be. This narrow definition is only relaxed in connection with the subsequent discussion of the price system and of the other decentralized incentives bearing on socialized enterprises and on the other organs subordinate to the Planning Commission.

How realistic are the models developed in Chapter One and how applicable are they to the other Soviet-type economies?

The first part of this question should not be judged solely in the light of such conceptions as the planners may themselves entertain of the way their planning scheme operates. Most businessmen in a capitalist economy would fail to recognize their own behavior in the rules for maximizing profits devised for them by theorists; yet they behave as if they adhered to these rules, or come close enough to doing so to allow useful predictive statements to be made about their reaction to changes in their economic environment (e.g. to changes in the prices of their inputs or in the demand for their product). The ultimate test of the model developed in Chapter One would be its predictive value. If, for example, an unexpected shortfall in the productive capacity of a sector or in the supply of foreign exchange became known to the planners, the model, if all the data in the possession of the planners were available, should enable us to predict their reaction to this shortfall—

the general direction and magnitude of the reallocation of resources which they would resolve upon as a consequence.

The problems faced by the planners in any situation where the output plans of producers are centrally coordinated and materials and other factors are rationed out to producers by a central coordinating agency seem to be of essentially the same character. If, however, institutional parallels are thought to be a better criterion for assessing the relevance of a model based on the Polish experience to other economies in the Soviet bloc, it may be in order to point out that the general framework of Polish planning during the Six-Year Plan was laid in 1949 by an economic committee of the Polish Council of Ministers which "based its work above all on Soviet models (*wzory*) and literature." [2] It is also known that Soviet experts helped to carry out the basic reforms which aligned Polish with Soviet economic institutions in 1949 and 1950. I cannot think of any essential difference between Polish and Soviet economic institutions between 1950 and 1955, at least outside the farm sector which, unlike in the U.S.S.R., was permitted to remain mainly in private hands in Poland. From 1956 on, the reforms aimed at administrative decentralization in the U.S.S.R. and in Poland led to certain divergencies. None of these divergencies, however, seem to have had a decisive effect on the nature of the coordinating problems faced by the central planning agencies in the two countries.

A few words on the organization of the book may now be in order. Chapter Two contains a summary survey of postwar economic development in Poland. Planning institutions and methods, the financial system, and price-setting policies are described in Chapters Three to Eight. These chapters concentrate on the period from 1949 to 1956, although evidence from later years has also been introduced wherever it seemed appropriate. The majority of recent developments—since the advent of Władysław Gomulka to power in October 1956—are dealt with in the last two chapters. This arrangement offered the opportunity of discussing recent

2. *Zarys rozwoju metodologii planowania w Polsce Ludowej 1944–1954* (Outline of the development of planning methodology in Peoples' Poland 1944–1954). The word *wzór* means model, form, design, etc. The planning forms (also called *wzory*) reproduced in Appendix C, were said to be "patterned after the latest Soviet forms"; see K. Krygier, ed., *System zaopatrzenia w gospodarce planowej* (The procurement system in the planned economy).

reforms in the framework of a planning system already familiar in its complexity. This seemed a good way of synthetizing the material contained in previous chapters.

Finally, I should like to acknowledge my debt to the friends and colleagues who helped me in the research and writing of this book.

Foremost I wish to thank the many Polish officials, particularly in the Planning Commission, who, ever since my first trip to Poland in 1956, have assisted me with information, ideas, and advice. Some of them were good enough to read parts of the manuscript for this book: I always appreciated their comments, though I could not always take them into account. The least I can say is that they helped me to clarify a number of misunderstandings.

Among the American economists who helped me, I wish to thank Alexander Erlich of Columbia University for his supervision and his valuable criticism of my Ph.D. dissertation, from which Chapters Seven and Eight of this book were culled (together with bits and pieces of Chapters Two, Three, and Six), and for his perceptive comments on an earlier draft of the book itself. I am beholden to Lloyd G. Reynolds for his continuous encouragement and support in this project. My thanks also to David Granick of Wisconsin University and to Henry Oliver of Indiana University who commented on the first chapter and to Raymond Powell, my colleague at Yale, for his penetrating critique of a preliminary version of Chapter Four and for many stimulating comments on a variety of topics discussed in the book.

I am very grateful to Michael C. Lovell and Edwin S. Mills, who helped me get over several hurdles in the mathematical appendices. In particular, Edwin Mills found the key relation which allowed me to prove the general theorem of Appendix B. Michael Lovell's criticisms steered me back on a number of occasions to the straight and narrow road of mathematical accuracy. I hope, nevertheless, that I may be allowed to claim undivided debit for any remaining errors.

I also profited from the comments of Tjalling C. Koopmans and Trout Rader on the first chapter and appendices and from discussions with a number of graduate students at Yale.

The California University Press kindly permitted me to reproduce several pages of my article "Producers' Prices in a Centrally Planned Economy: The Polish Discussion," in *Value and Plan,* ed. by G. Grossman (Berkeley, 1960). I also wish to thank *Problems of Communism* and *Soviet Survey* for allowing me to extract material from my recent articles in those publications. I am beholden to Marian Neal Ash and Elizabeth Hailey for careful editing and advice.

It is far from perfunctory for me to acknowledge the part played by my wife in bringing out this book. She typed, criticized, and corrected all the versions of the manuscript from yellow pages *cum* interwoven inserts to final form.

J. M. M.

August 1961
New Haven

Contents

Preface   vii

Chapter One.   Planning in Theory and Practice   1
    1. Introduction   1
    2. Short-Term Planning   6
    3. Long-Term Planning   33
    4. Prices in a Centralized Economy   39

Chapter Two.   The Political Background, Economic Growth, and Inflation   49
    1. Background   49
    2. The Six-Year Plan   56
    3. Hitches in the Six-Year Plan   63
    4. Inflation   68
    5. A Recapitulation   74

Chapter Three.   Current Planning I: The Distribution of Producer Goods   76
    1. Administration of the Economy   76
    2. Coordination of Current Plans   84
    3. Successive Approximations   91
    4. Resolution of Shortages   98
    5. Material-Technical Norms   102
    6. Execution of the Plans   104
    7. Vue d'Ensemble   112

Chapter Four.   Current Planning II: Employment, Wages, and Synthetic Balances   115
    1. Commands and Forecasts   115
    2. Manpower Balances and Wage Plans   119
    3. The Balance of the Population's Incomes and Outlays   122
    4. Formation and Distribution of the National Income   127
    5. The Financial Program   130
    6. Cost Planning and Problems of Financial Coordination   135

7. Short-Term Credits and the Cumulative Inflation   137
8. An Appraisal of Monetary and Fiscal Controls   140

Chapter Five.   Long-Term Planning and Investment Calculations   145
1. The Problem   145
2. The Early Postwar Years (1945–49)   146
3. Long-Term Planning   148
4. The Efficiency of Investments (1956–59) 160
5. Economic Calculations in Foreign Trade   165
6. A Synthesis   168

Chapter Six.   The Socialized Enterprise in the Centrally Planned Economy   172
1. Pressures and Propaganda   172
2. Bonuses Paid to the Management of Firms 174
3. The Place of Profits in Managerial Incentives   178
4. Profits, Working Capital, and Bank Credits 182
5. Conflicts of Incentives and Their Resolution   186
6. Conclusions: Prices and Management Decisions   187

Chapter Seven.   The Origins and Development of the Price System   190
1. Introduction   190
2. Current Prices: The Initial Period (1945–49)   191
3. Fixed Prices   199
4. Current Prices: The Six-Year Plan   202
5. Prices of Consumer Goods   205
6. Who Pays Which Prices?   210
7. Calculated Prices and Prices of Small-Scale Industry   212
8. Prices of Construction Works   215
9. Summary and Conclusions   218

Chapter Eight.   The Pricing of Producer Goods   220
1. General Lines of Policy   220
2. Who Sets Producers' Prices?   221

3. Price Reforms of the Six-Year Plan (1950–55)   222
4. The 1956 Reform   231
5. Theoretical Conclusions   250

Chapter Nine.   The Polish Model: 1956–60   263
1. The Thaw: March to September 1956   263
2. Theoretical Discussions of the Polish Model after October   272
3. Producers' Prices (October 1956–July 1960) 279
4. Administrative Decentralization: 1956–59   294
5. The Workers' Councils (October 1956 to 1960)   307

Chapter Ten.   Counterreforms   311
1. Economic Developments: 1956–60   311
2. Recentralization: 1959–60   320
3. Conclusions   324

Appendix A.   Planning by Successive Approximations: Consistency Problems   335

Appendix B.   The Efficiency Problem   349

                Forms for Material Balances   371

Bibliography   375

Index of Names Cited   393

Subject Index   396

Abbreviations

GG	*Gospodarka górnictwa* (Mining economy)
GM	*Gospodarka materiałowa* (Material economy)
GP	*Gospodarka planowa* (Planned economy)
HW	*Handel wewnętrzny* (Internal trade)
IB	*Inwestycje i budownictwo* (Investments and construction)
MP	*Monitor Polski* (Polish monitor)
ND	*Nowe drogi* (New paths)
PS	*Przegląd statystyczny* (Statistical survey)
PCh	*Przemysł chemiczny* (Chemical industry)
RPG	*Rocznik polityczny i gospodarczy 1958, 1960* (Political and and economic yearbook 1958, 1960)
RS	*Rocznik statystyczny 1947, 1948, 1949, 1956–60* (Statistical yearbook 1947, 1948, 1949, 1956–60)
TL	*Trybuna Ludu* (Peoples' tribune)
WNBP	*Wiadomości Narodowego Banku Polskiego* (News of the National Bank of Poland)
WS	*Wiadomości statystyczne* (Statistical news)
ZG	*Życie gospodarcze* (Economic life)

CHAPTER ONE

Planning in Theory and Practice

1. Introduction

The development of planning methods in Poland and in the other
Soviet-type economies of Eastern Europe may conveniently be
divided into three stages. In the first stage, which corresponds historically to the years of reconstruction after World War II, the
state expands its direct control of the economy by nationalizing
large-scale industrial and commercial enterprises. Even after the
state has taken over these "commanding heights," the private and
cooperative sectors are still well enough entrenched to hamper
comprehensive planning; market elements coexist with the centralized deployment of the resources under the direct command
of the state. To guide the economy as a whole, the authorities must
resort to financial planning and indirect controls. At this stage the
price system and economic calculation still have an important role
to play in the allocation of resources.

At the beginning of the second stage, the government legislates
crucial reforms aimed at recasting the economic system in the
Soviet mold. From then on, the basic institutions of the Popular
Democracy will be identical with their Soviet models. Comprehensive physical allocation of all essential materials, long-term plans
geared to perspective balances, budget grants to enterprises for
major investment outlays, and centralized price-fixing are characteristic features of the newly refurbished system. But market functions, though relegated to a modest place, are not totally abrogated
in the Soviet-type economies: wages and fringe benefits exercise a
decisive influence on the movement of workers, particularly of
unskilled grades; available supplies of consumer goods are sold in
state shops at, or in the neighborhood of, market-clearing prices,

with the exception of periods of great stress when administrative rationing temporarily prevails.

Planning methods in the second stage are colored by the enthusiasm and optimism of the Communist planners who have now replaced the old cadres, holdovers from the previous period when they were needed to run the technical operations of the system. The new planners, bent on removing what they are apt to call the "subjective" obstacles standing in the way of rapid industrial expansion, frame plans designed to "mobilize" workers, managers, and higher administrators toward the fulfillment of their tasks.[1] Well-balanced, efficient plans will be scrapped if they are not likely to coax out the maximum effort from the participants in the system. A rigorous priority system is applied to switch resources to essential uses: the brunt of planning errors falls on the low-priority sectors.

In the third stage, the planners, having exhausted the immediate tangible benefits of organizational improvements, or having come to recognize that many of these improvements were contingent on an extraordinarily liberal use of labor, face up to the resource scarcities constraining the development of the economy and concentrate on how to make the best use of the resources at hand to achieve the goals laid down by the political authorities. This is the stage where models of rational and systematic decision making come into their own.

The change in emphasis is so gradual that the stages, although generally consecutive in time, can hardly be marked off from each other. The Polish economy, which entered the second stage in 1948–49, has now reached the third stage; but it would be impossible to say whether the crisis precipitated by the New Course

---

1. Cf. the characteristic arguments used by Hilary Minc in 1948 to justify more ambitious plans (Chap. 2, p. 55). A recent editorial in *Red Flag*, the Chinese Communist newspaper, also illustrates a typical second-stage attitude. The editorial, "Persist in Placing Politics in Command, Strictly Carry Out Concrete Measures," stresses the ideological role played by the Party in boosting production. It points out that "the success and failure of production . . . are determined not only by material provisions but also, more importantly, by the workers and peasants who control and use these material provisions. . . . Under given material conditions, the development of production is determined by the ideological consciousness, morale and subjective efforts of men." (Monitored broadcast of *Red Flag* editorial, March 15, 1961.)

in 1953–54 [2] or the inauguration of the Gomulka regime in October 1956 opened this new era.

A wide assortment of factors may be invoked to account for the buoyant expectations of Communist leaders in the second stage and for their frequent disregard of the "objective limitations" blocking their way to progress:

1. With the exception of East Germany and Czechoslovakia, all the newly installed Communist regimes, at the beginning of their industrialization drives, disposed of a reservoir of underemployed agricultural population, which could be tapped to staff the construction sector and to increase output in industries formerly operated below maximum capacity. The benefits of this maximum employment policy can at first be quite impressive in overcoming bottlenecks.

2. The standardization of output and the deterioration in the quality of consumer supplies initially helped to produce great increases in output with relatively modest inputs.

3. The lack of statistics relating efforts to performance in the beginning stages of industrialization encourages a certain degree of self-deluding optimism. Since there is little or no previous experience by which to gauge how long it should take to build a plant or drive a mine shaft, it is natural to take as a norm the performance of countries more advanced technologically and to exert pressure from the top down to see that these norms are achieved. (They usually are not, but it may take some time to realize this.) The same applies to trends in labor productivity and in the consumption of materials per unit of output. Organizational changes in the administration of the economy, which usually occur more frequently in the early part of an industrialization program, tend to blow up indexes of gross output because of the usually observed trend toward vertical disintegration, which magnifies errors due to double counting. This again makes for rapid apparent gains at little cost.

4. In the early phases of a development program, the demand on the part of nonpriority sectors for factors of production—particularly for materials and investment funds—is easily compressible; it is possible to plan less accurately and to let the burden of

2. Chap. 2, pp. 65–66.

plan failures fall on the neglected sectors. Since cooperatives, workshops, small private industry, and plants under the control of local authorities work mainly for the consumer market, or are only one stage removed from this market, and since there is at this pass a "hunger for goods" which makes almost any item salable, these enterprises can absorb almost any rejects, remnants, and surpluses—left over after satisfying the demands of the priority industries—and turn them into marketable commodities. To a certain extent, even large-scale nationalized enterprises producing consumer goods or engaged in housing construction may be treated as second-priority buffers whenever important deficits in raw materials or other resources arise.

5. The planners of the newly installed Communist regimes inherit physical plant and equipment adapted to a totally different structure of demand from that which they now intend to impose on the economy. From their viewpoint the capacity of light industries, often working on imported materials, is overexpanded relative to that of the engineering branches of heavy industry. It is thus possible for some time to neglect the input needs (replacement of worn-out or obsolescent machinery, imported raw materials, and so forth) of these industries and dole out to them only such investment funds and foreign exchange as may remain after priority requirements have been met.

In the second stage, where nonpriority sectors tend to function as buffers, exact planning, if called for at all, will be essential only in the priority sectors of the economy. Inasmuch as the best engineers, the most politically faithful activists, the bosses most capable of getting out the goods will be shunted to these industries, precision planning may be discouraged even in these sectors.

Little by little these initial advantages are dissipated. Labor becomes scarcer as the surplus of agricultural labor gets skimmed off, and the lack of housing and other facilities in the new industrial centers begins to inhibit migration from the countryside. Inadequate supplies of consumer goods must be made good to avert labor unrest. Cooperative workshops, small artisans, and the remains of private industry, starved for materials and equipment, can no longer perform their function as stopgap suppliers for the consumer market (poorly or unevenly provided for by nationalized industry). Indexes of output become more reliable, as do norms of materials-consumption, estimates of construction costs, and forecasts of labor-productivity trends. Increases in output become more regular, also proportionately smaller, as they no longer hinge on the launching of one or two new plants whose output tends to swamp the rest.

As growth becomes smoother, the planning process becomes less hectic, less dependent on special drives or campaigns to eliminate this or that key bottleneck. The central planners, furnished with more abundant and reliable data on the recent utilization of materials and investment funds by ministries, central boards, and individual enterprises, can trim with greater discrimination than in the past the exaggerated demands for inputs submitted by economic organizations. They are able to confine the scope of bargaining with lower organs within increasingly narrow limits.

A characteristic of this more mature stage is that growth can no longer be generated by taking advantage of slack in the economy: all sectors have a valid claim on investment funds; long neglected repair needs—in housing, in machinery, or in overworked human labor—must be remedied. Even agriculture, the poor relative of industry in every East European economy, must be allotted more resources lest food output decline. The planners must budget their resources more carefully, since even small changes in the bill of goods they desire to produce may create new bottlenecks.

At this point the search for ways and means of economizing materials and manpower takes on new forms. In casting about for more effective means of husbanding their resources, the planners tend to pay increased attention to the price system which can be used to guide socialized firms toward a more discriminating application of their efforts to save on materials, labor, or equipment. We shall show in Chapter Eight how difficult a task price-setting turned out to be in Polish practice, in a system where virtually all producer goods were still administratively rationed and firms had only a weak incentive to reduce their costs.

Increased reliance on the price system is only one of the elements of a gradual trend toward decentralization. Whatever contribution political events in the Soviet Union and in the satellites may have made historically to this trend, it is believed that it was also a natural consequence of the economic transformation accompanying the third stage of development. At first, centralization had been effective in tightening up discipline, in diffusing among producers the more advanced technologies of industrially mature countries, in recasting the old economic system adapted to consumer needs into a pliable instrument for carrying out the industrialization and rearmament policies laid down by the Party authorities. But once these first aims had been achieved, the shortcomings of hypercentralization—the stifling of local initiative and the waste in channeling information back and forth between the peripheries and the center—began to outweigh the waning benefits of the system. In their search for new sources of efficiency, the authorities were certain to discover the advantages of delegating administrative responsibility and of developing local initiative.

2. Short-Term Planning

a. *Consistency of Material Balances.* The following model of short-term planning, which schematizes the results of Chapter Three, assumes a centralized allocation of the principal resources of the economy. The planners seek to frame an internally consistent plan for all sectors, fulfilling both the high-priority objectives, or "leading links," and the less essential components of the approved bill of final demand. The model corresponds to the third stage of planning, where input-output coefficients, no longer responding decisively to administrative pressure, are known in advance with a certain degree of precision. These coefficients are assumed to be invariable for a given planning period. For purposes of this model, capacity output in every sector is fixed within narrow limits; the supply of material inputs together with the availability of plant and equipment are the principal bottleneck factors of production. A more flexible model, where shortages of labor, of transportation facilities, of foreign exchange, or of other factors may also become the decisive impediments to growth will be considered in the next section dealing with the efficiency problem in central planning.

The outputs in this model correspond to individual commodities or to aggregated groups of commodities. It should be kept in mind throughout the following discussion that the planning of outputs with the aid of centrally made-up material and machinery balances does not usually encompass the entire production of each industry. On the other hand, where the balances are so aggregated that they cover an entire industry's production, this is incompatible with the assumption of stable input coefficients, since highly aggregated coefficients are likely to be sensitive to changes in the relative importance of components in the groups. In this and in some other points, the model below involves a certain degree of idealization of the planning practices discussed in Chapter Three.

We begin with a short summary of the planning mechanism described in Chapter Three. In Poland, the administrative machinery of the yearly plan is set in motion toward the middle of the preceding year by a set of directives issued by the Council of Ministers via the Planning Commission. These directives stipulate the year's targets for the growth of national income, the gross output of industry, transportation, construction, and agriculture; they also set the investment budget, the wage fund, and the cost-reduction tasks assigned to each ministry in charge of an economic sector. They lay down targets for the output of a large number of important producer and consumer goods, which socialized enterprises, organized under ministries of large-scale (key) industry, will be responsible for turning out. These directives are in the nature of minimum assignments, which may later be adjusted upward; but in practice, as bottlenecks come to light in the coordinating process, some of the targets may also be scaled downward before the plan-year begins.

The model set forth below deals only with the setting of targets for the output of individual commodities. The relation between these targets and the "synthetic indices" (investment budgets, wage funds, etc.) laid down by the Council of Ministers and the Planning Commission will be discussed in Section 2b below and in more detail in Chapter Four.

After receiving these directives, the ministries of key industry, cooperating with their subordinate organs—the central boards of industry—and with the producing enterprises themselves, report to the Planning Commission the materials requirements corresponding to the directive targets. It is now the task of the Planning Commission, with the aid of the ministries, to construct a consistent plan that will satisfy the minimum quotas of materials needed for investment purposes (mainly machinery and building materials), for armaments, for export, and for the consumer market, and will also meet the industrial requirements for the material inputs which will be capable of supporting all this final demand. Once the requirements for materials as inputs in the production process of key industry have been subtracted from the output targets of the directives, the quantities of output left over in every industry may be earmarked for final demand. These "net outputs" may be sufficient to satisfy the planners, in which case the program may be approved without further ado; but this fine coincidence of supply and demand will not usually come about in the normal course of planning, since the planners will be unable to set mutually consistent output targets in advance of the entire planning process. (We must also keep in mind that in the third stage of planning, with which we are dealing, the demands of the consumer market or of other traditionally low-priority sectors are no longer as flexible as they were earlier. These sectors can no longer be treated as buffers, satisfied with any allotments left over after the requirements of priority sectors have been met.)

It is taken for granted, therefore, that in some sectors the net output left over for final demand in the first approximation will be too low to satisfy minimum requirements. The total, or "gross," output of those sectors must then be raised. But this will set off a whole chain of repercussions, since each industry depends, directly or indirectly, on all the others for material inputs. These repercussions will have to be estimated in advance if the central planners are to hit upon a new set of outputs which will support the desired level of final demand. It is shown in Appendix A that this may be done through a series of successive approximations. We first assume that there are no bottlenecks in physical capacity that would prevent the planners from setting gross outputs consistent with their final-demand orders. Then, at each round, the estimated requirements of material inputs derived from the previous estimates of gross output may be added to the minimum needs for final demand. This sum yields a new set of gross outputs, from which the next estimate of materials requirements may be calculated. Eventually the process converges to a consistent set of gross outputs, capable of yielding the desired final bill of goods. If the original targets are not too far out of line with each other and there are no major adjustments to be made to the original bill of final demand generated in the first approximation, a satisfactory degree of consistency can be achieved in the second or third round, or "iteration."

The entire procedure may be represented as the solution of a set of simultaneous equations whose fixed coefficients are the input-output relations, the known variables are the final demands, and the unknown are the gross outputs. The set of target outputs used in the first approximation is merely a tentative solution.

Normally, however, capacity limitations in a number of major industries will impose a ceiling on the mutual adjustments just described. If this is the case, there will be some gross outputs in the simultaneous equations which will be known in advance. Since there cannot be fewer unknowns than the total number of equations (one for each production sector), some of the final-demand requirements will have to be flexible. (We exclude for the time being the search for alternative production processes which would allow all minimum requirements of final demand to be satisfied despite the output limitations.) In Poland, for instance, the metallurgical and the building-materials industries were operated at full capacity, while metal-fabricating industries, working for final demand, frequently had to adjust their volume of output to the steel supply. It is shown in Appendix A (Section 4) that mutual consistency can also be achieved by successive approximations where gross outputs in a given number of sectors are set equal to capacity ceilings, while tentative levels of final demand in the remaining sectors are chosen by the planners with an eye to the level of residual net outputs in the capacity-limited sectors.

The iterative procedure in this case will be even simpler, and convergence will be more rapid, than where the unknowns consist solely of gross outputs. In the event all sectors producing raw materials and semifabricates were capacity-limited, whereas the output of sectors producing mainly for final demand depended not on their productive capacity but on the supply of their material inputs, then a program meeting reasonable consistency requirements might easily be found on first try. These conditions could be approximated in practice. A concrete example, based on the technology matrix for 1958 prepared by the Polish Planning Commission, has been worked out in Appendix A.

In general, whatever the iterative procedure used, we may observe that as the industrial structure of an economy grows in complexity—as its various sectors become linked with each other in more numerous and roundabout ways—the residual error left after a given number of trials tends to become larger. In a simple economic structure, finished goods are sold on the consumer market or are earmarked for investments; they rarely reappear as inputs in the production of other commodities. As the economy develops, finished products are increasingly used as inputs in manufactures and services (e.g. textile fabrics in automobile making, food in restaurants), and semifabricates as inputs in the production of raw materials (steel supports in mining, fertilizers in agriculture). These feedbacks evidently complicate the planning process, since one sector's output hinges on the other, and neither can be set in advance. For instance, the output of steel supports and the output of coal are mutually dependent: coal goes to make coke and coke to make crude steel, which is rolled in the shape of supports, used in the mining of coal. In view of this growing complexity, successive-approximations methods for achieving consistency, though they may be adequate at an earlier stage of development, should eventually give way to more systematic mathematical solutions obtained with the aid of electronic computers.

Whatever the ease or difficulty of framing an internally consistent version of the national economic plan, there is still the matter of making final adjustments in the plan before the beginning of the plan-year for unforeseen changes in final demand or in output capacities (due, for example, to delays in the completion of key investment projects). It is here that the difficulty of tracing rapidly and exactly the effects of changes in one sector's output on all the other sectors affected manifests itself most acutely; it is also in this respect that formal methods of input-output analysis might be most helpful.

b. *The Efficiency Problem.* Plans balanced to a nicety may be far from efficient, in the sense that by reallocating available factors more output could be targeted in one or more sectors without sacrificing output elsewhere. Strictly speaking, central plans can never be fully efficient since the information communicated to the planners must necessarily be aggregated and simplified. They cannot represent all possible alternative processes for producing tens of thousands of commodities differing from each other not only in their intrinsic qualities but also in their location in time and space. A more modest, and operationally more useful, criterion is that the planners should make efficient use of the information at their disposal. According to this criterion, the shape of the production-possibilities surface, mapping out all possible combinations of efficient targets for centrally planned commodities, will be determined not by the supplies of scarce factors that will actually be on hand during the plan-year nor by the production processes that will actually be employed but by the estimates of these supplies and by the planned use of certain more or less aggregated processes as they may be anticipated some months before the plan-year begins. Resources will be allocated efficiently by this criterion if the planners can select output targets corresponding to points on the hypothetical production-possibilities surface generated by these data.

As will be shown in the latter part of this chapter, prices in Soviet-type economies cannot be used as a reliable instrument for drawing up efficient programs. The only trustworthy scarcity indicators the planners can rely on are the surpluses and deficits in their balances for materials and factors of production. None of the planning commissions in the Soviet Union or in Eastern Europe has so far made use, for purposes of operational planning, of electronic computers, which would be capable of sifting through and choosing among a much larger number of alternative programs than a bureaucratic organization could ever consider. In the absence of computers, it is reasonable to ask how close the planners can come to framing efficient plans within the limitations of the information at their disposal. To describe such a method, which will be consonant with what is known of planning practice in the Soviet-type economies, is the basic task of this section and of Appendix B, where the basic propositions stated below are formally stated and proved.

How detailed is the information channeled to the central planning organization?

In Poland the Chief Statistical Office provides data to the Planning Commission on the output of specific commodities or commodity groups and some, but rather more limited, data on the expenditure for the chief inputs consumed in production (including labor, fuel, etc.). Information on the consumption of materials and factors and on the material-technical norms linking inputs to output also percolates to the Commission through the central boards of industry and the ministries. These statistics, however, tend to be aggregated according to the organization furnishing them. They seldom provide information on the different processes— amounts of the several inputs used and by-products generated per unit of the chief output—that individual plants may be using. Information on the possible alternative processes that might conceivably be operated with the equipment at hand is not normally collected. The aggregation of the input coefficients that are transmitted to the central planners presents special problems where the individual plants are organized under more than one central board or industry (i.e. cement made by plants in the Ministry of Metallurgy from slag and in the Ministry of the Building Materials Industry from limestone). For key products such as electricity, steel, and sulfuric acid made according to well-known, standardized alternative processes (thermal and hydroelectric power, open-hearth and furnace steel, contact- and chamber-process sulfuric acid), the Commission is in possession of at least some of the relevant data. It is often possible for officials of the Commission to obtain supplementary data from subordinate echelons—although the time lost in so doing tends to limit the usefulness of direct interventions.

As we understand it, the allocation of resources for the forthcoming year is planned mainly in terms of a single process for producing each commodity or group of commodities. The simplifying, but not unrealistic, assumption will be made that the first phase of the planning procedure consists exclusively in testing the feasibility and desirability of tentative programs on the basis of a single (aggregated) production process for every good; the search for alternative processes will be confined to the second phase, where the planners may take advantage of the results of the single-process analysis (e.g. the presence of bottlenecks and surpluses in factor supplies) to choose alternative processes more in keeping with prevailing factor scarcities.

In the single-process production method postulated for every good, the same quantities of inputs and by-products are consumed or generated per unit of output of the main product, no matter how small or large this output may be. Indivisibilities as well as increasing or decreasing returns to scale are ruled out. (Decreasing returns may be analyzed with the same technique as alternative processes in the second phase.) It is assumed that the physical capacity of plants, the supply of labor of varying skills, the availability of land for agricultural products, the transportation facilities on hand at the beginning of the year, and the supplies of all other exogenous factors can be treated as constant for the purposes of short-run planning. Each production process may be represented by a column (vector) of inputs and outputs per unit level of operation of the process. Each process is assigned one main type of output; to produce one unit of this output, certain quantities, or input coefficients, are required of various materials, skilled and unskilled labor, transportation facilities, and so forth. In addition, each unit of output absorbs a given percentage of the plant capacity available in this sector. Certain quantities of by-products may also be produced in fixed proportions with the principal product. The availability of each factor is known and sets a ceiling to the sum total of all allocations of the factor among the different sectors.

The preferences of the ruling authorities, loosely termed "planners' preferences," determine the pattern of final demand that will ultimately be selected. It is not assumed that a clearly delineated preference function is consciously present in the minds of the authorities, but only that allocation decisions are made as if they were subordinated to such a function. For the time being, we shall restrict this function only in three respects:

1) Only net outputs are desired. Surplus productive capacity and other unused factor supplies have no utility.

2) Satiety for any good is ruled out.

3) The preferences of the planners are mutually consistent. All feasible combinations of net outputs may be ordered transitively: if one combination X^0 is superior to another X^1, it must be superior to all those combinations inferior to X^1.

In addition it is assumed that excess factor supplies have no disposal cost. This implies, for instance, that although unemployed labor may receive consumer goods from available supplies, in-efficiency will not be condoned for the sake of maintaining full employment.[3]

A simple procedure is now outlined, the systematic application of which will ensure that efficient sets of net outputs will be gen-erated. The planners, or their superior political authorities, may choose among these efficient outputs an optimal set according to their preferences. This procedure is believed to be consistent with planning practice in the Soviet-type economies. The main prob-lem, as in successive-approximations methods for achieving con-sistency, is how systematically the rules may be applied and to what degree of precision.

1. A trial set of gross outputs—or a mixed set of gross and net outputs—is tested for feasibility. If this program is not feasible, the planners undertake to reduce one or more of the gross outputs, according to their scale of preferences, until all levels of net out-put turn out to be positive or zero. If certain minimum levels of net outputs are required, the gross outputs are chosen so as to sat-isfy those constraints.

2. If the program elaborated in the first step utilizes the en-tire supply of every centrally balanced exogenous factor, it is ef-ficient. If the net outputs calculated from the gross output targets turn out to be in satisfactory proportion (i.e. if they happen to concord with planners' preferences), the program is also optimal. If it is not optimal, a new efficient program producing net outputs in more desirable proportions will have to be prepared by reallo-cating available factor supplies.

3. If all factors are not fully utilized in the program prepared in the first step, the planners allocate excess factors to various sec-tors in such a way as to increase gross output wherever possible. (Evidently this must be done with an eye to the relative desirability of increasing the net outputs of different industries and maintain-ing nonnegative net outputs in all sectors.) When it is no longer possible to allocate an additional amount of any factor to build up gross output in a sector without reducing the quota of this factor, or of some other factor, assigned to another sector, this is the signal

3. This is not a very restrictive assumption, since labor left in surplus in the single-process analysis may be fully committed in the second phase where alterna-tive labor-intensive processes may be introduced.

that an efficient program has been achieved.[4] To achieve efficiency, it is necessary and sufficient that *at least* one exogenous factor should be fully employed, as long as all sectors of the economy are directly or indirectly related. (It is most doubtful, however, that the pattern of planners' demand could ever be such that only one factor should be fully employed.) Efficiency, it is important to note, is defined in terms of net outputs. Yet the trial-and-error search for efficient solutions need involve only gross outputs (except for the constraint that net outputs must never fall below zero or below the established minimum). It is of course much easier to work with gross outputs, since they—unlike the net outputs—can be used to compute input requirements directly.[5]

4. The bottleneck-creating procedure of step 3, if it were carried out mechanically (e.g. by an electronic computer), would generate all possible efficient solutions.[6] However, insofar as the planners can predict the approximate configuration of net outputs associated with a given set of gross outputs, they will allocate their resources toward the sectors likely to yield more of the priority net outputs; they need only investigate a small group of efficient solutions to reach an apparent optimum.[7] (This point is elaborated at the end of this section.)

If one or more of the production processes yield several goods simultaneously, the above conditions for attaining efficiency do not remain valid in all cases. The crucial point in the analysis of joint products is whether or not the same good is produced in more than one process. If it is, then feasible solutions may be inefficient even though they may meet the requirements for efficiency stated above for programs excluding joint products.[8] But if

4. This proposition holds strictly only in the absence of joint products. See below, pp. 15–16.

5. For details, see Appendix B, Sect. 1b.

6. Since every convex linear combination of any two contiguous extremal points representing efficient solutions will generate another efficient solution, the number of solutions is infinite. Mechanical search could grind out all extremal solutions, from which all other possible solutions could be obtained by combination.

7. If the input-output matrix contains few zeros and many relatively large coefficients, it is always possible that the priority standing or the relative desirability of the various net outputs will be poorly expressed by the gross outputs. In this case, there may also be difficulties in achieving consistency.

8. If all the elements of the inverse of the Leontief matrix derived from the technological matrix are positive—which they may well be, even where joint products are involved—solutions satisfying efficiency conditions for the case excluding

each good is a product of only one process, then, no matter how many goods may be produced jointly by the same process,[9] efficient solutions will be generated under the same set of conditions as in the absence of joint products.[10]

So far we have glossed over the relation between the material and factor balances and the "synthetic balances," by means of which the planners seek to preserve macroeconomic equilibrium at prevailing levels of consumer retail prices. Theoretically, it would be no trouble to add new constraints to the formal program already examined: (1) total wages (derived from the labor-allocation equation) should match the value of the net output of consumer goods available to the population, allowing for personal taxes and increases in monetary circulation; (2) total foreign exchange earned in both minimum and above-minimum net outputs should match total foreign-exchange requirements in the program; [11] (3) the quotas of labor and materials allotted to the construction sector plus the net output of machinery for domestic disposal should correspond to the value of investment expenditures. These and other constraint equations would make the model more comprehensive, but they would add little to its realism. The departments of the Planning Commission charged with preparing synthetic balances must necessarily draw on the tentative plans made up for the allocation of materials and labor; some of the macroeconomic decisions they will make must also have feedback effects on the material and factor balances. However the interaction between physical and value planning is not close enough for us to claim that the elimination of slack and the choice of alternative processes are

---

joint products are also efficient in the joint-products case. For details, see Sect. 1c of Appendix B.

9. A closely related problem is discussed in Appendix A, Sect. 5.

10. Appendix B, Sect. 1c.

11. It may be stipulated that the foreign exchange used up in the program should not exceed the exchange earned from the export commitments in the minimum bill of net outputs. This would seem to imply that above-minimum output would either be consumed domestically or, if sold abroad, would only contribute exchange to next year's program. This is too formal an assumption. A minimum level of foreign trade may be provided for in planning the economy's main proportions for the coming year. This does not mean that consumer goods cannot be bought out of surplus exchange, which must also cover any unforeseen requirements in priority industries. The point is that the over-all balance of foreign exchange—including all proceeds and anticipated needs—will be struck only after the search for the optimum proportions has been completed.

effected with full cognizance of the macroeconomic repercussions they involve. This bureaucratic compartmentalization is not necessarily a weakness of the system: it permits specialists to focus on the problems that are of particular concern to their own branch —problems the "general coordinators" might neither have the time nor the expertise to cope with.

Generally, there is no assurance that a feasible program affording a desirable bill of outputs will satisfy conditions of monetary equilibrium.[12] Whether or not it will do so depends in part on the prevailing level of retail prices, which are in large measure arbitrary. If the attainment of macroequilibrium is less crucial than the formulation of programs that satisfy the physical constraints to the system, it may be better to superimpose the synthetic balances on the physical plans and use monetary circulation, price and wage policy, and other financial instruments to maintain macroequilibrium than to try and mesh the two types of plans.[13]

Inasmuch as the search for an optimal program in the second phase of the planning procedure, as it is represented in the present model, will depend on the surpluses and bottlenecks discovered in the first phase, it may be worthwhile to speculate on the character of the programs initially prepared. To say anything meaningful on the subject, we have to describe more concretely than we have done so far the nature of planners' preferences. The simplest case to analyze, which will be dealt with first, is the one where the planners' choice is limited to extremal points, or vertices, in the net-output space. This choice, as it happens, is less restrictive than it might at first appear. Insofar as the preference function can be approximated within certain limits by a linear function, only extremal points will be selected, or, more exactly, no point lying on a line connecting two extremal points will be preferred to all other feasible points.[14] By assigning a minimum net-output target in all sectors where declines in output below a certain point would

12. See Sect. 1d of Appendix B.

13. In the last resort, part of the population's cash balances may be confiscated through a monetary reform.

14. S. I. Gass, *Linear Programming: Methods and Applications*, pp. 39–40. In the diagram below, representing all feasible combinations of the net outputs Y_1 and Y_2, the only extremal points satisfying the minimum output conditions are A, B, C, and D. Point H is efficient but not extremal. It will never be preferred to one of the extremal points if the preference function can be approximated by a straight line. (See footnote continuation on next page.)

become increasingly irksome to the planners, we can make this linearity assumption somewhat more realistic.

The extremal points selected under these conditions will correspond to basic feasible solutions to the problem of maximizing a linear function of net outputs, subject to the restraints imposed by the minimum requirements for net outputs, by the mutual consistency of the gross outputs, and by the initial supplies of the exogenous factors. Such basic feasible solutions are characterized by the property that they include no more processes at positive levels than there are restraints to the program. Denoting by n the number of goods and by f the number of exogenous factors, we see that the number of processes actually operated cannot exceed $n + f$.[15] If the technology matrix is indecomposable, that is, if every product is used directly or indirectly in the making of every other product, all n gross outputs must be included in any solution. The number of net-output activities plus the number of partially unemployed factors included in the solution can at most equal f. If the only exogenous factors in planning practice were the half dozen to a dozen factors that are normally parceled out among sectors, such as machinery, technological personnel, or foreign exchange, the chances for any of them to remain unemployed would be slim, as the number of above-minimum net outputs would be most likely to be greater than twelve. But the number f embraces all the capacity limitations constraining the volume of output in each sector. There can be at most n such limitations. If there were as many as that and the number of priority sectors where above-minimum outputs were produced equaled half the total number of outputs, more than half the productive capacities might be partially unemployed ($\frac{1}{2} n$ plus the number of exogenous

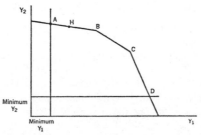

15. See Appendix B, Table B:1.

factors other than productive capacities). Generally speaking, for a given set of measurement units, the more unequal the weights attached to the net outputs in the planners' preference function, the fewer goods will be produced in above-minimum volume and the more factors will turn out to be in surplus availability.

We may now revert to the most general preference function that can be represented in two-dimensional space by convex, concave, or straight-line indifference curves. Every point—not just the extremal ones—on the production-possibilities surface now qualifies as an optimal point, potentially preferable to every other point.[16] Since the coordinates of every point on the surface can be expressed as a convex linear combination [17] of extremal points representing basic feasible solutions, we can easily extend the foregoing analysis to cover this general situation. If the optimal point is not extremal, as may well happen if the preference function is characterized by increasing marginal rates of substitution for one or more pairs of commodities, then, assuming that the number of restraints should be the same as in the case of the linear preference function already studied, the sum of the net-output activities plus partially unemployed factors included in the solution will be *larger* than f, the number of exogenous factors. However, since more commodities are now liable to be produced in above-minimum outputs, due to the increasing marginal utility of diminishing outputs, it cannot be predicted whether the number of partially unemployed factors will be greater than in the linear case.[18]

16. The point H in the diagram of note 14 is potentially preferable to points A, B, C, and D.

17. Convex linear combinations of s solutions in an n-activity model will be generated by multiplying each solution vector by a fraction (the sum of the fractions adding up to unity) and summing each of the n components over all the solutions. Thus for three solutions in a four-activity model we have:

$$\begin{pmatrix} x_1^c \\ x_2^c \\ x_3^c \\ x_4^c \end{pmatrix} = r_1 \begin{pmatrix} x_1^1 \\ x_2^1 \\ x_3^1 \\ x_4^1 \end{pmatrix} + r_2 \begin{pmatrix} x_1^2 \\ x_2^2 \\ x_3^2 \\ x_4^2 \end{pmatrix} + r_3 \begin{pmatrix} x_1^3 \\ x_2^3 \\ x_3^3 \\ x_4^3 \end{pmatrix}$$

$$r_1 + r_2 + r_3 = 1$$

where the vector on the left-hand side of the equation is the convex linear combination of the three solution vectors on the right.

18. Cf. the diagram in note 14 above. At B and at H both commodities are produced at above-minimum net outputs. At B two factors are fully employed and

Underemployment of factors is clearly a consequence of our analysis in terms of unique production processes. So far we have said nothing about whether or not this underemployment would be large enough to matter, or whether it would even be noticed by the planners. If the growth of production capacities in the various sectors had been reasonably well coordinated in the past, the extent of unemployed capacity in the sectors where above-minimum output was not pushed to its maximum might be negligible. This is all the more likely if one considers probable errors involved in measuring capacity. But if capacities had been poorly meshed or had been built up to satisfy a different order of priorities than the one prevailing at the time the current plans were being laid, the problem of bottlenecks and surpluses could not be disposed of so easily. In Poland before 1953, poor balancing methods in the long-range plans and unexpected delays in the completion of key projects caused imbalances in productive capacities. After the death of Stalin, the order of priorities changed in favor of a more rapid development of consumer-goods output; this policy shift created new discrepancies, which were only gradually eliminated in the course of the first Five-Year Plan (1956–60).

The foregoing discussion of extremal points leads straight to the problem, only briefly touched on before, of picking the optimal solution out of the complete set of feasible solutions.

The difficulty of the problem obviously hinges on the number of feasible solutions. We shall concentrate only on basic solutions, from which all other solutions can be derived by combination. Using the same notation as before, we recall that there are $2n + f$ possible activities in any program (n gross outputs, n net outputs, f disposal activities for the exogenous factors) and $n + f$ equations or restraints (n equations for the disposal of the gross outputs, f for the employment of the exogenous factors). The maximum number of basic solutions, some of which will not be feasible, will be $\frac{(2n + f)!}{n!(n + f)!}$, which is the number of different combinations of $n + f$ activities that may be chosen out of $2n + f$ activities. This

---

one partially unemployed (output is not constrained by line CD). At H, there is only one factor in bottleneck supply (the one corresponding to line AB) and two partially unemployed factors (neither line BC nor line CD impose a ceiling on output at H).

number quickly grows very large. For instance, a program comprising five goods and five factors will already possess 3003 different basic solutions. But there will be a much smaller number of basic solutions if all the gross-output activities have to be operated at positive levels, either because the input-output matrix is indecomposable or because minimum net outputs must be delivered for each good. In this case, all valid combinations must comprise the n gross-output activities, together with any f activities chosen out of the $n + f$ remaining activities. There will be $\dfrac{(n + f)!}{n!f!}$ such combinations, or 252 for the above example where n and f were both equal to five. (But if n and f were both equal to 15, the number of basic solutions would rise to over one hundred and fifty million!) These numbers reveal the enormous range of alternative patterns of allocation that may have to be tested for feasibility prior to the selection of an optimal program; they should dispel any notion that the planning problem is essentially trivial where only one process has to be considered for making each good.[19]

Suppose that one good dominated the preference function of the planners, so that in the program for the plan-year all net outputs, except for this priority good, could be fixed at zero or at a given minimum. It may easily be verified that f would be the maximum number of basic solutions to such a program.[20] If each sector had a capacity limit, f might be a significant number. The interesting point, valid only in the single-process case, is that there would be at most one *feasible* solution to this program and it would be optimal; any planners worth their pay should be able to find this solution after one or two trials.

19. The number f includes capacity limits of individual sectors. As a higher f will tend to raise the number of possible solutions, one would expect that the more capacity limits have to be taken into account, the more complicated might be the task of finding an optimal solution. But this reasoning overlooks the fact that it will generally be easier to maintain consistency in the trial programs and to find the gross outputs corresponding to desired changes in the final bill of goods if a number of outputs are capacity limited (Appendix A, Sect. 4).

20. Out of $2n + f$ possible activities, a total of n gross outputs plus one net output have already been selected. A basic solution being limited to $n + f$ activities, there remains only $f - 1$ activities to be chosen. Since there are f surplus factors among which to choose, the number sought equals $\dfrac{f!}{(f - f + 1)!\,(f - 1)!}$ or f.

This extreme case exhibits the essential advantage the planners derive from only having to choose among efficient solutions. The experience they have acquired in constructing the preceding year's plans and the data they have gathered on their fulfillment can normally be used to guide the search for feasible solutions in the current program for the year. If the ruling scale of preferences does not change radically from one year to the next, the feasible solutions considered will contain bills of goods that are in more or less desirable proportions. Since they are all efficient, any such program will be a candidate for ultimate selection. This contrasts with the situation where inefficient solutions are possible (e.g. where joint products are present), for then the planners must winnow through a larger number of possible solutions to be sure that they have not only hit upon the correct proportions of output but also that they are getting as much output as possible.[21]

Another way to express the advantage of working exclusively with efficient solutions is to conceive of such a solution as an opportunity cost that correctly reflects the alternative foregone in choosing some competing solution. Just as it is easier to shop

21. This intuitive reasoning may be formalized as follows: First we make the reasonable assumption that the planners' preference function is concave (in the net-output space, indifference curves for any pair of goods are either convex to the origin or straight lines). It may be shown that the set of feasible outputs is also convex (cf. Gass, p. 38). To simplify the problem, only two net outputs are considered, although there may be any number of exogenous factors. Three feasible points A, B, and C, located in the net-output space, are picked at random (this may be done by trying out different allocations). The points need not necessarily be extremal but, in the general single-process case, they must be efficient. The most desirable of the three points is now selected in accord with the planners' preference function. Suppose this optimal point, say B, shows less net output of the first good than A and less output of the second good than C. Then any other point in the space with a larger net output of the first good than at A or a larger output of the second good than at C must be inferior to all three of the original points. On the other hand, if the net output of one of the goods was greater at B than at either A or C, the net output of that good being smallest at C, any point with a net output of the other good larger than at C would be inferior. Starting from these three points, the planners, if they have any notion of the effect of changes in allocation on the bill of net outputs and can avoid inferior points such as have been described, should be able to narrow down the range where the optimum is likely to be found. This method cannot be guaranteed to work if one or more of the initial points are inefficient. In that case, as can easily be verified, no points yielding more of some net output can be rejected a priori as inferior. By increasing the number of points initially selected, this line of analysis can be extended to any number of goods.

in a market where every price for a good is the lowest price prevailing in that market, so the search for optimality is facilitated by confining trials to efficient solutions.

It should not be inferred from this discussion that an optimal solution can be picked out on first try. On the contrary, there is evidence that in the Soviet Union as well as in Poland several versions of the yearly plans are prepared before a final draft is approved. What is claimed here for the single-process case is that the theoretically optimal solution has a good chance of being included among the versions submitted to the authorities for final approval.[22]

c. *Foreign Trade and Alternative Processes.* The opportunity to trade with the rest of the world, even in a situation where every good must be produced according to a unique production process, adds a new dimension to the planning problem. Trading opportunities may be thought of as alternative processes for acquiring net supplies of desirable goods. It will not come as a surprise to learn that efficient solutions cannot be ground out by any simple mechanical rules where trading alternatives come into play. Inefficient solutions are more than plausible, they are likely, for there are no signals informing the planners of the comparative advantage the economy enjoys in one or another good. They may be capable of exporting goods whose net output is in relatively low-priority demand in exchange for more desirable goods also

22. The entire analysis so far has steered clear of normative principles, unrelated to our schematic interpretation of planning practice. Actually, it is possible to state some guiding rules that would help the planners direct available factors toward their optimal employment. One of the more perplexing tasks they must perform, for example, is to decide correctly whether an increment in the supply of a factor should go to the industry producing the good whose net output they wish to increase or to the industries producing the raw materials, semifabricates, or other material inputs needed to make the desired good. First, starting from any efficient solution, they should try allocating the factor directly to the end product, together with any other cooperant factors that may be required to step up the production of this good. Then they should check what effect the new allocation may have on material requirements and how much, on the assumption these requirements were satisfied, the net outputs of other goods would have to be curtailed. If this cost is too great (in terms of prevailing preferences), they should try and allot the factor to the semifabricate mainly responsible for the decline in the other outputs. Checking each time on the impact of a reallocation on the bill of net outputs, they would proceed backward to the most essential raw materials indirectly required by the good in demand.

destined for final consumption; but where they may go wrong is in reallocating their resources to increase the output of exportable goods to the detriment of the domestic production of commodities that it is more advantageous to import.[23] Once a feasible program has been prepared relying exclusively on domestic production, there will be a temptation to let it go at that, even though a careful calculation would show that a larger supply of some desirable good might be made available from imported sources by stepping up the output of exportables without reducing the net available supply of any good, as compared to the initial program. Only an exhaustive trial-and-error search for all the alternative bills of goods that might be delivered to final demand from domestic production and from imports would guarantee that an efficient solution would be worked out.

We shall now consider a model where goods produced domestically may be put together according to more than one process. Alternative processes may be introduced *before* consistency has been achieved in order to reduce the demand for factors or materials in deficit supply. While this procedure will obviously be advantageous if it makes it possible to generate a bill of goods which could not otherwise be attained, the consistent plan arrived at by this substitution may still be inefficient. Let us suppose that a consistent plan fully employing one or more exogenous factors has been struck. If some factors are still partially unemployed, the planners may try to improve the solution by substituting processes making less intensive use of the bottleneck factors. There is no guarantee that this new solution will be more efficient than the last unless, in the case of each alternative process introduced, all input-output coefficients but those corresponding to factors in excess supply happen to be smaller than or equal to their counterparts in the processes initially considered. A higher material coefficient in the alternative process may, under certain conditions, more than offset the advantage of economizing on the bottleneck factors.[24] Wherever this may occur, only a systematic calculation of the net outputs produced before and after the introduction of the new process, in conjunction with the initial process or by itself, will reveal the correct solution. From the impossibility of blindly testing every alternative process,

23. An open-economy model is summarily analyzed in Appendix B, Sect. 1e.
24. See Appendix B, Sect. 2.

if only because of the time limitations imposed on the task of laying out the plans, it may be predicted that certain unprepossessing alternatives will be glossed over if they fail to economize directly on deficit factors and do so only through the economies they effect in the consumption of intermediate goods.

Another difficulty, illustrated in the example below, is that factor surpluses may disappear before the most efficient solution has been discovered, and the planners may have no signal to guide them toward further improvements.

In this elementary case of programming with alternative processes, only two factors and two products will be considered.[25] This restriction is not clamped on the scope of the model merely to simplify the exposition: we have observed that in Polish planning practice the decisions to try out alternative technologies or processes at the highest level—to substitute thermal for hydroelectric power, to step up the output of low-cost plants situated at a great distance from raw material sources, and so forth—are made on the basis of comparisons which are limited to a very small number of factors and products. A more or less consistent plan is struck; bottlenecks are discovered; attempts are made to circumvent them one at a time by substitution, by small, quickly maturing investments, by imports, or by any other means the planners may contrive. A major reshuffling of resources with the simultaneous introduction of a large number of new processes might be a better way of raising the efficiency of allocation, but this is out of the question at the present time: no bureaucratic machine could cope with the intricate consequences of such a redeployment even in the initial stages of planning the "main proportions."

In the case now analyzed, factors A and B, available in limited quantities $\overline{A}$ and $\overline{B}$, must be allocated between the two products X and Y. Neither product's output is used as an input in making the other. To begin with, we shall search for the optimal allocation, as if each good were made with one process. Once this has been done by the methods already explored, an alternative process will be introduced for making each of the two products.

The more clear-cut case to deal with is the one where in the original single-process solution, one factor turned out to be in surplus and the other one in short supply. There will then be an

25. For details, see Appendix B, Sect. 2 ("Alternative Processes").

inducement to find at least one alternative process calling for
more intensive use of the abundant factor and economizing on
the scarce supply of the other.

This potential improvement and the various alternatives involved may be illustrated by means of the box-diagram below.

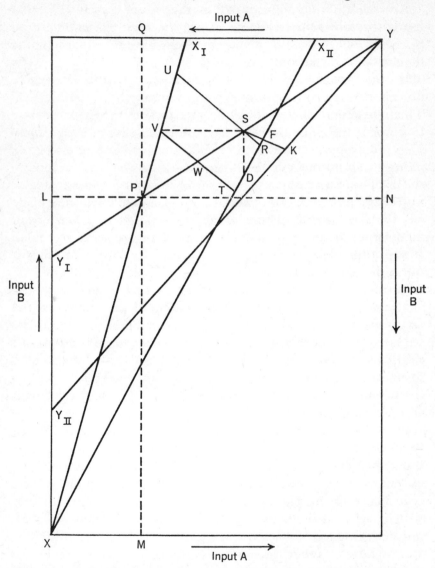

DIAGRAM 1:1. *Efficient Allocation for Two Inputs, A and B, Two Products,
X and Y, and Two Processes for Making Each Product*

The rays drawn from the origins X and Y show the various processes for making these two products with different combinations of inputs A and B. Each point farther out on a ray shows a higher level of output, increases being proportional to the quantities of inputs employed in the appropriate ratio. Increases in X are measured from the X-origin and increases in Y from the Y-origin in the upper right-hand corner. The amount of inputs A and B used in making X increases from the X-origin along the horizontal and vertical axes respectively. Inputs used in Y are measured from the Y-origin. At point P, for instance, where first-process rays X_I and Y_I intersect, both inputs are fully utilized. The total supply of B is divided between X and Y in the proportion MP to PQ. The total supply of A is divided between X and Y in the proportion LP to PN. If, starting from P, we desire to increase the output of X at the expense of Y, possibly because the minimum desired output of X exceeds the level at P, we shall find that factor B will be in short supply and factor A in excess. Let us take point V as the optimum the planners had attained before they began to investigate alternative processes. At point V, the output of X has been maximized for a given minimum output of Y (represented by the length YS). VS units of A are now in surplus. It will not take much imagination to introduce process II in making X which will use up excess A and release scarce B. But if process II for making X is used exclusively in combination with process I for making Y, there will be a shortage of A and a surplus of B (equal to SD). The correct and natural thing to do is to switch resources gradually to the second process until the supplies of both A and B have been just exhausted. Optimal points, such as S and W, will lie on the ray Y_I between rays X_I and X_II.

At any point along the isoquant-line VT, product X may be produced at the same output as at point V by a combination of processes I and II. UR is an isoquant corresponding to a higher output of X. The point S will be selected if X is more valuable than Y, and the minimum demanded output of Y is at S. Point W will be selected if the output of Y is to be maximized for the minimum output of X shown by point V. Finally, the line SK is an isoquant for product Y, showing the different combinations of inputs A and B which will make it possible to produce the same level of output Y as at S using a mixture of processes Y_I and Y_II.

Note that if the introduction of the second process does not lead to the elimination of the factor initially in surplus, then it will pay to use this process exclusively—and then to look for still other processes susceptible of taking up the remaining slack.

Polish officials have described to the author various cases taken from their routine work where, in order to obviate a shortage or to make fuller use of available resources, they made the type of allocation decisions that has just been analyzed. However, these decisions usually stopped short of a refined calculation of gains and losses. For instance, the planners might be willing to settle for an allocation such as the one at S in Diagram 1:1 as long as it satisfied minimum requirements with no factor left over, even though the substitution of factor A for factor B, indicated by the latter's *relatively* greater scarcity, might generate a higher level of output of both products. Furthermore, there is little chance that a point F, on the Y-isoquant SK, would be tried out, even though it could yield more X than at S while simultaneously maintaining the same minimum output of Y. For, to reach this point from an initial point such as V, one would have to make a complicated change-over from exclusive dependence on the first process for making X to exclusive dependence on the second, together with the introduction of a mixture of two processes for making the lower priority product Y. The best that might be hoped for is that point F should be reached in two steps. First, the planners might aim for point S. Then they might grope their way to point F by blind trial and error. But there would be no inducement or signal—such as the presence of factors in excess supply normally provide—that would make the planners look for point F once they had alighted upon point S. Only a quantitative comparison of gains and losses for every possible alternative would be sure to lead them to the optimum.

This does not mean that the planners cannot make intelligent guesses as to which of the fully employed factors are scarcest (i.e. have the highest marginal productivity or implicit price). Clearly, factors used intensively in making goods in high priority are *likely* to be in short supply. The search for substitutes will probably go on in this direction. But it may well bypass more advantageous, if less obvious, opportunities. The flair and experience of planners, who have some feeling for the marginal contribution of individual factors, will henceforth play a key role in the search for improvement. But no simple rules can make up for a lack of these talents.

An interesting point, raised by a Czech planner in an interview, is that the pool of consumption goods earmarked for the retail market may be adapted to bottlenecks and surpluses in factor supplies without necessarily sacrificing minimum consumers' demand. As an example, this planner cited the possibility of making furniture out of metal or out of wood, depending on the relative scarcity of the two materials. (Since the state has a monopoly on the retail market, it is probable that all the furniture made would be sold, whichever type consumers preferred.)

In actual cases involving interdependent systems, the formidable job of maintaining a semblance of consistency in the balances at all times militates against any sophisticated experimentation with alternative processes unlikely to produce very tangible gains in priority outputs. The search for efficiency must be confined to a small number of sectors. Beyond twenty to thirty sectors even the relatively simple methods described above would become unmanageable. How is this limitation to be reconciled with the unwieldy mass of material and factor balances (around 1,500 in Poland in 1956) prepared in the centrally planned economies? Key decisions involving alternative resource allocations during the plan-year are made at least six months before the beginning of the plan-year, before directives are issued for the year, on the basis of which the detailed balances will be struck. At this early stage, where the planners are concerned with establishing the "main proportions" for the coming year, they may operate with broad value aggregates for most industries with a complex output-mix (e.g. machine building, textiles, food processing, small-scale industry, and handicrafts) and confine the number of commodities expressed in physical quantities in the trial programs to a few of the most essential raw materials and semifabricates (coal, rolled steel, sulfuric acid, cement, bricks, etc.). Once these proportions have been set—growth targets and quotas of raw materials and other factors have been assigned to each economic sector organized under a ministry or comparable agency—more detailed work on disaggregated balances becomes possible. Further search for efficiency may then go on within the organizations in charge of economic sectors, which in much the same way as the Planning Commission at an earlier stage must try to uncover "reserves" in output by programming the most efficient use of the resources tentatively assigned to their sector during the plan-year.

We should also keep in mind that, at all stages in this planning process, the planners' imperfect knowledge of production functions necessarily imposes a limit on their search for optimality. Even where "organizational improvements" no longer have a major role to play as a source of progress, it may still be a good thing to plan with an optimistic bias—to count on slightly larger supplies of bottleneck factors than can reasonably be expected and to set tight technological and labor-productivity norms even though they may not be strictly adhered to. These overoptimistic plans will maintain the necessary tension in the system. In fine, the plans may not be battened down to the ultimate linkages; a few resources may be overcommitted; yet all the key targets may still be hit if the lowest echelons in the economic hierarchy—particularly the enterprises directly responsible for production—exert themselves to cut down on the input coefficients or have enough leeway to make the minor substitutions of abundant for scarce factors that the planners have neither the time nor the information to provide for. (Project-making organizations in charge of designing investment works may be enjoined to replace critical building materials with materials in more abundant supply; enterprises short of high-grade fuels may be instructed to use up more labor to make available supplies stretch further.)

Some of these improvements can be carried out without any interference by higher authorities at all. When plans are overtaut and the allotments of scarce material inputs appear too small to fulfill the plans, enterprises by substituting labor for materials are apt to salvage their production plans, though as a result they will frequently fail to achieve their labor-productivity tasks. If managers in their groping attempts to fulfill their assigned targets create a demand for factors that are not fully committed in the yearly plans, they are working in essential harmony with the spirit, if not the letter, of the plans.[26]

26. Cf. D. Granick's discussion of "free goods" in a linear-programming sense in his article "An Organizational Model of Soviet Industrial Planning," *Journal of Political Economy*, 47 (1959), 116.

The officials at the lower echelons who are responsible for doing some of this substituting often have much better knowledge of production functions than the central planners relying on statistical reports and correspondence: imperfect coordination of central plans, leading to moderate deficits of materials and factors, may be a blessing in disguise if it provokes the substitution of processes tending to mitigate these shortages. With this strategy in view, it may be judicious to decentralize the allocation of factors perennially in excess. A case in point is the allocation of unskilled labor, whose supply is unlikely to be fully committed in the central plans in an industrialization period.[27] This may help explain why the employment and distribution of unskilled labor in the Soviet Union and in the other Soviet-type economies have traditionally been a good deal more influenced by market forces than other inputs—unlike in Great Britain during World War II when labor was conscripted.

Administrative decentralization entails a certain division of the responsibility for setting detailed targets and for allocating factors of production between the central planning organs and subordinate agencies. This is not without its danger. The resulting loss in coordination may more than cancel the advantage of making decisions with better knowledge of conditions in the field. When, to choose an example from the Polish experience, the marketing organization for solid fuels in Katowice was allowed to distribute extra consignments of coal during the course of the year (either out of above-plan production or by depriving some consumers of their normal share), it could not clear these ad hoc decisions with the organizations marketing other materials in Warsaw or with the financial organs setting the wage funds that would determine the amount of labor that coal-consuming enterprises would be able to hire. Some plants used a great deal of labor to economize on coal while more privileged plants received more than enough coal to meet their needs. Although an exchange of

27. The rapid expansion of capital-intensive heavy industry with a limited supply of physical plant and equipment requires a much fuller utilization of machinery and equipment than in the pre-industrialization period when there was less pressure on capital resources. But the input-output coefficients and the information on processes at the disposal of the planners still partly reflect the earlier state of affairs. This will generate a tendency to underestimate labor needs (or to project excessively optimistic gains in productivity).

coal for labor between the two types of plants might increase production all around, neither the central planners nor their delegates would normally have had an inkling that this was worth doing. This state of affairs will be perpetuated as long as the technological norms sanctioned for each type of plant reflect the coal- and labor-intensive processes actually in use.

It may be in order now to summarize the advantages along with the systematic shortcomings of the model of administrative planning set forth in the foregoing pages.

1. The planners act in response to three signals: a) the feasibility of gross and net outputs, b) factor surpluses, and c) bottlenecks in factor supplies. Generally speaking, if the underlying data are correct, the decisions they take on the basis of these signals will guide them *toward* efficient solutions, among which they may choose the most desirable. Exceptionally, where joint products are involved or where a special configuration of material coefficients obscures the choice of alternative processes, the signals may lead to inefficient solutions.

2. The procedure is simple and it may be carried out with a minimum of calculation.

3. Once the signals disappear—outputs are feasible and all factors are employed—the guidance system breaks down. There is no *modus operandi* for finding combinations of processes that are superior to those already selected. In the absence of guiding signals only a mechanical trial-and-error search, which the planners have neither the time nor the computing facilities for carrying out, can lead to efficient solutions, if there is a significant number of alternative processes.

4. Alternative processes are considered a pair at a time. While this is an acceptable procedure for large-scale electronic computers that may sieve through hundreds of efficient programs before they finally arrive at an optimum,[28] it will be less than satisfactory for a ponderous and slow-moving organization with a limited capacity to absorb and process new data.

5. Information is available in the Planning Commission on

28. In linear programming, one new process-vector is added and one withdrawn for each iteration. It can be proved that if each new combination yields a higher value in the linear function to be maximized, an optimal solution will be attained in a finite number of steps.

only a few of the many alternative processes accessible to the economy as a whole.

6. Where foreign trade opportunities are present, there are no reliable signals guiding the planners toward an efficient allocation of resources.

7. While it may be desirable to maintain some tension in the plans—by keeping materials allocation down to the "irreducible minimum"—there is no way to tell ahead of time how far out of balance the plans can afford to be without actually disrupting production.

These principal obstacles to efficient planning would not be removed no matter how much the collection of technical coefficients might be improved. Even if one hundred per cent of the output of each balanced commodity could be traced to its final destination—as final demand or as input in the production process of some other industry—the problem of allocating factors among competing uses would remain acute. The fact that for many goods only a fraction of total uses can be so traced merely aggravates the problem.[29]

3. Long-Term Planning

The difficulties that stand in the way of making up consistent and efficient yearly plans are multiplied many times when long-range plans have to be constructed. In the long-range plans, the future supply and demand for each centrally planned material must be coordinated. A significant difference between short- and long-term plans is that in the latter the output of machines and the work performed by the construction industry no longer make up a part of final demand, exogenous to the system, but are organically linked with the outputs of subsequent years. Only consumer goods sold on the market, armaments, exports, and current social consumption represent final demand in any year. Plans must be consistent at a point of time and through time: the output of steel sheets in a given year must be sufficient to supply the metal input for the production of boilers, which in turn will be expected to provide their share of the steam power planned for a few years hence. The links between present and future output are the capital coefficients that tell the planners how many units

29. Chap. 3, p. 97.

of output must be invested today in order to increase gross output by one unit tomorrow.

The analysis of long-range planning summarized below is restricted to unique processes for making each good. For the purpose of this analysis, a multiperiod program will be said to be efficient if no alternative program can be found which would produce more net output in some time period or a larger terminal stock of some endogenously produced factor without foregoing the net output of any desirable good in any period or reducing the terminal stock of any factor. It is assumed that, in each period, every good is used directly or indirectly in making every other good, that there are no joint products, and that the longest gestation period for producing any new capacity is shorter than the length of one period.

The following are the general results of Appendix B holding for feasible programs: (1) If there is only one *endogenously produced* factor (e.g. one reproducible capital good), then any program fully employing at least one *exogenous* factor in every period will be efficient. In this case, the requirements for static and dynamic efficiency are identical.[30]

(2) If, in a given program, the capacity of every reproducible factor in period 1, as well as the endogenously produced capacity of such factors in all subsequent periods, is fully employed, such a program will be efficient.[31]

(3) If a program encompassing several endogenously produced factors (e.g. various types of capital goods) leaves at least one such factor partially unemployed, then, even though one or more exogenous factors may be fully committed in each period, the program may be inefficient.

(4) To ensure efficiency in the above case, it may be ruled that no program leaving capacity, newly created in period t, unemployed in periods $t + 1$, $t + 2$, . . . , should be considered, unless this capacity were expected to become relatively more expensive to produce in a subsequent period. By "more expensive"

30. Technically, one proviso should be added to tighten up the case, namely, that capacity produced during the plan period cannot be scrapped before the end of the period. Otherwise, the stronger assumption must be made that any endogenously produced capacity must be fully utilized during the last period of its operation.

31. Cf. R. Dorfman, P. A. Samuelson, and R. M. Solow, *Linear Programming and Economic Analysis*, pp. 341–42.

we mean that the opportunity cost of producing this capacity, measured in terms of any other type of capacity slated for full employment in period $t + 1$, $t + 2$, . . . , would be higher in a later period than at t. Barring the expectation of significant fluctuations in demand,[32] no other reason can be discerned why the planners in actual practice should want to consider any program which failed to fully employ capacity produced during the course of the plan period.

These various alternatives may be illustrated by a single example. Crude oil and refined gasoline, both valued as net outputs in the planners' preference function, are initially produced from two types of capacity, oil wells and refining plants. Oil is obviously required to make gasoline. We shall take it that some gasoline is also consumed in extracting crude oil. If only refining capacity can be expanded during the plan period, our first principle states that any feasible program operating existing oil wells at capacity in every period must be efficient, no matter how many other exogenous factors may be involved. (An alternative program must reduce the net output of petroleum or gasoline in some period or curtail the amount of refining capacity available at the end of the plan.) If more wells can be drilled, that is, if extracting as well as refining capacity can be expanded, the second principle states that any program fully utilizing the two types of newly created capacity will be efficient.

Possibilities of inefficiency will arise if refining capacity is built ahead of extracting capacity and some refining plant is left idle for one or more periods until the extraction of crude oil catches up with the demand. This strategy certainly need not be inefficient: the opportunity cost of producing refining capacity in the first period may be smaller than at any later time and it may be advantageous to build it early in the game. Nonetheless, it may also happen that a poorly constructed initial program would stand to be improved by cutting back the expansion of refining capacity in the first period. With the resources released in this initial period, the planners could (1) step up the pace of new

32. Surplus capacity in the food-processing industries might have to be built up to meet changes in the demand for the services of this industry due to crop fluctuations. To fit this stochastic element into the model, it might be desirable to redefine full employment of an endogenously produced factor in terms of the minimum capacity required to meet the mean expected demand for its service.

well-drilling and (2) produce, and perhaps even refine, more crude oil. In the next period, the first-period loss in refining capacity might be made good by a greater expansion of this capacity than in the original program. This could be done at the cost of a curtailment in oil drilling, but in such a way as to leave the terminal capacity of the oil wells equal to or larger than in the original solution. This profitable manipulation would only be apt to succeed if the cost of an increase in refining capacity, reckoned in terms of extracting capacity foregone, was *smaller* in the second period than in the first.

These results, it must be stressed, all hinge on a generous definition of efficiency. A program whose only advantage over its competitors was that it could generate an extra ton of petroleum today might be efficient even though some alternative program could produce hundreds more tons tomorrow. For there might be some ordering of planners' preferences—for example, in wartime—which would move them to select the program squeezing out the most immediate benefit.

It is hardly necessary to draw attention to the wide range of alternatives open to the planners preparing a long-term program even if the range of planners' choice is restricted to efficient solutions. In the two-good, two-factor model described in Appendix B, Section 3, the upper bound to the number of basic solutions (feasible and unfeasible) is six for each period taken separately and 924 for the three periods taken together.[33]

In general, there are fewer restraints on alternative processes in the long-run than in the current plans. Given enough time, as old equipment wears out and new projects are launched, the entire technology of a country can be transformed. The new techniques may be drawn from the current state of the arts or may be developed to fit concrete needs. There is a host of possible programs to be considered. Even if the planners have a very flexible pattern of development in mind and they target for gross outputs of the principal raw materials and semifabricates with-

33. There are altogether eighteen activities and twelve restraints. However, the number of solutions is restricted by the fact that both goods must be produced in all three time periods (the submatrices for each period being indecomposable). The choice is confined to any six activities out of the twelve remaining net-output or surplus-factor activities. The number of possible combinations equals $\frac{12!}{6!6!}$ or 924.

out worrying excessively about the exact composition of the final bill of goods that these levels of output will generate, they are likely to find that there exist faster and slower, more or less costly means of attaining the same goal.

The lack of knowledge of the relevant variables is still more manifest than in the case of current planning. Estimates of capital-input coefficients and of the gestation periods of investment projects are subject to an appreciable margin of error; little can be told in advance of the future course of technological progress. In view of these uncertainties, it would be unreasonable to waste time in over-refining the plans, in striving for a spurious consistency out of keeping with the fragile nature of the underlying data.

But even if the plans are going to be framed in round estimates and a wide allowance made for contingency factors in all the perspective balances, it may still be desirable to search for what appears to be the cheapest, most efficient road toward the goals contemplated. One need not have had a very precise idea of the future pace and character of technological progress to have foretold back in 1950 that Poland's economy, about to be launched on the capital-intensive development of its heavy industry, would have to adapt itself for years to come to a relative shortage of capital and to a relative surplus of unskilled labor. Even the most cursory examination of the long-range balances and the study of a few alternative variants should have revealed the necessity of introducing labor-intensive processes wherever possible in order to spare investment funds. Many of the disproportions in Poland's economy that arose during the course of the Six-Year Plan were due to poor balancing prior to the launching of the plan and to excessively optimistic forecasts of productivity trends.[34] Others were due to the inability to predict the fundamental changes in final demand that were impelled by the Korean War. The New Course inaugurated after Stalin's death also necessitated many unanticipated adjustments. But some of the troubles that eventually occurred can be laid to strategic errors which common sense

34. These are disproportions that the planners recognized as such, since they eventually disrupted the course of industrialization. Disproportions between heavy and light industry, which observers with a different scale of values from the authorities in charge might object to, will not concern us here.

and economic experience could have avoided. A highly placed Communist official concluded from his study of the disproportions which had plagued the Polish economy in the 1950s that the transformation industries created during the Six-Year Plan had been too material-intensive and ill-adapted to the resource-base of the country; they could not presently be operated at capacity because they depended on materials that had to be exported to pay for other essential imports. "The fuel and power base available at the end of the Six-Year Plan might have better fitted the needs of the transformation industries, if the production profile of the latter had developed along different lines." [35]

At least during the latter years of the Six-Year Plan, only the yearly plans had operational significance. The bottlenecks discovered each year in the process of making up the short-term plans had as much to do with the orientation of investment plans and generally with the expansion of productive capacities as the increasingly obsolete long-range plan. This lack of a clear perspective was an obstacle to smooth and efficient short-term planning, particularly in industries with a long production cycle, which were afflicted with frequent and costly changes in their production plans.

The five-year plans for 1956–60 and 1961–65 seem much more consistent internally, and were based on more reasonable expectations of productivity trends, than the Six-Year Plan. Rather than try by manipulating the balances to gauge the effect of alternative patterns of allocation on resource supplies and output, the planners found it more convenient to select processes and output mixes on the basis of calculations of costs and returns expressed in value terms. Once these calculations were made, the results were incorporated into the balances to check whether consistency could be maintained with the desired pattern of allocation. These value calculations for achieving efficiency were extremely inexact because they rested ultimately on a price system, which did not, and probably could not, reflect the opportunity costs of shifting resources to alternate uses.[36] Still, in the absence of electronic com-

35. S. Kuziński, *Główne proporcje rozwoju gospodarczego Polski Ludowej* (Chief proportions in the economic development of Peoples' Poland), p. 42.

36. Official transfer prices are unlikely to express current scarcities. They are still less likely to express the future scarcity relations pertinent to calculations involving long-range projects. This stricture also applies to the investment plans laid

puters to try out variants in the long-range balances, this was about the best the planners could do.

4. *Prices in a Centralized Economy*

So far we have seen that the balances may be—but are usually not—fully coordinated, and that there is at best only a crude attempt at achieving an optimal allocation with the resources at hand.

We must now ascertain whether the price mechanism can be used in conjunction with physical planning to bring about a more rational allocation. Prices may be thought of as signals transmitted from planners to producers with a view to provoking input and output decisions at the plant level in harmony with central policy. For a price message to have a suitable impact on producers, certain rules must be established governing their reactions to these stimuli. Producers may be enjoined to react to the prices themselves or to changes in certain magnitudes, such as costs, sales, and profits, which combine prices with input or output data. They may be told to maximize profits. Then again they may just have to minimize costs in current prices, their output performance being measured with the aid of some other units (such as the "fixed" or "plan" prices of Soviet practice). In principle, uniform prices should be quoted to all producers, and if more than one price system is introduced, the different systems should not act at cross purposes with each other. As we shall see, these principles are frequently violated in practice.

In all the economies under Soviet tutelage, there are two levels of prices: a higher level for consumer goods sold to the population and a lower level applying to all goods in transactions between socialized firms. The difference between the price of a consumer good sold to a socialized firm for processing and of the same good sold to the public consists of purchase taxes (the "turnover tax") and of the profit margins of the marketing network. Consumer goods are sold in retail shops at market-clearing prices, or at prices that come fairly close to this norm, except in periods of great stress when rationing and queuing supplant prices as a

---

by capitalist enterprises in market economies that have neither future prices to guide their investment calculation nor a central board to coordinate their projects with those of other investors.

means of distribution. Prices of goods circulating among firms
do not bear any direct or mechanical relation to the retail prices
of consumer goods. The indirect taxes levied vary widely as a
percentage of cost or of the final price. The planners do not make
direct use of consumers' prices as a basis for setting producers'
prices.[37] We shall mostly deal with the latter, since they are more
closely linked with the planning problems that interest us.

Prices, ideally, should provoke input and output decisions on
the part of socialized enterprises whose effect would be to improve
on the pattern of allocation achieved by trial-and-error methods.
Short of bringing about this improvement, prices might at least
be expected to provide an incentive for fulfilling the plans. They
should reinforce, not counteract, central directives. Our analysis
will show that even this limited objective cannot always be won,
since a set of unique prices cannot be found that will sustain a
program of inefficient outputs; the equilibrium point may turn
out to be more or less efficient than the program initially ordained.

We must first of all go beyond our previous conception of efficiency limited to the best possible utilization of the information
funneled to the Planning Commission. Efficiency must now encompass all outputs, whether centrally planned or not; it must
take into account the full range of substitution possibilities open
to the individual plant and to the economy as a whole. If we
assume that each enterprise faces a continuum of potential processes, each with its characteristic input-mix, then we can no longer
represent the entire range of allocation possibilities as in Diagram
1:1 by means of a few rays. Instead of trying to draw a closely
packed bundle of these rays, we may link equal-output points at
intervals on the hypothetical rays, to trace a series of isoquants all
convex to the origin. This has been done in Diagram 1:2.

The greater the distance of an isoquant from its origin, the
higher the output it stands for. Efficient points of allocation in
the diagram lie on the curve drawn between points where an X-
isoquant is tangent—back-to-back—with a Y-isoquant. At such
points, the ratio of the marginal products of inputs A and B
in making X is equal to the ratio of the marginal products of
these two inputs in making Y. The planners, with their limited
knowledge of alternative production processes have settled on

37. Exceptions to these general rules are discussed in Chap. 7, Sect. 5.

point P_1, which is inefficient, at least in the light of the full range of substitution possibilities open to the plants. By increasing the allocation of input A to makers of X at the expense of a reduction in their supply of B, and by allotting makers of Y this extra supply of B in exchange for the amount of A they lost to X, it would be

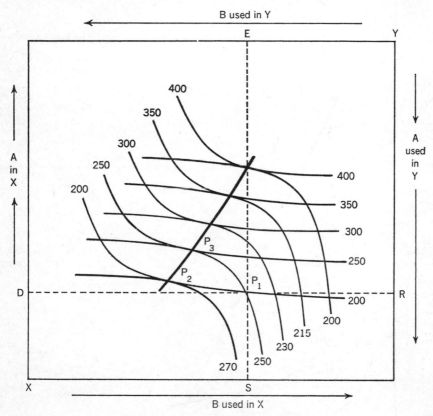

DIAGRAM 1:2. *An Inefficient Program*

possible to reach points on the efficiency locus between P_2 and P_3 where more of both products could be produced.

Consider now Diagram 1:3, in which a part of the previous diagram has been magnified, showing (inefficient) point P_1 and surrounding territory.

The "budget line" KL, tangent to the X-isoquant at P_1, traces all the combinations of inputs A and B which could be purchased for a fixed sum if the prices of these two inputs were in the proportion *OL* to *OK*. If the enterprise making X were enjoined to minimize its costs for any given level of output and if it were allowed to buy its inputs at stable prices, it would consume inputs

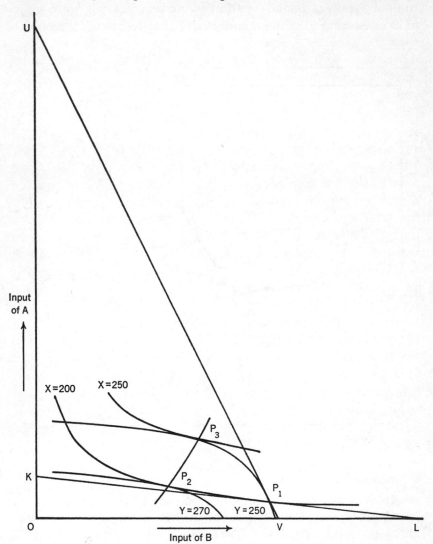

DIAGRAM 1:3. *Prices and Inefficient Outputs*

A and *B* in the amounts shown at point P_1. On the other hand, prices would have to be in the proportion *OV* to *OU* to induce makers of *Y* to land at P_1. Different prices would have to be charged to producers of *X* and *Y* to bring about the allocation corresponding to point P_1. But price discrimination of this kind is not practiced in the Soviet-type economies. The imposition of a unique set of prices, such as that represented by the slope of the line KL, must engender a deviation from P_1. If this price happens to equal the slope of the tangents at P_2, P_3, or intervening points, then the induced deviation may be in the direction of an optimum. However, if prices were fixed in the proportion shown by line UV, they would not lead to an efficient point between P_2 and P_3. The exhorbitant price charged for B might cause this input to be left in surplus. If Y were the priority good, it might still be produced at P_1; the output of X would then have to be cut to a point where one of its isoquants was tangent to a line with a slope equal to the ratio of OU to OV; this point would have to be chosen in such a way that the output of X would not consume more of scarce input A than remained after satisfying the large requirements for making Y at P_1. The allocation induced by the use of irrational prices would be inferior to that reached at P_1 by physical-planning methods.

We need not have dwelled on this point if it were not that its significance seems to have escaped economists in the Polish Planning Commission who casually argue that prices should always be set in such a way as to induce producers to fulfill their output plans (presumably whether these plans are rational or otherwise).

One short cut to optimum pricing is worthy of consideration. If it happens that the production frontier between goods X and Y forms a straight line, then setting relative prices of X and Y equal to the slope of this line will turn out to be efficient irrespective of the relative demands for these two goods. This condition will hold provided that there is only one scarce factor limiting the output of X and Y, or if the various factors are used in equal proportions in making X and Y, but under no other circumstances. If labor is the scarce factor, then the relative prices will be equal to the ratio of the direct and indirect labor costs of making X and Y.[38] This is in essence the principle of pricing

38. The total demand for the unique factor may be expressed as follows:

$$(1) \quad X_0 = a_{01} \ x_1 + a_{02} \ x_2 \ldots + \ldots a_{0i} \ x_i + \ldots + a_{0n} \ x_n$$

where X_0 stands for the total demand for the factor (in this case, say, labor); a_{0i} for direct labor requirements per unit of product i, and x_i $(i = 1, \ldots, n)$ for the gross outputs. The latter can be written in terms of the net outputs as follows:

$$x_i = A_{i1} \ y_1 + A_{i2} \ y_2 + \ldots A_{ij} \ y_n + \ldots + A_{in} \ y_n$$

according to Marx's labor theory of value adopted in all economies of the Soviet bloc, where prices of producer goods are, as
a general rule, set to cover the average unit cost of output in
an industry, exclusive of capital charges or rents.[39]

Constant rates of transformation between products presuppose
the absence of bottlenecks in productive capacity and of shortages
of farm or mined products (all shortages can be made good forth-
with by shifting labor and materials at constant cost to the critical
industries). In other words, there must be such an abundance of
capital, land, and other productive assets that their marginal productivity has dwindled down to zero.[40] This state of affairs is
hardly typical of backward or semideveloped countries undergoing
industrialization.

If there are capacity limitations in certain industries or other
factor scarcities, the problem presents itself as in Diagram 1:4.

Here the curve that is concave to the origin shows the production frontier [41] for producer goods A and B while the convex
curves are the isoquants showing the various combinations of
A and B that can be used in the making of quantities X_1, X_2, etc.
of product X. A line RS has been drawn tangent to both curves.
The slope of the production frontier at any point equals the
ratio of the marginal costs of producing A and B. The highest
level of X that can be produced with existing resources must be
X_1. At that level, the ratio of the marginal costs of A and B equals

---

where the A_{ij} are the direct and indirect requirements of input i per unit of net
output j. Equation (1) can be rewritten as follows:

$$(2) \quad X_0 = a_{01} \ (A_{11} \ y_1 + \ldots A_{1n} \ y_n) + \ldots a_{0n} \ (A_{n1} \ y_1 + \ldots A_{nn} \ y_n) =$$
$$(a_{01} \ A_{11} + \ldots a_{0n} \ A_{n1}) \ y_1 + \ldots (a_{0n} \ A_{1n} + \ldots a_{0n} \ A_{nn}) \ y_n =$$
$$A_{01} \ y_1 + A_{02} \ y_2 + \ldots A_{0n} \ y_n$$

The terms A_{0i} $(i = 1, \ldots, n)$ are the direct and indirect requirements of labor
necessary to increase the net output of the i'th good by one unit.

The relative prices of any two goods i and j should equal the ratio of A_{0i} to A_{0j}
(Dorfman, Samuelson, and Solow, pp. 222–23, 232–33, 248–52).

39. If labor is the only scarce factor, average cost must equal marginal cost and
there can be no rents to any factors of production.

40. In terms of the model of the previous section, this would imply that the only
binding restraint was the labor equation. On the contrary, this is just the equation
that is likely to show a surplus in practice.

41. The production frontier, also called transformation curve or production-
possibilities curve, shows all the combinations of levels of output of products A
and B that can be produced in a given period of time with available resources.

the ratio of the marginal products of A and B in the production of X.

If the price ratio equaled the slope of the line RS, firms would minimize the cost of inputs in producing the quantity of output X_1 by consuming OT units of input A and OM units

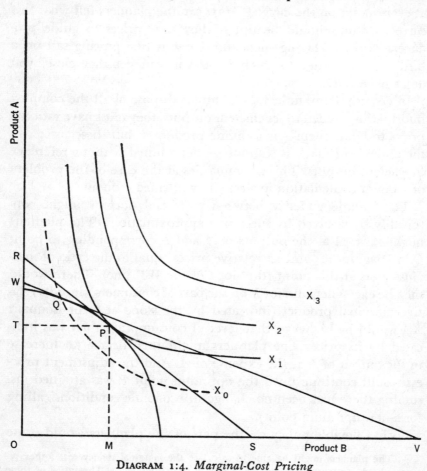

DIAGRAM 1:4. *Marginal-Cost Pricing*

of input B; if firms were enjoined to maximize profits, this price should also call forth the correct relative outputs OT of A and OM of B.[42]

Suppose information were available on the relative costs of pro-

42. Unless profits are maximized, firms will not equate marginal cost to price and the marginal costs of any two goods need not be proportional to their prices.

ducing A and B but little was known about the relative demands for the two products (i.e. about the production functions of consumers of A and B).[43] Could prices be set at marginal cost? Not unless the planners already knew the correct levels of output of A and B (respectively OT and OM), since relative costs will differ at every point on the curve.[44] How can the planners tell what this correct output should be unless they have prices to guide producers thither? Having such knowledge is like putting salt on a bird's tail in order to catch it: if you can get that close, you don't need salt.

In essence, then, unless the planners dispose of all the complex information needed to set efficient outputs, they must have rational prices to guide them—or to guide producers; but these prices, in the absence of markets, cannot be determined without reference to efficient outputs. This dilemma lies at the core of the problem of economic calculation in a centrally planned economy.

The interdependency between costs and outputs might conceivably be resolved by successive approximations. The planners might start off at the outputs of A and B corresponding to point Q in Diagram 1:4 and set relative prices equal to the ratio of marginal costs at this point (the slope of the WV line). There would then be excess demand for B on the part of consumers, since its relative marginal product (indicated by the slope at Q of isoquant X_0) would be higher at that level of consumption than was indicated by its price. The planners might then decree an increase in the output of B at the expense of A. And the adjustment process would continue until the optimum point P was attained (assuming there had been no change in economic conditions calling for a new optimum point).

Such a flexible policy on the part of the planners would come

43. The planners might be able to calculate the marginal money cost (other resources held constant) of producing A and B at various levels. The ratios of these marginal costs for every combination of outputs would yield the transformation curve of the diagram.

44. Note, however, that if any two products were always required in the same proportions, it would be sufficient to know their marginal costs at every point to price them correctly. One would only need to find the ratio of marginal costs corresponding to the given output proportion. If, for instance, only the transformation curve for mined products exhibited strong convexity and these products were consumed in fairly rigid proportions from one year to the next, this short cut might be operationally valuable.

perilously close to mimicking a market mechanism. Rapid and frequent changes would invite all those so-called "chaotic" and "spontaneous" effects of a market that the communist authorities are bent on eliminating. Actually, prices have never been allowed to play such an active role in the Soviet-type economies. We shall see later on that it would be in conflict with the accounting and control functions prices are expected to perform in a Soviet system.[45]

So far we have conceived the managers of socialized firms as reacting to prices in much the same way as profit-maximizing entrepreneurs in a capitalist system. Centralized price-setting, in the absence of markets or of administrative procedures designed to imitate the workings of markets, was responsible for all the theoretical difficulties discussed so far. In Soviet-type economies, however, there are other institutional factors hampering the operation of an efficient price system; among these may be mentioned the rationing of producer goods and the setting of production targets *in natura*. The price system can only function in the interstices of physical planning; but even in these narrow confines the monetary incentives set up for managers are not such as would lead them to maximize profits. Managers, we shall find in Chapter Six, are rewarded for fulfilling and overfulfilling their production plans, even if this entails high costs and lower profits. In Poland, at least up to the Gomulka reforms, the profit motive played a minor role in the complex of incentives contending for the manager's attention. In the early 1950s, management decisions were largely insulated from the influence of current prices. Since prices, according to a Polish economist, were set "practically at random," it was perhaps a good thing that enterprises were quarantined from their harmful effects.

Gradually prices were relegated to a subordinate function. Instead of reinforcing physical plans, they came to serve mainly as

45. Another theoretical solution consists in the application of formal linear-programming methods that would simultaneously generate optimum outputs *and* rational prices. A by-product of the solution of a linear-programming problem is a set of implicit prices, which, for a common set of assumptions, will be identical with the rational prices we have been investigating. Providing that all the production functions of enterprises had been correctly estimated in the matrix of coefficients utilized to generate the solution, the prices so calculated would lead producers to efficient outputs and to optimum input-mixes (assuming, of course, that managers had been instructed to follow a profit-maximizing policy).

units of account (for figuring out costs, sales, the value of investment outlays, and so forth) and as value-weights in aggregating
heterogenous outputs. Later, after Gomulka assumed power, there
was a chance to reactivate the price system. But apparently the
new authorities did not recognize that an essential condition for
doing this was, first, to scrap the institutions that had grown
up to supplant the allocating functions of prices and, second,
to remold the system of incentives that had come to distort or
to deaden the influence of prices on the decisions of management. This point was never made explicitly but it lay under
the surface of the controversy that, for several years, divided the
"value-men," who wanted to increase the influence of the price
system, from the adherents of planning by direct command and
rationing decisions. In Chapter Nine, which deals with the evolution of the Polish "economic model" since 1956, we shall come
back to this heroic debate, which was prematurely cut short by
political circumstances.[46] After the Third Plenum of the United
Workers' Party in October 1959, when Gomulka recommended
a tightening up of central controls to check inflation pressures
and to re-establish a greater degree of coordination in the plans,
any further discussion of the merits of decentralized planning
would have been out of place.

The Poles now realize they will have to improve their system
"from the inside," since they cannot count on a drastic overhaul
of the model they inherited from their Soviet allies. There is
considerable room, as we have seen in the first part of this theoretical introduction, for making improvements within this framework. For one thing, a better grasp of the theoretical nature of
the approximations procedures used in planning would permit a
more rational and systematic search for internally consistent and
efficient solutions. Moreover, prices, no matter how modest their
place in the economic system, can be made to fulfill their function
more adequately if this function is correctly apprised. The studies
conducted in the Planning Commission in recent years may help
to fill these gaps in the planners' understanding.

46. See Chap. 9, pp. 263–68.

CHAPTER TWO

The Political Background,
Economic Growth, and Inflation

1. *Background*

Poland until 1914–18 was partitioned into three zones, annexed to Russia, to Germany, and to Austro-Hungary respectively. Industry was built up in each of the zones to service the market of its hinterland. In the Russian zone, for instance, an important textile center grew at Lodz, which depended for its outlet on the vast markets of the Russian Empire. World War I and its aftermath brought havoc and destruction to Polish territories. A new independent Poland was hammered together by the Allies at the Treaty of Versailles, but war with Soviet Russia postponed a peace settlement until March 1921. The economic condition of the new country was critical: the old hinterland markets were gone and the productive facilities of the country, which had been augmented by the acquisition of a large part of Silesia from Germany, were ill-adapted to the needs of an impoverished internal market. By the time a runaway inflation had been brought to a halt and the country was back on its feet and ready to export its surpluses on advantageous terms, the world-wide depression of the 1930s was on its way, and Poland's new markets were again cut off. The conservative leaders heading the government resisted all pressures to devaluate the national currency; as a result, the zloty was left stranded on high ground after the American and European devaluations of 1931–34. To prevent a catastrophic drop in exports, domestic costs had to be compressed. Prices and wages actually fell by about half from 1930 to 1934. Considerable unemployment ensued: 343,000 workers, or approximately one-fourth of the working force outside agriculture, were registered on the dole in 1933. Some improvement set in from 1934 or 1935 on, but full recovery was delayed until at least the time of the Munich crisis.

The country was mainly agrarian and poor: nearly two-thirds of the population worked in agriculture and forestry at the time of the 1931 census. The national income per head in 1938 did not surpass $250 of 1960 purchasing power. With a yearly steel output of 1.5 million tons in 1937–38 or 43 kilograms per head, Poland was one of the less industrialized European countries, distinctly lagging behind its neighbor Czechoslovakia (1.7 million tons or 120 kilograms per head). Its main natural wealth consisted of abundant bituminous coal deposits, from which an output of 36 million tons was extracted in 1937, or 2.8 per cent of the world output of coal at the time.

Prior to World War II, cartels, monopolies, state ownership, and state controls pervaded the Polish economy, which bore only passing resemblance to the classical model of competitive capitalism. At the end of 1934, there were 342 cartels in Poland controlling 27 per cent of the total number of industrial and trade corporations, 28 per cent of the banks, and 69 per cent of the insurance companies.[1] Coal, sugar, wool spinning, and steel were completely cartelized industries.[2] The state owned 93 per cent of the railways, 95 per cent of the merchant marine, and all commercial aviation; it controlled around 70 per cent of steel output, 30 per cent of the coal industry, 99 per cent of the salt mines, and at least 50 per cent of the chemicals and metals industries.[3] Only a few branches of industry, such as brickkilns, manufactures of woolen fabrics, sawmills, and tanneries were fully competitive. Farming and handicraft trades were the traditional strongholds of competition.

With World War II and the German occupation, many of the factories that had escaped destruction passed into the hands of the Reich and of German nationals: nearly all Jewish establish-

1. Z. Charłap and E. Szturm de Sztrem, "Statystyka karteli w Polsce" (Statistics of Cartels in Poland), *Statystyka Polski*, series C, no. 28 (1935), 37.

2. The state made memberships in the coal, sugar, petroleum, and alcohol cartels compulsory.

3. These percentages were estimated by F. Zweig, *Poland Between Two Wars*, p. 109.

ments suffered this fate. The Russian depredations of the liberation and the political uncertainty of the months that followed the creation of the Lublin Committee under Soviet auspices in the summer of 1944 caused many owners of enterprises to decamp and abandon their holdings. Enterprises owned by German nationals, collaborators, and Fascists were taken over by the state immediately upon the liberation of Polish territories. By the time a coalition government had been formed in 1945, with the participation of socialist and peasant-party elements but dominated by the Lublin Communists, there were relatively few industrial enterprises in Polish hands, particularly in the newly acquired western territories.[4] The early socialization of the economy was as much a consequence of the war as it was a manifestation of doctrinaire communism.

The "new Poland" was indeed a lot different from the old. The population had become culturally far more homogeneous than it had been before the war. The Germans had killed or deported all but about 100,000 Jews out of a population in prewar territory of over 3,000,000. The Ukrainian and Byelorussian minorities in the East had been incorporated into the Soviet Union, along with the eastern territories Poland had been compelled to cede to Russia in exchange for the western "Recovered Territories" placed under Polish administration at Potsdam. Poland's population had declined from 35 million in 1939 to 25 million inhabitants at the close of the war. Economically, Poland was now a richer country, for the exchange of territories had been vastly profitable: coal and zinc mines, steel mills, and power plants were gained in Upper and Lower Silesia in the West against poorly cultivated farm lands and moderately rich oil and potassium deposits lost in the East. Normally, one might have expected that, after the recovery of war damage, the standard of living of the country should have been higher than the prewar average, which was depressed by the appallingly low levels of the eastern provinces.

From the time of the formation of a coalition cabinet in 1945, which included, besides the Communists, members of the Socialist, Peasant, Democratic, and Labor Parties, up to the end of 1948 when the Socialist and Workers' (Communist) Parties were fused

4. *Życie gospodarcze* (Economic life), no. 1 (1946), 183.

into the monolithic Polish United Workers' Party and the remaining parties were stripped of all influence, the Communists consolidated their power, worming themselves into key positions, ousting "reactionary elements," and gradually dwindling down the opposition.[5]

Economic power in this early period was divided between two warring factions: on one side, the Central Planning Office (C.U.P.), headed by Czeslaw Bobrowski, a Socialist and former official in the Ministry of Agriculture before the war, who had surrounded himself with academically trained economists and professional people; on the other side, the Ministry of Industry and Trade, headed by Hilary Minc, an old-time Communist and advocate of all-out industrialization on the Soviet model and a trusted partner of Bierut, Berman, and Gomulka, the Communist team gradually pre-empting power under Moscow's tutelage. Minc had gathered under his fold a number of young Marxists and technicians who were to form the cadres of the planning apparatus in future years.

In 1944 and 1945, the economy was run by emergency measures reminiscent of Soviet War Communism, during the period following the October Revolution. The country was in chaos: Germans were fleeing the western territories in droves; refugees were pouring in from the territories ceded to Russia; a land reform was sweeping the countryside with hardly any supervision or arbitration by competent government organs; and Russian troops in former German areas, dismantling machinery and rounding up cattle for transfer to the East, were constantly running into conflict with the Polish authorities.[6] Forced deliveries were imposed on the peasants; rationing of consumer goods prevailed in the towns; and the government financed a large part of its expenditures by the printing of "fresh money" with inflationary effects.

Starting with 1946, some degree of stability was restored to the economy. In planning the national economy, Bobrowski's Central Planning Office seemed to have the upper hand over Minc's Ministry of Industry and Trade. The nationalization decree of January 1946, which had placed all enterprises employing more than fifty workers in the custody of the state, legislated a *fait accompli;*

5. For a full description of the political events of this period, see M. K. Dziewanowski's *The Communist Party of Poland, An Outline of History,* chap. 10.
6. Władysław Gomulka for a time was in charge of reconstruction in the formerly German territories in the West. His measures opposing excessive Soviet depredations are said to have antagonized Stalin.

paradoxically, however, it helped the revival of small-scale private industry by defining the scope in which it might freely operate. The nationalization law was officially advertised as a "durable basis for private initiative." [7] Promises were held out to private and cooperative trade of unfettered development. Farmers were given repeated guarantees that their land holdings and cattle would not be collectivized. These were the main features of the "three-sector model"—large-scale state industry, producers' cooperatives, and small-scale private enterprises—propounded at the time by Bobrowski, by Oskar Lange, and by many other professional economists.

The Three-Year Plan of Reconstruction, decreed in September 1946, was the first long-range plan undertaken. It consisted of a set of construction projects and targets for the development of basic state-run industries. The plan was to guide the private sector by "general recommendations" rather than by concrete orders. The yearly capacity and output balances underpinning the plans were only crude estimates, but at least the targets did not overtax the productive potential of the country. As it turned out, the principal objectives of the Three-Year Plan were reached on schedule.[8] The plan provided for both industrial growth and improved standards of living; by 1949 standards of living were probably higher than before the war for a large part of the population but especially for the peasants. Despite the great progress made toward recovery, industrial output as a whole did not come up to prewar levels for comparable territory until about 1950.[9]

The gains made during the period of the plan were achieved despite what the Communists termed a "sharp intensification of the class struggle." Against the opposition of the non-Communist minority, the Polish Parliament (*Sejm*) passed a law in mid-1947 requiring all private traders to register and obtain licenses. These licenses took months to get, when they were granted at all. Pending the award of a license, firms engaged in foreign and wholesale trade were not allowed to operate. Trade actually carried on was

7. ZG, no. 1 (1946), 541.

8. The plan for heavy industry was fulfilled by 101 per cent, for light industry by 97 per cent. Agriculture and forestry surpassed expectations. See table 15 in T. P. Alton's *Polish Postwar Economy*.

9. M. C. Ernst, "Measurement of Polish Industrial Growth 1937, 1946–1955," p. 100. Including handicrafts, output in postwar territory did not reach 1937–38 levels until 1951.

hit by arbitrary taxation measures, including prohibitive levies exacted from private business at the end of the year against allegedly unrecorded sales. Retailers were also liable to fines and incarceration for selling at "speculative prices" (higher than cost plus a standard profit margin). There was no redress against all these administrative orders. Various discriminatory bureaucratic measures also contributed to the decline of private industry, which was allowed to buy only a fraction of the raw materials it needed from the output of the state sector.

The statistical results of the socialization campaign, which had been masterminded by Berman and Minc, were the following: from 1946 to 1950 the share of private shops in retail trade fell from 78 to 15 per cent; wholesale private trade was practically eliminated; and private firms in industry and handicrafts, which were still responsible for 21 per cent of total output in 1946, had been reduced to 6 per cent by 1950.[10]

In the summer of 1947, Poland, under Soviet pressure, turned down the American offer to participate in the Marshall Plan. As partial compensation for the loss of this assistance, the Soviet Union extended to Poland a $450 million loan repayable in ten years at 3 per cent interest; the Russians promised to deliver equipment and to provide technical assistance for the building of a gigantic new steel mill at Nowa Huta.

Early in 1948, the long-standing dispute between Hilary Minc and Czeslaw Bobrowski came to a head. A crucial debate on "Planning Methods in Poland" took place on February 18 and 19, 1948, in the presence of Prime Minister Cyrankiewicz. The most important economists belonging to the Polish Workers' (Communist) Party and to the Socialist Party were present. Minc assailed the National Economic Plan for 1948 prepared by the Central Planning Office for significant deviations from Marxist principles. National income, he alleged, was still constructed according to "bourgeois" methods, which inflated the importance of the nonsocialist sector in the total product. Instead of assigning top priority to increasing production, which would sooner or later pull up consumption, national income had been projected from the estimated rise in its components (private consumption and

10. For details and sources, see W. J. Stankiewicz and J. M. Montias, *Institutional Changes in the Postwar Economy of Poland*, pp. 11–25.

investments). Minc argued that the rapid expansion of the producer goods sector was the only way to increase consumption in the long run. Bobrowski, on the other hand, favored a more balanced pattern of growth, ruling out heavy sacrifices in the present for the sake of doubtful future gains. Finally, Minc objected that the 1948 plan was a farrago of operational decisions for the state-controlled sector mixed with recommendations, projections, and estimates for the rest of the economy. According to him, not one word was said in the draft project about the means for carrying out the plans and controlling their execution, or about the concrete forms for mobilizing the masses toward fulfilling the plans.[11]

Hilary Minc voiced much the same arguments against the plans of the Central Planning Office as the "teleologists" had raised against the partisans of "genetic" planning in Soviet Russia in the mid-1920s.[12] Ambitious plans must be drawn up, and concrete measures, including institutional reforms, must be devised to carry them out. "To plan," Minc concluded, "means first of all to mobilize the masses whose creative energy and enthusiasm are the most important factor in the realization of the plans."[13] The teleologist, unlike the geneticist, is loth to recognize any objective limitations to economic expansion; if they exist, they can be overcome with Bolshevik ingenuity and with the enthusiasm of the masses.

This debate marked the end of the first, or reconstruction, stage of Polish planning, described in Chapter One; it inaugurated the second stage of ambitious industrialization plans. Bobrowski had to resign his post.[14] He was replaced for a few months by Tadeusz Dietrich, who later became Minister of Finance. In the fall of 1948, Hilary Minc was named head of the State Commission for Economic Planning, which was created to replace the old Central Planning Office. Minc kept a few technicians of the old C.U.P.,

11. Hilary Minc, "O właściwą metodę planowania w Polsce" (For a correct method of planning in Poland), *Nowe drogi* (New paths), no. 8 (1948), p. 36.

12. For details, see E. H. Carr, *A History of Soviet Russia, Socialism in One Country, 1924–1926, 1,* 496–98.

13. Minc, p. 36.

14. Bobrowski was named Polish envoy to Sweden; immediately upon reaching his post, he left for Paris where he spent the years 1948–56. He returned to Poland in the fall of 1956. For a summary of his recent work, see Chap. 9.

including the officials in charge of procurement and investment planning; but for most of the key posts he brought along the faithful Marxists who had worked with him in the Ministry of Industry and Trade. From now on, the theory and practice of planning was to conform to Soviet-Marxist precepts.

In mid-1948 the political situation took another turn for the worse. Soon after Stalin had launched his crusade against Tito, Gomulka was attacked for his nationalistic deviations and was forced to resign from his post of secretary general of the Polish Workers' (Communist) Party in August in favor of Boleslaw Bierut, a Stalin man. After the purging of Gomulka and of other communists tainted with Polish nationalism, Poland had to knuckle under to Soviet rule. The merger of the Socialist and Communist parties in December 15, 1948, eliminated the last remains of formal political opposition in the country. Old Socialists inimical to the newly formed United Workers' Party were purged.[15] After this, universities, professional journals, and other centers of intellectual activity, deprived of their former autonomy, became responsible for disseminating Soviet doctrine in all fields. "Bourgeois economics," which had been tolerated within certain narrow limits until the end of 1948, was now banished from books, periodicals, lectures, and university courses. From early 1949 to late 1955, all economic writing had to conform to the letter and spirit of Soviet-Marxist doctrine. Censorship was thorough, and writers soon became accustomed to molding their thought to the prescribed pattern. Articles and books on planning, larded with quotations from Marx, Engels, Lenin, and Stalin were almost totally emptied of substantive content. An intellectual low point was reached in 1951 and 1952. For information on this barren period, we are forced to rely largely on more recent works reviewing the historical development of planning. After the death of Stalin, controls were relaxed, and, in small doses, facts and empirical analysis again found their way into economic writing.

2. The Six-Year Plan

Encouraged by the success of the Three-Year Plan, the Communists soon turned their attention from reconstruction to gen-

15. The dramatic political events of 1948 are described in some detail in Dziewanowski's study, pp. 208–22.

eral development. They naturally opted for development according to Soviet principles, which entailed an all-out industrialization drive, spearheaded by the growth of heavy industry.

The first draft, or "guiding principles," of the Six-Year Plan, presented to the First Congress of the United Polish Workers' Party at the end of 1948, was still reasonable in scope; it was the upward revisions of the next three years that overtaxed the country's strength.[16] But even the first version suffered from serious defects. Hilary Minc later conceded that

> in the years 1948 and 1949 [when the plan was first prepared] the state of technical knowledge was marked by a certain provincialism . . . There was an excessive tendency to build new objectives without regard to existing capacity; this led in many cases to planning on the basis of technology which was not quite up-to-date, and which in certain cases was obsolete. Investment outlays were not realistically estimated . . . There was a shortage of project-making organizations, a lack of exact information on the state of technology in the East and in the West.[17]

16. It is common knowledge in Poland that Hilary Minc went to the Soviet Union in late 1949 to seek approval for a set of targets that were already more ambitious than those contained in the first draft. But Stalin is said to have demurred and called for the still higher targets that were incorporated in the final official version of the plan. Boleslaw Ruminski, minister of the chemical industry in the 1950s, argued at the Eighth Party Plenum in October 1956 that Minc could not disculpate himself entirely from the blunders of the Six-Year Plan.

> In Comrade Kuzinski's speech, which was widely disseminated in Warsaw factories, it is said and written that comrade Minc was the author of the first version of the plan, of the good plan. Then a second plan was imposed, of which Minc was not the author. Who imposed it? The friends did . . . I understand that comrade Minc worked under special conditions. Much was imposed in connection with special industry. But comrade Minc is also the author of the second version of the plan. Moreover we know what sort of policy comrade Minc carried out. Were the friends guilty there? We all remember the prodigality, the gigantomania, and the romanticism which characterized the period of Minc's rule.

In this citation "special industry" stands for armaments and "the friends" for the Soviets. See the stenographic report of the debates of the Eighth Plenum, *ND*, no. 10 (1956), p. 70, and A. Erlich's "The Polish Economy after October 1956: Background and Outlook," *American Economic Review*, 49, no. 2 (1959), 110.

17. Speech at the Eighth Plenum of the United Polish Workers' Party, October, 21, 1956. *ND*, no. 10 (1956), 121.

The revisions were hastily prepared and reinforced certain of the shortcomings of the original version.[18]

The principal targets of the first draft and of the final version are shown below, together with official statistics of plan fulfillment.

TABLE 2:1. *Initial and Final Six-Year Plan Targets for 1955 and Official Statistics of 1955 Performance*

			December 1948 draft	July 1950 plan	Actual official results for 1955
National income	index (1949 = 100)		170–180	212	174 [a]
Gross investment	"	"	230–250	350	232 [b]
Gross output of so-socialized industry	"	"	185–195	258	274
Agricultural output	"	"	136	150	113
Steel	millions of tons		3.8	4.6	4.4
Crude petroleum	thousands of tons		170	394	180
Hard coal	millions of tons		90–95	100	95
Cement	"		n.a.	5.0	3.8

[a] Computed at 1956 prices.

[b] Index of gross investments in the national economy computed at 1956 prices.

Sources. J. Marczewski, *Planification et croissance économique des démocraties populaires, 1,* 188; Alton, p. 117; *Rocznik statystyczny 1959* (Statistical yearbook 1959), pp. 58, 64, 75, 87, 92, 168.

Further revisions in the plan were made in 1951 and 1952 as a result of the deterioration of the international situation. Projects for the construction of a number of war plants were added to the investment budget without any of the basic objectives of the plan being cut back to make room for the newcomers.[19] The output plan for 1952 was raised nearly 17 per cent above the target specified in the approved version of the Six-Year Plan.[20]

At the July 1950 plenum of the Party, which was devoted to a discussion of the Six-Year Plan, the decision was taken to go ahead with the collectivization of agriculture. The plan set a target of 20 to 25 per cent of the cultivated land to be collectivized by 1955.[21] In the meantime, to meet the growing urban demand

18. Cf. Chap. 5, Sect. 3.

19. A. Karpiński, *Zagadnienia socjalistycznej industrializacji Polski* (Problems in the socialist industrialization of Poland), p. 11.

20. Alton, p. 118.

21. Dziewanowski, p. 233.

for foodstuffs, the government had to rely on compulsory deliveries from private farms. The heaviest exactions fell on the richer peasants who normally marketed the largest share of their production.

The results of the Six-Year Plan, though they fell short of expectations, were still impressive. But so was the cost of their achievement.

Let us first examine the credit side of the ledger. The official index of the gross output of socialized industry rose by 174 per cent from 1949 to 1955, the growth rate declining from about 20 per cent per year at the beginning of the period to 11 per cent in 1955. National income in 1956 prices, measured according to Soviet precepts, rose by 74 per cent, or at a compounded rate of almost 10 per cent per year.[22] The official index of industrial output overstates the actual extent of growth.[23] An index for basic industry built up by Dr. Maurice Ernst from basic production statistics shows an increase of 78 per cent for the Six-Year Plan or a little over 10 per cent per year; according to this index, the rate of increase eased off from 15 per cent in 1950 to 8.5 per cent in 1955.[24] Ernst's adjusted index, covering a wider sample of industry and including handicraft production, shows a slightly higher growth—84 per cent for the six years. If Ernst is correct, even the target for 1955 output in the 1948 draft of the Six-Year Plan was not reached. An economist of the Planning Commission, on the basis of unpublished calculations, arrived at an increase

22. At 1950 prices, national income rose by 82 per cent or a little over 10 per cent per year. See *Dochód narodowy Polski 1954 i 1955* (National income of Poland 1954 and 1955), p. 47—henceforth referred to as *Dochód narodowy 1954–1955*. These estimates exclude the value of all "nonproductive services," which probably increased more slowly than the other components of income during the Six-Year Plan.

23. The official index, weighted with "fixed prewar prices," suffers mainly from the introduction of new or modified products at prices appreciably higher than prewar levels; it is also distorted by changes in the importance of double counting, due to the trend toward the vertical disintegration of enterprises during the early 1950s, and by the usual biases associated with base-year weights in a period of rapid growth. The first two of these biases are recognized by A. Karpiński, p. 47.

24. Ernst, p. 100. In this index, commodity series are aggregated into industrial groups by means of 1956 prices weights and the groups are in turn consolidated into a series for all industry by weighting them with their corresponding labor costs. (According to Ernst, weighting with value-added weights including depreciation does not affect the index substantially.) The final index is the median between an index weighted with 1948 labor costs and an index weighted with 1955 labor costs. (Ernst, pp. 80–83, 133.)

for the period of 120 to 130 per cent.[25] Another unofficial Polish calculation indicates that output just about doubled during the period.

Significant changes in the structure of production took place between 1949 and 1955. The rise in farm output, which averaged only about 2 per cent per year, lagged far behind the pace of industry. The 13 per cent increase achieved between 1949 and 1955 was far short of the 50 per cent mark that had been targeted for this sector; [26] the proportion of agriculture in national income also fell more than had been planned. According to Ernst, the output of the producers' goods industries (group A of the official industrial classification) rose by around 100 per cent, while the output of consumer goods (group B) rose by slightly less than two thirds.[27] The metal-working industries' output almost tripled. Chemicals, rubber, construction materials, and leather all went up by over 130 per cent; the production of textile, clothing, fats, salt, and fuels rose by less than 50 per cent.[28]

Labor productivity (defined as average production per employee) showed substantial improvement according to Ernst's calculations: over-all, it rose by 20–30 per cent in six years, a compounded rate of 3 to 4 per cent.[29] By Western standards such a rate would be quite respectable. However, we ought to keep in mind that productivity in 1949 was still at least 30 per cent below prewar (in comparable territory); at best, the Six-Year Plan raised productivity back to prewar levels. In power plants, mining, and metallurgy, productivity was still a good deal below prewar in 1955; but the greatly expanded industries, such as metal working, chemicals, and rubber products, did show some gains over prewar productivity.[30]

This spurt of industrialization required a vast redeployment of resources. Over a million persons, nearly a tenth of the farm population, left agriculture to find work in other occupations. Of

25. A. Karpiński, p. 49. On biases in the official index, see below, p. 313 n. 4.

26. For details on plan fulfillment in agriculture, see the United Nations, Economic Commission for Europe, "The Polish Economy since 1950," *Economic Bulletin for Europe, 9*, no. 3, 22, 27–28.

27. Ernst, p. 103. The official index shows increases of 196 per cent and 171 per cent respectively (*RS 1956*, p. 81).

28. Ernst, p. 103. Official statistics show much larger increases for all categories.

29. Ibid., p. 183.

30. Ibid., p. 191.

these new workers, 50 to 70 per cent got jobs in industry.[31] Registered unemployment, which still numbered 118,000 in 1949, was virtually wiped out.[32] The number of women holding jobs rose from 747,000 in 1949 to 2,000,000 in 1956. Over 200,000 persons formerly engaged in private handicrafts were recruited for work in industry, construction, transport, and trade. Altogether employment in the socialized sector (outside of agriculture) grew by 2,232,000 persons—or by 61 per cent—during six years; it is remarkable that over half of this increase occurred during only two years, 1950 and 1951. Employment in the typical investment sectors, such as construction and the building materials and machine-building industries, more than doubled, almost all the increase taking place before 1953.

New capital, the other ingredient of Poland's growth, was marshalled mainly by allocating an increasing proportion of national income to investments. Capital for new projects was also mustered by cutting down on the resources formally allotted to replacements and repairs, especially in agriculture, housing, road-building, and other low-priority sectors. This reallocation raised the share of net to gross investment at the cost of temporary decapitalization in the neglected sectors. The share of net investment in national income, calculated at 1950 prices, is estimated to have risen from 22.7 per cent in 1949 to a high of 38.2 per cent in 1953 and then to have subsided to 31.2 per cent in 1955.[33] The cost of all state investments, reckoned in 1955 prices, averaged 29 billion zlotys a year; this was estimated to equal four times the prewar rate for 1937 territory.[34] Of total investments, 46 per cent were given over to the development of industry, and in this latter

31. A. Karpiński, p. 118. A fair number of them continued to live on the farm and commuted to work.

32. Ibid., p. 111.

33. "Net investment" is defined in the official computation as new investments and capital repairs plus increases in working capital and reserves minus recorded depreciation. The national incomes of different years in this official calculation have all been computed in 1950 prices, which are much less affected by the incidence of turnover taxes than the prices of subsequent years. (Turnover taxes levied on consumer goods blow up the relative share of consumption and artificially reduce the share of investments.) In terms of 1956 prices, the ratio of net investment to national income rose from 15.6 per cent in 1949 to 27.9 per cent in 1953 and 22.2 per cent in 1955. See Dochód narodowy 1954 i 1955, p. 47, and Rocznik polityczny i gospodarczy 1958 (Political and economic yearbook 1958), p. 461.

34. A. Karpiński, p. 63.

portion, 85 per cent went to heavy industry, as against 75 per cent originally planned. The farm sector got only 10 per cent of total investments, which were laid out almost exclusively for the development of collective and state farms; in 1952 and 1953, total private investment (mainly in agriculture) dropped to less than half of what it had been in 1949.[35]

Since new capital was concentrated overwhelmingly in the machine-building and metal-working, chemicals, metallurgy, and power industries, whose capital-to-labor ratios all increased, the neglected sectors, mainly consumer goods, building materials, and fuels, could only increase their output by employing a good deal more labor with substantially the same plant and equipment. Less than 16 per cent of the rise in the industrial labor force during the Six-Year Plan went to newly constructed enterprises (as against 32 per cent of the investment).[36] The bulk of the increase in output during the period was obtained by working old plant and equipment more intensively.[37]

This substitution of labor for capital on a large scale is relevant to the planning problems that interest us: it shows that the planners must take into consideration the possibility of radically altering factor proportions if they wish to find the shortest path to their goals; and they cannot do so by relying on fixed capital-to-output coefficients or on any crude devices of this type. They must at least have a conception of how labor productivity in each industry will be affected by a more or less intensive use of existing assets.

Another point we may deduce from the change in proportions is that the rate of growth is dependent not only on the fraction of investments given over to building up capital goods industries, but also on the average proportion of national income invested. In other words, a country with a poorly developed capital goods industry, cut off from sources of import of such goods, is still capable of investing a high proportion of its national income to

35. A. Szerwentke, "Wykonanie 6-letniego planu inwestycji" (Fulfillment of the Six-Year Investment Plan), *Gospodarka planowa* (Planned economy), pp. 15–16.

36. A. Karpiński, pp. 83 and 113.

37. In 1955, only 23 per cent of output came from new or reconstructed enterprises. The latter are defined as enterprises undergoing more than 50 per cent expansion in capacity. (Ibid., p. 69.) These reconstructed enterprises are not included in the share of investments in new capacity cited in the text.

accelerate growth insofar as labor can be substituted for capital in the investment sectors.[38] But when there are limited opportunities for the substitution of labor for capital, and the capital goods are already worked at or near capacity, it takes a disproportionate increase in the share of income invested to achieve a higher rate of growth. Similarly, for a limited capacity in the consumer goods industries, a substantial decrease in the investment rate is needed to achieve any short-run improvement in the supply of consumer goods.[39]

3. Hitches in the Six-Year Plan

We have already seen that the fulfillment of the officially approved version of the Six-Year Plan was exceedingly uneven, the farm sector trailing farthest behind in the completion of its appointed tasks. Plan failures had direct repercussions on the real wages of workers and employees which, instead of rising by 50 to 60 per cent in six years as planned, plummeted in 1951 and 1952 and had barely recovered 1949 levels by 1956.[40]

Another consumer sector of the economy that had to bear some of the impact of the failure to fulfill plans elsewhere was residential construction, which suffered from lags in the production of building materials. From 1950 to 1956, the stock of urban housing increased by only 800,000 rooms, while the urban population grew by 2,400,000 persons. Three additional urban residents had to be accommodated for every newly constructed room; this ratio was almost double the *average* number of occupants per room in 1949, when the losses due to World War II still had not been made good. According to Gomulka, the stock of rural housing was lower in 1955 than in 1949: the new construction of rural housing had failed to keep pace with the attrition rate of old housing.[41]

38. E. D. Domar, "A Soviet Model of Growth," in *Essays in the Theory of Economic Growth,* pp. 230–40.

39. Cf. Erlich, pp. 98–101.

40. "The Polish Economy since 1950," *Economic Bulletin for Europe, 9,* no. 3 (1957), 35. The Secretariat of the Economic Commission for Europe estimates that real wages were 18 per cent lower in 1953 than in 1949. This does not take into account quality deterioration and queuing for goods whose prices were set too low to equilibrate demand.

41. October 20 speech before the Eighth Party Plenum of the Polish United Workers' Party; see *ND,* no. 10 (1956), 25, 26. Gomulka's estimate of the deprecia-

In the first three years, household consumption took the brunt of plan failures. "Disproportions" during this period were caused in large part by the unanticipated expansion of the armaments program linked with the Korean War. Defense plants swallowed up 11 per cent of total industrial investments from 1951 and 1955, most of which for projects not foreseen in the Six-Year Plan. This proportion was as much as all the light industries together received in those years.[42] Investments in the light and food-processing industries had to be trimmed in 1952 and early 1953 to free resources for the expansion of the armaments industry.[43] As a result investments in consumer goods industries in 1953 only reached 50 per cent of the amount originally scheduled in the Six-Year Plan.[44]

According to Hilary Minc,

> The building up of the defense industries, of armament production, and of the armed forces skimmed the cream of output—alloy-steel plate, roller-bearings, pipes, the most precise machinery, etc. It took the best technicians and engineers and also contributed to the non-fulfillment of investment plans in a number of branches of industry . . . This situation, it has to be said clearly, led to the creation of a half-war economy in 1951–1953.[45]

Stanisław Kuzinski, an economist in the Secretariat of the Central Committee of the Party, has recently pointed out that 80 per cent of the output of the machine-building industry went to make armaments, military equipment, means of transportation, and machine tools, and only 20 per cent was left to meet equipment needs in the coal-mining, chemicals, and power industries as well as in agriculture.[46]

Another source of difficulties was the Western embargo on strategic exports to the Communist bloc. "This forced us," Minc said,

tion of housing was apparently based on a service life of one hundred years, a generous estimate tending to minimize anticipated losses.

42. "The Polish Economy since 1950," p. 26.
43. Investments in these consumer-goods industries did not recover their 1951 level until 1954. A. Karpiński, p. 89.
44. From a speech by Hilary Minc quoted in Dziewanowski, p. 237.
45. Speech at the Eighth Plenum, October 21, 1956, ND, no. 10 (1956), 123.
46. Kuzinski, Główne proporcje . . . , pp. 49, 50, 60.

"to develop domestic production in a number of branches hastily and at high cost; on the other hand . . . this was one of the factors which hindered our contacts with Western technology." [47]

From the fall of 1953 on, however, in keeping with the more liberal policy pursued by Stalin's successors in the Kremlin, a new order of priorities was established.[48] At the Ninth Plenum of the Central Committee of the United Workers' Party in September 1953, it was resolved to switch investment funds scheduled for 1954 toward consumer industries and residential construction at the expense of heavy industry. The investment budget as a whole was to be scaled down. Nevertheless, substantial sums were allotted for the further expansion of the "socialized sector" in agriculture.[49] Besides serving obvious political ends, new investments in collective and state farms were to help increase the supply of marketed grain, a shortage of which had compelled the authorities to devote large amounts of critically scarce foreign currency to food imports. Further cuts in the investment program were made at the Second Congress of the Party in March 1954. The congress also called for renewed efforts to "socialize the countryside."

These political turmoils are reflected in year-to-year changes in the level of gross investments. Investments in socialized industry, which had been rising at an average rate of about 25 per cent per year from 1950 to 1953 (at 1956 prices), remained practically constant in 1954 then fell by 6 per cent in 1955.[50] On the other hand the total of state and private investments in agriculture, which had declined since the beginning of the Six-Year Plan, recovered their 1950 level in 1953 then rose sharply in 1954. It

47. H. Minc, p. 123. As an example of the effects of the embargo, Minc cited the construction of the Zeran works. It had initially been planned to produce automobiles at Zeran on license from the Fiat works in Italy. But the Western embargo on lathes and other precision machinery for making automotive equipment had been "one of the causes" which impelled the Poles to apply for a Soviet license instead.

48. This turning point nearly coincides with the launching of Malenkov's New Course in the Soviet Union.

49. Dziewanowski, pp. 92–94.

50. All these and the statistics which follow in the text are taken from the RS 1960, p. 75. Of the total investment fund earmarked for industry, a larger share, from 1953 on, went to light industry which had fared poorly in this respect in the preceding years.

is significant that the New Course only succeeded in stemming
the tide of rising industrial investments; the trend was not reversed until late 1954 or early 1955.[51] Indeed, as we have already
seen, the percentage of the national income invested was higher
than ever in 1953. Once a great number of projects had been
launched and investment funds had already been earmarked for
their completion, it was embarrassing to the regime to have to
starve them of funds and leave half-finished hulls gaping at the
sky. Such a policy, by creating temporary dislocation and unemployment, might have attracted even more criticism than another
year or two of enforced austerity.

The way the cuts in the investment program were made casts
an interesting sidelight on long-range planning. Instead of re-
trenching on a handful of postponable projects and finishing off
all jobs nearing completion, the Planning Commission trimmed
outlays on a few dozen projects, delaying their achievement for
an unreasonable length of time. On the average, the construction
of plants classified as priority objectives took two years longer than
had been foreseen in the Six-Year Plan. Low priority objectives
suffered even more delays "since they experienced special difficulties in the procurement of materials and bore more than their
share of the financial reductions." [52]

One might have expected that heavy retrenchments on a few
construction sites would have upset the perspective balances even
more seriously than scattered cuts, which could be ordered in
such a way as to effect an internally consistent reduction in the
investment effort. This would be misleading because the economies of scale derived from concentrating mechanized equipment
as well as engineering and managerial talent on a few sites more
than offset any disadvantages due to the lack of synchronization
in the launching of interdependent projects.[53] Such at least was

51. According to H. Minc, this delay was due in part to a failure to keep investment expenditures within planned limits. Speech at the Eighth Plenum, *ND*, no. 10
(1956), 124.

52. A. Karpiński, p. 89. A case in point is the Warsaw Subway, on which enormous
sums had been expended prior to 1953. After 1954 its construction was not entirely
discontinued but went on at snail's pace. According to a 1956 report, *Trybuna Ludu*
(People's tribune), May 12, 1956, the length of the tunnels advanced "a few dozen
meters a month."

53. Professor Kalecki, at present a high official of the Polish Planning Commission,
stresses this point in his article, "Czynniki określające tempo wzrostu dochodu na-

the experience of planners in Poland, where indivisibilities in the supply of resources may have been a more bothersome factor to contend with than in a vast and varied economy such as the Soviet Union.

By the mid-1950s, disproportions in the development of industry that could not be remedied in the short run had already come to light. At best they could have been palliated by a concentration of investments in the lagging sectors; but, as a matter of fact, they were probably aggravated by the policy adopted in 1954 at the Second Congress of the Party of shifting resources toward collectivized agriculture and light industry. The failure to dovetail the growth of interdependent industries was made evident by the recurrent deficits of certain materials and by the appearance of surplus capacity in processing industries that had expanded faster than their raw-material supplies. Most typical was the machine-building industry, some of whose branches were reduced to working at 30 to 50 per cent of capacity, an average of one shift per day, for lack of steel and nonferrous metals.[54]

One of the worst failures of the Six-Year Plan was the underfulfillment of targets for the production of building materials, which became a bottleneck for certain types of construction. The plan foresaw an output of almost 5 million tons of cement but only 3.8 million tons were actually produced in 1955. The situation was also critical for bricks, tiles, and lime, as many small privately or cooperatively owned factories producing these materials had been forced to cut back output for lack of funds to repair or to modernize equipment in the early 1950s.[55] Shortages of these building materials held back residential housebuilding; the pace of industrial construction was only maintained by the wide substitution of lumber for cement and bricks, with consequent damage to Poland's already depleted timber resources. The third

---

rodowego w gospodarce socjalistycznej" (Factors determining the rate of increase of national income in a socialist economy), *GP*, no. 8 (1958), 3.

54. S. Kuzinski, "Niektóre dysproporcje sześciolatki w naszym przemyśle" (A few disproportions of the Six-Year Plan in our industry), *ND*, no. 9 (1956), 5. According to Lissowski, the machine-building and metal-processing industry as a whole was working at 45 per cent of capacity in 1956. See "Metody rachunku ekonomicznego w perspektywicznym planowaniu regionalnym" (Methods of economic calculation in the regional long-range plan), *GP*, no. 1 (1958), 13.

55. A. Karpiński, p. 23.

bottleneck, a shortage of imported raw materials, was caused by the failure to expand exports at a rate commensurate with import requirements. Notable among these shortages were cotton, rubber, and zinc concentrates. The capacity for refining ore concentrates was much in excess of domestic ore supplies, but a part of the available equipment had to stand idle for lack of imported concentrates. The main source of export earnings was coal mining, whose output lagged behind plan and whose exports failed even to keep abreast of production increases.

From 1953 to 1956, investment outlays in the socialized sector, measured at 1956 prices, showed practically no increase; the rise in the total volume of investments in the country was due mainly to the reactivation of private spending in farm buildings and equipment and in housing.

As we have seen real wages rose again from their 1952–53 low point and nearly recouped the losses sustained in the first years of the plan. But the recovery was not fast enough to pacify the urban proletariat, bilked of the generous gains in living standards the authorities had promised at the inauguration of the plan. Their discontent was shared by the intelligentsia, chafing under the totalitarian controls imposed by the Party. From 1956 on, as will be shown in detail in Chapter Nine, criticism of waste and inefficiency in planning began to undermine the dogmatic optimism of official pronouncements. A high point of popular resentment was reached with the Poznan riots of June 1956, which laid bare the failure of the planners to remedy the excesses of the early years of the Six-Year Plan by halfway compromises and stopgap measures from 1953 on.

4. *Inflation*

Throughout the postwar period, marked by so many institutional changes and by violent turns in economic policy, prices and money wages steadily pursued their upward course. Inflation, some time repressed, some time open and running, has always been a problem to contend with, a problem the planners were never able to solve satisfactorily.

In retracing the course of the inflation, we shall go over some of the historical ground already covered, this time concentrating on the way changing economic conditions influenced the market for consumer goods, farm incomes, and urban wages. We dwell on the inflationary problem at this length because it undermined every attempt to use prices as guides to resources allocation; as we shall see in Chapters Seven and Eight, inflation distorted the structure of production costs and caused producers and lower administrative organs to make decisions that were inconsistent with the broad decisions taken by the highest authorities.

The inflation of the war years and of the liberation had boosted retail prices over one hundred fold from 1938 to early 1945. The pace of the early postwar inflation, though rapid, abated somewhat from the chaotic period that had preceded it. During the Three-Year Plan (1947–49), investment costs, consisting mainly of wages, rose by over 400 per cent; retail prices of clothing and footware tripled; food prices were held to a 50 per cent increase by direct controls and rationing.[56]

Data available on the free-market prices of agricultural and industrial products show that prices began to steady toward the middle of 1948. This relative stabilization was made possible by substantial gains in the output of consumer goods (especially textiles, shoes, and sugar) and by the excellent grain and beet sugar harvest of that year.[57] The budget surpluses accumulated in 1947 and 1948 reflected these improvements and contributed to checking the inflation. Rationing was temporarily abolished.

The increased purchasing power released by a sudden acceleration of the investment program in 1949, preparing the way for the Six-Year Plan, was neutralized by continued improvement in the supply of industrial consumer goods and, again, by a bountiful harvest. But soon after the launching of the ambitious Six-Year Plan in 1950, strong inflationary pressures began to spill over into price increases.[58]

By the autumn of 1950 so much surplus currency was already in circulation that the government found itself compelled to carry out a highly unpopular monetary reform. All prices, wages, and savings accounts were converted at a ratio of 100 old zlotys to

56. *RS 1948*, pp. 4–5; *RS 1949*, pp. 4–5; K. Secomski, *Planowanie inwestycji* (Investment planning), pp. 72, 81, 104.

57. *RS 1949*, pp. 2, 62–63.

58. In 1950 textile prices went up on the average by 25 per cent (woolens by 40 per cent). *Wiadomości statystyczne* (Statistical news), various issues of 1950; index of retail prices, *TL*, February 3, 1956.

three new zlotys. For their cash holdings, which made up most
of the population's liquid assets, citizens received one new zloty
for every 100 old zlotys. By this means, two-thirds of the people's
cash holdings were confiscated.[59] Even the reform was not successful in arresting the upward movement of prices, which picked up
added momentum in 1951 and 1952. The situation was aggravated during these two years by the failure of the potato harvest
and by a marked decrease in the amount of meat contracted by
the state. Urban rationing of meat and of certain basic food
products was "temporarily introduced" in September 1951, extended in December and again in March 1952.[60]

In January 1953, rationing was abolished and the index of retail prices which had been artificially maintained at 135 per cent
of the 1949 base jumped to 192 per cent of that level. (The index
of food prices sold in government stores increased from 130 to
209.6).[61] The United Nations' Economic Commission for Europe
estimates that the cost-of-living index rose by 132 per cent from
1949 to 1953.[62] It declined by 2 or 3 per cent from 1953 to 1956,
although the divergence between the indexes of official and free-
market prices testifies to renewed inflationary pressures.[63] In 1957
and 1958, after substantial wage increases had been granted to
several categories of industrial workers, prices rose again, by 6
per cent in the first year and by 3 per cent in the second, according to the official index of retail prices.[64]

Among the forces building up inflationary pressures, we must
distinguish between those that tended to bring about once-for-all
price increases and those making for continuous self-feeding expansion. Failures to hit targets of consumer goods output belong

59. The amount of money kept in government savings accounts was relatively
small. The time of the year picked out to carry out the reform (October) fell hard
on urban workers who had been saving to buy winter clothing and to lay in stores
for the cold season. It was also the right season to mulct farmers who were still
holding a good share of their harvest proceeds in cash.

60. *TL*, May 2, 1952.

61. *TL*, February 3, 1956, and *RS 1956*, p. 245. Free-market prices rose from 240
(on a 1949 base) in 1952 to 270 in 1953 and then inched up to 283 in 1956. The
much more moderate increase of free than of controlled prices from 1952 to 1953
brings out the extent of the suppressed inflation prior to the removal of rationing.

62. "The Polish Economy since 1950," p. 35.

63. From 1953 to 1955, official food prices were cut by an average of 6 per cent.
They rose by 5 per cent on the free market. (*RS 1956*, p. 244.)

64. *RS 1959*, p. 97.

to the first category. For example, urban food supplies in the early 1950s were much lower than had been anticipated in the Six-Year Plan; their shortage caused a disequilibrium between purchasing power and the available provision of consumer goods at fixed prices; as we have seen the government introduced rationing to hold the price line in 1951 and 1952 but was eventually compelled to allow prices to rise to restore balance in the market. Unless it can be shown that these shortages also forced up wages, which again brought pressure on prices, there is no reason to conclude that a cumulative process of inflation had been set off by the initial disturbance. We shall find in Chapter Four that the cumulative forces mainly operated through the monetary system. For the time being, we shall concentrate on the factors that tended to build up the purchasing power of the population and the demand for consumer goods.

Reference has already been made to the phenomenal increases in the nonagricultural labor force that took place during the first few years of the Six-Year Plan, particularly in the typical investment sectors. From 1949 to 1953 employment in construction rose from 308,000 to 771,000 workers and in machine building and metal processing from 220,000 to 515,000.[65] Young people from the farm, women, and persons formerly self-employed (particularly in handicrafts and trade) made up most of the new recruits to the working force. The total increase in the nonagricultural labor force was held to 50 per cent from 1949 to 1955 because a number of traditional consumer goods industries, such as textiles and garment making, showed little rise when handicraft production is included in the statistics.

The wage bill for all nonagricultural workers (but excluding handicrafts) rose almost exactly threefold from 1949 to 1953 and a little more than fourfold from 1949 to 1956.[66] If the average wage which prevailed in 1949 outside of agriculture had remained at the same level all the way to 1956, the wage bill would have

65. A. Karpiński, p. 107.
66. Comparable wage fund and employment data are available for the years 1949, 1953, and 1956, except that in the first two years they include employment in state farms and in auxiliary farms attached to factories and other institutions, but not in 1956. To net out these agricultural workers, it has been assumed that their average wage (available for 1956 only) bore the same relation to the average wage of all workers in 1949 and in 1953 as in 1956. (RS 1957, pp. 267, 269.)

risen by only 44 per cent from 1949 to 1953 and by 61 per cent from 1949 to 1956. Hence at least three-fourths of the rise in the wage bill was due to higher wages and only about one-fourth to wider employment.

It is roughly estimated that more than half of the rise in current investment outlays was caused by higher investment costs between 1949 and 1951 and somewhat less than half between 1951 and 1953.

Other budgetary expenditures also contributed to the inflationary pressure. The provision of working capital for new enterprises and the financing of losses of state-run enterprises took an increasing share of total outlays in the national economy from 1949 to 1953. In 1953 when they reached their peak, these expenses came to 40 per cent of total investments.

Investments were not the only source of surplus purchasing power that had to be mopped up by turnover taxes and by monetary reform. Substantial sums were also spent on armaments and on the upkeep of the armed forces. Even communal services (from crèches to dining halls), which were only partially self-sustaining financially, fed fresh purchasing power into circulation. In 1953, when about 38 per cent of national income calculated in 1950 prices was invested, an additional 6.4 per cent was "consumed socially," leaving only about 55 per cent of national income for individual consumption.[67]

Altogether, during the Six-Year Plan, the urban population rose by three million inhabitants; over a million of the latter were new wage earners. The upward pressure on retail prices of the increased wage bill due to this influx might have been held in check had the farm sector been induced to market a sufficient amount of foodstuffs to meet the swollen urban demand or if the supply of industrial consumer goods and of imports had been large enough to close the gap in newly released purchasing power. Actually, the planners gauged the total supply of consumer goods required to maintain financial equilibrium on a widely optimistic recovery of agricultural output (which was supposed to grow by 50 per cent during the Six-Year Plan). It is also likely that they overestimated the share of total produce that they would be able to draw from the countryside. The laggard collectivization drive,

67. *Dochód narodowy 1954–1955*, p. 47.

together with the disappointing performance of state farms and of such collectives as were formed, all contributed to this failure to tap the peasants' surplus for the needs of the industrialization program.

It is significant that the terms of trade between manufactures and farm produce shifted strongly in favor of the peasants, both on the free market and in government shops.[68] While there is doubt as to how much the absolute level of living of the peasantry rose after 1948 [69]—it dropped up to 1953 but rose rapidly thereafter—it is certain that, on the whole, the peasantry fared better than the rest of the population during this most intense period of industrialization. Faced with a chaotic and generally inadequate supply of unattractive industrial goods, deprived in large measure of access to investment goods to improve his farm, the peasant "withdrew into his shell," ate more, and fed a part of his surplus to his hogs.

The supply price of the young agricultural laborer on the margin of choice between staying on the farm and seeking urban employment must have risen if not absolutely (in terms of a real wage), at least relative to the wages of "intra-marginal workers," that is, of employees with a more limited range of choice, who were already rooted in their city jobs. This in part explains the reduced spread between the wages of white-collar and skilled workers on the one hand and of "green" workers on the other. Socialized plants competed with each other for young farm hands, and, by raising unskilled wages, preserved the necessary inducement to attract fresh labor supplies.

Another force pushing up wages was the demand for experienced workers on the part of expanding industries, which was to some degree requited at the expense of plants that were lower on the planners' scale of priorities. The average wage of workers in metallurgy rose from 1.18 times the over-all average in the socialized economy in 1949 to 1.38 times the average in 1955, while at the same time wages in the cotton and food processing in-

68. In 1955 the official index for food prices in socialized trade stood at 210.5 per cent of the 1949 base, as against 145.6 per cent for industrial goods (*RS 1956*, p. 245).

69. See W. Styś, "Zagadnienie intensyfikacji i opłacalności produkcji rolnej" (The problem of the intensification and profitability of agricultural production), *Ekonomista*, no. 4 (1957), 115–19.

dustries were falling behind the average increase in all branches.[70]

By 1953, despite the upward scramble of unskilled wages (at the relative expense of already established workers), the real-wage differential between city and farm jobs had fallen so low that the spontaneous influx of labor from the countryside no longer satisfied the demands of the industrialization program. The "enlistment action" carried on in the countryside to recruit workers for industry was only a palliative and had little success in remedying this deficit. To a limited extent, the shortage was made good by increasing the proportion of women in industry.[71]

The rising cost of attracting fresh labor reinforced the inflationary pressure created by the large proportion of the total labor force that had been switched to the production of armaments and producer goods. An increase in productivity in consumer goods industries might have helped to fill the inflationary gap, but this increase could not be achieved without diverting investment funds from heavy industry to retool obsolete processing and textile plants. This the authorities were unwilling to do before 1953 and unable to do rapidly enough thereafter.

5. A Recapitulation

After completing in good time their Three-Year Plan for reconstruction, the Poles plunged headlong into a six-year industrialization program, which probably could not have been fulfilled even if, following the outbreak of the Korean War, new assignments in defense and heavy industry had not been loaded on to the original targets.

During the first years of the Six-Year Plan, the United Workers' (Communist) Party ruled the country by violently repressing all signs of dissidence in political or in economic matters. In the plan, consumers' needs were systematically sacrificed to achieve the regime's main goals, the building up of heavy industry and the strengthening of the country's defense capability. The growth of output—10 to 15 per cent per year in this initial period—was remarkably rapid. It was realized not only by deflecting resources

70. *ND*, no. 2 (1956), 29.

71. The peasant's choice is between two types of work (farm and nonfarm) and two real incomes. A woman, faced with a choice between unpaid household work and a job in industry, may enter the labor market when real wages fall. The income effect of falling real wages is likely to be stronger than the substitution effect.

away from agriculture, handicrafts, small-scale consumer industries, and housing but also by the capital-saving method of crowd-
ing hundreds of thousands of new laborers each year into existing plants for the sake of any marginal contribution they might
make to raising output. Irrepressible wage and price increases revealed the miscalculations the planners had made in their excessively optimistic expectations of labor-productivity gains and
in their forecasts of farm output and marketing.

The end of 1953 marked the inauguration of a softer policy,
which was designed to make good some of the economic losses
sustained by the population in the preceding years. Charged with
the implementation of this new policy, the Planning Commission
cut back investment outlays on a wide assortment of projects
(some of which were already long started) and aggravated the disproportions that had been developing in preceding years—mainly
between the capacity of industries producing raw materials and
semifabricates and the capacity of processing industries. Output
still grew at nearly 10 per cent per year; but real wages recovered
too slowly to suit industrial workers, who were ready to rebel by
mid-1956.

When we consider all the sharp political changes that left
their mark on economic policy during the postwar period, we
must conclude that the planners never worked for more than
two years under the same directives or with the same order of
priorities. We should have this constant uncertainty in mind
when we come to appraise the planning system through which
policy was translated into practice.

CHAPTER THREE

Current Planning I: The Distribution
of Producer Goods

1. *Administration of the Economy*

The routine planning of a centralized economy of the Soviet type consists primarily in coordinating the current production plans of the different sectors of the economy and in parceling out materials and equipment among producers to enable them to fulfill their assigned tasks. These operational functions are the hallmarks of a Soviet system. A market economy might be compatible with a fair degree of planning, as long as targets were implemented through a market mechanism, but no such economy could accommodate itself to hidebound rationing and to administrative commands for effecting the short-run allocation of resources.

To understand these routine operations, one must know the various parts of the bureaucratic machine and how they relate to each other. First the economic administration must be assigned its proper place in the constellation of forces governing the country.

The United Polish Workers' Party, made up in majority of Communists and in minority of ex-members of the Socialist Party, rules Poland. The Party is headed by its first secretary,[1] who presides over the Politbureau (9 to 13 members). This body in turn represents and acts in the name of the Central Committee of the Party (65 to 80 members). At the headquarters of the Central

1. The names of the first secretaries who served since the end of World War II and the dates of their tenure follow: Władysław Gomulka, 1945–48; Bolesław Bierut, 1948—March 1956; Edward Ochab, March 1956–October 1956; Gomulka 1956 to date (1961).

Committee in Warsaw, a number of Communist experts help the Party frame its economic policy, keep a close watch on the execution of Party directives, and advise on personnel matters affecting the economic administration. Another typical para-executive organ is the Warsaw Party Committee which has various industrial departments and its own economic experts supervising the carrying out of central policy in the region of the capital. Similar Party organizations function at the level of the province (voivodship), the county, the township, and the factory. They parallel—when they do not supersede—the rule of the state's executive organs at these different echelons.[2]

In principle the source of all governmental power is the popularly elected Parliament or *Sejm*, though in practice this body, under Communist control, has played a compliant role in the performance of its legislative duties. Since October 1956, it has been reactivated to the extent that some of its specialized commissions have begun to keep a close tab on government finances and on developments in the national economy. The Supreme Control Chamber, which had been transformed into the Ministry of State Control in 1952, recovered its original status in December 1957; it again reports to the *Sejm* on the economic, financial, and administrative activity of state organs "from the viewpoint of their legality, economy, appropriateness and equity."[3] The State Council, a 15-man body, issues decrees while the legislature is not in session, orders elections, convenes the *Sejm*, and generally acts in its name as the supreme organ of state power. Since the promulgation of the constitution of 1952, the Council of Ministers, which also draws its mandate from the *Sejm*, has been deprived of its basic political character and has been turned into an administrative organ for carrying out state and party policy. Indeed, its large size (43 members under Bierut, 31 under Gomulka) and its specialized composition[4] would have made it unwieldy as a political instrument.

2. Since October 1956, the role of the Party in carrying out economic policy is said to have diminished and many Party specialists have gotten jobs directly in the administration.

3. *RPG 1958*, p. 51.

4. From 1952 until 1956 there were eleven industrial ministries: Mining, Power, Metallurgy, Machine-building, Meat and Dairy, Wood and Paper Products, Building Materials, Chemicals, Food-processing, Light Industry, and Small-Scale Industry

Attached to the Council of Ministers are three top-level economic agencies: (1) the Planning Commission,[5] (2) the Economic Committee, and (3) the Economic Council.

The Planning Commission, whose chairman (at present S. Jędrychowski) is an ex-officio member of the Council of Ministers, draws up national plans for the approval of the council and supervises their execution. Before 1956, when it was known as the State Commission for Economic Planning (P.K.P.G.), it held sway over the entire economic field, wielding power over the economic ministries. It reached its heyday in the early 1950s under the rule of Hilary Minc, who became a virtual economic czar of Poland. Under Gomulka, some of the Planning Commission's prerogatives have been turned over to the Economic Committee, headed by the prime minister and made up of the vice-chairmen of the Council of Ministers together with four of the economic ministers (Finance, Foreign Trade, Heavy Industry, and Agriculture). The supreme coordination of economic policy is now vested in this inside cabinet. The Economic Council, headed by Oskar Lange, was founded in late 1956 to introduce reforms in the economic organization of the country and to offer expert advice on economic policy. It acquired a measure of influence soon after its institution, most of which it lost in 1958 and 1959, once the Party began to veer toward a harder line in political and economic matters.

From now on we shall be mostly concerned with the Planning Commission, the economic ministries and their subsidiary organs, which were jointly responsible for carrying out the state's economic policy during most of the period covered in this study. We shall have frequent occasions to discuss the Gomulka reforms, particularly in Chapters Nine and Ten, but our discussion will

and Handicrafts. Since 1956, some of these ministries have been amalgamated. The first two industries on the list have been joined under the Ministry of Mining and Power and the next two under the Ministry of Heavy Industry. For the changes that took place in the composition of the Council of Ministers from 1945 to 1955, see Alton, *Polish Postwar Economy*, pp. 78–80.

5. In 1956, in connection with the partial decentralization of the economy, the State Commission for Economic Planning was renamed Planning Commission of the Council of Ministers. The changes that occurred at that time in the nature and competence of the top planning organization were not important enough to warrant making a consistent distinction between the old and the new commission, which, throughout this work, are both referred to by the name of "Planning Commission."

be focused on the hypercentralized planning system of the early 1950s.

There are now only around 800 persons working in the Planning Commission, some 300 of whom have substantive jobs. In 1954–55, the personnel of the Commission numbered around 1,800 persons, many of whom went to work in the economic ministries and in lower organs after the 1956 reform. There were, at this earlier time, twelve departments in charge of industrial production, corresponding roughly to the ministerial breakdown of industry. The Department of Balances and Procurement was responsible for coordinating the current (yearly and quarterly) plans of socialized industry and for balancing the supply and demand for materials and equipment. It was divided into six branches: metallurgy and metal ores, fuels, machinery, building materials, food-processing industries, textiles and light industry. Altogether these branches employed about 250 persons.[6]

Among the other important subdivisions of the Planning Commission may be mentioned the Section on Perspective Planning, the Department of Regional and Local Planning, the Department for the Coordination of Investment Projects, and the Department for the Coordination of Price Policy (known before 1956 as the Department of Costs and Price Policy). These organizations were less affected by the personnel retrenchments of 1956 than the departments more directly linked with production and supply planning.

We shall now descend the hierarchical ladder, first to the ministry, then to the central boards of industry (equivalent to the Soviet *glavk* or directorate), down to the enterprise and the plant and indicate how these organizations fitted into the planning scheme for 1950 to 1955.

Diagram 3:1 shows the typical organizational structure of "industrial ministries," responsible for the operation of large- and medium-scale nationalized enterprises in their sector.

In the chemical industry, for example, there were ten central boards of industry directly subordinate to the ministry. These were the central boards for inorganic products, pharmaceuticals,

6. Before 1955, according to David Granick's report of a 1958 interview in the Planning Commission, there were 60 persons working on metal balances, 30 of whom dealt with rolled ferrous metals alone ("Polish Interviews, July 1958," pp. 2–3).

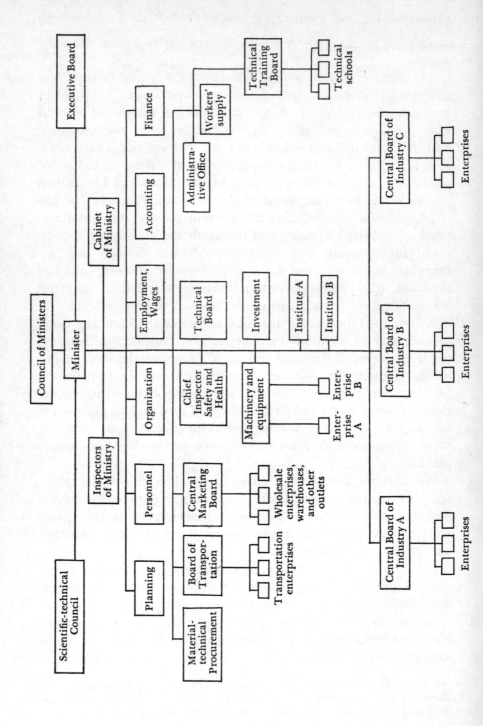

DIAGRAM 3:1. *Structure of Industrial Administration (1955)*

synthetics, rubber, artificial fibers, organic products, plastics, minerals, salt, and technical gases. There was one central marketing board (*centralny zarząd zbytu*) with headquarters in Warsaw, which supervised the distribution of chemical products by several marketing offices (*biura zbytu*),[7] generally located near large chemical centers (e.g. the Office for the Marketing of Inorganic Products in Gliwice). There were also a few sales offices (*biura sprzedaży*) under the Central Marketing Board, which sold chemical products (i.e. coal derivatives) originating in enterprises subordinate to different ministries. Note, however, that foreign trade in chemical products was the exclusive province of the Ministry of Foreign Trade and of its specialized import-export corporations.

The Central Board of the Inorganic Industry directed 26 producing enterprises (e.g. the Torun Phosphate-Fertilizer Works). These enterprises were on "full cost-accounting," in the sense that they had their own bank accounts, drew up income statements and balance sheets, and were linked with the government budget only through their net taxable profits and subsidized losses. All the higher organizations were on "budget account," with the exception of the sales offices. The operating costs of organizations on budget account were charged to the general upkeep of the administration and were financed by the central budget.

As a rule, small plants (*zakłady*) located in the same city were merged under the same enterprise. Plant autonomy was restricted. All banking transactions, balance sheets, and income statements were centralized at the enterprise level. Only unit costs of production were computed in each plant—and then solely in industries where "internal cost-accounting" had been introduced.

In several ministries, including the Ministry of Mining, there was one more echelon in the hierarchy, the trust (*zjednoczenie*), which was wedged between the central board and the enterprise. In the Ministry of Mining, these trusts supervised as many as a dozen bituminous coal mines located in one district of Silesia. Until 1950 the trusts had been responsible for the financial transactions of their subordinate mines; they had kept the mines' cost accounting records for them, leaving managers free to devote themselves to their production tasks (which, at that time, were

7. These subordinated marketing organizations are not shown in the diagram.

assigned a much higher order of priority than lowering costs or earning profits). When financial responsibility was once again vested in the mine in late 1950, the trust was retained as a convenient administrative agency for subdividing material allotments, planning the level of individual mines' subsidies, and setting wage and cost limits.

In April 1950, a planning commission was organized in each of the voivodships (provinces) as a small-scale replica of the Planning Commission in Warsaw. These commissions, administratively subordinated to the presidia of the Peoples' Councils (*Rady narodowe*) of the provinces, were charged with the coordination of local supply and production plans and manpower balances. In point of fact, they exercised little independent power; their principal function in the planning process was to work out balances of materials and other factors for the voivodship on the basis of detailed directives issued by the State Planning Commission and the ministries. They also helped to run small-scale industry and to supervise private agriculture and handicrafts. At a still lower level, the county planning commissions had similar duties and even fewer prerogatives.

Although the Peoples' Councils of voivodships and counties were in principle responsible for the management of local industry, the Ministry of Small-Scale Industry and Handicrafts (reformed in 1958 as the Committee for Small-Scale Production) exercised detailed supervision over small-scale enterprises through its control over their investment outlays and through its materials-allocating functions.

In 1954, 13.9 per cent of the value of gross industrial output of socialized enterprises was attributed to enterprises run by the Peoples' Councils. State enterprises accounted for about one-third of the output of local industry and producers' cooperatives for two-thirds. It was estimated that private industry (excluding handicrafts) produced less than one per cent of total industrial output in the mid-1950s.[8]

The increased financial autonomy granted to state-run enterprises in 1950 was part of a wider reform, which sought to awaken the interest of managers in reducing costs and paring down losses. This principle was bound up with other organizational moves.

8. *RPG*, pp. 472, 528–33.

Prior to 1950, both the procurement of materials needed as inputs by industrial producers and the sales of industrial products to the "nonmarket sector" (i.e. to socialized firms) were highly centralized. Procurement centrals, which were responsible for supplying materials to enterprises in "their" ministry or central board, controlled a wide-flung network of warehouses and supply points. They often interceded directly with producers for extra consignments of scarce materials, getting around the red tape of the central marketing boards, which were supposed to keep tabs on all sales within their sector.

The reforms of 1950 aimed at a drastic reduction in the role of procurement organizations of all varieties. The enterprise was henceforth to have its own procurement division, which was authorized to do business with the central marketing organization of its suppliers or directly with so-called "cooperating producers" which dealt with the enterprise on the basis of "planned contract." Furthermore, producers no longer had to sell their wares to a sales or marketing organization. They could sell straight to their industrial clients, as long as the marketing board of their ministry was properly notified and approved of the transaction. A companion reform provided for the elimination of "accounting prices": most sales were now made at uniform prices (including the cost of railway delivery). The new system was called "organized transit" to distinguish it from the old "accounting transit," which had required the financial participation of marketing organizations in every transaction.

Many of the warehouses and supply points of the recently liquidated procurement centrals were turned over to marketing organizations in 1950 and 1951. Some are said to have been closed or transformed to serve other purposes, leaving a gap in the provision of these facilities which was never entirely closed.[9]

9. For further details on the 1949 and 1950 reforms, see Chap. 7, Sect. 4. Also, Z. Deutschman, "Z zagadnień zaopatrzenia materiałowo-technicznego" (Selected problems in material-technical procurement), GP, no. 7 (1955), 24; H. Witkowski and K. Krygier, "Z zagadnień organizacji zaopatrzenia materiałowego w przemyśle" (Selected problems in the organization of material procurement in industry), ZG, no. 1 (1951), 39–40. It should be pointed out that the 1949 decree on the liquidation of the procurement apparatus was not fully carried out. As late as 1955, the procurement offices of certain ministries were still maintaining their own warehouses and supply points and keeping personnel in key industrial centers to intervene in favor of the plants they represented (Deutschman, p. 24).

2. Coordination of Current Plans

The reforms just alluded to, while they delegated certain accounting and financial functions from higher agencies to the
enterprise, were not devised with the object of decentralizing
the allocation of resources. Quite to the contrary, planning, if anything, became more centralized in the ensuing years, up to the
crisis of 1953 [10] which precipitated a reversal of this trend. In
the first years of the Six-Year Plan, the bureaucratization of planning was in full swing. In official circles, the answer to all shortcomings in the centralized system was "deeper," more detailed,
and more comprehensive planning: given enough time, it was
held, consistent plans could always be elaborated. There was not
much point in holding out incentives and inducements to enterprise managers, who were responsible for performing the tasks they
were allotted and who could always be dismissed if they failed to
deliver the goods. Decisions on what, how, and for whom to produce were up to the central planners; managers supplied with
certain quotas of factors and equipment were chiefly expected to
transform these resources into the desired product-mix with the
highest possible technical efficiency.

The planning procedure for commodities subject to centralized
supply [11] was divided into three phases, which took up about nine
months of the year preceding the plan-period: (1) The Planning
Commission in the early spring issued "directives" to ministries
and central boards for the forthcoming year. (2) A draft, called
"project," of the National Economic Plan was prepared by the
Commission from materials submitted by lower organs. (3) Once
the National Economic Plan had been approved by the Council
of Ministers and promulgated, final detailed plans of production
and procurement were drawn up by ministries, central boards,
marketing organizations, and enterprises.

There is enough evidence, based on personal interviews with

10. Above, Chap. 2, pp. 65–67.
11. As we shall see below, pp. 89–90, many commodities of secondary importance
were planned and distributed by ministries and lower organs. From 1952 to 1955
all commodities for which material balances were drawn up were "administratively
distributed" (rationed). Up to 1951 and from 1957 on, a number of commodities
that were balanced were not subject to distribution. See also p. 107 below.

officials of the Planning Commission long active in the same line of work, to outline the procedure generally followed in the preparation of these directives.

The work done on the material balances in the earliest phase of the planning period was confined to about two dozen trial-balances struck for key materials. Three sources of data were used in working out these balances: (1) targets fixed for the long-range plans; (2) current statistics of plan and performance for the current year; (3) summary balances of the national economy, comprising preliminary forecasts of the growth in national income, consumption, investments in fixed capital, and inventories for the forthcoming year. Particular attention was paid at this stage to the problem of planning a correct level of investment expenditures, consistent with the anticipated supply of building materials and with the capacity of the construction industry. It was desirable also, though this consideration was sometimes relegated to the background in the early 1950s, that investment outlays, most of which were in the form of wages, should not be so high as to upset equilibrium in the retail market. (To guard against this happening, the planners had to prepare a trial-balance of the disposable income and outlays of the population, making use of such estimates as they may already have had on hand on the volume of retail sales planned for the coming year, in keeping with tentative consumption targets.) [12]

It was also at this stage that the first feasibility tests were made to ascertain whether the output targets were consistent with capacity estimates, whether enough labor would be available during the plan-year to hit these targets at expected productivity levels, and whether the transportation network was adequate to move the planned outputs to their destination. Balance of payments estimates had to be drawn up to check whether the proceeds from planned exports would be sufficient to pay for the volume of imports needed to support domestic production and for the minimum import requirements of consumer goods. The work involved at this stage was, and still is, necessarily crude, partly because the statistics available so early in the year are not an adequate guide for the level of performance that may be banked on for the forth-

12. The elaboration of these synthetic balances is discussed in the next chapter.

coming year. But the estimates can be refined at later stages, and it is convenient to have a broadly consistent program ready from the start.

The directives for 1951, a year of increased centralization, laid down not only the principal production targets but also labor productivity and other basic indices. The idea was to avoid the necessity for multiple revisions of the projects prepared by lower echelons by framing as early as possible a fairly consistent master-plan within which all subsidiary plans would eventually dovetail.[13] Each subsidiary organ was to consider the set of directives it received as its minimum assignment: deviations could only be approved if they were at least broadly consistent with the "general proportions" of the original plan.[14] In the second stage, ministries, central boards, and enterprises worked up their concrete plans on the basis of the directives.

The enterprise was an essential first link in this chain of planning; its procurement needs, based on the tentative production targets of the directives, were written up in applications for materials and other factors and dispatched to its supervising central board. Once the needs had been checked, they were consolidated for all enterprises subordinate to the board and passed on to the procurement department of the ministry. Finally, the ministry transmitted the industry's total requirements to the Planning Commission.

At each echelon, a procurement-technical plan was drawn up—which was the supporting document for the applications—establishing the kind and quantity of inputs that would have to be made available to producers under the central board or ministry to allow them to fulfill their production plans. Since these various procurement plans, which were expressed in physical units, also had to be translated into cost plans, they had to be more comprehensive and include more minor, hard-to-plan input needs than the bureaucracy could possibly cope with intelligently. As a result, most of the work done consisted in the mechanical summation of submitted applications.

13. S. Róg, "Przemysł" (Industry), in *Zarys rozwoju metodologii planowania w Polsce Ludowej 1944–1954* (Outline of the development of planning methodology in Peoples' Poland 1944–1954), ed. by B. Minc et al., p. 29.

14. Róg, pp. 34–35.

The work of the balancing departments of the Planning Commission consisted in meshing the supply and demand for all centralized commodities (a much larger number normally than the number of key commodities for which the first trial-balances were prepared). The material balances they drew up were supposed to reconcile the output targets for individual commodities with requirements, as expressed in the procurement plans submitted by ministries. These balances served as the supporting document for dividing up the available supply of centrally allocated materials among ministries. (In the case of important materials in short supply, the allotments portioned out to ministries were subject to the approval of the Council of Ministers.)

The full-fledged version of this scheme proved unworkable: it put too much pressure on the limited time and personnel of the organizations drawn into the planning process. Procurement planners were so busy revising requirements for every new draft of the national production plan [15]—there were more than ten versions of this plan in 1953 [16]—that, by March or April, when they were through planning for the current year, it was already time to start planning for the next. They rarely had time to analyze plant performance or to study the possibilities of economizing on materials.[17] The procedure was so lengthy that the third phase of planning—the translation of the National Economic Plan into detailed operational plans—could never be carried out before at least three months of the plan-year were over.

As early as 1952, the list of materials planned "from the bottom up" was pruned down to basic raw materials and semifabricates.[18] This still did not block off the traffic of bureaucratic minutiae shuttling back and forth along the lines of the administrative

15. In 1951, every single item in the initial version of the various machinery balances had had to be re-estimated before the final version of these balances was approved. See A. Holzer, "Bilans maszyn w planowaniu gospodarczym" (The balance for machines in economic planning), *GP*, no. 4 (1952), 36.

16. R. Zalewski, "Uwagi o sposobie opracowania narodowego planu gospodarczego w przemyśle" (Remarks on the method for elaborating the national economic plan in industry), *GP*, no. 4 (1953), 8–9. Zalewski points out that "versionism" increased in 1953. This was of course linked with the political and economic crisis referred to in Chap. 2 (pp. 65–67).

17. K. Krygier, ed., *System zaopatrzenia w gospodarce planowej* (The procurement system in the planned economy), pp. 99–100.

18. Krygier, p. 99.

hierarchy. Stronger measures had to be taken. In 1954 the enterprise was cut off for all practical purposes from the initial stages
of planning. Planning was now organized "from above" (*od góry*).
The enterprise could make suggestions to its central board concerning its needs, its production capacity, and its consumption
norms, but it was the board's undivided responsibility to frame
the procurement plan of its wards. According to a 1955 report,
"the central board makes fewer mistakes in planning requirements from above on the basis of the comprehensive data at its
disposal than in summing up the applications of individual enterprises, as was the practice in the past." [19]

The second reform aimed at reducing the time and paper work
needed to "finalize" the yearly plans. The notion was to insulate
the ministries and the central boards from day-to-day changes in
governmental directives affecting the Planning Commission's work
until the last stages in the planning process, at which time all
plans could be properly coordinated. Thus, a change in the postulated rate of growth of the producer goods' sector would influence
the trial-balances of the Planning Commission but would not normally be transmitted to the ministries concerned. The ministries
and the Planning Commission were enjoined to draft separate and
partly overlapping plans. Starting in May of the year preceding
the plan-period, each ministry was to prepare draft balances and
supply plans on the basis of Six-Year Plan targets as well as of
any other information in its possession concerning the demand
of consumers both in and out of the industry for its products. In
June, these projects would be handed down to the central boards,
whose responsibility it was to discover "reserves" and to help
tighten up the technical norms and labor productivity forecasts
underlying the ministerial projects. By late August or mid-Sep-
tember the revised projects were to be submitted by the ministries
to the Planning Commission. They would then be reconciled
with the independent draft worked up by the Commission from
plan-fulfillment data for the current year and from routine information gathered from ministries and central boards during the
course of the year. Close liaison between the Planning Commission and the ministries was to be maintained throughout the

19. Ibid.

period during which the parallel plans were being elaborated.[20]

Once the differences between the Planning Commission and the ministries had been ironed out by the Council of Ministers and by other high state organs, the National Economic Plan was at last promulgated. Enterprises received their concrete directives toward the end of the year; and as we have already seen, detailed production and supply plans were finally made ready three to six months after the plan-year had already begun.

As more experience was gathered with this parallel-planning method, a certain degree of specialization developed. The ministries became chiefly concerned with technical problems—establishing the "true capacity" of plants, reviewing consumption norms, binding consumers to their suppliers—while the Planning Commission was more involved in balancing interindustry needs, imports, exports, and final demand. However, for a large number of commodities consumed exclusively within one industry (e.g. fluxing materials in the metallurgical industry), balances were prepared by officials in the ministry; if they were submitted to the Planning Commission at all, they were usually perfunctorily examined and approved.

Frequently also, the Planning Commission delegated to the marketing organizations the task of preparing the first draft-balances of the products in which they specialized. They were instructed to work in close conjunction with their customers, in particular with the ministries drawing up supply plans for their firms. Unfortunately, the ministries were usually working behind schedule and the marketing organizations had to be content with fragmentary and unreliable estimates of the future needs of their sector.[21]

Table 3:1 below shows that the responsibility for drawing up balances was quite diffused, at least for machines and equipment; there was obviously a trend toward increasing the number of balances during the course of the Six-Year Plan, due to the planners' aspiration toward an ever greater degree of detail and accuracy,

20. R. Zalewski, pp. 7–9.

21. A. Issa, "Analiza ekonomiczna stanu zbytu i zaopatrzenia" (The economic analysis of marketing and procurement), *Gospodarka materiałowa* (Material economy), no. 14 (1956), 473.

but the proportion of the balances handled directly by the Planning Commission remained fairly stable.

TABLE 3:1 *Number of Machinery Groups or Subgroups Balanced by Listed Institutions, 1950–54*

	1950	1951	1952	1953	1954
State Planning Commission	5	8	8	11	18
Central Board of Machine Economy (C.B.O.M.)	4	7	11	10	14
Departments of ministries	3	5	5	3	3
Central boards of industry	3	8	9	9	9
Procurement centrals	1	3	3	2	4
Central marketing boards	1	2	3	3	5
Sales centrals	2	5	7	7	9
TOTAL	19	38	46	45	62

Source. H. Piklikiewicz, "Metodologia i organizacja bilansowania maszyn i urządzeń" (The methodology and organization for balancing machines and equipment), *GM*, no. 21 (1954), 650.

In 1956, when hyper-centralization had already come under heavy fire from revisionist writers, Bronislaw Minc, who, as former head of the coordinating department of the Planning Commission, had played a key role in designing the planning scheme described in this section, wrote a popular article deriding the fastidious detail of the scheme and the arbitrary division between commodities planned centrally and commodities whose balancing remained at the discretion of the ministries.[22] Minc pointed out that 1,500 commodities were balanced by the Planning Commission, but in addition 3,300 commodities had to be submitted by the ministries to the Commission for approval. Among the latter, he listed sauerkraut, two kinds of cucumbers, soda water, lemonade, buttons, combs, and tooth paste. (Interestingly enough, the orangeade plan, unlike the lemonade plan, was the exclusive responsibility of the ministry for food-processing.) The agricultural plans, though they might lack in precision, made up for it in pettifogging detail. For auxiliary sources of meat such as deer, hares, and foxes, separate balances were drawn up with the aid of natural-increase estimates computed according to prescribed norms.[23]

22. B. Minc, "W sprawie metod planowania" (On the subject of planning methods), *TL*, March 20, 1956. See also Chap. 9, Sect. 1.
23. Ibid.

These picturesque aberrations should not mislead us as to the real nature of the balances and the quality of planning. The agricultural balances were noteworthily unreliable because the statistics on which they were constructed were poor and because the vagaries of nature would have tended to upset even the most carefully established coefficients relating factor inputs to crops or meat production. These restrictions applied a fortiori to the task of planning the private sector of agriculture (over 80 per cent of farm output in 1956), which was almost totally refractive to central controls. Industrial commodities that were low in the planners' priority scale, such as tooth paste and combs, were also planned mechanically and were subject to a wide margin of error. But in all fairness, we should test the success of the central planning scheme by the coordination of the plans for key producer goods, and consumers' staples, which together numbered far less than the 1,500 groups and items that were allegedly balanced in the Planning Commission. (Most of these detailed balances were actually prepared by lower organs and were only submitted to the Commission for final approval.) [24] It is on these key commodities numbering at most two hundred goods (such as coal and pig iron) and consolidated groups (such as "rolled steels") that we shall now dwell.

3. *Successive Approximations*

Between 1957 and 1959 the research department of the Planning Commission conducted a study on the methodology of planning with material balances. This work was carried out by economists familiar both with planning procedures and with the theory of input-output economics essential to an understanding of the balances. We shall quote extensively from the work done by K. Porwit and W. Sławin on this subject which contains the most candid statements found in the literature of the practical problems faced by the planners in their efforts to achieve consistency in the balances. Porwit's main conclusions are set forth in the following paragraphs:

> When the method of balances was first employed, the basic notion was to strive for maximum accuracy: every planned

24. Cf. Table 3:1 above.

expenditure of a material had to be justified in detail by reference to the concrete use for which it would be consumed
and to the consumption norms corresponding to this use.
The individual consumers represented by their ministries
prepared detailed procurement plans containing thousands
of calculations and justifications. It turned out, however, that
this degree of detail and accuracy was largely deceptive. The
procedure for building up the project of a plan consists essentially in the examination of successive variants involving
changes in the proportions among different magnitudes. Detailed and drawn out calculations became unreal soon after
they were completed. Since there was neither the time nor
the possibility of introducing changes with the same accuracy
as in the first version, corrections were made by approximate
percentage adjustments. . . .

The method of balances, based on an exhaustive comparison of requirements and production tasks, poses a baffling
problem: how to coordinate deadlines and schedules for completing the work on interdependent balances. Every consumer
who was asked to calculate his requirements demanded the
prior establishment of his level of output, since this was
the basis on which he could calculate his requirements. But
the level of this output depends on the results of the balancing process itself. More than once, the question came up as
to whether production plans and procurement plans should
be elaborated simultaneously (i.e. whether they should proceed from the same version of the National Plan) or in successive stages. In theory, there can only be one correct solution:
the coordination of production and requirements is one, in-
divisible process. But in practice, the balancing of a couple
of thousand products cannot be a simultaneous operation. In
other words, it is hard to achieve a state of affairs where every
one of the balances corresponds to the same, mutually coordinated version of the draft-plan.

Work on the balances is parceled out among a number of
agencies in the ministries responsible for the production of
allied groups of materials. In striving for the mutual consistency of the balances, a steady contact must be maintained
between organizations drawing up balances and organizations

representing procurement needs. The balances in the course of the work on the draft of the National Plan pass through the Planning Commission but only a moderate (*niewielka*) number of balances are directly worked on in the Commission. These balances are undoubtedly the best coordinated of the lot and those grounded on the most consistent set of assumptions.[25]

In connection with the work done in the research department on the balances, W. Sławin and his collaborators prepared tables of technological coefficients for 1957 and 1958; these tables were based on 195 material balances elaborated in the Planning Commission. After certain closely related goods, such as soap and soap powders, white and gray salt, had been consolidated, the 195 original balances were boiled down to 95. The technological input-output coefficients extracted from these balances were arranged in matrices of 95 rows and columns (one matrix for 1957 and the other for 1958). It was observed that when the rows and columns of the matrices were arranged in suitable order, the matrices of coefficients exhibited a remarkable degree of "semi-triangularity": most nonzero coefficients occurred on or below the main diagonal of each matrix. The conclusions of the authors bear on the general consistency problem as well as on these structural properties of the input-output system.

The semi-triangular form of the table of coefficients points to the possibility of improving and accelerating the process of successive approximations. The method of successive approximations at present in use is in fact an iterative procedure (*postępowaniem iteracyjnym*). This iteration process may be facilitated by dividing the balancing system into a number of consecutive stages. The appropriate sequence is indicated by the triangular form of the coefficients. The system of interdependencies widens going from the apex to the base of the triangle.

In our balancing system, the groups of products belonging

25. K. Porwit et al., "Uwagi o metodach centralnej koordynacji planu gospodarczego" (Remarks on the methods for the central coordination of the economic plan), *Prace i materiały zakładu badań ekonomicznych* P.K.P.G. (Papers and materials of the economic analysis section of the State Commission for Economic Planning), no. 11 (1958), 33–35.

to the first four branches (machine-building, construction, textile, and leather industries) may be balanced in the first approximation and independently of other branches. This is possible since these products are basically allocated to final demand.

The materials . . . may be balanced . . . in such a way that the level of production of materials established in preceding stages may serve as a basis for allocating materials in successive stages.[26] It should be noted that we did not take into account the consumption in productive uses corresponding to the above-diagonal coefficients. If we follow the indicated sequence of balancing, the feedback effect (*wtórny wpływ*) of this [above-diagonal] consumption will be insignificant, since its quantity and relative weight—with the exception of pitprops used in coal-mining—are insignificant. This consumption may be introduced into the balances in the next approximation, or suitable correction factors may be applied to the estimates derived in the first approximation.[27]

If we understand our informants in the Planning Commission correctly, the kernel of the balancing problem lies in the dependence of manufacturing industries producing mainly end products on the material inputs sold by mining, metallurgical, chemical, and other industries specialized in making intermediate goods. If the latter are operated at full capacity, their output can be taken as given. This eliminates any feedback effect for this group of industries. The problem of sequence—aside from the manifestly superior strategy of starting the computation of material requirements from finished products and working back toward raw ma-

26. At this point the authors refer to an aggregated table of coefficients showing for each of thirteen aggregated branches the number of linkages with every other branch. The table is arranged so as to minimize the number (not the importance) of linkages above the diagonal. Out of 301 linkages, 26 were above the diagonal, 156 along the diagonal, and 119 below the diagonal. The order of the branches listed was as follows: metal-working and machinery, construction, textile, leather, food-processing, building materials, rubber, nonferrous metals, metallurgy, lumber and paper, chemicals, power, fuels.

27. W. Sławin et al. "Tablice przepływów materiałów w naturalnych jednostkach miary" (Tables of materials-flows in natural-measurement units), *Prace i materiały zakładu badań ekonomicznych*, no. 18 (1960), 12.

The method advocated in the citation is equivalent to the Gauss-Seidel iterative procedure described in Appendix A, Sect. 2, at the end of this volume.

terials and semifabricates—only matters for those industries that
are not expected to maintain their output at or near capacity
during the plan period. (Any circular interdependencies among
industries in this category will cause the underestimation of output levels computed from the direct requirements of other industries and from final demand.) The little evidence there is suggests
that the circular dependencies among these industries are relatively
unimportant.[28] The errors incurred in making insufficient allowance for them may not be significant in view of the lack of precision of the input-output coefficients and of the frequent failure
on the part of the planners to trace even the direct effects on
materials requirements at successive stages of manufacture of the
many changes that get to be introduced in the final bill of goods
in the course of preparing the final draft of the plan. (Revisions
in the targets were frequently made during the planning period
in line with new political instructions and with the latest estimates of industrial output, agricultural crops, norms, and capacity.)

According to one source, it was common practice for the planners in a specialized industrial department of the Planning Commission to draw up their first trial-balances in anticipation of
increased requirements in subsequent versions. They consequently
underestimated the production possibilities of the sector for which
they were responsible. As the demand for "their" products rose,
they uncovered "reserves" in production which allowed them to
meet these new demands. The art consisted in releasing the last
tons of concealed reserves for the ultimate version. If the extra
output could be realized without the support of additional material inputs, the procedure just described was likely to cut down
the extent of "versionism." Otherwise, it was just an expedient
device for managing capacity reserves and for forestalling painful
reappraisals late in the planning process.

A closer look at the make-up of a typical material balance will
help to bring out certain concrete problems faced by the planners
in their search for consistency. The two tables reproduced in
Appendix C, said to be patterned after Soviet models, were adopted
in Polish planning in 1954. The first is a summary balance (Form
B-1) for use in the Planning Commission. It recorded for each

28. See Appendix A, Sect. 4.

material balanced the total production and consumption slated in the current year, broken down according to ministry, as well as the production and consumption targets assigned to individual ministries for the forthcoming plan-year. Besides domestic production, the other sources of supply for the balanced material listed in the table were imports and changes in suppliers' inventories. Current allocations to domestic users were broken down between "nonmarket" and "market" supply. The former refers to deliveries for productive uses (mainly consumption of materials by industry, construction, and transportation); the latter refers mainly to deliveries of consumption goods to the wholesale and retail markets. Ministries consuming small amounts of a product were pooled in a miscellaneous category. They received most of their supplies from wholesalers. Contrary to pre-1954 practice, quotas of materials earmarked for increases in inventories of industrial consumers were bunched with other deliveries in Form B-1. It should also be noted that state and Planning Commission reserves (items III and IV of Table C:1) were not actual stockpiles but unallocated supplies, most of which were used in the course of the plan-year to bail out consumers in short supply.

Form B-2 was filled out separately for each ministry. (Since the column headings are identical with those in Form B-1, only the main headings are listed in Table C:2.) This form, strictly speaking, was not a balance at all: it merely broke down the disposals side of Form B-1. Even in Form B-2, the most detailed of the forms approved by the Planning Commission up to that time, only the most important types of output for which the balanced material served as input were itemized separately. In planning coal deliveries, for instance, only the principal products for which coal is used as a basic input (coke, cement, bricks, steel, etc.) were singled out.

It is evident that it was only for the products separately itemized that anything like a consistent program could be drawn up by successive approximations.[29] They were, in effect, the only products for which input-output coefficients were available in the Planning Commission. For some materials, requirements were measured in terms of tons of input per million zlotys worth of

29. The theoretical problem involved (and some suggestions for solving it) are discussed in Appendix A, Sect. 5.

output of the ministry, a measure which was too sensitive to changes in the composition of ministerial output to be an exact guide to allocations. For others no coefficients were available at all in the Planning Commission. For instance, quotas of materials balanced centrally that were used in the making of goods balanced by lower organs were automatically pooled with the undifferentiated allocations to individual ministries or miscellaneous consumers. This reduced even further the proportion of total disposals that could be traced to its ultimate destination as inputs used in the making of particular products and that could be regulated by technical coefficients.

Important statistical evidence on this subject has lately been released in conjunction with the theoretical and empirical study of material balances already referred to. The compilers of the study computed for 95 centrally balanced materials the percentage of "normed" allocations. These were allocations to industry, construction, and other "productive uses" regulated by a norm of consumption per unit of output of the particular product in the making of which the material was to be used. The results showed great disparities among materials in the coverage of the norms, disparities which appeared to be related to the degree of fabrication. Productive uses of iron ores and nonferrous ores, pig iron, steel, rolled steel products, lumber, cement, cellulose, sulfur and phosphorus, cotton, raw hides, petroleum, tobacco, wheat, and potatoes were almost totally covered by Planning Commission norms. Over 65 per cent of the allocations to productive uses of coal, coke, electricity, rubber, tin, scrap, calcium carbide, sulfuric acid, caustic soda, cotton and silk yarn, tanned leather, and alcohol were normed. But norms regulated less than 20 per cent of the consumption for productive uses of aluminum, lead and zinc alloys and semifabricates, graphite, roller bearings, plastics, textile fabrics, shoes, petroleum products, and meat. Finally, 45.9 per cent of the allocations of the composite industry described as "metal products, machines, and equipment" was normed.[30]

All these technological norms were either statistical—i.e. computed as the ratio of the allocation made to an industry divided by this industry's output during a given period—or aggregated from the technological norms set by ministries and central boards

30. Sławin, et al., pp. 24–27.

for individual plants. The complex problems the planners encountered in setting and controlling these lower-level norms will be discussed in Section 5.

4. *Resolution of Shortages*

In general the consolidated applications for materials reaching the Planning Commission exceeded available supplies—although the reverse also occasionally happened.[31] So far, no figures relating to this gap have been published. A Polish official once estimated in an interview that between 1953 and 1955 the Planning Commission could only satisfy around 80 per cent of the ministries' requests for metallurgical products.[32] Some information is also available concerning the balance of supply and demand at the level of the marketing offices responsible for the detailed supervision of the distribution of small groups of products. We learn for example that the applications for steel castings reaching the Marketing Office for Forged and Cast Steel Products exceeded planned supplies by 50 per cent in 1953, by 30–35 per cent in 1955 and by 10–20 per cent in 1956 and 1957.[33] As late as 1957, when the supply situation for most goods had improved, only 25 to 30 per cent of the requirements for Carnauba waxes could be satisfied.[34] But this was an exceptional case. By that date, deficits rarely exceeded 5 to 15 per cent of demands.

How were these shortages resolved by the organizations responsible for keeping supply and demand in balance? The handbook for procurement workers recommended—in the order listed below—the following means of dealing with shortages: a reduction in material consumption achieved by means of economies; replacement of the good in shortage by substitute materials; paring down of less essential domestic needs; an increase in production; the exploitation of "reserves" (i.e. higher efficiency); a cut in exports (if any); a stepping up of imports. Since none of these measures taken in isolation were susceptible of doing away with

31. Cf. Krygier, p. 85.

32. Granick, "Polish Interviews," p. 2. This gap was reported to have narrowed down to an "infinitesimal" discrepancy by 1958.

33. J. Nowak, "Odkówki i odlewy staliwne" (Steel forgings and castings), *GM*, no. 3 (1957), p. 95.

34. C. Aleksander, "Artykuly chemii organicznej," *GM*, no. 5 (1957), 158.

a shortage, it was suggested that they should be tried out in combinations.[35]

The handbook might have mentioned that increases in production, where extra capacity was not immediately available, were sometimes achieved by small, quickly maturing investments or by accelerating the completion of investment projects already started.

In the concrete example cited in the handbook, a reduced volume of exports took the brunt of the adjustments made to deal with a deficit. This was also in practice the line of least resistance; for the adverse effect on imports of the failure to earn foreign exchange by exports was less immediate and less obvious than the production breakdowns that might result from a drastic cut in material allotments to domestic industries. According to another source, the officials of the Planning Commission earmarked for exports those quantities of goods that could be drawn off from the pool of domestic allotments "without prejudice to procurement needs at home." Exports of "very many goods" came out as a "resultant item" of the balances.[36] Even where long-term commitments had been undertaken to export certain quantities of goods, they still would not necessarily figure as an irreducible element on the outlay side of the balance. If approved domestic requirements were rising, then exports had to be scaled down, no matter what the cost. (In 1955 certain items had to be imported and then re-exported to honor foreign-trade contracts, which otherwise could not have been fulfilled owing to increased domestic consumption.) [37]

An interesting case involving substitution of a productive service for a material in short supply was described in a Planning Commission interview in response to a question about the importance of the search for alternative processes in the planners' attempts to circumvent or widen bottlenecks. The more recently built sugar refineries are mostly located close to consuming cen-

35. Krygier, p. 85.

36. A. Rolow, "Ulepszyć współpracę przy planowaniu i realizacji zadań eksportowych" (Improve collaboration in planning and in carrying out export tasks), *GP*, no. 7 (1956), 25.

37. H. Lipczyński, "Nowe zadania handlu zagranicznego" (The new tasks of foreign trade), *GP*, no. 1 (1957), 30–31.

ters, away from the beet-producing areas in the western parts of Poland. Their coal consumption per ton of sugar produced is significantly smaller than in western plants refining local beets. Up to 1959–60, whenever the beet harvest fell below average, only the plants closest to the producing areas were operated at capacity. Fuel balances were particularly strained later on, and efforts were made to pare down the industrial consumption of bituminous coal. Transportation facilities being available for the purpose, it was decided to ship a larger proportion of the beet harvest to outlying plants which would require less coal to process the same amount of material than local refineries. Transportation services were thus substituted for the scarcer coal.[38]

What were the "less essential domestic needs" alluded to in the procurement handbook's list, which could be foregone when the plan was overstrained? Up to about 1953, consumer goods industries, producers' cooperatives, and private handicrafts were the principal buffer sectors. This was not publicized, and no citations can be invoked to support the point, but it was freely acknowledged by a number of Polish economists interviewed between 1956 and 1959. The crisis of 1953 forced a reappraisal of this policy. It had become evident that the maintenance of the expansion plans mapped out in 1950 would cause real wages to fall below the political danger point. A new constraint was superimposed on the short-range plans: that a minimum amount of consumer goods should be produced. Work was halted on many construction sites and many factories had to do without the equipment for which they had applied. Finally, the priority system was worked with greater discrimination than in the past.

This new policy was more beneficent to large-scale socialized enterprises in consumer-goods industries than to so-called "in-

38. In the model of Appendix B, transportation services would be classified as a "good" produced with certain inputs including network capacity, labor, and fuel. The alternative processes for making sugar were distinguished mainly by different coal and transportation coefficients. In the given circumstances, the capacity coefficients were immaterial since the harvest was too small to strain capacity in either group of plants. Even if labor was fully employed, its input requirements were not large enough to predetermine the choice of processes. This is then a case (the possible occurrence of which is suggested in Appendix B, Sect. 2) where the indirect demand for exogenous factors is the correct criterion for choosing the alternative process rather than the direct demand for labor or for beet-processing capacity (In this case the capacity of coal mines was the principal bottleneck).

ferior social forms," such as cooperatives and private undertakings. The results of a 1955 survey showed that central allotments covered only 60 per cent of the submitted requirements of industrial cooperatives and that, of the total allotted, no more than 95 per cent was actually delivered in the course of the year.[39]

Discrimination in the dosing out of materials by the Planning Commission was not, incidentally, the only form in which the system of priorities manifested itself. We shall see in the latter part of this chapter how lower organs could exercise a good deal of power in favoring certain groups of customers above others in the course of carrying out the plan.

It should be pointed out that many requests to satisfy "nonessential needs" never had a chance to manifest themselves. "Prohibitions by use," for example, ruled out the allocation of non-ferrous metals as inputs for making a long list of consumer goods, including compacts, cigarette boxes, children's toys, book ends, wastebaskets, hangers, and perambulators.[40] Many materials, subject to "restrictive regulation" (reglamentacja), could be expended only for a few circumscribed uses. Copper plate, for instance, was issued to the Ministry of Machine-building exclusively for use in shipbuilding. Finally, special permission had to be obtained from the Planning Commission to purchase special high-quality steels; prospective buyers had to prove that no cheaper steels—or steels in more abundant supply—would do for the purpose they had in mind.

In all these instances, applications for low-priority uses never got off the ground.

When all the measures taken to bring the demand for a material into balance with its expected supply had been exhausted —or, more exactly, when a point had been reached where only the most painful ablation of demand, with complex, hard-to-trace repercussions in many sectors, could eliminate the apparent shortage—the planners normally gave up the search and "closed the balance on paper." By this was meant that a mechanical closure was effected by compressing the technological norms of consum-

39. W. Ilecki and Z. Machoń, "Zagadnienie zaopatrzenia w Centralnym Związku Spółdzielczości Pracy" (The procurement problem in the Central Union of Work Cooperatives), *GM*, no. 11 (1956), 383.

40. *Monitor Polski* (Polish monitor) (1953), A-32, *poz.* 415.

ing industries: a smaller material quota was allotted than these consumers normally required to fill their plans. In such a case, everybody from the minister down was expected to exert "bolshevik ingenuity" to fulfill the industry's output targets even under these straitened circumstances.

The effects of this enforced austerity may have been beneficial in the days when requests for materials were egregiously inflated and methods of control were in their infancy. But by 1955, when the situation on this score had improved, the ritual closing of the balances had lost its magic. Consumers threatened with production breakdowns exerted their ingenuity in interventions and pressures with the authorities responsible for allocation decisions, as they tried to pre-empt supplies from other consumers. Insofar as they succeeded, the plans of the alternative recipients were disrupted; if they failed to get extra rations and they had to cut back output, their own consumers suffered. In either case, the coordination of output and supply plans fell off.[41]

5. *Material-Technical Norms*

The efforts of the planners to knock together a consistent plan will be of no avail if the basic data on which they rely are faulty or if, in the course of executing the plan, the political authorities intervene with fresh directives and upset the balances. We shall first consider the errors caused by the failure to transmit accurate information about the production functions of individual producers; in the next section we shall survey the obstacles that habitually crop up during the plan-period itself.

In the first heady days of the Six-Year Plan, when the young technicians running the Planning Commission under Hilary Minc still believed in drawing up ideally consistent plans, which would correspond to the true "engineering capabilities" of the economy, norms of consumption for all planned materials were supposed to be derived from technological data. These norms were to be sufficiently taut to mobilize producers to their fulfillment. In the first three years of the plan "tens of thousands of materials" were normed in the chemical and machine-building

41. Cf. "Prace przygotowawcze do Krajowej Narady Ekonomicznej Zbytu i Zaopatrzenia" (Preparatory studies for the National Economic Conference on Marketing and Procurement), *GM*, no. 24 (1955), 828–29.

industries (even if only "a few dozens" were actually controlled).[42] By 1955 the industrial consumption of coal was covered by norms to the extent of 82 per cent, although deviations from norms in certain industries ranged from 100 to 200 per cent.[43]

A 1951 decree published in the compendium of laws, *Monitor Polski,* gave precise directions as to how the type, make, and age of equipment, the size breakdown and the ash content of the coals fired in the furnaces should be taken into account in norm-setting.[44] The trouble was that, for every one of the elements considered, at least one had been left out of the reckoning altogether. Nothing was said of the condition of the equipment, of the frequency of its repairs, of the stone, sand, and humidity content of the coals, or of the ambient temperature of the boilers. Besides, many plants had no control instruments and no exact record was kept of the kinds and amounts of coal expended. The director of a plant visited by the author in 1956 explained that his coal ration consisted of fine grades with a high ash-content, which were not particularly suitable for the firm's equipment. "We try and keep a stock of better coals on hand, which we mix with the slack and slurry when the quality of regular deliveries falls so low that we cannot keep up the head of steam called for by our production process." The matter of norms was a theoretical nicety he did not bother very much with.

As late as 1956, a major item of complaint on the part of procurement specialists was that the norms were predicated on a "fully standardized quality of delivered materials"; the smallest failure on the part of suppliers to meet standards caused consumers to exceed their quotas.[45] The "mobilizing" features of the norms reinforced this tendency. The norms, according to the letter of a 1953 decree, were to be "progressive" in keeping "with the experience of the advanced science and technique of the Soviet Union."[46] It was never made clear how norms geared to

42. Z. Deutschman and H. Witkowski, "Zagadnienia oszczędności zużycia materiałów w gospodarce Polski Ludowej" (Problems in economizing the use of materials in the economy of Peoples' Poland), *Ekonomista,* no. 4 (1955), 42.

43. W. Olczakowski, ed., *Gospodarka węglem w przemysle* (Coal economy in industry), pp. 33–34.

44. *MP* (1951), A-22, *poz.* 270.

45. Issa, p. 470.

46. *MP* (1953), A-33, *poz.* 421.

better-than-average performance could serve the needs of exact planning.

Even where the norms for individual producers were correct, there was still a long way from the plant to the Planning Commission. The plant norms were supposed to be combined into industry-wide norms by weighting them in proportion with the volume of plant output. But this injunction was frequently ignored.[47] These norms were seldom adjusted for changes in the relative importance of the output targets assigned to producers with different technological coefficients.

Last, but not least, there was inadequate control of norms at the level of the enterprise. Since the scale of allotments was subject to vigorous bargaining at every echelon in the administrative ladder—each inferior organ trying to get as large a quota as possible from its immediate superior—there was plenty of pressure to jack up the norms on any plausible pretext in order to justify larger applications. This pressure usually met with at least partial success, since, no matter how frequently the norms were checked, the age and condition of available equipment, the poor quality of the materials received and other intangible factors could serve as a likely pretext for loosening the norms.

6. *Execution of the Plans*

Once the National Economic Plan had been promulgated by the Council of Ministers, normally in the last quarter of the year preceding the plan-period, the Planning Commission portioned out to each ministry all the materials to which it was entitled for the year, holding back only the small emergency reserve stipulated in the balances approved by the Council of Ministers.[48] Each ministry then distributed the allotments it had received among its subordinate central boards, which in turn subdivided their share among the enterprises they supervised. Ministries and central boards also kept emergency reserves, which they expended during the course of the year.[49]

47. *GP*, no. 11 (1953), 30.

48. In the metallurgical industry, these reserves came to one to three per cent of total allocations in 1958 (Granick, "Polish Interviews.")

49. David Granick reports that in the machine-building industry, the ministerial reserves around 1958 were in the range of five per cent. In the central boards, reserves were regularly kept at about five per cent of the total allocation to the

The yearly allotments at each stage were broken down into four quarters, which took into account the seasonal pattern of the consuming industry's demand. These quarterly allotments were the supply counterpart to the quarterly output targets, which had filtered down to the enterprise by a similar administrative procedure.

From the viewpoint of the enterprise, the quarterly plans were more operational—and hence more important—than the yearly plans: on the supply side, they conditioned their purchasing authorizations; on the output side, they set the standards according to which their performance was appraised and the bonuses paid to their managers were determined.

Yet the yearly plans were far more important than the quarterly plans at higher echelons. The balances underlying the quarterly plans rarely amounted to more than a seasonal breakdown of the yearly plans: they were not regularly revised to take into account performance in preceding quarters.[50]

Most enterprises did not get their materials allotments until the end of the first quarter or the beginning of the second. By that time, of course, their orders had long been put in for the first six months of the year, since industrial suppliers and marketing organizations normally demanded advance notice of ninety days or over before delivery.[51] (These earlier orders were made on the basis of tentative output and consumption plans drawn up by the central board for the firm.) Thus, the final version of the yearly plans, which was supposed to be the best balanced, governed allocation for little more than six months out of the year. This was one of the many sources of discrepancy between plans and fulfillment.

The nomenclature of the orders received by authorized suppliers were more detailed than that of the limits themselves. (The thousands of rolled-steel items of different dimensions, sizes, and

board. These reserves were apparently earmarked for the use of individual plants, but Granick suspects that the central board could shuffle the reserves among plants ("Polish Interviews," p. 2).

50. According to Granick's informant, the Planning Commission reluctantly reworked its balances once a year to adjust for any important unforeseen supply or demand changes that had occurred in the process of fulfilling the plan (Ibid.).

51. Certain marketing organizations demanded that exact orders by size and type be submitted five months before delivery; see GM, no. 5 (1955), 130.

shapes cannot be separately rationed by any central authority.)
It was therefore possible for supply and demand of a given commodity (e.g. thin steel sheets) to balance aggregatively, but if the
marketing organization was short of the desired sizes or specifications and if the substitution that had to be forced on consumers
called for a greater expenditure of the material than had been
foreseen, this might still result in an excess of demand for the
commodity as a whole. There was always an element of discretion
in the decisions of suppliers, since they operated with a greater
degree of detail than any warrants or instructions binding upon
them.[52]

No matter how carefully the yearly plans had been laid, certain
discrepancies were bound to come up during the course of their
execution. We have already considered inaccuracies in the balances due to the difficulty of conveying exact information about
the production functions of enterprises to higher organs. Related
sources of disruption—due to unavoidable errors on the resources
side of the balances—may be mentioned at this point:

1) Natural events, such as fluctuations in the harvest yield of
beets, flax, and potatoes (which affected the output of the sugar-
refining, linen, and alcohol-distilling industries); flooded mines
and other catastrophes; disruptions in the transportation system
due to inundations, etc.

2) Significant changes in export or import prices on the world
market. A precipitous drop in the price of Polish export coal (such
as occurred in 1958) was apt to compel a curtailment of certain
industrial imports, which would have repercussions in the rest of
the economy.

52. The following percentages relate availabilities to requirements for specific
types of steel castings in 1957 (as reported by the marketing office in charge of
their distribution):

Weight (per casting)	Castings of alloy steel (per cent)	Castings of carbon steel (per cent)
up to 5 kgs.	75	50
5–25 kgs.	88	81
25–100 kgs.	85	78
100–500 kgs.	96	105
over 500 kgs.	104	71

Source. Nowak, p. 96.

3) The failure to complete new industrial projects on time. Since production from new enterprises scheduled to go into operation during the course of the year was counted on in the balances, any delays in construction or "bugs" in the initial stages of production upset the balances and forced a redistribution of available supplies of the deficit goods among consumers.

4) The beginning-of-year inventories of materials held by consumers that were banked on in the balances were "no more than a fiction in a majority of cases"; [53] the demand for building up stocks and reserves (not to speak of hoards) cut into allotments for current operations and sometimes caused shortages.

Shortfalls that occurred because of errors on the disposals side of the balance were due mainly to two causes: (1) above-plan output and (2) the receipt of materials whose quality was below standard and which were not fully suitable for the plant's equipment. In general, if equipment was not working satisfactorily, if workers were negligent, or if production was in any way disorganized, consumption of materials inputs surpassed their norms and the enterprise suffered a shortage.[54]

Certain auxiliary materials and components were never formally balanced or rationed. From 1956 on, an increasing number of less important primary materials were taken off the rationed list (although their balances were still drawn up). These "non-limited" materials, one might have expected, should have been in adequate supply, but this was not the case, and though there was no formal distribution, marketing organizations and supplying enterprises (where they were sole producers) had to cut requests down to size.[55] In 1955 screws and bolts, for example, were so short that they were a limiting factor in the production of boilers—and ships! [56] Two years later, requirements for these

53. R. Karski, "Planowanie produkcji a organizacja zaopatrzenia i zbytu" (Production planning and the organization of procurement and marketing), *GP*, no. 9 (1956), 22.

54. K. Krygier, A. Tafet, and H. Witkowski, "Podstawowe tezy do programu Ogólnej Konferencji Zbytu-Zaopatrzenia" (Basic theses for the program of the General Conference on Marketing and Procurement), *GM*, no. 9 (1956), 294.

55. Marketing offices were said to favor the formal rationing of all articles in short supply in order to reduce the arbitrariness of informal allocation. See B. Warzecha and W. Tyc, "Bilansowanie materiałów nie bilansowanych centralnie" (The balancing of materials not balanced centrally), *GM*, no. 18 (1955), 602.

56. Deutschman, p. 23.

materials were only being met to an extent ranging between 30 to 60 per cent for pressed and 20 to 40 per cent for machined screws.[57]

The cumulative effect of all these sources of disturbance was to provoke a scramble for scarce materials by the supply staff of enterprises that had not received a full complement of the materials and components they required. Some of these materials could be obtained by exchange, since most firms received certain items—in excess of their requirements—which they could trade with. (This practice though not officially sanctioned, was tolerated.) [58] In other cases, the wholesale points and sometimes even local retail stores normally catering to private consumption were raided for any stocks they might be holding.[59]

But the most common resort was to personal interventions, either to obtain extra consignments by drawing on the reserves of the Planning Commission and of the ministries, or simply to put pressure directly on producers to obtain favored treatment, e.g. to obtain supplies from above-plan output. To bring more effective pressure on their suppliers it was common practice for enterprises to station expeditors in Katowice and in other Silesia industrial centers, where they could intervene directly to make sure that their employers got the goods they needed. Occasionally, where nothing else availed, the supply officials of enterprises bent on obtaining materials at any cost were reduced to bribing employees in the marketing section of supplying firms to achieve their ends.[60]

The reserves held by higher echelons were usually inadequate to deal with shortages, particularly where the balances were "strained" and the materials were in short supply, since, in effect, reserves were fixed at a level that was inversely proportional to their necessity.[61] Hence, many of the interventions succeeded only

57. J. Jarno, "Wyroby metalowe" (Metal goods), *GM*, no. 7 (1957), 228.

58. According to one of Granick's informants, centrally distributed materials had to be exchanged "through the intermediaryship of the central board." This was said to be common practice.

59. Deutschman, p. 24.

60. Issa, pp. 470–71.

61. We have already seen that Planning Commission reserves amounted to one to three per cent of total allocations. Reserves stipulated in the 1957 plan for steel plates and sheets (very scarce items) came to only 0.11 and 0.27 per cent of output respectively. See *GM*, no. 3 (1957), 98.

at the expense of less powerful clients. The allotments of the latter were not necessarily formally reduced; however it often turned out that their orders simply could not be filled by suppliers, who had already switched their share to more privileged customers.

Inventories held by producers were also exceedingly meager or nonexistent. Coal stocks at the pit (which had equaled 24 days' output in 1938) were down to one or two days' backlog in the 1950s. In the Central Board of the Metallurgical Industry, stocks of pig iron had been scaled down from 41.5 days' output in 1938 to 7 days' in 1952, raw steel from 15 days' output to 9 and rolled products from 33 days' output to 16.[62] With small stocks, the supplying firm could not wait to fill orders until a full assortment of goods had been produced; it had to dispatch very small consignments at any one time. This fault in the system was partly offset by the accumulation of inventories in the consumers' warehouses.[63]

When allotment plans broke down during the course of the year because of unforeseen lapses in production or excessive requirements by consuming firms, the sales centrals and the marketing office, were usually allowed to exercise some discretion in the distribution of available supplies. Whether they supervised direct turnover or organized transit, they were deluged with requests for additional allotments and with complaints on delays in deliveries. An official of the sales central for the chemical industry stated in an interview that when there was a deficit, he would first seek to discover whether any unjustified demands might be cut down.[64] Once this was done, he would lop off quotas according to a list of priorities by industry. Metallurgy, chemicals, and the textile industry, for example, were arranged in descending order or priority. However, if a plant from a lower group

62. H. Fiszel, "Srodki obrotowe przemysłu i ich struktura jako wyraz wyższości socjalistycznych stosunków produkcji nad kapitalistycznymi" (Turnover funds and their structure as an expression of the superiority of socialist over capitalist production relations), in *Materialy i studia*, 2 (Materials and studies), Instytut Nauk Społecznych przy KC PZPR, 180, 181.

63. On the tendency for inventories to shift from producers to consumers, see K. Tomanek, "Ceny, rozliczenia i finansowanie" (Prices, settlements of accounts, and financing"), *GM*, no. 15 (1956), 507.

64. A client, for example, may have unused stocks or may be unreasonably transgressing his material-consumption norms.

was in danger of having to close down for lack of a chemical, it would get special priority. With this exception, there seemed to be no awareness of the need to equalize the marginal productivities of the allotments made to different consumers. There was no reason to expect that the last ton of lye used by the metallurgical industry would have the same value product (in terms of planners' preferences) as if it had been allotted to the low-priority fats and soaps industry.

A frequently voiced complaint was that materials in short supply were dosed out to consumers without taking into account the level of their production costs; inefficient producers working on obsolete equipment were given the same chance as everybody else to "compete" for rations. In many cases, a policy of concentrating allotments of deficit materials in the most efficient plants would have permitted a higher total volume of output to be produced with the same amount of inputs.[65]

Of the three plants the author visited in the fall of 1956, a producer of electrical instruments was in a relatively high priority industry, a modern key-industry brick factory and a soap-making plant were much lower on the scale. Talks with the directors and operational planners of these firms confirmed previous expectations: the instrument plant could get its materials with little trouble, not excepting coal, which it managed to receive in sufficient quantities during the coal crisis of 1955–56; the brick factory complained of the quality of the coal it received and of the failure to get the grades and profiles of steel its repair shop had ordered; the soap-making plant seemed to be the worst off, especially with respect to coal which was so full of sand and stone that it gave off far less heat than was necessary to operate the boilers at the prescribed pressure.

Shortages are not the only manifestation of planning errors and of unforeseen difficulties. Since enterprise managers were often in a position to "push" those products they found most advantageous to produce (or which they were forced to produce for lack of the materials necessary to put together the items stipulated in their production plans), unexpected surpluses sometimes arose in the midst of prevailing shortages. "The problem of overproduction," writes a supply specialist, "is among the most im-

65. *ZG*, no. 16 (1957), 8.

portant in the economy . . . It is often encountered starting with investment goods and tools all the way to shoes and buttons." [66] Warehouses were filled with little wanted items, often in open storage.[67] Sometimes these surpluses were unloaded on clients who could not afford to refuse consignments from their suppliers for fear of incurring their bad will. In this sellers' market, tied sales were an easy way of getting rid of little wanted items and of boosting the value of a firm's output.[68]

The evidence collected in this chapter on the operation of the supply system has been very fragmentary. What we should like to have is a record of applications, allotments, and actual deliveries for each important category of materials. Such a record, as far as could be ascertained, has never been assembled, let alone published. Occasional data, such as we have cited, have appeared on the proportion of planned availability to requirements, but data on the fulfillment of planned deliveries have been even harder to come by.[69] About the only concrete piece of evidence indicating that the defects we have alluded to are not just isolated phenomena is the report of a sample survey of 395 industrial enterprises made by the Economic Council in the first half of 1958. At that time, as we shall see in Chapter Nine, the economic system was still working much in the same way as in former years, but the slower pace of industrial expansion put into effect since 1956 and the partial decentralization of procurement had already made for moderate improvement in the supply situation for producer goods. Nevertheless, of the 395 enterprises canvassed, 334

66. B. Himmel, "W sprawie produkcji pozaplanowej i ponadplanowej" (On unplanned and above-plan production), ZG, no. 16 (1955), 654.

67. S. Hortyński, "Gospodarka materiałowa w Bielskim przemyśle włókienniczym" (Material economy in the Bielsko textile industry), ZG, no. 7 (1955), 255–58. See also ZG, no. 14 (1955), 570, for an extensive review of the marketing problems of the tools and instruments industry.

68. R. Basztoń, "Problemy zaopatrzenia" (Procurement problems), GM, no. 14 (1956), 482. A common device was to hold up consignments, then announce to the client that the goods were substandard and could not be delivered. If the client, to save his output plan, accepted deliveries, sight unseen, the producer was free from any further recriminations. In 1954, this situation was said to be "industrywide." See J. Liwowski, "Normalizacja w przemyśle włókien sztucznych" (Standardization in the artificial-fibers industry), Przemysł chemiczny (Chemical industry), no. 6 (1954), 293.

69. It was occasionally alleged that deliveries ran to over 95–98 per cent of allotments (cf. Granick's "Polish Interviews," p. 3; and Nowak, p. 95).

still pointed to procurement difficulties as a factor holding back the expansion of their output, the majority of enterprises singling out this factor as their principal hindrance. By way of contrast, it may be noted that only one-tenth of the enterprises pinned the chief blame for their insufficient output on obsolete equipment (although most respondents listed this shortcoming as one of the output-limiting factors). The third most frequently mentioned difficulty—the lack of adequate inventories used in production—chiefly tended to reinforce the first, namely the pervasive shortage of materials.[70]

7. Vue d'Ensemble

A few main conclusions can be unraveled from the web of institutional factors described in this chapter.

1) The average firm had little control over the material inputs it received from distributing organizations: as a rule, the scarcer the material, the more its consumption was hemmed in by administrative regulations, and the more rigidly its supplies were rationed by distributing organizations. Even when materials were not on the rationed list, they were usually hard to get and informal distribution took the place of formal rationing.

2) Production plans were imperfectly coordinated, but there were a number of loopholes in the distribution setup that allowed consumers to get extra consignments of materials. Such sources included central reserves, the above-plan output of suppliers, exchanges, and supplies obtained by raiding the warehouses of state-operated wholesale points. Some materials and components might also be bought from producers' cooperatives and from private sources at higher prices. These informal arrangements made for a greater degree of flexibility in the system.

3) The mechanical compilation of the materials requirements of individual enterprises based on preliminary output plans was too cumbersome and time-consuming a procedure to succeed in practice. As a result of the drastic changes in output and consumption that had to be made in the Planning Commission to "close" the balances, the preliminary summations lost their usefulness. "Planning from above," which went into effect at the

70. M. Malicki, "Hierarchia trudności" (A hierarchy of difficulties), ZG, no. 49 (1958), 1–2.

beginning of 1954, seemed better suited to cope with the twists and turns in economic policy that frequently upset the preliminary work on balances prepared six months or more before the plan-year. It also left the Planning Commission more time to carry out the successive approximations aimed at achieving full consistency.

4) There were essentially two kinds of shortages: first, shortages that could be eliminated by better balancing and coordination without the need to cut back allotments to end-uses; and second, shortages, caused by serious disproportions in the economy, that could not be cured without significant retrenchments in the demand for certain end-uses. The first would be amenable to input-output techniques or to other improvements in balancing methods; the second would not. It is clear that the shortages in nonferrous metals and semifabricated steels from which industry suffered during the Six-Year Plan were of the chronic type. Direct and indirect sources of demand for these products exceeded availabilities; but the planners were reluctant to make the painful cuts in final demand that would have been necessary to maintain a balance. The basic fault here lay in the long-run plans and in the radical changes in plan priorities ordered by the government from time to time in keeping with the vagaries of political conditions.[71] Planning errors, of course, tended to aggravate maladjustments, although they were not primarily responsible for them. On the other hand, shortages of electrical instruments and components, screws, spare parts, tools, chemicals, and other items whose short-run supply should have been elastic were probably caused mainly by the inadequacies of the planning system. In short, the large gaps—of the order of 30 to 50 per cent—between availabilities and requirements for certain materials reflected mainly disproportions; failures to realize planned allotments, which seem to have caused shortfalls limited to 5–10 per cent, were mainly due to planning errors and faulty forecasts.

5) So far the material balances have been discussed mainly from the viewpoint of consistency. But, as we saw in Chapter One, balanced plans may be inefficient if the wrong processes are operated or if full advantage is not taken of the opportunities offered by foreign trade. In fact, the planners in Poland did not limit their

71. See Chap. 2, pp. 65–67.

task to the achievement of statistical consistency. Whenever they hit a bottleneck in a given type of capacity or in a scarce factor, such as skilled labor or foreign currency, they tried to find suitable alternatives to reach their objectives. In choosing among these alternatives they had to keep in mind the order of priority of the different goods whose output they could retrench or expand to get around the obstacle. They also considered the substitution of materials or factors in more abundant supply for the deficit items. Though they could only do this in the crudest way, this was better than if they had confined themselves to the construction of harmonious plans.

To succeed in their sempiternal efforts to achieve rapid industrial growth, the planners had to use their ingenuity wherever they were confronted with shortages and bottlenecks. We should be deluding ourselves if we were led to conclude from the evidence of waste and misallocation that has come to light in recent years that experienced planners were incapable of marshaling the nation's resources expeditiously toward the goals laid down by the political authorities.

CHAPTER FOUR

Current Planning II: Employment, Wages, and Synthetic Balances

1. *Commands and Forecasts*

We saw in the last chapter that the planners exercised comprehensive controls over the distribution of materials and equipment. To the warrants, allocation orders, and other bureaucratic paraphernalia, there was a real counterpart: goods moved from suppliers to warehouses, to stores, and to consuming enterprises. With the exception of the allocation of foreign exchange and the planning of transportation services, the other balances were not so operational. The allocation of labor, the wage bill, and the purchasing power of the population could be regulated by the state—but they could not normally be dictated on short notice. Labor, for instance, was to an important degree allocated by the market, except for some categories of skilled manpower, such as graduates of politechnical schools, who were centrally assigned to their jobs. The decision of the farmer's son to hire himself out in a steel mill, of the housewife to teach part-time, of the consumers to buy on the market according to their tastes—all of these actions could at most be influenced by the state, but they could not be canalized into the narrow grooves of the plans. Even the cost plans, which should at least in part have been derivable from schedules of materials allotments, could not be set with any degree of precision because they also depended on more elusive components, such as wages, maintenance and repairs, and decentralized investments, which were only loosely planned.

Although the decisions of individual consumers or job-seekers could not be directly controlled by the state, the planners, by regulating the population's purchasing power, the wage fund, or the total bill of goods available for consumption, could try and maintain an over-all balance between the supply and demand for labor or for consumption goods; surpluses or deficits for specific commodities or categories of workers could be dealt with as they arose. Aggregated, or "synthetic," plans were meant to preserve this over-all balance.

In a centralized economy, the most common symptoms of a disequilibrium between the purchasing power of the population and the retail value of consumer goods in state shops (sold at fixed prices) are a reduction in the shops' inventories, an increase in the currency holdings of the public, and a rise in (uncontrolled) food prices on the peasant market. Whether state-controlled retail prices are permitted to rise to avert queuing and shortages or whether consumers' rationing is introduced, the authorities will find the consequences of inflationary pressures politically and economically harmful. The economic consequence that may be most worrisome to the regime is the drop in labor efficiency that is generally associated with declining real wages and with reduced incentives. These undesired effects, though, are hard to measure. During the greater part of the 1950s, the bias, wherever a conflict arose between financial stability and the pressure to realize immediate output gains, was not to let financial restrictions get in the way of production. The discussion of the synthetic plans, to which the bulk of this chapter is devoted, concentrates on the financial and fiscal controls the state can apply to curb inflation without holding back economic growth.

The principal money flows in the Polish economy, from which the aggregate balances may be constructed, are shown in Table 4:1 below:

Since the total payments made by a sector must equal its total receipts plus any net change in its assets, the row sums and the column sums of the table must match for any sector. For example, the "balance of the population's incomes and outlays," a basic instrument of Soviet and Polish planning, is made up from the first row and column of the matrix. This balance, net of internal transactions, states that the wages, salaries, and other benefits realized by households from state enterprises and from the budget can be expended in three ways: (1) as outlays on purchases from state and cooperative enterprises, (2) as tax payments and other contribu-

TABLE 4:1. *Matrix of Intersector Transactions for the Polish Economy*

Payments ↓ \ Receipts →	Households, private farms, small-scale private enterprises	State and cooperative enterprises	State budget and Treasury accounts	National Bank of Poland and specialized banks [a]
Households, private farms, small-scale private enterprises	Transactions within sector	Purchases in state and cooperative stores	Direct taxes, social security payments, and other direct contributions	(Increase in currency held by public) (Increase in savings deposits)
State and cooperative enterprises	Wages and salaries, purchases from private sector	Sales and purchases of intermediate goods, capital goods, construction and transportation services	Turnover taxes and profit levies	Repayment of loans, interest payments (Increase in currency holdings and bank deposits of enterprises)
State budget and Treasury accounts	Wages, salaries, and social security benefits	Purchases of goods from enterprises, budget-financed investment outlays and subsidies to enterprises	—	(Increase in Treasury deposits with National Bank)
National Bank of Poland and specialized banks [a]	Interest on savings deposits and withdrawals (Decrease in currency held by public)	Gross increase in loans to enterprises	(Decrease in Treasury deposits) (Net increase in loans to state [b])	Interbank transfers [b]

[a] Investment Bank, Agricultural Bank, PKO (Savings Bank), and saving-credit cooperatives. The Investment Bank manages and dispenses the investment credits granted by the state to enterprises and finances the short-term credit needs of the construction sector. The transactions shown in the matrix for the Investment Bank involve only its short-term crediting business. Investment grants to enterprises made through the Investment Bank are entered in the matrix as a direct expenditure of the state on enterprises.

[b] The savings of the public in the Savings Bank, which are redeposited with the National Bank of Poland, are automatically transferred to the Treasury account at the bank. This is the principal form of government borrowing.

Note. Items in parentheses denote an increase in the assets or a decrease in the liabilities of a row-sector and a corresponding decrease in the assets or increase in the liabilities of a column-sector. These changes need not involve an actual payment-transaction between the two sectors.

tions to the state, or (3) as additions to savings in the form of currency holdings or deposits in savings banks.[1]

The second row and the second column generally correspond to the "balance of the incomes and outlays of ministries" (discussed below), except that the latter excludes the payments and receipts of very small enterprises under the management of the local peoples' councils.

The transactions in the third row and column are all included in the consolidated budget of the central and local authorities. (A surplus in the budget increases treasury deposits with the National Bank, a deficit reduces these deposits.)

Finally, the fourth row and column reproduce the principal elements of the credit plan of the National Bank, with this important distinction that the plan balances the total sum of credit outstanding against the sum of Treasury and enterprise deposits, while the table only shows the changes in these magnitudes scheduled to occur during the course of the plan-year.[2]

Some of the most important flows of funds going in the economy are not reflected in the highly aggregated matrix of Table 4:1. In particular, attention should be drawn to the triangular pattern of payments between light industry, the budget, and heavy industry. In the 1950s the food-processing and textile industries paid into the budget the bulk of the turnover and profit taxes contributed by state enterprises, but most subsidies and investment funds paid by the budget to state enterprises went to construction and heavy industry.

The "balance of national income," defined in accord with Soviet practice to encompass only the material sphere of production, cannot be directly read off the table but may be reconstructed from its detailed components, insofar as payments for goods can be segregated from payments for personal and government services which are excluded from official computations of national income.

The next section is devoted to a description of two essential building blocks in value planning: the labor balance and the wage fund, which is itself dependent on labor plans.

1. For details, see below, Sect. 3.
2. Another item on the liabilities side of the credit plan, whose net increase has been omitted from the table, is the capital owned by the bank, which can also be lent out.

2. Manpower Balances and Wage Plans

The balancing of the supply and demand for skilled and un-skilled labor matters not only for aggregate planning: it is also a tool used in making up the current plans, though far less pliable a tool than the planning of materials supply. For one thing, labor is not normally conscripted and must be pulled to and fro by in-centives. For another, it is not enough to strike a nation-wide balance of the labor force. As long as the transportation system could bear the brunt, materials in surplus in one part of the coun-try could always be transferred to deficit regions; but a surplus of labor in one region could not easily compensate a shortage in another. The critical housing situation and the desire on the part of workers, newly arrived from the farm, to find jobs close to their home and land placed a low ceiling on labor mobility. A surplus of hands in one region could coexist for years with a deficit in an-other. From 1949 on, the industrial districts of Silesia suffered from a labor shortage while pockets of unemployment subsisted in southeastern Poland.

The first regional manpower balances were prepared in 1951; due to the lack of census data—the results of the December 1950 census were still not available—the balances had to rely on "far-reaching estimates," which were so crude they could not serve as a basis for labor-recruitment plans.[3]

The nation-wide balance drawn up in 1953 revealed that the reservoir of surplus farm labor had been nearly exhausted and that a serious disproportion was developing between the relative scarcity of labor in the Recovered Territories in the west and the relative abundance of labor in the rest of the country. Similar balances broken down by regions date back to 1954; but they were chiefly limited to the supply and demand for graduates of technical schools.[4] Attempts were also made at that time to plan the supply of skilled labor on a nation-wide scale on the basis of the man-power tables prepared in the central boards and ministries.

No local (county) balances of manpower were prepared in 1953.

3. A. Rajkiewicz, "Zatrudnienie" (Employment), in *Zarys rozwoju metodologii planowania w Polsce Ludowej 1944–1954*, ed. by B. Minc et al., p. 246. Most of the material in the following pages is taken from this source.

4. Rajkiewicz, pp. 247–48.

In 1954, they were resumed, but they apparently proved more useful as a working document for the elaboration of the Five-Year
Plan (1956–60) than as a prop for the current employment plans.
This lack of data did not prevent the Warsaw planners from balancing their employment plans: on the outlay or demand side of
their balance they put down the requirements of the different
ministries for additional labor and on the supply side the sources
of manpower that would be tapped to meet the requirements,
such as organized recruitment in the countryside, laborers offered
by labor exchanges, and so forth. What was missing was an estimate of the capacity of the labor reservoir. In official thinking, as
long as this capacity held out, new workers could always be attracted to industry by suitable incentives, if need be by paying
out higher wages.

Efforts to relocate manpower to meet the needs of the industrialization program did not get very far. The program for redis-
tributing the labor force by economic region, which was part of
the Six-Year Plan, "despite its highly attractive character, was fulfilled to an insignificant extent." [5] This lack of success caused the
planners to reduce the scale of their ambitions in the Five-Year
Plan. By that time, it was freely owned that the movement of
labor responded—insofar as housing and other conditions allowed
—mainly to the pressure of economic opportunities, and that little
more could be done at the planning stage than to anticipate shortages before they arose and suggest ways and means of alleviating
their severity (e.g. by accelerating the building of houses and by
providing more consumer goods in labor-deficit areas).

When wages and labor norms had to be manipulated by enterprises in labor-short regions to attract the number of laborers
stipulated in the plan, a conflict sometimes arose between the
constraint imposed by the approved wage fund and the necessity
of getting hold of the required labor. As has already been mentioned, the financial constraints were usually allowed to give way
when they clashed with production drives. Until the end of 1953,
the quarterly wage plans of the ministries were subject to upward
revision in proportion to the overfulfillment of output plans in

5. B. Wełpa, "Kierunki zmian w rozmieszczeniu sił wytwórczych w latach 1961–
1975" (Trends in changes in the allocation of productive forces in the years 1961–
1975), GP, no. 9 (1958), 8.

the sector. This practice was curbed in 1954: enterprises could still obtain extra funds if they surpassed their production quota, but the total wage bill of the ministry was not to exceed the limit set for it by the National Economic Plan (except with the permission of the vice-chairman of the Council of Ministers).[6]

The method for planning the wage fund finally crystallized around 1954. Each industrial ministry and central board had to justify its projected wage expenditures on the basis of its employment plan and of the detailed analysis of the average wages planned for each category of workers. (There were eight such basic categories in industrial plants.) Supporting data had to be submitted on the value of output in fixed and in current prices, on labor productivity (measured in physical and in value units), on the proportion of workers working on piece rates and on straight time, and, last but not least, on the average overfulfillment of the piece-rate norms. These data had to be made up separately for workers in industrial jobs, for workers engaged in investment projects and major repairs carried out decentrally, and for the personnel of budgetary organizations administering the reporting industry.[7] The wage fund so built up was still not fully comprehensive. It included neither the bonuses paid to management nor the wages of workers employed by enterprises to carry out small-scale decentralized investments.[8]

Among the items included in the plan, the projection most likely to be off the mark was the "average overfulfillment of piece-rate norms." Workers typically overfulfilled their norms by 50 or 60 per cent,[9] and there was no exact way of estimating how much they would be overfulfilled (on the average) in any forthcoming period.[10] The government, on the other hand, was hesitant about

6. T. Leszek and S. Pudlik, "Płace" (Wages), in *Zarys rozwoju* . . . , pp. 275–76. In recent years, above-plan increases in the wage fund have been permitted ranging from 0.6 to 0.9 per cent in different industries for every percentage-point overfulfillment of production plans in the industry. See *GP*, no. 10 (1959), 2–4.

7. Leszek and Pudlik, pp. 277–78.

8. S. Frenkel, "Niedoskonała kontrola" (Imperfect control), *ZG*, no. 34 (1959), 6.

9. For sources and further details, see Stankiewicz and Montias, *Institutional Changes in the Postwar Economy of Poland*, pp. 70–82.

10. The following statistics reveal how little progress had been made as late as 1958 in tightening up the norms and in putting them on a uniform basis. The average fulfillment of piece-rate norms in the metal-working industry (319 enterprises) was 199 per cent in September. The average fulfillment of norms was less

tightening up the norms as often as technical progress warranted their revision because of the workers' opposition to such speedup practices.[11]

A recent post-mortem of the 1953 wage reform in the machine-building industry revealed the looseness of the plans underpinning this reform. Both the wage fund and the labor-productivity forecasts were poorly estimated. After the reform, labor productivity per hour was expected to rise appreciably faster than wages; but, at least during the first year, wages rose faster than productivity. In the first nine months of 1954, productivity forged ahead of wages in only three central boards out of thirteen.[12]

The continuous upward drift of average wages in periods when no wage increases were officially sanctioned testifies to the weakness of wage controls.[13] As late as 1958, illegal wage payments were estimated at slightly less than a half billion zlotys compared to a total wage fund of 124 billion zlotys. But the mass of the unplanned excesses in the wage fund were perfectly legal; the following year, due to larger investment expenditures than had been anticipated and to the overfulfillment of production plans (entailing bonuses to workers and management), the unplanned excess in the total income of the population was running at a yearly rate of ten billion zlotys, the overwhelming part of which was attributed to the wage fund and to the social security payments tied to wages.[14]

3. *The Balance of the Population's Incomes and Outlays*

During the Six-Year Plan, the balance of the population's incomes and outlays omitted transactions within the private sector (e.g. among households, farms, and small private enterprises). It mainly balanced the wages, salaries, and social security payments

---

than 150 per cent in 11 enterprises, 151 to 170 per cent in 47 enterprises, 171 to 200 per cent in 117 enterprises, 201 to 230 per cent in 94 enterprises, 231 to 250 per cent in 22 enterprises, and over 250 per cent in 28 enterprises. See L. Kazalski, "Podstawy eksperymentów płacowych" (Principles of the wage experiments), *ZG*, no. 10 (1959), 5.

11. On the impediments to carrying out the 1953 reform of piece-rate norms, see M. Wajs, "Przyczyny i skutki pewnej reformy płac" (Causes and results of a certain price reform), *ZG*, no. 36 (1959), 3.

12. Ibid.

13. See Chap. 2, p. 71.

14. J. G., "Konsekwencje i niekonsekwencje" (Consequences and inconsequences), *ZG*, no. 40 (1959), 1; see also Chap. 10, Sect. 1.

made by the state to the private sector against purchases by house-holds in state stores, taxes, and other payments to the state effected by the income recipients of the sector. A slightly abbreviated ver-sion of the official form used in 1954 and 1955 is shown in Table 4:2, as well as estimates of the payments involved by broad cate-gories for the year 1956.

TABLE 4:2. *Balance of Money Incomes and Outlays of the Population: 1954 Scheme, Actual 1956 Data*
(in billions of zlotys)

Incomes		Outlays	
A) 1. Wage fund	98.0	A) Purchase of goods from the	
2. Other remunerations not		socialized sector	133.2
included in wage fund	n.a.		
3. Fund earmarked for distri-			
bution in cooperatives	n.a.	B) Outlays on services from the	
4. Travel allowances and per		socialized sector	9.7
diems	n.a.		
Total of wages and assimilated			
incomes (Socialized sector)	112.5	C) Taxes on wages and salaries	6.5
B) 1. Pensions	3.9	D) Taxes on private farms	3.6
2. Family allowances, sick-			
ness benefits, etc.	8.4		
3. Students' stipends	1.1	E) Other payments to the finan-	
Total social insurance and		cial system, of which:	
security benefits	13.4	1. Land and real estate taxes	1.0
		2. Payments to State Land	
		Fund	.1
C) 1. Agricultural goods sold		3. Income taxes from the	
by farmers to the so-		nonsocialized sector	.6
cialized sector	30.2	4. Insurance payments	1.2
2. Nonagricultural goods		5. Social security payments	n.a.
sold by the population		6. Payments to social or-	
to the socialized sector	1.0	ganizations	n.a.
3. Commission stores [a]	n.a.	7. Increase in savings	
Total of C) (not including 3.)	31.2	accounts	1.3
		8. Other taxes and pay-	
		ments	n.a.
D) Money incomes of members		9. Turnover taxes from the	
of collective farms [b]	n.a.	nonsocialized sector	.7

TABLE 4:2 *(continued)*

Incomes		Outlays	
E) Receipts from the financial system, of which:		10. Payments for electrification	.04
1. Net increase in credits received	3.4	11. Repayments of credits	n.a.
		Total of E)	8.1
2. Insurance for damage to life and property	1.1	F) Other outlays	1.9
3. Government obligations	0.1		
4. Fund for reconstruction	n.a.	G) Increase in the cash holdings of the population	6.7
5. Increase in consumers' installment credits	n.a.		
Total of E)	5.6	TOTAL	169.7
F) Sales by the nonsocialized sector of goods and services to the socialized sector	4.3		
G) Other incomes	1.7		
H) Statistical discrepancy	.9		
TOTAL	169.7		

ᵃ Mainly sales by individuals of packages received from abroad to state-owned commission stores.

ᵇ Included in item C). In 1955, the money incomes of collectives were of the order of 1.7 billion zlotys, but by the end of 1956, four-fifths of the collectives had been disbanded and money incomes of the remainder had dropped to a yearly rate of about 0.3 billion zlotys. (*RS 1959*, 198–99.)

Note. Independent farmers are classified as part of the "population"; the non-socialized sector includes handicrafts, private shops, and other small enterprises together with the free professions.

Sources. The scheme is from: J. Czarkowski and B. Oyrzanowski, *Bilans pieniężnych dochodów i wydatków ludności* (The balance of money incomes and outlays of the population), p. 164. The data are from: Zieńkowski, *Jak oblicza się dochód narodowy*, Appendix, Table 1; and *RS 1959*, pp. 330–31, 359–81.

The main source of information for the balance of incomes and outlays was the cash plan of the National Bank, which records all payments to the state (via state stores, taxes, etc.), all outlays by the state on wages, salaries, and social security benefits, and changes in monetary circulation.[15]

The lack of data on transactions within the private sector and the consequent failure to balance the incomes and outlays of the peasantry separately from the incomes and outlays of the urban population were a decided inconvenience for Communist planners, concerned as they were with the relations between the different classes of the population, particularly between peasants and workers. From their point of view it would not be satisfactory just to predict that a contemplated increase in wages paid to workers in state enterprises would have the ultimate effect of raising the currency holdings of the population by a given sum, if it could not be ascertained how much of the extra money would end up in the possession of peasants, workers, speculators, and black-marketeers. Practically speaking, a balance of incomes and outlays limited to payments between sectors was an inadequate guide for setting the proportion between industrial and food products in retail trade or for dividing the available supplies of consumer goods between village and town shops.[16]

15. See below, p. 131.

16. The following budget proportions are based on sample surveys of the incomes and consumption of peasant households (1955–56) and of urban workers and employees (1958):

	Percentage of total cash outlays expended on three items:	
	Peasant households	Workers and employees
Food (excluding alcohol)	27	44–55
Clothing	25	10–13
Shoes	11	5–7

The proportion of food in the total budget of peasant households comes to 60–62 per cent if the value of food grown on the farm is included. But only cash purchases of food affect the balance of incomes and outlays of the population. These data have been calculated from: *GP*, no. 10 (1958), 36–40; *GP*, no. 4 (1959), 60–61; and *RS 1959*, p. 355. Also relevant in this connection are the estimates made in 1958 of the ratio of total expenditures to currency holdings for the urban and rural populations. It was found that this ratio was three times as large for wage and salary earners as for the agricultural population; see *Finanse*, no. 9 (1960), 50.

For 1956 a more comprehensive balance was drawn up in the Chief Statistical Office which used the recent results of family budget data and of special sample studies. The items listed in Table 4:1 were broken down according to three classes of income recipients or consumers: workers, peasants, and members of the nonsocialized sector. Internal transactions in the private sector, which were not recorded in the cash plan of the National Bank, were also estimated. Although it is not possible to reconstruct this new balance with the data at hand, a brief mention of the principal flows will give an idea of the importance of the materials omitted in the old scheme. In 1956 farmers sold 10.6 billion zlotys worth of goods on the urban "peasant markets" (targowiska),[17] most of which was bought by workers and employees. Of the total consumption expenditures of workers and employees amounting to 130 billion zlotys, 19 billion were expended outside the state sector (on the peasant market, on direct purchases from farmers, on handicrafts, and on articles of private commerce).[18]

The balance of incomes and outlays, whether in its shortened or its long form, will reveal a threatened excess of disposable income over the available supply of consumer goods. But it is still of little help in detecting or remedying a partial disequilibrium. This became clear in the summer of 1959 when meat prices had to be raised by 20–25 per cent to choke excess demand in the market. An editorial article in Zycie Gospodarcze, published soon after the operation was completed, revealed that the sudden increase in the demand for flour products and rice that had followed the boost in meat prices had taken the planners by surprise. The attempt to cure one disequilibrium had given rise to another.[19]

An article written earlier in the year by Mieczysław Lesz, the minister of internal trade, made no pretense as to the exact nature of plans in this domain:

17. The government supervises hygienic conditions, law and order in the peasant markets, but the prices of goods sold in these markets are free to move in accord with supply and demand. The peasant markets should not be confused with the rural markets and fairs where peasants trade mainly with each other.

18. L. Zieńkowski, Jak oblicza się dochód narodowy (How national income is computed), Appendix, Table 1.

19. "Prognoza i plan." (Prognosis and plan), ZG, no. 45 (1959), 5. See also Chap. 10, pp. 318.

Our instruments of market analysis are still very weak. We do not know what results an increase or a decrease in price will have. We only know that a price reduction will increase demand and vice-versa, but we have no way of predicting the extent of this rise or fall in demand . . . We have no way of determining the market effects of an increase in the wages of given categories of workers.[20]

4. Formation and Distribution of the National Income

National-income analysis is used in the early stages of making up the yearly plans to test the inflationary potential of alternative levels of investment activity. It serves more generally as an essential link between production planning and the synthetic balances, including particularly the balance of the population's incomes and outlays.

National-income accounting would be a better instrument for planning the main proportions of the economy, if it were not for the exclusion of unproductive services from the basic accounts. Although the familiar accounting identities of Western income analysis still hold in the Marxist framework—*ex post*, national income produced equals national income distributed, and saving equals investment—the operational predictions that can be made from the accounts are not as helpful as they would be if their coverage were more comprehensive.

National income produced in Polish accounting covers the net output (gross output minus material expenses and depreciation) of the "productive sectors," namely, industry and handicrafts, agriculture, forestry, construction, transport of goods, communication, and "economic trade" (the sale of material goods). Each sec-

20. M. Lesz, "W rok po reformie handlu" (A year after the reform of trade), *ND*, no. 3 (1959), 116. It is interesting that price and income elasticities for many food products including meat had been calculated on the basis of published family-budget data by a Polish econometrician, sometime prior to the price increases of June 1959. The officials who had planned the operation had apparently not availed themselves of these results. See J. Łoś, "Zmiany w spożyciu robotników przemysłowych w związku ze zmianami zamożności" (Changes in the consumption of industrial workers in relation to changes in their income), *Handel wewnętrzny* (Interior trade), no. 6 (1957), and "Wyniki badań budżetów rodzinnych a planowanie spożycia" (The results of family-budget studies and the planning of consumption), *Ekonomista*, no. 2 (1958), 364–89.

tor's net output equals its yearly sales plus the increase (or minus the decrease) in inventories, including goods in process, that has taken place during the year. Investments, besides increases in inventories, comprise the value of capital goods sold by industry and the services rendered by the construction sector. (All domestic investment must obviously be included in the material sphere.) The net income of the productive sectors may be broken down into the following components: wages and salaries, profits of enterprises, taxes and other remittances to the state. The sum of these components equals national income received. The bulk of the income received by wage-earners, by enterprises, and by the state will directly revert to the productive sphere in the form of purchases from this sector; but a part will go to pay for services in the nonproductive sphere, and some of it will be taxed away or saved. Recipients of incomes in the nonproductive sphere will also divide their earnings among these different lines of expenditure. It is evident that if all the receipts in the productive sphere were traced to their eventual destination, they would resolve into purchases of goods and services sold by the productive sectors, additions to saving (in the form of currency holdings and bank deposits), taxes, and other remittances to the state.

Saving, or "accumulation" in Marxist terminology, is the sum of: (1) wages and salaries received by employees in the productive sphere minus the value of consumption goods sold and productive services rendered to the public (private saving); (2) enterprises' profits, net of depreciation, after payment of taxes and receipt of subsidies (saving by enterprises); (3) gross receipts of the state minus wages and salaries paid in the state sector and purchases of consumer goods and productive services by government organs (state saving). The sum of these three components of total saving is identically equal with net investment (sales of investment goods plus the value of construction services plus increases in inventories plus net foreign investment, minus depreciation).[21]

The possible effects on *ex post* saving and investment of an in-

21. The inclusion of net foreign investment, the excess of exports and services sold to foreign nationals over imports and services purchased from foreign nationals, introduces the possibility that a part of total investment might consist in nonproductive services exported (i.e. certain types of tourist expenditures) which would not be included in national income. In that case of course the saving generated by this nonincluded income would also be omitted.

crease in investment outlays on new construction may be traced through this scheme. The construction sector will spend part of the new outlays on wages and salaries and part on purchases from other enterprises; it may also have to pay taxes and remit some of its profits to the state. Any profits retained go to make up the contribution of the sector to "saving by enterprises." The wages and salaries paid out from the new outlays may be spent on goods in state shops, on purchases from unproductive sectors (not included in national income), or saved. If they are spent on state shops, inventories will decline, offsetting a part of the original investment; if they are saved, the increased saving will be a counterpart to the original investment. Purchases from sectors not directly covered in the national accounts give rise to incomes, which may be broken down according to the same categories of expenditure as the initial receipts. What matters of course is the pattern of these expenditures and the way they will eventually be resolved into increased government saving, reduced inventories, higher enterprise deposits, or a larger volume of currency in the hands of the public. If, for example, construction workers spend their increased earnings on railroad travel [22] or on movie or theater entertainment, most of this expenditure will revert to the state in the form of profits and taxes from state enterprises,[23] thus adding to government saving. But if they spend their money on private services, the new incomes generated are more likely to swell monetary circulation and reduce the inventories of shops than to build up budget surpluses.

A subsidiary set of accounts has been devised, which, at least in theory, should help to caulk the holes in the official estimates of national income limited to the material sphere. This is the "secondary distribution of incomes" (*wtórny podział dochodów*), which attempts to track down the expenditures of income recipients in the material sphere on all goods and services—productive and non-productive—and then to resolve the incomes generated by these expenditures during the course of the year into material consumption and saving. This redistributive scheme, though it has long been taught in the planning schools, still offers the planners nothing more than theoretical guidance: as late as 1959 it had not

---

22. Passenger travel is not included in Poland's national-income accounts.
23. It is assumed that the supply of these services is fixed in the short run.

yet proved possible to collect the data necessary to put flesh on the theoretical skeleton.[24]

5. *The Financial Program*

The financial program is also called the consolidated financial plan: it subsumes the principal financial accounts of the government, including the national budget, the balances of incomes and outlays of the different ministries, the cash plan, and the credit plan. All but the last consist of money flows and are expressed in zlotys per year or per quarter. The credit plan, shown in outline form in Table 4:3, records the total volume of credit outstanding at any given time rather than the net change per year or quarter as it appears in the financial program.

TABLE 4:3 *The Credit Plan*

Liabilities	*Assets*
Capital of the National Bank of Poland	Short-term credits to enterprises
Deposits of enterprises and institutions	Credits to specialized banks
Currency in circulation	

Since long-term investments are nonreimbursable—they are essentially budget grants—they do not appear in the credit plan, except, indirectly, through the short-term loans extended to the Agricultural Bank, which may then be used to finance long-term lending to the farm sector. The short-term credits extended by the National Bank, which has a monopoly of this business for all state enterprises outside the construction sector, help to finance above-seasonal inventories, goods in transit, and various unanticipated working-capital needs.[25]

The following data on the liabilities of the National Bank at the end of 1955 will give the reader an idea of the relative importance of the different sources of finance in the credit plan. Total liabilities amounted at that time to 55 to 60 billion zlotys. The deposits of the Treasury and of the specialized banks equaled 46 per cent of this total, the deposits of enterprises 19 per cent, currency in circulation also 19 per cent, and the bank's capital 9.7 per cent. Deposits of enterprises earmarked for the financing of major repairs and other specialized accounts made up the rest.[26]

24. Zieńkowski, p. 46.
25. See below, pp. 137–40.
26. Total liabilities have been calculated from published data on currency

We have already seen that increases in monetary circulation appear on the expenditure side of the balance of the population's incomes and outlays. An unanticipated increase in the public's currency balances corresponding to a failure on the part of consumers to buy as much from state stores as the planners had forecast is likely to have its counterpart in an unanticipated rise (or smaller-than-planned reduction) in consumer-goods inventories. As these inventories are normally credited, forecasting errors in the balance of incomes and outlays will be correlated with errors in the credit plan.

An increase in monetary circulation will also figure in the cash plan which registers all the receipts and payments in currency of the National Bank. Since all the cash receipts of state stores, enterprises, and institutions must be deposited at the bank within twenty-four hours and all wages and transfer payments are paid from bank accounts, cash transactions between the state sector and the population are comprehensively recorded in the cash plan.

TABLE 4:4. *The Cash Plan*

Receipts	*Payments*

1. Sales of goods by socialist enterprises
  a. in stores
  b. in catering establishments
	1. Wages

	2. Pensions and stipends

2. Sales of services by socialist enterprises
  a. trains
  b. trucks and buses
  c. theaters, etc.
	3. Payments from the accounts of farm collectives and cooperatives

	4. Purchases of goods and services by the socialized sector from the private sector
3. Compulsory payments (taxes, etc.)	5. Retirement of bonds, lottery prizes, etc.
4. Voluntary payments (loans, savings)	6. Decrease in monetary circulation (if any)
5. Increase in monetary circulation (if any)	

Source. Czarkowski and Oyrzanowski, p. 24.

---

circulation [*Finanse*, no. 9 (1960), 48] and from the percentage of currency in circulation to total liabilities [*Wiadomości Narodowego Banku Polskiego* (News of the National Bank of Poland), no. 3 (1957), 120]. The other percentages are also taken from this latter source.

The state budget [27] is probably the most operational of the balances consolidated in the financial program. An indication of its relative importance is that budget expenditures amount to over 50 per cent of national income, as estimated by the statistical office. The main elements of the state budget for 1955 are set forth in the table below.

TABLE 4:5. *The 1955 State Budget: Closed Accounts*
(in millions of zlotys)

Receipts		Expenditures	
Turnover taxes:		Investment grants	27,745
socialized sector	56,460	Subsidies to cover losses in	
private sector	815	the national economy	13,477
Profits of state enterprises	10,785	Increases in the working cap-	
Positive budget differences		ital of socialized firms	8,946
(including profits on		Negative budget differences [a]	13,218
sales of imported con-		National defense	12,578
sumer goods)	19,259	Administration	11,062
Income taxes	5,747	Social and cultural services	29,045
Real estate and land taxes	4,022	Government debt services	537
Other receipts	27,194	Other expenditures	6,586
TOTAL	124,282	TOTAL	123,194
		Surplus	1,088

[a] Negative budget differences arise in the export trade (wherever the purchase price of goods exported is higher than the foreign currency prices translated at the official rate into zlotys) and in state purchases of agricultural goods (wherever the sales price of the good to state industry is lower than the purchase price).

Sources. *RS 1957*, pp. 290–91; and *RS 1959*, pp. 360–61.

Budget surpluses are deposited in the government's account at the National Bank, where, as we have already mentioned, they appear on the liabilities side of the bank's balance sheet as a source of finance for the credit plan. The greater part of the deposits accumulated in the Treasury account by 1955 (which amounted to some 23 billion zlotys) [28] accrued from budget surpluses dating back to the early 1950s. The significance of these surpluses will be discussed in the next section.

27. The state budget subsumes the central budget and local budgets. The proportion between the two in the latter years of the Six-Year Plan was about 80–85 to 15–20.
28. The Treasury deposit is calculated from the sources cited in footnote 26. The surpluses are from *RS 1960*, pp. 414–15.

One building block of the financial program remains to be considered. This is the balance of incomes and outlays drawn up separately by each ministry. It shows on the receipts side: (1) the total value of output sold and services rendered by the enterprises and other subordinate units of each ministry; (2) funds obtained from the budget for investment purposes, for increasing the working capital of enterprises, for current subsidies, and for the administration of the ministry; [29] and (3) new credits received by enterprises from the banking system. Outlays include costs of production (material inputs, wages and salaries, interest and marketing expenses), expenditures on plant and equipment, major repairs, additions to inventories and other short-term assets, disbursements of the enterprise fund,[30] administrative expenses, payments to the budget from profits, turnover taxes, and credits repaid.[31] The difference between the total receipts and outlays of a ministry for any period equals the change in the deposits of its subordinate enterprises and of its administrative organs with the banks plus the change in their currency holdings.

The balances of the ministries are the only ones in the financial program to record costs and sales. All the other balances, which settle with the budget on a net basis, essentially rely on the accuracy of costs and sales planning in the ministerial balances. The state budget, for example, depends on estimates of the consolidated profits and losses of enterprises in the different ministries. The accuracy of these estimates will determine the reliability of budgeted expenditures on subsidies to the national economy and of tax receipts from this same source.

A summary version of the financial program or consolidated financial plan is shown in Table 4:6 below.

State income in the program is made up to comprise the entire "product for society," or Marxian surplus value, generated by socialized enterprises, as opposed to the other balances, which record the part of surplus value that is actually collected by the state. All profits, including those remaining at the disposal of enterprises, are covered in the program. On the expenditure side, the

29. The administrative expenses of ministries, central boards, and marketing offices were paid from budget funds during the Six-Year Plan.
30. See Chap. 6, Sect. 3.
31. Czarkowski and Oyrzanowski, p. 164.

program shows all investment outlays including those made from decentralized funds.

Unlike most of the other plans and balances from which data are drawn to construct the financial program, the program is only

TABLE 4:6. *The Financial Program of the State (Simplified Scheme), 1954*

Incomes	Outlays
I. Income from socialized enterprises	I. Social-cultural expenditures
1. Taxes and retained earnings	
a. Profits (all)	II. Administrative expenses
b. Turnover taxes	
c. Other	
2. Depreciation allowances	III. National defense
3. Others (e.g. social insurance deposits)	
	IV. Gross investments
	1. Increase in the gross value of physical assets
II. Income from the private sector	a. Investment outlays (all)
1. From agriculture	b. Major equipment repairs
a. Real estate taxes	2. Increase in inventories, goods in process, etc.
b. Payments for electrification	
c. Other	
2. Outside agriculture	
a. Turnover taxes	
b. Income taxes	V. Net excess of the value of exports over imports at domestic prices
c. Increase in bank deposits	
III. Income from the population (fines, licenses, payments for services, fees of trade unions and other professional organizations, etc.)	
IV. Net increase in monetary circulation	

Source. Adapted from Czarkowski and Oyrzanowski, p. 29.

an analytical document submitted to the government along with the budget and the National Economic Plan: it does not have the force of law.[32] It is not promulgated by the council of ministers (as is the National Economic Plan), nor is it sent to the *Sejm* for its approval (as is the state budget).[33] In the past, revisions in the budget introduced by the *Sejm* were usually not coordinated with the financial program. Such revisions might have inflationary effects even though the budget remained balanced. For example, the *Sejm* might resolve to raise social or cultural outlays and decide to finance the additional expenditure by channeling into the budget a larger part of the profits accumulated by enterprises than had been planned in the program. In the course of the year, unless production costs were reduced beyond expectations, enterprises would be likely to experience a shortage of funds, which might be reflected in an abnormally low level of their inventories or in extraordinary borrowings from the National Bank. Any unplanned extension of credits by the National Bank would inject liquidity into the system which, through above-plan wage expenditures of enterprises, would eventually be transformed into excess demand.[34]

6. *Cost Planning and Problems of Financial Coordination*

A close connection between cost planning on the one hand and material balances and supply plans on the other might be supposed, inasmuch as costs are computed from material, labor, capital, and transportation inputs, which are planned, while value aggregates correspond to output targets, which are also planned. Since producers' prices are fixed, the physical plans should be readily translatable into costs and values by weighting inputs and outputs with their respective prices.

This exact correspondence could only be realized if physical plans were perfectly comprehensive. As we saw in Chapter Three, one lesson the Polish planners learned in the early 1950s was that

32. Z. Rajewski, "Powiązanie N.P.G. z systemem finansowym Państwa" (The link between the National Economic Plan and the state financial system), *GP*, no. 7 (1958), 35.

33. In recent years, the National Economic Plan has also been subject to the approval of the *Sejm*.

34. Rajewski, p. 35.

planning "from the bottom up," coupled with the systematic aggregation of supply and output plans, was unmanageable. Krzystof Porwit, whose candid comments have already been quoted in a similar connection, recently deplored this failure to tie in the synthetic with the physical plans, both as regards cost estimates and the synthetic balances:

> In past years when the procurement plans of the different sectors were fully developed, detailed quantitative data were translated into values. This method was given up a couple of years ago, because it did not produce the desired results. First, despite the far-reaching expansion of the list of distributed materials in the procurement plans, the evaluation of these materials only yielded a part of total [material] costs. Secondly frequent changes in the physical plans compelled laborious and complicated corrections in the value-estimates.[35]

For lack of detailed and comparable physical data, the synthetic balances had to be worked up from bookkeeping and financial statistics, which were poorly suited to the analysis of intersector flows.[36] It sometimes happened that all the material balances were "closed," yet the total value of gross outputs of the sectors involved differed from the sum of labor and material costs, amortization, indirect taxes, and net profits; or consumption plus investment came to more than net national product; and no one could be sure whether the incomplete coverage of the material balances or errors in the data underlying the synthetic balances were at the root of the discrepancy.[37] Because the various synthetic balances were prepared in separate various government departments, it sometimes occurred that identical components were estimated independently. These estimates usually diverged because of conflicting assumptions. (The officials in the Planning Commission who were responsible for planning costs and sales had only loose contact with the Ministry of Finance where taxes and profit levies were being budgeted on the basis of the ministry's own estimates of costs and sales.)

35. K. Porwit, "Międzygałęziowa koordynacja planu zaopatrzenia" (Interbranch coordination of the supply plan), *GM*, no. 10 (1958), 338.

36. Porwit et al., "Uwagi o metodach . . . ," *Prace i materiały* . . . , no. 11 (1958), 113.

37. Ibid., pp. 109–10.

The way increases in real wages were planned reveals an interesting aspect of the synthetic balances. The same prices and wages were usually entered in the plans as in the preceding year; but a surplus was left open in the balances, which could be allotted in the course of the year either to wage increases or to price reductions, depending on how the economic situation developed. This method, it was alleged, afforded more flexibility and facilitated comparisons in the costs and profit rates of enterprises from one year to the next.[38] If wage boosts were actually granted during the year, with repercussions on costs, profits, and credit requirements, all this was beyond the ken of the yearly synthetic plans.

7. Short-Term Credits and the Cumulative Inflation

We now return to the inflationary mechanism briefly mentioned in Chapter Two. The National Bank, besides being charged with the provision of short-run credit to industrial enterprises, wholesale organizations, and retail shops, shares with the Ministry of Finance the responsibility for supervising the financial operations of these various enterprises.

All enterprises are assigned a "norm of working capital," a certain value of assets which they may hold in the form of inventories, goods in process or in transit, or deposits in the branch of the bank with which they do business. In addition, they can borrow from their bank to acquire seasonal (above-norm) inventories, to raise their depleted working capital to the level of the norm they are permitted to hold, and to finance trade bills and other items in transit.[39] The reason the norms need to be repleted frequently is that taxes and the bulk of planned profits have to be turned over to the Treasury, whether or not planned costs have been exceeded and sales targets have been hit; inferior performance in either of these respects compels firms to dip into their sanctioned quota of working capital; enterprises short of working capital must wait until the end of the year for a chance to obtain funds from the budget to bring their capital up to norm. In the meantime they resort to bank borrowing.

38. *Finanse*, no. 6 (1956), 14.

39. Of total National Bank credits outstanding at the end of 1955, 28 per cent belonged to the first category, 36 per cent to the second, and 23 per cent to the third. The only other important category consists of renewed (overdue) loans amounting to 10.5 per cent of total credits. See *WNBP*, no. 3 (1957), 120.

An interest rate of 3 to 4 per cent was charged by the National Bank on short-term credit, but the level of this rate was never manipulated to effect a balance between the supply and demand for credit. The rationing of credit by the bank was supposed to achieve this goal. In principle the bank lent only on certain types of inventories—mainly of a seasonal nature—not on unsalable remnants or on materials hoarded by producers to forestall failures in the distribution of supplies. These controls were—and still are—largely ineffective, because it is a simple matter for a firm to finance all its "bad" inventories with its own funds and all its "good" inventories with bank credit.[40] But even if firms were not in a position to obtain all the credits they desired and the volume of short-term credits was strictly tied to approved requirements for seasonal inventories, bills in transit, or other worthy purposes, there would still be no reason to suppose that producing enterprises and trading organizations would be left with exactly the minimum balances they needed to carry on their business.[41] This minimum depends on the schedule of receipts and payments of each enterprise and on the fluctuations in these variables. An automatic crediting policy may pump excess liquidity into the system, which enterprises will take advantage of to purchase more than their allotted share of inputs.[42] If they hire extra labor,[43] the monetary overhang will be immediately translated into excess purchasing power (unless the supply of consumer goods is increased correspondingly). If the firm buys materials or other inputs, the initial excess is spread over a number of enterprises, which, after

40. S. Ficowski, "Struktura zapasów w gospodarce narodowej w latach 1950–1955" (The Structure of inventories in the national economy in the years 1950–1955), *WNBP*, no. 1 (1957), 25.

41. This point and the discussion that follows are based largely on Raymond Powell's study of the Soviet monetary system, "Soviet Monetary Policy." It is believed that the Polish financial system is a close enough replica of the Soviet system to apply Powell's analysis.

42. According to Powell, there will be excess liquidity in the system if the ratio of credits to the total volume of inventories is larger than the quotient of two ratios: (1) the ratio of desired cash and deposit balances to the value of output and (2) the ratio of inventories to the value of output.

43. Wage expenditures in excess of the planned wage fund were authorized for above-plan output and in many other exceptional cases. The various opportunities enterprises have for overfulfilling the wage plan are described in E. Dąbrowski's "Kontrola funduszu płac w walce o obniżenie kosztów własnych" (Control of the wage fund in the struggle for the compression of costs), *WNBP*, no. 9 (1956), 491.

the level of their minimum balances has been met, will wish to spend the surplus. If bank controls are not stringent enough to keep firms from spending this money, the excess liquidity will eventually be resolved into wages, profits and taxes. In the Polish economy, where virtually no taxes are paid on producer goods and profit rates are minimal, most of the excess liquidity passed into wages.[44]

The resulting upward drift in wages was reflected in higher production costs, which raised the value of certain types of inventories estimated at cost, including mainly goods in process and finished goods held by producers.[45] When this drift was serious enough, it eventually forced the government to decree price increases in order to wipe out subsidies in producer goods industries and to do away with queues and shortages for consumer goods. Price increases for raw materials and consumer goods automatically raised the value of inventories stocked by producing and trading enterprises. Whatever the cause of the rise in the value of inventories, credit usually had to be expanded to enable firms to finance the increased cost of holding their normatives. The new credits were likely to make a fresh contribution to excess liquidity, which, once translated into unplanned purchases of inputs, would again push up wages; and another round of inflation would get underway.

This cumulative mechanism was probably at work during the Six-Year Plan, particularly during the first few years when prices of producer goods and retail prices of consumer goods were adjusted to rising costs at fairly frequent intervals.

The resulting inflation would have been much more serious if budget surpluses had not blotted up a good part of the excess liquidity. How important this excess must have been may be judged by the relative size of the surpluses (18 per cent of total

44. The mechanism whereby the excess volume of bank credit eventually spills over into purchasing power is described in detail by B. Oyrzanowski in an unpublished paper on "Problems of Inflation under Socialism," prepared in 1960 during his stay at the Center for International Studies of the Massachusetts Institute of Technology.

45. Inventories of materials used as inputs by producers were valued at fixed transfer or purchase prices and were not immediately affected by cost increases. The same remark applies to inventories of consumer goods held by trading organizations. Accounting rules for the valuation of inventories are given in *Informator Księgowego* (Bookkeeper's manual) (Warsaw, 1956), pp. 360, 478, 717.

revenue in 1951 and 13 per cent of total revenue in 1952) and by the proportion of this surplus to the total assets of the National Bank (around 25 per cent in 1952). The budget surplus in 1951 and 1952 must have been a good deal larger than the total increase in the volume of credits extended.[46]

The Ministry of Finance seems to have used the budget surplus quite deliberately as an instrument for offsetting inflationary pressures, but there is some doubt as to whether the responsible officials understood the complex causes that forced them to rely on this fiscal device.[47] The surpluses were planned by the ministry not only for the purpose of controlling inflation but for two other reasons: (1) as a safeguard against the failure to fulfill cost-reduction plans which would usually entrain above-plan losses in deficit enterprises and shortfalls in payment of planned profits to the budget on the part of normally profitable enterprises; (2) to finance possible wage increases and price reductions (the counterpart to the safety margin already discussed in the balance of the population's incomes and outlays).

8. An Appraisal of Monetary and Fiscal Controls

The budgetary surplus, we have concluded so far, is the main instrument available to the financial authorities which can be manipulated to preserve financial equilibrium without jeopardizing the investment, inventory, and output targets stipulated in the National Economic Plan. Granted that there exists a level of planned surplus which would do just that, if all other physical and value plans were exactly fulfilled, one may still question whether the planners can forecast the government's revenue and outlays, changes in inventories, and other relevant magnitudes accurately

46. Computations based on data in *WNBP*, no. 3 (1957), 120.

47. The explanation usually adduced by Polish officials to account for the budget surpluses was that the Treasury account at the National Bank had to be built up each year as a "financial cover," on the liability side of the bank's balance sheet, for newly created assets in the form of credits extended. According to one specialist in the ministry, the other liabilities of the bank, such as the deposits of enterprises and the bank's capital, "formed too narrow a base for the expansion of credit." See M. Kucharski, "Ekonomiczne znaczenie nadwyżki budżetowej" (The economic significance of the budget surplus), *Finanse*, no. 6 (1956), 13. This is not a very helpful explanation if one considers that any extension of credit had to have its exact counterpart as a deposit liability (of the Treasury, of enterprises, and of the specialized banks), or as an increase in currency in circulation.

enough to keep the actual surplus within sight of the amount budgeted and, in the last analysis, whether they can curb unanticipated inflationary pressures arising during the plan-period. It would be simple if the National Bank or the Treasury could mop up excess liquidity in the system by arbitrarily confiscating above-plan profits or by depriving enterprises of their norm of working capital. But in order to give the managers of enterprises sufficient autonomy to induce them to lower costs, strive for profits, and pay their bills on time, the allocation of profits and the disposal of working capital must be governed by fairly stable ordinances and regulations on which enterprises may base their financial plans. Tax yields must also be set by law. Hence, from day to day, the maneuvering power of the financial authorities is quite constricted. They usually are not in a position to contain the inflationary pressures released by unforeseen expenditures or by the failure of the ministries to keep within their cost plans.

In point of fact, the statistics show extremely large discrepancies between planned and realized budget surpluses, at least for the early 1950s. In 1951, for instance, the surplus actually collected was twelve billion zlotys against four billion budgeted; in 1953 the surplus came to three times as much as had been anticipated; by contrast, the year 1954 closed with a negligible surplus although a record surplus of 11.9 billion zlotys had been budgeted. (From 1951 to 1953, actual expenditures were more or less held within budget limits, whereas receipts were grossly underestimated; in 1954, receipts were slightly higher than planned, but this time expenditures exceeded plan by 13 per cent. In 1958 both receipts and expenditures were about 6 per cent larger than plan.) [48] Some of the differences between forecasts and results were due to changes in investment policy decided in the course of the year; others might be traceable to the under- or overfulfillment of cost-reduction plans; still others were caused by unpredictable fluctuations in the harvest, which partly determined the volume of purchases from the agricultural sector. It may also be that such leeway as the financial authorities had to increase receipts above plan was used to repress inflationary tendencies as they developed during the course of the year.

The grand test of the central authorities' control over financial

48. *RS 1960*, p. 414; O. Halecki, ed., *Poland*, p. 437; *RPG 1958*, p. 733.

variables lies in their ability to plan the volume of currency in circulation. Two Polish analysts claimed in 1957 that this was a high-priority objective and that the financial planners were capable of achieving it.[49] But the statistics do not bear them out. According to interview information from the Planning Commission, it was customary to plan proportional increases in currency in circulation and in personal incomes (the receipts side of the balance of incomes and outlays). As a rule of thumb, the department in charge of synthetic balances in the Planning Commission set a target of 10 per cent increase per year for both monetary circulation and personal incomes. A look at Table 4:7 discloses quite different results, especially for 1956 when circulation apparently got out of hand and strong inflationary pressures developed. (Note the small rise in retail inventories for 1956 coupled with the unusually high rise in incomes.) From these data we cannot infer that the more operational plans prepared by the National Bank and the Ministry of Finance, particularly for individual quarters, were as wide off the mark. Still, unless the Planning Commission and the financial organs operated on quite different assumptions, which in itself would also be bad, the evidence suggests that the accuracy of the prognostications in the yearly financial plans was not high. In fact one may wonder how high it could be, considering the large spreads between planned and actual yearly increases in inventories (shown in the first column of Table 4:6). These spreads must have had their counterpart in the credit plans, most of the actual rise in inventories normally being credited. Unless the credits supporting the unplanned rise in inventories were matched by increases in treasury deposits unanticipated in the yearly budget, the chances were that the volume of currency in circulation would also expand beyond plan.

However approximate the fulfillment of the yearly plans may

49. "A few years ago, when many more failings afflicted our economic planning than today, the credit plan was the main determinant of monetary circulation, since the quantity of money in circulation increased whenever the need to augment the volume of short-credits arose. Nowadays monetary circulation—more exactly, the extent of its rise or fall—is determined by the balance of the population's incomes and outlays, and the cash and credit plans must be adjusted to this volume of circulation. The National Bank, for example, may under no circumstance open credits over and above the credit plan (which has been concerted with the balance of incomes and outlays), since this could result in an increase in circulation." (Czarkowski and Oyrzanowski, p. 43.)

TABLE 4:7. *Yearly Changes in the Level of Inventories, Personal Incomes, and Monetary Circulation*

	Yearly increases in total inventories (billions of zlotys)		Percentage increase in total inventories (preceding year = 100)	Percentage increase in retail-trade inventories (preceding year = 100)	Percentage increase in personal incomes (preceding year = 100)	Percentage increase in currency in circulation (preceding year = 100)
	PLAN [a]	ACTUAL [b]	ACTUAL [b]	ACTUAL [a]	ACTUAL	ACTUAL
1954	n.a.	n.a.	n.a.	108.8	109.8	108.9
1955	4.9	11.0	110.7	115.0	107.8	114.9
1956	4.1	7.6	106.7	104.2	117.0	150.0
1957	7.7	21.6	117.8	112.5	126.7	113.2
1958	11.2	19.7	113.8	124.1	111.9	114.7
1959	9.2	15.9	109.8	118.5	109.8	102.7

[a] Computed from inventories at current prices. Retail trade inventories in constant prices rose by 13 per cent in 1957, 28 per cent in 1958, and 19 per cent in 1959.

[b] Computed from inventories at constant prices.

Note. Increases in inventories and currency were computed from end-of-year data.

Sources. A. Zwass, "Szybkość obiegu pieniądza gotówkowego w Polsce, N.R.D. i Jugosławii" (The velocity of monetary circulation in Poland, the German Democratic Republic, and Yugoslavia), *Finanse*, no. 9 (1960), 48, 55; L. Bogobowicz and W. Pruss, "Zapasy przedsiębiorstw uspołecznionych w 1959 r." (The inventories of socialized enterprises in 1959), *WNBP*, no.7 (1960), 314.

be, one would suppose that the planners could still reach their objective—financial stability for a given level of output and investment outlays—by providing for a budget surplus large enough to meet all the contingencies likely to arise during the course of the year.

Actually there may be disadvantages in budgeting such a large surplus which would more than offset its practical benefits. For one thing, the *Sejm,* which in recent years has been more vocal in its criticism of state plans, might be reluctant to give the Ministry of Finance a blank check to spend at its discretion the important sums corresponding to the uncommitted receipts. A more serious objection is that large surpluses might come into conflict with the regime's growth objectives. For it is inconvenient to let the pace of investment activity be determined by monetary conditions. The planners want to be able to rely on the production of newly launched enterprises: they cannot allow the completion of plants to be accelerated or retarded because the volume of currency in circulation is falling or expanding beyond schedule. Even if there is a risk that cost limits will be exceeded, the planners may still prefer to take this chance and, if worse comes to worse, permit a drop in retail inventories and let currency expand during the course of the year rather than curb investment activity ahead of time. Whether they adopt this policy or budget their resources more prudently will depend on how far they are willing to tolerate increases in the prices of foodstuffs on the peasant market, the shift of purchasing power from urban workers to peasants that normally results from these high-price sales, and the flourishing speculative and black-market activities opened up by the inflation. Since late 1959, as will be shown in the last chapter, the Polish government has opted for more stringent controls, even apparently at the expense of scheduled investments. But in the past the more adventurous policy prevailed—with inflationary consequences that anyone could have foreseen.

CHAPTER FIVE

Long-Term Planning
and Investment Calculations

1. *The Problem*

Which is better, to plan ahead with perspective balances that suffer from all the pitfalls of current physical planning together with a much greater degree of uncertainty, or to base the expansion of the economy's capacity on calculations of investment efficiency grounded on prices that reflect correctly neither the scarcities of today nor those of tomorrow? This is the chief dilemma of investment planning.

In the early postwar period, prices were distorted by a rapidly unfolding inflation; yet physical plans could hardly be framed at all for lack of statistics and lack of experience. This first period was one of compromise between the two extremes: both material balances and price calculations were utilized at an exceedingly primitive level. The second period, which lasted from about 1949 till 1954 or 1955, marked the eclipse of economic calculation (although hardly enough progress was made in the methodology of the perspective balances to warrant their exclusive employment). Since 1955, both physical and price planning have been much improved, and some success has been achieved in combining the two approaches.

We shall not dwell at any length on the crude tools forged in the first ten years of postwar planning. Our first systematic description of long-range planning relates to the current efforts to frame a five-year plan for 1961 to 1965 and a long-range plan for 1961 to 1975.

2. *The Early Postwar Years (1945–49)*

If prices and investment profitability were neglected during the first postwar years, the chief blame rests not on the planners' doctrinal prejudices but, for the main part, on the inflation and on the distortions in the price system that made economic calculation well-nigh impossible.

That at least some of the planners had every intention of getting the most work out of the price mechanism was evident from the reports made at a conference of the top economic advisers of the Central Planning Office as early as November 1945.[1] One department head admonished the planners to be guided by profitability considerations in the choice of investments and warned against the "technocratic approach" of choosing expensive investment alternatives just for the sake of being up-to-date. He called for the most stringent economy of investment funds, which must be reserved for projects yielding a very high return.

Financial considerations alone would have made it imperative to limit funds to bottleneck projects that were certain to contribute to the rapid increases in production needed to mop up the surplus purchasing power created by budgetary deficits.[2] Investments in ports and transportation, the principal bottlenecks in feeding raw materials to plants and raising production to prewar levels, took 41 per cent of planned investments in 1946 and 25 to 28 per cent in the following two years.[3] Bringing production back to capacity and patching up the transportation system did not require much economic analysis or very detailed physical balances.

In these first years, after the key sectors' minimum needs for investment funds had been satisfied, the rest of the economy was

1. Notes taken at the State Commission for Economic Planning from two of the papers delivered at this conference: Juliusz Pomorski's "Problem cen" (The price problem), and Bolesław Wścieklica's "Hierarchia potrzeb inwestycyjnych" (The hierarchy of investment needs).

2. The banks in general financed industry and trade with long-term credits while the government took care of the rest of the economy with outright grants. Long-term bank credits were not included in the budget and in the investment plan as such until the middle of 1946. In addition, private investments accounted for, about a third of total outlays. (See Secomski, *Planowanie inwestycji*, Part II, p. 74.

3. The hierarchy of needs in 1946 was established as follows: railroads, ports, communications, the spring sowing campaign, and industry (led by coal mining, metallurgy and electric power). See Secomski, "Na marginesie planu investycyjnego" (Remarks on the investment plan), *ZG*, no. 16 (1946), 559.

granted credits according to "the situation in the money market." In practice the inflationary threat frequently forced the planners to trim the tentative plans drawn up for nonpriority sectors. In 1945 and 1946, long-range plans amounted to little more than a collection of blueprints, left over from prewar days and from the German occupation, which were only loosely coordinated in a national program. The Three-Year Plan of Reconstruction (1947–49) was the first attempt to build a general plan mobilizing the country's principal resources for rebuilding the economy. There is evidence that even this plan was founded on only a limited number of summarily elaborated balances.[4]

The general policy in this early period consisted in holding down investment outlays by the dubious device of charging low official, so-called "rigid," prices for investment goods. This was a way of favoring nationalized firms (which got their materials at cheaper prices than private enterprises) and of building up critical sectors of the economy at an apparently lesser cost. But as a result prices became far removed from opportunity costs, at a time when physical planning was still too primitive to ensure the material support for the investment plans. Consequently, there was only a very loose correspondence between investment outlays and the economic efforts they were assumed to represent. Financial plans were overfulfilled while the actual plans (in terms of buildings completed or machinery installed) fell ten to twenty per cent short of the mark.[5] Another aspect of the same phenomenon was that money could be found for many worthwhile projects but not the materials to carry them out.[6]

The shift from financial to "concrete" planning (by means of material and labor balances) began in 1948; it was at first dictated by the necessity of finding a real counterpart to monetary expenditures. As the years went by, the planners, instead of mending their price system and turning the financial plan into a basic economic tool for the regulation and apportionment of investments, shoved

4. Cf. the comments of Ignacy Borejdo on the Three-Year Plan in metallurgy, "Plan techniczny w hutnictwie" (The technical plan in metallurgy), *ZG*, no. 8 (1948), 348, 349.

5. This discrepancy was also due to the inflation. Secomski, *Planowanie inwestycji*, pp. 72, 80, 104.

6. Secomski, "Na marginesie . . . ," p. 558, and Jan Druto, "Zagadnienie bilansów materiałowych" (The problem of material balances), *GP*, no. 1–2 (1947), 8.

it to the background and, from 1951 on, suffered it to become little more than the blurred mirror of their physical plans.[7]

During the transition years 1947 and 1948, the state gradually expanded its holdings in the economy by nationalization of trade and by financial reforms, until it acquired almost complete control of all sectors but agriculture. Leaving aside the great political advantage that the United Workers' Party stood to gain from this socialization, it was a clear asset to the planners who could now draw up balances of factors of production and concrete investment plans with the assurance that they had the means to execute these plans and that there would be no more spontaneous, uncontrolled private activity to upset their calculations.

3. Long-Term Planning

a. *1949–55*. From 1949 on the Poles adopted most of the Soviet precepts, methods, and injunctions concerning investment planning. The basic principle was that the over-all volume of investments and its apportionment among the various sectors of the economy belonged to the exclusive realm of centralized political decisions. These decisions were not to be determined by, nor should they be judged in the light of, economic calculations based on prices and costs.

The central authorities required only one prop to make correct "programming decisions" (i.e. decisions involving the allocation of investment funds to different industries): they had to rely on perspective balances of output and plant capacity to check on the internal consistency of their investment plans, to ensure that investment outlays had a counterpart in the physical resources assigned to approved projects. The sphere deemed proper for investment calculations in value terms was confined to comparisons of investment alternatives yielding the same or essentially similar

7. Already in 1949 Bronisław Blass (the chief government spokesman on financial matters at the time) was ready to recommend that the financial plan of investments be prepared *after* all the physical plans had been approved "with the possibility of correcting the physical indexes" if it proved necessary to tailor them to the limited possibilities of the budget. There was no hint that the *choice* of projects might be determined by financial considerations. See B. Blass, "Plan finansowy w naszej praktyce planowania" (The financial plan in our planning practice). *GP*, no. 3 (1949), 148.

benefits, usually measured in output gains.[8] This cramping view of the role economic analysis can play in helping the planners to allocate their investment funds was rationalized on political grounds (there must be no objective standard to challenge the ultimate decisions of the Party leadership in planning investments). It was also argued that the price structure would tend to bias calculations in favor of investments in the highly profitable consumer industries and away from the subsidized branches of heavy industry.[9]

However, as the concrete example below will show, any attempt to stake out a narrow field for calculations of investment efficiency, as if the choice of alternative projects or techniques had no repercussion on the rest of the economy, rests on a superficial understanding of the investment process. The decision to produce a billion kilowatt-hours a year of electricity from coal-consuming thermal plants rather than from hydroelectric power will probably require a cut in exports of solid fuels; the resulting shortfall in foreign-currency earnings will affect the import program; at the same time, this decision will release high-grade steel (which would otherwise have gone in the making of steam turbines) for the further development of the machine-building industry, for tanks, or for the manufacture of hollowware. To produce exactly the same bill of final goods under either alternative would clearly be irrational and defeat the purpose of the original analysis. On the other hand, if targets for the year are going to be fixed with foreknowledge of the cuts in coal exports and of the increase in steel supplies, then it would be casuistic to claim that investment decisions had no influence on the composition of the final bill of goods.

Since 1950, when the general lines of the present administrative specialization in long-term planning were laid, there have been

8. This orthodox viewpoint is perhaps most intelligently defended by Józef Pajestka in his article, "Wprowadzenie do metod badań efektywności inwestycji produkcyjnych" (Introduction to the methods for studying the efficiency of productive investments), in *Zagadnienia ekonomicznej efektywności inwestycji* (Problems in the economic efficiency of investments), p. 47.

9. Cf. Secomski, "Uzasadnienie celowości zamierzonej inwestycji" (The justification of the purpose of a contemplated investment), in *Zagadnienia ekonomicznej . . . ,* pp. 41–42.

three basic stages in the preparation of investment projects. (1)
The department of perspective balances of the Planning Commission is charged with the elaboration of general plans of development for each industry and with their mutual coordination. (2)
The industrial ministries in Warsaw draft more technical and detailed plans mapping out the construction or expansion of individual plants and other objects. (3) The project-making organizations (*biura projektowe*) attached to the ministries but usually
located in the districts where the industries for which they prepare
projects are concentrated are responsible for detailed technical
documentation and cost estimates as well as for the exhaustive
analysis of the technical variants (including the size and location
of plants) which can accomplish the goals laid down in the perspective plans.

Although these various organizations are expected to work in
close contact with each other, the problem of insuring smooth
communication between them has remained critical: it is not infrequent for a lower organization to work on assumptions that
have already been rejected or modified at a higher echelon.

Little is known about the programming of the Six-Year Plan.
Some output and capacity balances were undoubtedly prepared
for the original version, but it is doubtful whether they were completely recast, as they should have been, after the radical revision
of output targets pressed on the Poles by the Soviet Politburo in
1950. The Six-Year Plan for the metallurgical industry, a top-
priority sector, was only promulgated in 1951. The blueprints and
cost estimates for the principal investment projects embodied in
the plan were made ready between 1950 and 1952. Yet, perspective
balances were not drawn up until 1952 and 1953, "when it was
desired to verify *ex post* whether the foundations of the plan were
geared to each other and were properly coordinated in the framework of the industry and within the national economy as a
whole." [10]

By that time it was manifest that the plans for this industry *were*
out of gear with each other: witness the disproportion between
the growth of pig iron, steel, and rolled metal output. In 1953,

10. A. Pospiech, "Z doświadczeń nad badaniami efektywności w 'Biprohucie'"
(Some of the experiences in studying the efficiency of investments in "Biprohuta"),
in *Zagadnienia ekonomicznej* . . . , p. 285.

40 per cent of pig iron production had to be shipped for processing to mills which had excess capacity in their open-hearth shops; 37 per cent of the output of blooming irons and other semifabricates was rolled in "cooperating plants." These are very large percentages by the standards of any modern economy, and the expense of unloading and reheating these masses of metal must have been considerable. We may note in passing that this particular disproportion was avowedly caused by the failure to launch new production facilities on schedule as well as by poor coordination in planning the expansion of the various branches of industry.[11]

In May 1954, Kazimierz Secomski, a vice-president of the Planning Commission in charge of investment planning, deplored the fact that capacity balances had not been drawn up for every industry in preparation for the Six-Year Plan and that the balances that had been prepared were deficient in a number of ways but especially in their failure to provide reserves for unforeseen contigencies. Many projects for new plants that had been embodied in the plan should have been postponed until the industries consuming their products had been further developed. Dye works and paints were among these "overdeveloped" industries.[12]

The first general instructions to project-making organizations were issued in August 1953 and remained valid until the last year of the Six-Year Plan. They stipulated that every project should be tied to a perspective balance of productive capacity (prepared by a higher organization). The project makers in the general justification for a project were to state the level of demand anticipated during the plan period for the products that would be generated by the new capacity and to analyze the potential of all existing plants in the same branch of industry (together with their projected rate of expansion).[13] The documentation on a project was

11. H. Fiszel, *Czynniki i rezerwy przyspieszenia krążenia środków obrotowych w gospodarce Polski Ludowej (na przykładzie hutnictwa żelaza)* [Factors and reserves in the acceleration of the circulation of turnover funds in the economy of Peoples' Poland (with special reference to ferrous metallurgy)], pp. 133–35.

12. K. Secomski, "Zagadnienia inwestycyjne i budowlane w świetle uchwał II-go Zjazdu P.Z.P.R." (Investment and construction problems in the light of the resolutions of the Second Congress of the United Polish Workers' Party), *Inwestycje i budownictwo* (Investments and construction), no. 5 (1954), 5.

13. P.K.P.G., *Instrukcja No. 98*, "O zasadach sporządzania i zatwierdzania dokumentacji projektowo-kosztorysowej dla inwestycji" (Principles for preparing and confirming the technical and cost documentation for an investment), p. 13.

to contain a "general section" in part devoted to economic analysis, though the instructions were far less specific on this point than on technical questions, requiring only "a description of the effectiveness of investments" and an inventory of basic technical-economic data. These latter were to include computations of the ratio of yearly costs of production to investment outlays, investments per unit of productive capacity, output per man and a few other technical indices.[14] There was no hint as to how these various criteria were to be combined for an over-all appraisal. The "branch instructions" put out by the Ministry of Metallurgy in 1954 were generally similar to the parent instructions; the only new recommendation was that the ratio of "accumulation" (prices minus variable costs) to investment expenditures should be analyzed in conjunction with the other criteria.[15]

The economic content of these instructions was so vague that project offices were soon forced to work out their own principles and devices for lack of central guidance.[16]

As we have seen, the project makers were asked to calculate several coefficients and indices to provide a many-faceted view of each project. This was a perennial source of confusion, for these various coefficients and indices did not all reinforce each other but often pointed to different optimal variants. As a result, one project-making organization found itself compelled to elaborate a "hierarchy of the importance of diverse indices in the whole national economy . . . for the next two Five-Year Plans." [17] In planning the complex development of water resources for transportation and for urban and industrial requirements, this organization singled out a "dominant" consideration on the basis of which it resolved whether to go in for a project at all, when to launch it if it did, and what technical variant to select. The dominant factor in 1956 was to be "the demand for water by industry

14. Ibid., p. 18.

15. Ministerstwo Hutnictwa, *Instrukcja branżowa Ministerstwa Hutnictwa o zasadach sporządzania i zatwierdzania dokumentacji projektowo-kosztorysowej dla inwestycji* (Branch instructions of the Ministry of Metallurgy on the principles for preparing and confirming the technical and cost documentation for an investment), no. 2, p. 16.

16. Pospiech, p. 23, and the article by W. Magiera and A. Dowgiallo "Ekonomiczna efektywność inwestycji wodnych" (The economic efficiency of water investments), also in *Zagadnienia ekonomicznej efektywności*, p. 263.

17. Magiera and Dowgiallo, pp. 259–60.

and by the communal economy, taking into account the rising
trend of needs consequent upon the further development of industry and of urban centers, with due regard to the impossibility
of replacing water for these purposes by any other means." [18]
These diffuse stipulations failed to provide a concrete all-purpose
criterion for appraising the economic effectiveness of investments
in this sector of the economy.

b. *Since 1955.* It was not until late 1954 or early 1955, when the
Planning Commission was faced with the task of preparing a Five-
Year Plan for 1956–60, that a systematic procedure for perspective
planning began to take shape.

The elaboration of the first Five-Year Plan fell into four
phases: [19]

1) In the first phase, the work consisted in setting an approximate limit to the investment outlays over the plan period and in
striking tentative balances of plant capacity and output to make
sure that the monetary expenditures should have a "real counterpart" in the physical plans.

2) The second phase involved a preliminary division of investment funds among the various sectors of the economy and the
drawing up of production programs for the individual branches of
industry. The size of the investment fund and the general production tasks served as the basis for this phase.

3) In the third phase, the planners strove to find the most effective way of using the investment funds earmarked for each industry, so as to fulfill all production tasks while achieving the maximum possible increases in labor productivity at the least cost.
Decisions were now made concerning the retirement of obsolete
machinery and the division of funds in each industry between new
construction, modernization, and expansion. Most of the work
done at this stage was still grounded on physical indicators and
on balances of capacity, although economic calculations were expected to reinforce the other techniques. Note also that, in order
to link up capacity expansion with its concomitant costs, investment outlays per unit of capacity (e.g. per spindle, per loom, or
per megawatt of electric power) had to be multiplied by the antici-

18. Ibid., p. 270.
19. *GP,* no. 10 (1955); *Ekonomista,* no. 2 (1955).

pated increases in productive capacity. This sort of calculation spanned the gap between value aggregates and physical indicators.

4) The fourth and last phase concerned individual investment projects: the choice of technical alternatives, the analysis of costs, and the various factors that have already been touched on in our earlier discussion of "project making." [20]

It was stipulated that there should be some "feedback" from lower to higher phases of making up the plan. For instance, if economic calculations in the third and fourth phases caused errors to be uncovered that had been made in drawing up capacity balances in the second phase, the balances were to be reworked to correct these errors. But such revisions were apparently quite infrequent.[21] According to one official, the long-range balances were drawn up exclusively from "administrative documents" (the projected requirements of ministries and subsidiary agencies) without the benefit of economic analysis.[22]

Of late, more detailed information has come to light on the first phase of long-term planning—where the main lines of economic expansion are blocked out. Starting with mid-1957, preliminary studies were begun on a fifteen-year "perspective plan" scheduled to run from 1961 to 1975, the first such long-term plan ever undertaken in Poland. The plan was to supply the general frame for the three five-year plans envisaged for the period.

The well-known economist Michal Kalecki directed these studies and was responsible for the theoretical formulations underlying the plan.[23] His basic equation relating the investment effort and the growth of national income was the following:

$$\frac{\Delta Y}{Y} = \frac{1}{m}\frac{I}{Y}\left(1 - c\frac{\Delta I}{I}\right) - a + u$$

20. Some of the economic analysis in stages 3) and 4) was entrusted to "Commissions on the Assessment of Investment Projects." These generally dealt with wider problems than the project-making organizations, which specialized in technical analysis and cost estimation.

21. M. Rakowski, *Zagadnienia planowania wieloletniego w Polsce Ludowej* (Problems of long-range planning in Peoples' Poland), p. 111.

22. *GM*, no. 23 (1956), 799.

23. At the beginning of 1957, prior to Kalecki's participation, a few rough calculations were made in the Department of Perspective Planning on the development of the Polish economy from 1961 to 1975. These calculations turned on output projections for about a dozen sectors of the economy; they were not tied together by any "synthetic" model for the growth of the economy as a whole, as were Kalecki's subsequent projections.

where Y is national income and ΔY its increment in the plan period; m is a marginal capital-to-output ratio; I stands for "productive investment outlays," gross of depreciation, and ΔI for their yearly increment; c is the average gestation period during which investment funds will be immobilized; u is a technological progress factor tending to raise national income independently of the investment effort; and a is a capacity-reducing coefficient connected with the retirement of obsolete and worn-out plant and equipment.[24]

According to Lissowski,[25] who cooperated with Kalecki in this work, the period 1956–60 served as a base for estimating the parameters in this equation, though some corrections were made in projecting m, u, c, and a from past trends. For instance, the marginal capital-to-output ratio m was adjusted in the light of what were termed "exogenous barriers" to development, such as balance-of-payments difficulties, raw-material shortages, and organizational problems. These barriers, Kalecki argued, would eventually tend to raise the value of m.[26] In addition, a, the factor

24. Cf. two articles by Michał Kalecki, "Dynamika inwestycji i dochodu narodowego w gospodarce socjalistycznej" (The dynamics of investments and national income in a socialist economy), *Ekonomista*, no. 5 (1956), and "Wpływ czasu budowy na współzależność inwestycji i dochodu narodowego a 'współczynnik zamrożenia'" (The influence of construction time on the relation between investment and national income . . .), *Ekonomista*, no. 1 (1957). If we exclude the term in parentheses, Kalecki's formulation becomes a variation of a Harrod-Domar growth equation, with this exception: Kalecki's I refers to investment outlays during the period, not to the value of investment projects completed, though it is only the latter that can generate a direct increase in output. The term in parentheses shows how the rate of growth is reduced—for a given investment ratio—as the average period c during which capital will be locked up in projects under construction is increased. Let ΔK stand for the volume of investments actually completed during the year. Then $I - \Delta K = \Delta B$ where ΔB is the increase in the volume of investment works "in process." Kalecki proves that, if c is constant and the rate of growth is small, ΔB will equal $c\, \Delta I$. But since:

$$\frac{\Delta Y}{Y} = \frac{1}{m}\frac{\Delta K}{Y} - a + u, \text{ then } \frac{\Delta Y}{Y} = \frac{1}{m}\frac{I - \Delta B}{Y} - a + u = \frac{1}{m}\frac{I - c\Delta I}{Y} - a + u =$$

$\frac{1}{m}\frac{I}{Y}\left(1 - c\frac{\Delta I}{I}\right) - a + u.$ This is the formula in the text.

25. W. Lissowski, "Metody rachunku ekonomicznego w perspektywicznym planowaniu regionalnym" (Methods of economic calculation in the regional long-range plan), *GP*, no. 1 (1958), 28.

26. The theoretical factors bearing on m are set forth in Kalecki's article, "Czynniki określające tempo wzrostu dochodu narodowego w gospodarce socjalistycznej" *GP*, no. 8 (1958), 2–4. Kalecki singles out coal mining, metallurgy, the chemical industry,

representing the retirement of plant and equipment, was raised compared to past experience in anticipation of the heavy replacement needs that would have to make good the failure to maintain physical assets and keep up with obsolescence during the Six-Year Plan. The residual element u was lowered on the supposition that there were fewer gains to be achieved in the future from fuller utilization of capacity than there had been at the beginning of the industrialization drive.[27]

The question arises whether the future ratio of gross investment to national product was to be established at some foreordained level, which would in turn determine the growth rate of income, or was to be calculated from a targeted growth rate. In making the Fifteen-Year Plan, the second sequence was followed: the primary directive concerned the growth rate. Kalecki prepared his first draft (August 1957) on the assumption that the growth rate of national income of 8 per cent planned for the first Five-Year Plan (1956–60) could be maintained throughout the perspective plan. He rapidly came to the conclusion that bottlenecks other than the capital supply would militate against such a high growth rate. The shortage of foreign exchange, the long gestation period of mining investments, and the lack of competent technicians to expand certain industries could only be compensated by a disproportionate increase in the level of investments. This heavy additional burden would not be warranted for the purpose of preserving a small increment in the growth rate.[28] By May 1958, when the second draft was made ready,[29] the planned growth rate had subsided to an average 6.6 per cent for 1961–65 (a fraction less for the entire fifteen-year period). The ratio of gross investment to national income computed at factor cost (excluding turnover taxes) was to average 31.5 per cent for 1961–75.

---

and agriculture as sectors afflicted with "technical-organizational ceilings" reducing their potential rate of growth (p. 5).

27. Interview material. Experts in the Planning Commission estimated that technical progress and other residual factors had increased national income by 3 per cent per year from 1950 to 1956. They foresaw a drop in u from three to two per cent for the long-term plan.

28. Interview material.

29. This draft is discussed in detail in Kalecki's article "Plan perspektywiczny na lata 1961–1975" (The perspective plan for the years 1961–1975), *ND*, no. 8 (1958), 27–45.

The planners in charge of preparing perspective balances had to comply with general directives on the size of the investment fund available for each year and on the growth of income to be attained (as set forth in Kalecki's original draft). Besides, they were given concrete instructions, which aimed at achieving the following goals: (1) Poland's consumption standards must catch up with the present standards of advanced West European countries by 1975. (2) There must be a "significant improvement" in urban and rural housing standards. (3) Poland must rely mainly on its own resources to achieve the goals of the Fifteen-Year Plan and must count on repaying all outstanding credits. (Foreign loans should only be relied upon to hit the plan targets ahead of schedule.) [30]

The second draft, which took into account bottleneck impediments to growth, was elaborated with the aid of hundreds of specialists in every sphere of economic activity. It was supported by a large number of perspective balances of output and capacity (for some 150 to 200 materials and factors of production), drawn up not only in the Planning Commission itself but also in the ministries and in other agencies.[31] Many calculations of investment efficiency went to test and reinforce the work done on the capacity balances and on the expansion of export industries.

These calculations were not perfectly synchronized. A good deal of work went on in the different industrial ministries along independent lines before any serious attempt was made to mesh the various forecasts with each other and to fit them to Kalecki's

30. W. Buch, "Kierunki rozwoju przemysłu w planie perspektywicznym 1961–1975" (Growth trends for industry in the perspective plan 1961–1975), *GP*, no. 8 (1958), 1.

31. According to the official instructions for making up the long-term plan for 1961–65, supply plans were to be prepared for 156 materials or groups of materials. This number involves some double counting. For example, the supply plans for metallurgical products were divided into eight items: (1) finished rolled products (planned as a group), (2) rolled steel products of ordinary steels, (3) rolled steel products of quality steels, (4) steel pipes (a subgroup), (5) steel conduits of 165–521 millimeters diameter, (6) welded pipes of 400 mm. and above, (7) galvanized sheets, and (8) tin plate. Material balances were to be drawn up in the ministries for all products for which physical output targets were to be stipulated. These numbered— including groups, subgroups, and detailed profiles—over one thousand items. See *Załączniki do instrukcji pięcioletniego planu rozwoju gospodarki narodowej na lata 1961–1965* (Annexes to the instructions for elaborating the project for the Five-Year Plan of development of the national economy for the years 1961–1965) (Warsaw, Komisja Planowania przy Radzie Ministrów, 1959), pp. 1–22, 48–56.

investment limits.[32] It was frankly conceded that some of the work started in 1957 would have to be revised in late 1958 and in 1959 after the planners from the other countries of the Soviet bloc had been consulted and the separately drawn up national plans had been reconciled with each other.[33] Some of the planners interviewed by the author in 1960 claimed that satisfactory coordination was achieved through successive approximations, but the published evidence does not fully support their assertions.

Soon after the second draft of the Fifteen-Year Plan had been hammered out, a draft of the second Five-Year Plan (1961–65), which had initially been framed as the first phase of the long-term plan, was discussed at the Twelfth Plenum of the Central Committee of the United Workers' Party (October 1958). Eugeniusz Szyr, who had been chief of the Planning Commission before Jędrychowski, led the partisans of an accelerated pace of industrial expansion in an assault against this draft. Jędrychowski, in answer to Szyr, warned against a return to the policy of 1951–53, when the economy had been strained by an excessive investment burden: "We all know what is involved in such excessive investments: open or concealed price increases, a drop in real wages, chronic market shortages etc. . . . Do we wish these phenomena to occur again? I believe we do not." [34]

32. Efforts made in early 1957 to plan long-range electricity consumption were hamstrung by the lack of "crystallized views" concerning the growth of power-consuming industries; see *GP*, no. 3 (1957), p. 24. A detailed description of the first attempts to map out a fifteen-year plan for the metallurgical industry is to be found in the special number of *Problemy projektowe hutnictwa* (Project-making problems in metallurgy), no. 1 (1957), devoted to this problem. J. Gwiaździński, "Perspektywy rozwoju hutnictwa żelaza w Polsce" (Perspectives for the development of ferrous metallurgy in Poland), pp. 2–16, started off by assuming future rates of growth of industry approximately equal to those planned for 1956–60. He also made very rough projections of the expansion of the chief consumers of steel (machine-building industry, shipyards, automobiles, construction, and mining) and estimated the changes that were likely to occur in the norms of steel consumption per unit of output in each of these industries. His final estimates of steel requirements were a summing up of the anticipated needs of these different industries together with some rough adjustments for the needs of "other consumers."

33. Buch, p. 1. These long-term plans were coordinated through the Council of Mutual Economic Aid (Comecon), which was founded in 1949 but only became effective in promoting industrial specialization in the bloc in recent years.

34. *XII Plenum Komitetu Centralnego Polskiej Zjednoczonej Partii Robotniczej* (Twelfth Plenum of the Central Committee of the United Workers' Party), Warsaw, November 1958, p. 192.

A technical conference on long-term planning took place in November 1958. At that time, a few economists, following the line of Szyr in the Central Committee, also chose to press for a higher growth rate and a greater investment effort to catch up with the West than had been provided for in the Fifteen-Year Plan. In particular, complaints were voiced concerning the forecasts laid for the farm sector and the lack of provision made for the mechanization of agriculture.[35]

Professor Kalecki took these suggestions into account in revising his estimates for the Fifteen-Year Plan. The result was the third draft issued in May 1959.

This third draft made only slight concessions to the advocates of faster growth. The average growth rate for 1961–75 was notched up only from 6.6 to 6.9 per cent, with correspondingly modest increases in the investment ratio. However, the new plan envisaged a much more intensive drive to mechanize agriculture and to remove surplus manpower from the farm.[36] This was the most carefully prepared version, which was summarized in an internal document numbering over one thousand pages.

More work still had to be done on the Five-Year Plan. In June 1959, the Politbureau of the United Workers' Party resolved on a full-scale farm mechanization program, which was to gravitate around the newly instituted "Agricultural Circles," a government-sponsored type of farmers' cooperative for the joint use of equipment. To give effect to this policy, the Party caused 24 billion zlotys to be added to the plan for 1961–65. It was commonly acknowledged by planning officials in Warsaw in the summer of 1959 that the added burden had not been fully balanced to test the feasibility in each sector of realizing these new objectives. The "synthesis section" of the draft for the Five-Year Plan, which made up about one tenth of the plan document, was reworked but the

---

35. J. N., "Ogólnokrajowa konferencja w sprawie planu perspektywicznego" (The national conference on the perspective plan), *GP*, no. 12 (1958), 38–39.

36. Kalecki had postulated earlier that the farm population would remain about constant during the plan period: the other sectors of the economy would draw no more than the natural increase from the countryside. In the third draft, the agricultural population declined by a substantial number in fifteen years. Note that neither the second nor the third drafts were predicated on a collectivization drive to eliminate private farming.

remaining sections, the underpinning of the plan, were circulated in their previous form.[37]

However crude these latest attempts at perspective planning may seem, it should be remembered that their theoretical foundations were more solid and the degree of coordination exercised in harmonizing the plans for the different sectors of the economy was better than anything that had been tried in the past. The care taken in relating the allocation of investment funds to capacity changes and the growing sophistication of foreign-trade and investment-efficiency calculations also testify to this progress. Since the perspective plans were subject to frequent, politically motivated, changes, the more careful balancing of estimates at an early stage would have been of limited benefit in any event.

4. *The Efficiency of Investments (1956–59)*

We have already seen that up to 1955 the official instructions set a narrow compass to synthetic calculations of costs and returns in investment planning. In February 1956, a new set of instructions was issued which loosened these prescriptions.[38] The selection of projects was to take place in two stages. The first stage would eliminate from consideration all the projects whose initial investment could only be recouped after a period longer than that officially sanctioned for the branch of industry under consideration. This meant that if the investment outlays on a project were to exceed those made on an existing "standard project" with a similar composition of output, then its operating costs (compared to the standard project's) had to be low enough to make up for the extra investment costs in less than a given number of years. The second stage consisted in choosing among the projects meeting the first test the project with the lowest total cost per unit of output. (This

37. Oskar Lange, speaking before the June 1959 plenum, pointed out that even though the additional investments called for by the new plan might be relatively modest, the needs for machinery and equipment were so concentrated in the metal-consuming branches of industry that bottlenecks were likely to arise in this sector if present calculations were not carefully revised. [Report to the Second Plenum of the Central Committee, June 22–25, 1959, *ND*, no. 8 (1959), 97.]

38. The text of these instructions is not available but their general outline can be discerned from A. Wakar's critical article, "Wskaźniki efektywności ekonomicznej inwestycji" (Coefficients of investment efficiency), *Ekonomista*, no. 1 (1957), 12–14, 36–37.

total unit cost was defined as the sum of investment outlays plus total operating costs over the service life of the asset divided by the total output over the same period.) The minimum recoupment period recommended by the instructions for the Five-Year Plan (1956–60), was to be two to three years for plant modernization and other small projects and five years or more for larger projects.

Polish economists were quick to point out the theoretical weaknesses of the instructions: (1) They made no attempt to distinguish the time rate at which cost savings would be expected to accrue from a given investment. (Of two investments, both of which could be recouped in ten years, no preference would be indicated for the project that would reap most of its cost savings in the early years.) (2) The gestation period of the investment project was left out of consideration altogether. A project maker would have no ground for preferring a project, that would start yielding benefits before it was completed and whose outlays would be distributed over several years, over a project that would tie up capital during a protracted period without affording any benefits at all. (3) Comparison with a standard existing project (as enjoined by the instructions) was perfectly arbitrary, since the selection would usually have to be made among alternative projects, all of which were clearly superior to projects already completed. (4) The decision to reject or to accept a given project should be determined by the funds available for investment as well as by the rates of return or recoupment periods of the several alternatives; there was no reason to assume that the arbitrarily set recoupment period would bring about a balance between the supply and demand of investment funds. (5) The built-in discrimination in favor of large projects through the differentiation of recoupment periods could not be justified on any grounds.[39]

A revised version of the instructions came out in August 1956. It is on this version that most of the economic calculations of the first and second Five-Year Plan have been based. As before, the scope of the calculations was confined "mainly to the analysis of all projected variants to achieve a given effect with minimum outlays of productive resources."

The basic formula prescribed was the following:

39. Ibid., pp. 15–16, 35–37; and *GP*, no. 10 (1956), pp. 59–64.

$$E = \frac{I + Iqn + \sum\limits_{i=1}^{n} K_i + \sum\limits_{i=1}^{n} R_i}{\sum\limits_{i=1}^{n} P_i}$$

where E is the efficiency index to be minimized; I stands for the investment expenditure, q for the profitability coefficient applied, K_i for the yearly operating costs, R_i for yearly repairs and maintenance on the equipment, and P_i for yearly output. Since the project is expected to be in operation for n years,[40] yearly costs, repairs, and output are summed over this entire period. For the duration of the first Five-Year Plan (1956–60), the instructions set an upper bound of 10 per cent and a lower bound of 7 per cent to the profitability coefficient q. The product Iqn was assumed to represent the cost of immobilizing investment funds. (It was of course tantamount to an interest charge on the capital invested.)

The main advantage of the new formula was that it combined the two equations of the old without loss of generality. For a given recoupment period, it favors the choice of projects with a longer service life. This is substantially correct. But the same charges can be brought against the new formula as against the old: it also ignored the time pattern of investment outlays, operating costs, and output produced; and q, the virtual interest rate, was just as arbitrarily set as the recoupment period, for neither had been assigned the essential function of rationing off the supply of investment funds.[41]

Soon after the new instructions came out, a whole flurry of de-

40. In case the gestation period of the investment project was to last longer than eighteen months to two years, n was to include the average period during which investment funds would be locked up. This average period could be calculated by weighting the gestation period of the different works by their respective investment costs and dividing the sum of these components by the total cost (Wakar, pp. 15–16, 21).

41. As we have seen the magnitude of q was to fall between 7 and 10 per cent. According to one article, for each extra year during which investments were immobilized, the economy sustained a loss in foregone opportunities of 15 to 20 per cent of the value of these investments. This leads the authors of this article to the conclusion that q was usually set much too low; see M. Bartnicki and M. Rakowski, "O aktualnych problemach efektywności inwestycji" (On actual problems in investment efficiency), *IB*, no. 5 (1959), 6.

tailed studies were prepared incorporating investment calculations made according to the latest precepts. Some of these studies emerged from the Planning Commission, others from the ministries, and still others from the project-making organizations. They covered every major industry. The main emphasis was given to the selection of optimum technologies. The chamber process of manufacturing sulfuric acid was compared with the contact process; the profitability of introducing the phosphorus process in the making of pig iron was investigated, as were the relative advantages of synthetic and natural gasoline. Detailed calculations were made to determine whether it was better to expand lignite output by investing in open-cast mines or by deepening and expanding existing mines. These and many others like them were typical of the studies carried out for the first time in this period.

After nearly three years of experience gained in carrying out these studies, a number of controversial points were still being debated and the lack of uniform principles to settle outstanding issues was still giving rise to arbitrary solutions. We have already mentioned the problem of setting q, the virtual interest rate, at a satisfactory level. There was also some question as to how n, the service life of equipment and structures, should be established. But the least consistent of all was the treatment of so-called "ancillary" and "indirect" investments. By ancillary investments the Poles denote works that are not directly connected with the core of a project. In industrial construction, such investments as workers' housing, electric installations, and railroad sidings are normally planned and executed by organizations independent of the industrial ministry supervising the main undertaking. When calculations were made for the purpose of choosing among several possible variants of a project, these ancillary investments were frequently left out of account altogether. This led to errors, particularly in selecting among competing alternatives for the location of a new project, as the necessary investments in housing, transportation, and electric power tended to differ significantly according to location.[42]

42. Ibid., p. 6. The question comes to mind where the line should be drawn between outlays that should be charged to an investment project and outlays that should not. What about the schools and the stores that will have to be opened in a newly opened locality? If wages were sufficiently flexible, then the workers' extra

By indirect investments are meant all those additional outlays that must be made to supply the requisite amount of inputs to a projected plant once it will be working at capacity. Among the first-order linkages of this sort, may be cited the expense of expanding coal output to supply coal for new thermal plants (an important consideration in choosing between hydroelectric and thermal power) and the cost of adding capacity to the cement industry in order to furnish the concrete needed for building dam sites for hydroelectric projects. Rakowski the chief expert on this subject, writes that the former expense was covered in calculations of investment efficiency but not the latter: a manifest discrimination in favor of capital-intensive hydro-projects. In general, wherever coal could be replaced by other sources of power, such as electricity and diesel oil in running locomotives, investments in these alternatives were made to appear more advantageous than they really were by burdening coal with ancillary and indirect investment costs and by overlooking such costs in the case of the other inputs.

To remedy this arbitrariness, Rakowski suggested that the projectmakers might use input-output methods to trace back all the direct and indirect investment needs to which each technological variant might give rise. But would it not be much more sensible to set the prices of material inputs at a level corresponding to all the investment costs, including interest charges, that went into their making? [43] The arbitrariness of investment calculations in the last analysis stems from weaknesses in the system of prices and

expense and discomfort from living with fewer amenities in a new community might be reflected in higher pay. The profitability of building new stores would become apparent to the Ministry of Internal Trade. This mechanism, however, cannot be relied upon in an integrally planned system and there is probably no way of getting around the necessity for coordinating the plans of all the different ministries affected by any project. This need for bureaucratic coordination in minor questions of technological choice and localization is of course just what economic calculation is supposed to obviate.

43. The branch instructions of August 1956 recommended that a comparison of the indirect investment costs of alternative projects should be limited to a study of the differences between the interest costs (Iqn in formula) of these indirect investments, inasmuch as differences in their depreciation costs were already reflected in the costs of inputs [*Ramowe wytyczne badań ekonomicznej efektywności inwestycji* (Branch rules for the study of the economic efficiency of investments), p. 11.] This was an implicit recognition that the complication was caused by the failure to register interest costs in transfer prices.

wages. We shall see in Chapter Eight that it was not solely, or even mainly, the failure to register interest costs that vitiated the use of current producers' prices in investment calculations: heavy subsidies in raw-material industries and the insulation of domestic prices from opportunity-cost relations in foreign trade had an even more perverse influence on the selection of investment projects.[44]

5. *Economic Calculations in Foreign Trade*

Until about 1955, as we saw in Chapter Three, the decision to import or to export a given commodity was governed almost exclusively by the state of its material balance. If there seemed to be a surplus in the balance after all needs had been met, it was exported; if there was a shortage, and the foreign-currency situation permitted, it was imported. Otherwise, domestic substitutes were sought to replace the commodity whenever possible. Ratios of domestic costs and prices were computed from 1953 on for certain types of commodities entering foreign trade, but these "effective rates" (*kursy wynikowe*) rarely served as a basis for making import or export decisions.

For calculations bearing on foreign trade, the instructions on investment calculations of August 1956 did not afford sufficient guidance, and certain special modifications had to be introduced into the formula. In order to test the economic advantage of exporting a given commodity, two key ratios were supposed to be analyzed: (1) the gross ratio of domestic costs per ton to the foreign price (expressed in accounting rubles [45] or dollars), and (2) the ratio of the potential export's processing costs to its net foreign-currency yield. This net yield was defined as the gross proceeds in

44. The new instructions of January 1960 for calculating the economy efficiency of investments are much more sophisticated than the old and meet several of the objections raised in the foregoing discussion. Its discount formula may even be more refined than the maintenance of an arbitrary interest rate (7 per cent) and the defects of the price system warrant. See *Instrukcja ogólna w sprawie metodyki badań ekonomicznej efektywności inwestycji* (General instruction on the methodology for analyzing the economic efficiency of investments) (Warsaw, Komisja Planowania przy Radzie Ministrów, 1960).

45. The accounting ruble, before the recent revaluation of the ruble, equaled a quarter of a U.S. dollar. Since trade within the Soviet bloc and Polish trade outside the bloc are both conducted at or in the neighborhood of world prices, accounting rubles are little more than a conventional notation for U.S. dollars.

rubles or dollars per ton minus the total foreign-currency value of the materials embodied in one ton of the good exported. (The materials whose cost is subtracted from the gross yield are of two types: materials imported at a direct foreign-currency cost and materials normally exported whose domestic processing entails the direct loss of foreign-currency earnings.)

With the aid of this analysis, certain flagrant errors were uncovered in the apportionment of resources between domestic production and foreign trade. It was found that the net yield in foreign currency of exporting aluminum produced during the winter months, when the coal intake of electric-power output is at its seasonal high, was negative. Calcium carbide and cement exports, particularly from high-cost marginal plants, also ate up more foreign currency than they contributed from their sale abroad.[46]

The next step was to introduce an interest charge that would record the cost of locking up capital in investment projects yielding exportables.[47] The "net coefficient of foreign exchange efficiency" (abbreviated E_{Dn}) was derived from the standard investment formula of the basic instructions by dividing the numerator (processing costs plus investment costs plus cumulative capital charges) by the net foreign-currency yield of the project throughout its service life (instead of by total output as in the formula).[48]

Finally, a measure of the net return in foreign currency was contrived as an additional check on the other formulae. The idea here was to convert the processing costs (including depreciation) into dollars or accounting rubles and to calculate the percentage return on the investment in export capacity. Since the bulk of processing costs was made up of wage outlays, their foreign-currency equivalent must equal approximately the import content of wages, or the foreign-currency cost of an average worker's budget. In previous studies it had been found that the purchasing power parity of Polish workers' consumption expenditures was about 50 zlotys to one dollar or 12.5 zlotys per ruble. This was the

46. M. Rakowski, "Tablice efektywności inwestycji eksportowych" (Tables of efficiency of export investments), *Prace i materiały . . .* , no. 1 (1957), 6–8.

47. As we have already seen, domestic prices included no interest or other capital charges. This limited their usefulness in calculations of comparative advantage.

48. Rakowski, "Tablice . . . ," p. 5. The adjusted formula was equivalent to the ratio of average processing costs, amortization, and capital charges to the foreign-currency yield, all these magnitudes being expressed on a yearly basis.

ratio adopted in the calculations. To arrive at a percentage return, the difference between the net accounting-ruble yield and the ruble equivalent of the processing costs was divided by the gross ruble proceeds of the goods exported.

The following table exhibits some of the flagrant discrepancies among the rates of return on investments in export capacity, which developed as a result of the lack of economic calculation in recent years.

TABLE 5:1. *Selected Profitability Indicators in Investments in Export Capacity* [a]
(1960 draft plan)

	Net domestic costs (excluding interest) per ruble of export proceeds (zlotys)	Net domestic costs (including interest) per ruble of export proceeds	Per cent return [b]	Total value of exports (1960 Plan) (millions of rubles)
Bituminous coal	2.03	2.98	+79.0	374
Coke	5.8	7.14	+14.0	82
Steel plate	3.5	4.94	+40.0	45
Steel sheets	6.13	8.63	+28.47	47
Zinc (electrolytic)	3.52	5.25	+26.5	18
Calcium carbide	12.5	18.3	0	1.4
Soda ash	14.0	21.5	−25.0	6.4
Cement	20.9	35.0	−11.8	4
Window glass	46.1	62.5	−29.0	1.8
Cotton cloth	50.7	60.7	−48.5	18
Woolens	10.9	11.7	+ 4.4	22
Canned ham	1.5	1.9	+33.4	23
Fresh eggs	17.7	17.8	−11.1	12
Brewing barley	4.7	4.8	+62.5	2.2
Buckwheat	21.4	21.5	−71.0	0.7

[a] Based on 1956 costs and foreign prices and on tentative plans for the volume of exports in 1960.

[b] Net ruble yield per ton minus value of processing costs (converted into rubles) divided by gross ruble proceeds (multiplied by 100).

Source. Rakowski, "Tablice. . . ."

By and large it turned out that the commodities distinguished by an above-average rate of return in these 1957 calculations were also the ones scheduled to be exported in the largest volume in 1960 (according to plans based on material balances). This should not surprise us, since a strong comparative advantage was likely to show up as a surplus on the resources side of the material balances underlying the draft-plans for 1960.[49] Still, important quantities of cement, cotton cloth, and eggs were exported at a frightful cost before 1956 and even in 1957 and 1958 after this study had been circulated.[50] For cotton cloth, the yield, excluding interest charges, was 51 zlotys of processing costs per ruble of net proceeds or 204 zlotys per dollar. This was twice as high as the black-market rate for the dollar at that time, which had been bid up by speculative and hoarding demand to over 300 per cent of purchasing-power parity. Including interest charges, cotton-cloth exports cost 243 zlotys for every dollar earned!

Admittedly, the marginal profitability of exporting these different goods would diverge less than the average; but even the roughest calculations made in terms of marginal costs indicate that substantial differences would remain. In any event, nothing could possibly justify the export of goods yielding a negative return on their foreign-currency earnings.

One conclusion that emerges from this analysis is that even crude measures of costs and returns can expose important errors in the allocation of resources. The decision taken by the Polish government from late 1957 on to curb cement and cotton-cloth exports [51] was sound, even though the calculations that led to this decision rested on a tenuous theoretical base.

6. *A Synthesis*

An argument flared up in a Polish mining journal in 1956 and 1957, which set in sharp relief the differences dividing the officials in favor of planning with physical balances from the advocates of economic calculation. The controversy turned on the respective merits of increasing the output of lignite and brown coal from open pits and from underground mines. The administrative personnel of the Central Board of the Lignite Industry, the organization directly supervising the lignite mines, favored investments in underground mines, which were expected to yield lignite in a very short time, but at a high cost per ton. The Central Board came to

49. See Chap. 1, Sect. 4; and Appendix B, Sect. 1e.

50. The volume of exports planned for 1960 and their composition were broadly similar to the exports actually realized in the years 1955 to 1958. In 1956, 93 million meters of cotton cloth, 343 million eggs, and 561,000 tons of cement had been exported.

51. *Mały rocznik statystyczny 1959*, p. 105.

this conclusion from an analysis of the perspective fuel balance, which showed that a fuel shortage would arise in the early 1960s if coal exports were to be maintained at or near present levels. The forecast was that this shortage would gradually ease off in subsequent years as supplies from newly opened bituminous coal mines became available. The demand for substitute fuels was therefore concentrated in the earlier period, when Poland's foreign-exchange position would be most critical and every shortfall in exports might jeopardize essential raw-material imports.[52]

On the other side, the project making organization in charge of drafting plans for the expansion of lignite output held the opposite view. Its calculations showed that investments in open-cast pits might be recouped in a short enough period to justify the choice of the more expensive alternative.[53]

This controversy cannot be resolved by any meritorious arguments. No "inherent superiority" of decentralized methods based on economic calculation can be invoked, because these methods depend on a rational price system and on exact formulae for testing investment efficiency. In their absence, the crudest perspective balances may give a truer answer to the problem than the analysis of costs and returns in national currency. Of course, the balances are also susceptible of leading the planners into error, since they are not likely to consider all the possible rearrangements of resources—each requiring an overhaul of interdependent balances —that are capable of yielding a more economic solution.

But at least the techniques for drawing up balances can be improved—and were in fact improved from 1955 on—by a more careful and systematic trial-and-error search for a satisfactory solution, while price-induced errors are harder to detect, except by checking against the balances, and harder still to correct. In practice, the balances afforded some safeguards against the incidence of acute shortages of materials, whereas economic calculation, though it might reveal certain inefficiencies, could not be relied on for preserving desirable proportions in the economy throughout a plan period.

We can look at the controversy from another angle. An im-

52. A. Strzemiński, "Efektywność inwestycji w przemyśle węgla brunatnego" (The efficiency of investments in the brown-coal industry), *Gospodarka górnictwa* (Mining economy), no. 2 (1957).

53. J. Przedpełski, "Efektywność inwestycji w przemyśle węgla brunatnego" (The efficiency of investments in the brown-coal industry), *GG*, no. 11 (1956), 327–32.

portant defect of the price system, which limited its usefulness for
investment calculations, was its failure to give expression to the
scarcity of capital and of other bottleneck factors besides labor.
Under these conditions price calculations were not likely to lead
to the choice of technologies or processes that pressed least on the
supplies of the most critical factors. The acute shortage of foreign
currency, for example, should have predisposed the planners toward technical processes which made more intensive use of domestic resources; but since the prices of imports did not reflect the
real extent of their scarcity, investment calculations could not be
expected to reveal the best alternatives. However, in the long run,
assuming that disproportions in the economy could gradually be
eliminated, extreme shortages would disappear, and prices based
on average production costs would provide a more accurate reflection of opportunities foregone. Investment calculations would
then come into their own again.

Whenever earlier planning decisions have created disproportions which can only be corrected by stopgap measures, the use of
prices and economic calculation must be held in abeyance. But if
the planners can start out with a clean slate and exercise a large
measure of choice in reshuffling resources according to their preferences, prices and economic calculation have a crucial role to
play. In this regard, postwar Polish investment policy may be divided into three periods. During the reconstruction period, which
lasted from the end of the war to 1950, the planners had relatively
little room for free choice: bottlenecks in transportation and in
the supply of raw materials overruled other considerations. At the
threshhold of the Six-Year Plan, the economy was less afflicted than
at any previous time with bottlenecks and disproportions, and this
would have been a good time to resort to economic calculation.
Unfortunately, this was just the period when the method of balances had come into fashion, and almost nothing was being done
in the way of investment calculations.[54] Poor balancing methods
in framing the Six-Year Plan and the drastic structural changes
imposed by the authorities in the midst of the plan period (from
1954 on) created a host of disproportions, which the planners of

54. The year 1950 also marked a low point of sophistication with regard to price-
setting (below, Chap. 8). Irrational pricing, of course, reinforced the planners' prejudice in favor of the balances.

the Gomulka period were left to grapple with. After 1955, the officials of the Planning Commission were more inclined than in the past to test the investment efficiency of alternative projects and the comparative advantage of their foreign-trade decisions, but the disproportions left over from the Six-Year Plan restricted their freedom of action.

It was recognized by one of the newly appointed officials of the Gomulka regime that the neglect of residential construction in the 1950s, the lagging expansion of export sectors, and bottlenecks in raw-material industries would place limits on the planners' freedom of choice for many years to come. One direct consequence of this state of affairs was that the location of new projects could not be resolved on the basis of cost-minimizing calculations, since an acute housing shortage made it practically impossible to move large numbers of workers to localities otherwise favorably situated for development.[55]

In short, the best hope for reinstating economic calculation to its "rightful place" lies in improving the balances and in raising the accuracy of long-range planning. Until then, barring a radical improvement in the price system, economic calculation, as in the past, will have to be relegated to a comparatively minor status among the instruments of planning.

55. C. Bobrowski, "Stopień swobody wyboru: Uwagi na marginesie wytycznych rozwoju gospodarczego na lata 1961–1965" (The scope of the freedom of choice: remarks on the directives for economic development for 1961–1965), *GP*, no. 1–2 (1959), 6–7. This article offers illuminating comments on an aspect of planning rarely discussed in the economic literature of the Soviet bloc.

CHAPTER SIX

The Socialized Enterprise in the Centrally Planned Economy

1. *Pressures and Propaganda*

We have already had many occasions to notice that the freedom of socialized enterprises to manage their own affairs was narrowly circumscribed by the system of central planning. In Chapter Nine, where the measures taken after 1956 to delegate authority and loosen centralized controls will be described, more will be said about the narrow leeway left to enterprises during the Six-Year Plan. For the purposes of the present chapter, we shall be interested mainly in the way managers exercised such initiative as they had in conducting their business. So much has already been written in the West on this subject as it pertains to the other economies of the Soviet bloc,[1] and the behavior of enterprise managers seems so alike in these various countries, that there is little knowledge to be gained in raking over these issues. Only the salient points will be brought out here.

Each year the enterprise received from its central board a set of detailed directives defining its tasks within the framework of the National Economic Plan. The central board, in addition to breaking down among its subordinate enterprises the directives it received from its ministry concerning the value of gross and marketed output, assortment plans, labor productivity, cost reduction, wage funds, profits, decentralized investments, and similar economic indicators of a more general nature, normally tacked on its own assignments. These assignments compassed the norms set for the consumption of materials, the technical improvements which

1. See, in particular, B. Balassa's *The Hungarian Experience in Economic Planning*, Chap. 5; and J. S. Berliner's *Factory and Manager in the U.S.S.R.*

172

were to be introduced at the plant level, minor and major repairs, cooperation with other firms, the health and safety of employees, and any number of other routine activities. There was in practice no limit to this barrage of directives ultimately directed at the enterprise by higher and lower authorities.

Socialized enterprises, bound as they were by a sheaf of directives regulating the bulk of their activities, were still not absolved from the duty of drawing up their own detailed plans. This took the form of a technical-industrial-financial plan, a document mapping out in the finest detail the entire production and financial operation of the enterprise contemplated for the year. Among other particulars, this plan was supposed to show by what concrete means the managing staff intended to implement the central board's directives. The detailed plan, prior to the Gomulka reforms, was subject to the approval of the director of the central board. Such approval did not, however, imply that the enterprise could schedule its operations on the basis of the plan and expect to be free of meddling for the rest of the year. For there was nothing to prevent the central board, either at the behest of the ministry or on its own accord, from imposing new directives during the course of the year. Even the quarterly technical-industrial-financial plans, elaborated from the latest directives, were subject to such changes at short notice.

The imposition of an excessive number of regulations by the Planning Commission and the ministries and of concrete directives by the central boards provided the enterprise with possibilities of evasion they might not have had if only a few rules had been imposed but strictly enforced. Because there were too many rules and directives to be simultaneously adhered to, managers could exercise a measure of choice· they could decide in a pinch what was essential and what was not. In so doing they took their cue from Party resolutions and from the campaigns in the press; they could fulfill or overfulfill the priority targets, observe the most essential rules, and ignore the rest.

During the Three-Year Plan and during most of the Six-Year Plan, the United Workers' Party, the press, and state organs exhorted workers and management to devote their efforts primarily to the fulfillment of production tasks and secondarily to material savings. Money economies were supposed to result from the reduced consumption of materials rather than from the substitution of cheaper inputs.

According to Bronisław Minc, pressures on cost savings were channeled through administrative organs, whose personnel, being themselves rewarded mainly for output gains, tended to press subordinate enterprises for an outstanding performance in increasing output, even if it had to be achieved at the expense of higher unit costs.[2]

Instructions were issued in 1954 requiring all enterprises to carry out the economic analysis of their activities, but they were generally ignored because no member of the staff was made responsible for carrying out this analysis. The accountants, who should most closely be concerned with costs, were so bent on "closing the books" before the deadline to get their special "balance-sheet" bonuses that they could not spare the time to attend to the profitability of the firm.[3]

2. Bonuses Paid to the Management of Firms

From 1945 to 1954, the managing staff of socialized firms got bonuses predicated exclusively on the output plan. The loose level of planning frequently allowed earnings from this source twice as great as basic pay.[4] In many industries, from 1948 on, the ability of the firm to raise labor productivity above plan was also rewarded by a special bonus.

Although certain features of the early schemes were modified and revised at frequent intervals (especially the ceiling on the share of the bonus in basic pay, the deductions from output bonuses for quality failures and for unjustified transgressions of the assortment plan), their main provisions were not basically reformed until the latter part of the Six-Year Plan.[5] It was only in

2. B. Minc, "W sprawie bodźców zainteresowania materialnego w gospodarce socjalistycznej" (On material incentives in a socialist economy), *GP*, no. 3 (1956), 20.

3. J. Zalewski, "Analiza ekonomiczna" (Economic analysis), *Rachunkowość* (Accounting), no. 8 (1956), 377.

4. M. Kuczyński, "Rozwój systemów premiowania personelu inżyniero-technicznego i administracyjnego w przemyśle polskim" (The development of bonus systems for engineering-technical and administrative personnel), *Ekonomika i organizacja pracy* (Management and work organization), no. 4 (1955), p. 164. This article contains a succinct summary of the provisions of the early postwar bonus schemes, which are not covered in the present study.

5. In a few industries, starting with 1953, the waste of materials was to be pe-

the middle of 1954 that a separate bonus was instituted, which was to be paid out to the managing staff [6] of each firm for reducing costs below the unit costs budgeted in the plan of the enterprise. In some industries, 80 per cent of the bonus earned by the employees for their work in increasing production was paid to them each month, while the rest was withheld until the results of the cost plan for the quarter were announced. If costs exceeded the plan, the remainder of the bonus was canceled permanently. But if costs had been kept within the planned allowance, the 20 per cent left over from the output plan plus an extra bonus, depending on any additional cost savings that might have been effected, were added to the pay of managing personnel. Elsewhere the production bonus was paid in full each month and an additional bonus accrued to the employees for cost compression at the end of the quarter. Bonuses paid out for reducing costs in light industry in 1956 averaged 8.7 per cent of total above-plan cost reductions actually achieved.[7]

In several industries, there was an almost immediate reduction in the costs of enterprises after the new bonus was introduced in 1954. In the first quarter of 1954, before the bonus came into effect, the chemical industry had exceeded its planned costs by 20 million zlotys; in the second and third quarters, reportedly as a result of the new incentive, there was an above-plan reduction in costs totaling 12 million zlotys. In ferrous metallurgy, where planned costs had been exceeded by nearly 7 per cent in 1953, costs went down by 1.5 per cent above plan in 1954.[8] It is not known how typical these sectors were of the general impact of

---

nalized by cuts in the bonuses, but even this sanction was rarely applied. In light industry, up to the middle of 1954, bonuses were still derived exclusively from above-plan output with deductions for failures to meet quality norms. See W. Mościcka, H. Niemira, and G. Gajda, "O niektórych zagadnieniach funkcjonowania systemu premiowego w przemyśle" (Problems in the functioning of the bonus system in industry), *Finanse*, no. 2 (1956), 18.

6. In the machine-building industry, the staff receiving bonuses was divided into three groups: (1) director and chief engineer; (2) chiefs of production departments and vice-directors; (3) engineering-technical personnel, chief of bookkeeping staff, and other middle and lower-rank administrative personnel.

7. H. Król, "Zagadnienie zainteresowania obniżką kosztów własnych w przedsiębiorstwie—nadal aktualne" (The problem of cost-reduction incentives in industry is still in order), *GP*, no. 9 (1958), 55.

8. Ibid.

the reform. Even the results of these selected industries should be taken with a measure of skepticism in view of the possible manipulation of accounting records—such as will be described in a moment—which may have contributed to the "cost savings" they reported.

According to Brus, the conditions regarding quality and assortment nominally regulating the payment of output and cost bonuses were seldom enforced, because they hinged on the director's decisions (for distribution of bonuses within the firm) or on higher officials who had a personal interest in maintaining the bonuses as large as possible. The authorities were reluctant to cut out the bonus altogether, since the employees counted on it as an inalienable part of their pay and suffered greatly by its loss.[9] In early 1955, for instance, bonuses from all sources came to about 70 per cent of the basic pay of white-collar workers in the machine-building industry.[10] If the bonus was subtracted from their pay, the chiefs of departments earned less than skilled workers.[11]

Even after the basic reform in the system of 1954, the resultant pull of all the incentives stimulated managers to concentrate on "beating the output plan." An example from the industry manufacturing automobiles and trucks may show why. In 1956 the director of a firm in this industry earned 2,300 zlotys a month basic pay; as a bonus, he got another 2,300 zlotys for 100 per cent fulfillment of his output plan; for each point above this target, he was paid an additional 10 per cent of his basic pay; for just fulfilling the cost plan, he received no bonus whatever; for every percentage point of above-plan reduction of costs, reckoned at the end of the quarter, he was paid 10 per cent of his basic pay, up to a maximum of 60 per cent. If we suppose he fulfilled the output plan of the firm by 106 per cent, his basic salary would be raised by 3,680 zlotys per month (2,300 zlotys plus six times 230 or 1,380 zlotys); this comes to 11,040 zlotys per quarter or to 60 per cent more than his basic pay for the whole three months. For a 6 per cent above-plan cost compression, his quarterly pay would only be raised by

9. W. Brus, "W sprawie bodźców zainteresowania materialnego" (On material incentives), *ND*, no. 12 (1955).

10. *ZG*, no. 14 (1955), 576.

11. *ZG* no. 10 (1955), 374.

1,380 zlotys or by one-fifth. And, as the source points out, it is harder to save on costs than to increase output.[12]

The incentive value of bonuses tied to planned costs was deprecated by Polish economists for a number of reasons. Many firms achieved fictitious cost savings by manipulating the amortization, maintenance, and purchase accounts.[13] Sometimes the quality of goods was allowed to deteriorate for the purpose of effecting cost savings. Goods might be acquired by "cooperation" from other firms rather than produced at home (at approximately the same real costs). This helped compress book costs, because most heavy industrial goods during the Six-Year Plan were bought at deficit prices, when they would have been entered at cost if they had been produced within the firm.[14]

Finally, the "very elastic boundary" between goods whose costs were comparable from year to year (and therefore entered the cost plans), and those which were not, encouraged schemes to prove nonexistent or meaningless cost reductions: this was true, for instance, of prototypes or of newly launched products whose initially high costs were pared down as soon as mass production was started. Frequent changes in the assortment plan imposed from above also rendered the analysis of cost performance difficult or impossible.[15]

To compensate for the tendency of firms to "conceal reserves" in cost compression when drawing up their plans for the year, the Central Boards often made across-the-board cuts in employment and cost plans. The result was that many firms could not get bonuses legally and were forced to resort to illegal tricks to receive their "fair share" of bonus funds.[16]

We have made only passing references to the incentive effects

12. Z. Oldakowski, "Bodźce antyprodukcyjne" (Counter production bonuses) *Głos Pracy* (The voice of labor), June 18, 1956. In one of the leading steel mills of the Ministry of Metallurgy, the bonuses on cost reduction were about one-sixth to one-tenth of the output bonuses paid to different members of the staff. See *Ekonomista*, no. 4 (1956), 115.

13. Mościcka, Niemira, and Gajda, p. 28.

14. W. Brus, "Oddziaływanie prawa wartości a bodźce ekonomiczne" (The influence of the law of value and economic incentives), *Ekonomista*, no. 3 (1955), 38.

15. B. Gliński, A. Nowicki, T. Marzantowicz, "W sprawie bodźców zainteresowania materialnego: Możliwości premiowania przedsiębiorstw socjalistycznych z zysku" (On material incentives: Possibilities of rewarding socialist enterprises from profits), *GP*, no. 1 (1956), 39.

16. *ZG*, no. 17 (1955), 698.

of the price system on the structure of production. If we assume that the assortment plan, which stipulates the product-mix the firm should deliver, reflects the planners' demand, then we must conclude that incentives ran counter to plan, since the output-plan bonus swamped all the others and induced deviations from planned assortment.[17] In former years, bonuses were computed from the value of output at fixed prices of 1937–38; more recently, bonuses were linked to the value of output at transfer prices in producer goods industries.[18] (The value of output on which the bonuses were based included rejects, goods sold at a quantity discount, or delivered to the sales central and then stored as surplus, etc.) [19] Whether one system of prices was used or another, many firms found it advantageous, in order to attain the principal bonus, to concentrate on goods that required the least labor costs, or, to look at the phenomenon from another angle, that incorporated as high a percentage as possible of materials purchased on the outside.[20]

On the whole, the bonus on cost reduction did not show very beneficial results, chiefly because both cost plans and their fulfillment contained too many arbitrary elements. In mid-1957 the cost bonus was scrapped.[21] In principle, its incentive role was to be taken over by the Enterprise Fund (accumulated from the firm's participation in profits). We shall see below that this reform met with only indifferent success.

3. The Place of Profits in Managerial Incentives

At least until the credit reform of July 1955, the personal interest of managers in making greater profits or diminishing planned losses was meager. There were only three inducements, and all

17. Brus, "Oddziaływanie . . ." p. 47.

18. Mościcka, Niemira, and Gajda, p. 18.

19. *Ekonomista*, no. 14 (1955), 44.

20. B. Minc, "W sprawie bodźców . . . ," p. 23. The suggestion that raw-material–intensive items are more "profitable" for management to produce was attributed by Minc to Kalecki.

21. In January 1957, new bonus systems had been set up in a number of "experimenting enterprises" (where new methods of organization were tried out). In most of these experiments, the bonuses on cost reduction were raised to parity or near parity with the bonus on output. It is doubtful whether the results of these experiments had anything to do with the elimination of the cost bonuses. See W. Jaworski, "Bank a przedsiębiorstwa eksperymentujące" (The bank and experimenting enterprises) *Finanse*, no. 2 (1957), 14.

were weak: (1) to keep staff and crew contented by accumulating profits in the Enterprise Fund, which could be spent for social improvements and special bonuses; (2) to maintain a sufficient supply of working capital to fulfill production tasks; and (3) to preserve a healthy financial situation—which made it easier to receive credits from the National Bank of Poland and protected the firm from the meddlesome interference of officials from the bank and from the Ministry of Finance.

Managers, in addition, were spurred to saving on labor costs by the fear of losing their bonuses. Since bonuses to management took last priority among all payments from the wage fund, when labor costs were exceeded (due, for instance, to newly imposed output tasks), the funds set aside for bonuses sometimes had to be depleted to meet the extra costs. Even when the bank finally unblocked the firm's account and made additional sums available for wage payments, there was often no provision made for paying out bonuses to management.[22]

The Enterprise Fund (*fundusz zakładowy*), established by the law of February 6, 1950,[23] supplied incentive for sound management, insofar as it helped to attach the staff to the firm and to keep down labor turnover. This was desirable from the viewpoint of managers, for keeping a good and stable labor force often turned the scale between fulfilling the plans and falling behind. Up to 1955, key ministries such as mining and metallurgy paid into the fund 4 per cent from planned profits and 30 per cent from above-plan profits. The share of the profits going to the fund, which was graduated according to the importance of the branch of the economy, declined to 2 per cent of planned profits and 15 per cent of above-plan profits for enterprises in the least privileged sectors. In enterprises working on a planned subsidy, the fund drew a part of the sums accruing from cost reductions. The reductions from profits going to the fund could not in any event exceed three per cent of the wage bill of any enterprise.[24] In February 1955, in recognition of rising costs and of the obstacles to earning planned profits, the part of the bonus from planned profits was replaced by one derived

22. *ZG*, no. 10 (1955), 373.

23. *Dziennik Ustaw*, no. 6 (1950), *poz.* 53.

24. A. Karpinski, *Plan techniczno-przemysłowo-finansowy* (The technical-industrial-financial plan), Part II, pp. 168–69.

from the wage bill, half a per cent of which was to be paid into the Enterprise Fund.[25] The system was revised again by the ordinance of 9 December 1955. The fund was to accumulate 30 per cent from above-plan profits (or reductions in losses) in mining, metallurgy, and chemicals, 20 per cent in defense and in light industry and 15 per cent in small-scale industries and handicrafts. In addition, all coal and ore mines were to earmark 4 per cent of the planned wage bill to the fund. Other sectors were entitled to do so only with the express consent of the Ministry of Finance.[26]

During the Six-Year Plan, the fund was small in almost all branches of industry: in 1952 only 226 zlotys per worker were paid out in industry for the whole year—less than 3 per cent of the average wage. A 1954 investigation by Brus and his associates revealed that there had been no improvement since 1952 and that the effect of the fund on the workers was still practically nil.[27] The failure of firms to accumulate any sizable sums may in part be explained by the harsh conditions which limited the right of firms to pay any sums into the fund unless they fulfilled their production and sales plans in the proper assortment, reduced their comparable unit costs, and kept within their cost allowance.[28] Exceptions were sometimes sanctioned but only with the approval of higher authorities.

In 1957, the fund was reinforced to fill the gap in incentives left open by the abolition of the cost-reduction bonus to management. If the profit plan was fulfilled, 1.5 per cent of the wage bill was to be paid into the fund, plus a share of above-plan profits averaging about 50 per cent in 1957. The fund could not, however, accrue a total of more than 8 per cent of the wage bill for any industry. As a matter of fact, this maximum proportion was not attained in most industries. In the Ministry of Heavy Industry, the fund accrued 3.7 per cent of the wage bill in 1957, 4.7 per cent in the

25. *Dziennik Ustaw*, no. 9 (1955), *poz.* 52 and 58. As will be seen in Chap. 8, many branches of heavy industry were working at a loss in 1955.

26. *MP*, no. 120 (1955), *poz.* 1584. It is noteworthy that the fund no longer received any part of planned profits (which, by and large, were high in consumer goods industries and low or nonexistent in enterprises turning out producer goods).

27. Brus, "W sprawie bodźców . . . ," p. 83. Workers in leading plants of the machine-building industry received cash awards from the fund equal to 0.4 per cent of the wage bill (J. Kwejt, *Analiza działalności gospódarczej przedsiębiorstw przemysłowych* (Analysis of the economic activity of industrial enterprises), p. 306).

28. *Finanse*, no. 5 (1956), 56.

Ministry of Mining, and as little as 2.8 per cent in the Ministry of Construction and Building Materials.[29]

A sample survey made by the Ministry of Finance and by the Ministry of State Control of "a few hundred enterprises" showed that 60 per cent of the enterprises covered had inflated their fund by illegal price increases or by submitting inflated cost plans (with the aim of eventually boosting profits by effortless "cost reductions").[30]

Nevertheless, the incentive effects of the fund were still weak. Not only were the total sums earmarked small, but a large part had to be given over to housing and social amenities. Since the part of the bonus paid in cash was usually distributed on an equalitarian basis among all the workers and employees, the sums received by the staff chiefly responsible for reducing costs and increasing profits were too modest to counteract the powerful influence of production bonuses.[31]

According to new regulations issued in 1958, which were aimed at discouraging "loose planning," a part of the fund was to be accumulated from year-to-year increases in actual profits and a part from planned profits; but total disbursements from the fund still were not raised sufficiently to swing the balance of incentives toward the maximization of profits.

Indeed, it is doubtful whether the Polish planners were prepared to take a radical step in this direction, at least as long as the price system remained in its parlous state. The opponents of profit-based bonuses quite properly pointed out that the efforts of managers to improve the efficiency of their firms had a comparatively small effect on profits. What really counted in most multiproduct firms was the proportion of highly profitable items in total production; the possibility of altering the product-mix to raise this proportion offered the best chance of increasing profits.[32]

29. S. Frenkel, "Mimo wszystko dobre wyniki" (Good results in spite of all), ZG, no. 12 (1958), 3.

30. Ibid.

31. Król, p. 58. In the metallurgical industry, 3 per cent overfulfillment of production plans each month would add 144 per cent to the basic yearly pay of technological personnel. But a maximum of one month's pay could be obtained from the Enterprise Fund.

32. Gliński, Nowicki and Marzantowicz, p. 45. Detailed statistics on the wide range of profitability for different items produced in the same firm are presented in Chaps. 7 and 8.

4. Profits, Working Capital, and Bank Credits

Socialized enterprises depend in part on profits (or on cutting down losses) for an adequate supply of working capital; theoretically, they should not neglect this aspect of their operations, for, if they are short of funds to pay labor or materials, they may not be able to fulfill their production plans, with all the losses to management and staff that this entails.

As we saw in Chapter Four, each enterprise was supposed to have at its disposal a minimum sum of working capital, called its "norm." This norm was determined by the volume of its operations and of its standard inventories (including goods in process) and by the speed of its turnover.[33]

If this quota was depleted for valid reasons or if the enterprise's expanded activities called for its increase, the manager was authorized by a 1951 regulation to retain 30 per cent of above-plan profits toward increasing these funds. However, if there had been unplanned losses and the enterprise had been losing some of its working capital, then the ministry had to examine the matter in detail and consider remedial measures before the quota could be replenished from budgetary sources.

Every enterprise, from 1951 on, was to pay its profits to and draw its subsidies from its central board, which in turn settled its net profits or losses with the state budget through the National Bank. At least 10 per cent of each enterprise's profits were to be paid to the central board's special account at the bank (after deducting certain sums for the Enterprise Fund and for sanctioned increases in working capital). This payment was to be made even when profits did not come up to plan. Thirty per cent of above-plan profits were to remain at the disposal of the enterprise. In practice, the account drew 90 to 95 per cent of all the profits of

33. The discussion of working capital, profits and losses which follows is based on the sources below: *MP*, no. A-17 (1951), *poz.* 225; *MP*, no. A-21 (1951), *poz.* 261; *Finanse*, no. 1 (1954), p. 13; Z. Piroźyński, "Budżet Państwa podstawowym planem finansowym Polskiej Rzeczypospolitej Ludowej" (The State Budget is the basic financial plan of the Polish Peoples' Republic), *Finanse*, no. 4 (1954), 9; E. Winter, "Niektóre zagadnienia systemu rozliczeń zysków i strat oraz środków obrotowych" (On the system for settling profits and losses and turnover funds), *Finanse*, no. 6 (1954), 36. See also *Prawo finansowe* (Financial law), 293.

enterprises in central boards showing a surplus in their settlements with the budget. The Minister of Finance was authorized
by a decree of February 1951 to raise budgetary expenditures for
financing increases in turnover funds and current subsidies to the
extent of any unforeseen surplus in positive price differences or
in profit payments from enterprises.

According to regulations issued in 1953, enterprises suffering
unplanned losses were to meet their obligations by drawing on
their working capital. It was only at the end of the year that the
excess of losses shown in the enterprise's financial statement over
subsidies received could be taken into account in determining the
correct level of working capital for the following year. By this
stringent monetary policy, the government hoped to force management to make up the above-plan losses of one quarter by earning
above-plan profits in the next. This pressure could be successful
only if enterprises knew in advance that no other source was available for replenishing their working capital until the end of the
year. Enterprises that had to pay more profits to the state than
they earned, or that suffered unexpected losses, would be pinched
by a shortage of capital. This would make it more difficult for
management to fulfill the output plan and to cash in on the bonus
for exceeding the plan target. This system, in practice, was vitiated
by the arbitrariness of the authorities in fixing the quotas and in
reshuffling profits and losses among enterprises and among central
boards. The size of the quotas hinged not only on the objective
factors listed above but also on the "actual financial capabilities"
of the Treasury and on the vagaries of the repartition of the quotas
at different administrative levels. As a result, in a significant number of cases the quotas were either too large or too small to suit
the economical operations of the firm.[34] Central boards of industry
sometimes requisitioned profits from their subordinate enterprises
to compensate unplanned losses in the board as a whole, or to meet
the demands of the ministry.

The fear of losing working capital did not always spur managers

34. M. Karczmar, "Problemy reformy systemu kredytowego" (Problems in the reform of the credit system), *Finanse*, no. 3 (1957), 14. One observer cites "the bank-
ruptcy of the quotas . . ." as a means of fulfilling the permanent needs of the firm
for working capital. See J. Dobrowolski, "O nowe zasady finansowania" (For new
principles of financing), *GM*, no. 5 (1957), 150.

to greater efforts, because they could usually obtain their regular allotments of materials from suppliers, who were not authorized to hold back deliveries to defaulting clients.[35] A state of near-bankruptcy did not necessarily disrupt the production activities of a firm or imperil bonuses to the managing staff.

Even though enterprises had to pay their suppliers 1.5 per cent per month on the value of overdue accounts, there was still a good deal of interfirm crediting going on, particularly in industries suffering from a chronic financial deficit (such as ferrous metallurgy). An extreme case in point was a steel mill investigated by H. Fiszel whose "working funds" on December 31, 1952 were made up as follows: [36]

1) Own funds	4.5 per cent	
2) Accounts payable	62.0 " "	
3) Bank credits	18.5 " "	
4) Overdue credits	15.0 " "	
	100.0 " "	

As we saw in Chapter Four, enterprises could also turn to the National Bank for short-term credits to supplement their working capital. The principal limitation on this source of funds was not the 4 per cent interest per annum charge levied on these loans—the impact of interest payments on an enterprise's total costs was usually negligible [37]—but the administrative criteria applied by the bank in dispensing the credits. As soon as an enterprise applied for credit, it was subjected to the careful scrutiny of officials whose functions in large measure duplicated the controls of the Ministry of Finance and of inspectors in the enterprise's own ministry. Whenever officials of the bank discovered "discrepancies," it was their duty to pass their reports along to the authorities supervising the enterprise or to the appropriate organs of state control.

One of the aims of the credit reform of July 1955 was to tie the

35. Karczmar, p. 13. In 1955, it was decreed that advances on the wage bill could be granted only to firms earning their planned profits. Furthermore, from 1956 on, suppliers might under certain conditions cut off deliveries to their consumers. But the limitations and exceptions written into these regulations were such that they were rendered largely ineffective.

36. Henryk Fiszel, "O oddziaływaniu prawa wartości na produkcję socjalistyczna" (On the influence of the law of value on socialist production), *Ekonomista*, no. 1–2 (1954), 170. The Poles include in "working funds" the sources of finance for a firm's inventories together with any short-term financial assets the firm may have on hand.

37. Ibid.

extension of credits more closely to the financial performance of socialized enterprises, and particularly to their profit record.

Henceforth, enterprises were to be appraised by the bank according to their fulfillment of the "accumulation plan" (i.e. the earning of profits including any sums earmarked for taxes). An auxiliary criterion was whether or not the firm was reducing its unit costs according to schedule. All industrial enterprises were to be divided into three groups for purposes of credit extension: (1) working well, (2) working poorly, (3) "others." The first group had no excess inventories or hoards, and no overdue payments. The "bad firms" were likely to be in debt both to their suppliers and to the bank and to be short of working funds. The rest were not good enough for the first group, but neither could they be placed in the second, a rather extreme measure that could not be taken without the special approval of the president of the National Bank. "Good firms" were to get credits for any worthwhile purpose with little paper work. "Bad firms" were to be controlled and hemmed in from all sides; in fact, their central board and their ministry would have to watch over them with special care, since they became in certain cases the coguarantors of credits extended to these firms by the bank to replenish their supply of working funds. If poor risks did not pay back the loans, the bank was authorized to debit the account of these superior authorities.[38]

To combat the extension of interfirm credits through unpaid accounts, the new regulations raised the priority of payments of debts to other socialized enterprises from last to third place, just behind payments of wages and of taxes and other obligations to the Treasury.

This last measure at least was effective in cutting down the defaults of clients toward their suppliers. The other measures, if we are to believe the criticism leveled at financial institutions after the events of October 1956, were not so successful. The carrying out of the reform "revealed in a most signal manner all the weaknesses of the credit system." [39] The principal obstacles to carrying out the reform were the bureaucratization of the banking apparatus, which caused delays in the making of crucial decisions, and the arbitrary exercise of the limited powers vested in the local ap-

38. *MP*, no. 65 (1955), *poz.* 853.
39. Karczmar, p. 25.

paratus of the bank. The unwillingness to implement the law with sufficient severity, if necessary by cutting back the output of "bad firms," emasculated the new regulations.[40]

5. *Conflicts of Incentives and Their Resolution*

Three principal forces contend for the attention and interest of the managers of Polish socialized enterprises: (1) directives from higher authorities, (2) bonuses, and (3) profits. These forces partly overlap; for example, the bonus for fulfilling the assortment plan rewards the staff for complying with the detailed directives of higher authorities. The bonuses on output and on cost reduction may or may not translate the will of the authorities: this depends on how the bonuses are fixed, whether managers can find an advantage in eschewing the production of onerous items, especially whether the prices used in computing the bonuses are such that it pays managers to break the assortment plan.[41] The profit motive may reinforce the bonuses but only if the bonus for cost reduction is fully as attractive as the bonus on output. This was generally not the case. For the most part, the net pull of the bonuses ran counter to the interest in profits.

To what extent do the various incentives help to carry out the planners' will and to what extent do they thwart it? The answer to these questions will be different for each industry, according to its financial position (whether generally deficit or profitable), to the bonus system in force, and to the personal relations between managers of enterprises and their superior authorities. In the metal-working industries, where each firm produces a large number of highly differentiated products requiring varying labor and material expenditures, the opportunities for manipulating the product-mix to boost bonuses are great;[42] in blast-furnace opera-

40. Ibid., pp. 13–14; and S. Ficowski, "Zmiana cen środków produkcji" (The reform of producer goods prices), *WNBP*, no. 6 (1956), 294.

41. The bureaucratic will of the central board or of the ministry may be expressed in the assortment plan, but deviations from this plan need not be inefficient from the vantage point of realizing "planners' preferences" at the least cost. This point was recognized by Glinski, Nowicki, and Marzantowicz (p. 35), who argued that the neglect of "unprofitable" (*niezyskowne*) items leads to the specialization of firms in products best adapted to their equipment, labor force, and facilities (i.e. in products which they can manufacture at the least cost).

42. In 1951 plan fulfillment for the output of four major groups of motors in one large factory varied between 51.6 per cent and 137.5; in the first half of 1954 between 86.8 and 120.9. See *ZG*, no. 21 (1954), 858.

tions and in the open-hearth shop of steel mills, products are standardized and there is little opportunity for great gains in output to be made by concentrating on low-cost, high-yield items. Even the slabbing, cogging, and rolling mills produce a relatively narrow range of products, no one being equipped to produce for example both light, labor-intensive products and heavy structural steels.[43]

All in all, the bonus for meeting and surpassing the output plan was the sharpest goad stimulating managers to greater exertion, swamping all other incentives. The stress on production performance was so ingrained in the administration of the economy that credit reforms were hamstrung for fear of the adverse effect they might have had on the volume of output of inefficient plants.

6. *Conclusions: Prices and Management Decisions*

During the Six-Year Plan, the chief task of the enterprise was to produce its quotas of output with the least possible waste of the materials and equipment placed at its disposal. If materials were in critical supply, they were sparingly rationed by the Planning Commission and by the ministries: the enterprise was not expected to alleviate the shortage to any significant extent by substituting more abundant for deficit materials. Since neither transfer prices nor plan (fixed) prices were faithful indicators of scarcity, plant managers, insofar as they were actuated by price incentives, were likely to make decisions out of tune with planners' preferences or with efficient allocation. Even the general price reforms had only a minimal effect on the demand of firms for materials and manpower, because substitution of the factors that had become relatively cheaper added very little to the bonus for reducing costs.

All these limitations notwithstanding, the demand of the firm for producer goods had some price elasticity. When substantial financial savings could be made by using one material rather than another, or from applying labor to cut material consumption, most

43. At a conference on price policy which took place in October 1955, Professor Ignacy Haendel, director of the Costs and Prices Division of the Ministry of Metallurgy, said that complaints about deviations from the plans due to the "riding" of prices had been exaggerated, at least as far as the steel industry was concerned; he supported this assertion by pointing out that in the first eight months of 1955 the assortment plan in the Central Board of the Steel Industry had been fulfilled by 95 per cent and in the Central Board of Quality Steels by 98.2 per cent. He suggested that these results must chiefly be credited to the incentive of the bonus for keeping production within the assortment plan.

firms responded to pressures from the central board and from the finance inspectors to do so, even if the savings added little to the bonuses or to other incentive payments accruing to the managerial staff. A number of cases were cited to the author where the price reform of 1956 had been fully effective in causing certain directives of the Planning Commission to be carried out which had hitherto been ignored. The price of cadmium having been raised twelvefold above its previous price, plants producing lead-cell batteries "found it possible" for the first time to eliminate cadmium as an auxiliary material. New price relations between amyl, butyl, and ethyl alcohols in the 1956 catalogues prompted consumers to shift their orders from amyl to butyl alcohol in some plants and from butyl to ethyl in others.[44]

In a soap plant visited in 1956, the author was told of many cost savings which would be effected during the forthcoming year by slight changes in the production process made profitable by the 1956 prices.[45]

The decline in the use of wall blocks made of light concretes by industrial construction enterprises from 19,000 cubic meters in 1953 to 16,500 in 1954 and 6,000 in 1955 is said to have been due to their high prices which discouraged consumption.[46] Though building firms were oppressed with more than one hundred regulations and circulars from the Planning Commission and from their ministry, these restrictions on the use of materials were infrequently applied. When it came to selecting materials, builders ignored regulations and ordered lumber because of its low price.[47]

Finally, the abundant literature on prices and the numerous

44. In the lacquer and paint industry, butyl acetate (made from butyl alcohol) was the chief solvent used in the production process. After the price change, consumers went over to ethyl acetate and cut out their purchases of butyl alcohol altogether (information from the Central Marketing Office of the Ministry of the Chemical Industry).

45. This factory was going to be placed on a new bonus system with emphasis on costs, so that the example is not typical. In general, by the end of 1956 the economic system had evolved a good deal and the situation was no longer representative of what it had been under the Six-Year Plan.

46. L. Kołudzki, "Jakość i cena materiałów a postęp techniczny" (The quality and price of materials versus technical progress), Budownictwo przemyslowe (Industrial construction), no. 1 (1956), 17.

47. M. Kaczorowski, "Główne problemy ekonomiczne produkcji i gospodarki materiałami budowlanymi" (The main economic problems in the production and economy of building materials), IB, no. 9 (1954), 9.

complaints on the waste of low-priced materials suggests that, at least in the long run, many managers did react to prices, within the narrow scope of decision-making left open to the enterprise under a basic materials-rationing system.

CHAPTER SEVEN

The Origins and Development
of the Price System

1. *Introduction*

In an economic system where all producer and consumer goods were strictly rationed, where long-range balances took the place of economic calculation, the functions of the price system would be confined to aggregation and control. Prices would help to summarize how well enterprises had put together the resources placed at their disposal but they would have no influence on the structure of a plant's inputs or on the composition of its output. Strictly speaking, once an assortment plan had been assigned to an enterprise, it would have to stick to the proportions stipulated in this plan, come what may. In assessing the performance of the enterprise, outputs in excess of the assigned proportions would have to be given a zero weight.

At one time, between 1949 and 1951, it looked as if the Communist authorities were seriously intent on eliminating the resource-allocating function of prices and on binding up the economy in a comprehensive system of administrative controls. But this policy, as we saw earlier, collapsed under the weight of the paper work necessary to carry it out. Whether the planners willed it or not, "the law of value" influenced input and output decisions; there was gradual recognition that prices should be set to reinforce physical plans rather than be allowed to induce managerial decisions at variance with the plans.[1] The crystallization of this view coincided with the trend toward administrative decentralization.

1. The theoretical limitations to such a policy were examined in Chap. 1, pp. 44–47.

The revival of the resource-allocating function of the price system would have been easier if the set of prices devised for this purpose could also have been used to perform routine aggregating and cost-accounting functions. This did not prove possible. For purposes of control and aggregation, prices must be simple to apply and constant for long periods of time; they should not correspond to the most detailed industrial nomenclature, or else accountants and supervisors at higher administrative levels will get lost in minutiae. As we shall see, the catalogue of "fixed 1937–38 prices" issued in 1949 and the cost-estimate prices used in construction satisfied this requirement. However, for the purpose of guiding enterprise managers to correct production decisions, prices must express current relative scarcities: at the very least they must not be so out of date as to lose their link with current costs. Prices of consumer goods must be close enough to market-clearing to avert queues and shortages on the one hand and stocks of unsold goods on the other. Finally, the prices used in investment decisions and long-range planning should reflect *future* scarcities, particularly for projects with a long gestation period. Even in recent years, requirements of price stability and bureaucratic convenience have tended to outweigh other considerations.

2. Current Prices: The Initial Period (1945–49)

The origins of the double price system (within the government sector and in the open market) can be traced to the controls imposed by the German occupants during World War II. In the western regions of prewar Poland which had been annexed outright by the Reich, a very systematic *Preisstop* was instituted—as in the rest of Germany—which embraced not only newly produced goods but even such items as secondhand clothing.[2] In the east, in the area known as the *General Gouvernement,* there developed alongside the controlled prices, which covered only the most important raw materials, industrial goods, and foodstuffs, a much higher level of semilegal prices for persons or institutions unauthorized to buy at the ceiling prices. Most Poles had to procure their principal needs in this gray market, while state-controlled enterprises and the German population bought in the privileged

2. E. Rose, "Problem dwoistych cen w Polsce" (The problem of two-level prices in Poland), ZG, no. 19 (1946), 725.

government market. Owing to the uneven pace of the country's liberation, the system in effect in the *General Gouvernement* was extended to all Poland, with this difference, that open-market prices were now sanctioned rather than informally tolerated as they had been in the past.[3]

By the middle of 1945, comprehensive regulations on a "provisional price system" had been issued. On April 14, the Economic Committee, attached to the Council of Ministers, and the Ministry of Procurement and Trade put out a joint circular on "stable prices" (*ceny stałe*). With the exception of coal, coke, steel products, cement, paper, petroleum products, lumber, tobacco, and alcohol, all wholesale stable prices were set equal to 1939 prices multiplied by a factor of six.[4]

These uniform "stable" prices were to be paid to domestic producers regardless of actual production costs. However, according to a regulation of March 1946, producers were to receive their "own prices" determined by the Ministry of Procurement and Trade to cover their factory production costs. Any excess of the "own" prices over the stable prices paid by consumers was to be financed on a monthly basis from an Equalizing Fund.[5] By the middle of 1946, the Commercial Centrals (the parent body of the marketing organizations whose functions were described in Chapter Three) were buying at the different accounting prices and reselling at uniform prices, settling positive and negative price differences through the Equalizing Fund.[6]

Many industrial products whose stable prices were not covered in the official lists had their prices set equal to their average costs of production calculated on the basis of stable input prices. These were the "controlled" or "calculated" prices.[7]

In June 1945 an important circular was issued by the Economic Committee of the Council of Ministers and of the Ministry of Industry on the operations of the price system in state-run indus-

3. Pomorski, "Problem cen," p. 1.

4. The appropriate 1939 prices were those listed in the *Rocznik statystyczny 1939*. In the case of items not listed in this source, other authentic prices of 1939 were to be applied.

5. *Dziennik urzędowy Ministerstwa Aprowizacji i Handlu* (Daily official gazette of the Ministry of Procurement and Trade), 1946, *ust.* 5, *poz.* 22.

6. "Ceny artykułów przemysłowych" (Prices of industrial articles), *ZG*, no. 16. (1946).

7. Ibid.

try. In addition to the stable prices already mentioned, the circular described and regulated the scope of "wholesale commercial prices," which were defined as free-market prices minus a 10 per cent trading margin.[8] Most basic industrial products (raw materials and semifabricates) were to be sold exclusively at stable prices, except for limited quotas fixed by ordinance of the Economic Committee, which could be marketed at commercial prices.[9] About half the current production of building materials was to go to industry and to the local population at the lower stable prices, while the rest might be sold at the higher prices. The city population could buy textile, pharmaceuticals, soap, and other *rationed* consumer goods at stable prices; farmers also enjoyed the privilege of buying at stable prices but only in exchange for deliveries of agricultural products. Additional quantities could be purchased at the higher price level. All other goods (including machinery and tools, leather goods and glassware, luxury articles, etc.) were to be sold mainly at commercial prices, a maximum of 25 per cent of production being subject to distribution within the Ministry of Industry at lower prices.

The gap between commercial and stable prices varied widely from commodity to commodity and from time to time. In May 1945, the ratio between the two was approximately three to one for coal and zinc, two to one for foundry coke and sulfuric acid, and 150 per cent for lead.[10] In practice, state enterprises receiving allotments of rationed materials directly from the Ministry of Industry and Trade and, after August 1945, from the Central Planning Office were authorized to buy all their requirements at official stable prices, but, for a few items, such as steel sheets and plates, they had to pay commercial prices for quantities above their allotted rations. Private firms, handicrafts, and cooperatives were charged commercial prices for all their purchases (whether rationed or free), except where they were fulfilling an order for

8. According to Pomorski, commercial prices might be either "fluctuating" (market-clearing) or "regulated," where the state had a monopoly position in the output of a given product (p. 3).

9. There were no commercial prices for most items in this category until August 1945.

10. For sources and details see Table 5 of my unpublished Ph.D. dissertation, "Producers' Prices in a Centralized Economy: The Polish Experience," referred to hereafter as "Producers' Prices . . . ."

large-scale state industry, when they were authorized to buy at official stable prices.[11] This was one of the many ways by which the
government sought to discriminate in favor of the nationalized
sector.

Once enterprises on cost-accounting had met their obligations
to the state arising from the price differences and from the turnover tax, which was set as a small percentage of total sales, they
were free to retain any remaining surpluses and to dispose of
them as they pleased.[12] Since at that time the capital and current
accounts of enterprises were not so carefully set apart as in later
years, profits could go to increases in turnover funds, to repayment
of investment loans from banks, or to the undertaking of small
capital projects, in addition to any funds distributed to the staff.

We have seen that stable prices were initially derived from 1939
prices multiplied by a factor of six; it soon became evident that
the price structure would have to diverge more radically from
that of 1939 if enormous differences in the profitability of different items were to be avoided. Starting with September 1945, the
multipliers were set with some consideration for the current level
of average costs in each industry, although the policy was still to
peg prices of investment goods as low as possible in order not to
increase the financial burden of investments.[13] An exception was
made for raw materials such as lumber "whose consumption must
be limited [through higher prices] for economic reasons." [14] By
October 1946, the multipliers varied from 35 for agricultural machinery to 18 for pig iron.[15]

Until at least the end of 1947 all the evidence points to the
chaotic nature of prices and costs. For one thing, a large percentage of wages was paid in kind, in the form of food rations, textile
coupons, and other articles of consumption (Table 7:1 below), so
that wages made up only a fraction of total labor costs.

Many of the industries suffered financial deficits in 1946 and

11. *Dziennik urzędowy Ministerstwa Przemysłu* (Daily official gazette of the Ministry of Industry), no. 12 (1946), *poz.* 102.
12. Leon Kurowski, ed., *Prawo finansowe* (Financial law), p. 47.
13. An unequivocal statement of the policy of setting low prices for producer
goods "which would favor rapid reconstruction" is to be found in the Chief Statistical Office's *National Income of Poland 1947* (English edition), p. 2.
14. Pomorski, p. 3.
15. "Producers' Prices . . . ," Table 6.

1947, not because of any outright refusal on the part of the Ministry of Industry and Trade or of the Central Planning Office to raise prices to cover costs but because the inflation was so rapid that if output prices were not raised for a month or two after input prices had gone up, producers were caught in a cost-price squeeze. The metallurgical industry could not cover even its out-of-pocket costs in 1945, in 1946, or in early 1948. Counting nominal amortization—which was derived from estimates of capital property well below replacement value—the mills also suffered losses in 1947. Significantly, the official report of the industry stressed that unit costs for individual products or groups of items could not be worked out during these years because of excessive fluctuations in the prices of its inputs and in wages and fringe benefits and be-

TABLE 7:1. *Percentage of Payments in Kind in the Total Wage Bill*

	Per Cent
July 1946	57.8
July 1947	42.4
July 1948	28.1
December 1948	24.0

Note. Wages include all supplementary allowances.

Source. E. Krzeczkowska, "Walka o regulującą rolę Państwa na rynku w latach 1947–1949" (The struggle for the regulative role of the state on the market in the years 1947–1949), *Materiały i Studia Wyższej Szkoły Nauk Społecznych przy K.C. P.Z.P.R.* (Materials and Studies of the High School for Social Sciences of the Central Committee of the United Polish Workers' Party), *2, 153.*

cause of the artificial exchange rates set for the purchase of imported materials. Furthermore, the profit-and-loss position of the industry was complicated by changes in commercial prices, surpluses from which were in part allowed to remain at the disposal of enterprises.

Until June 1946, there was no differentiation of the multipliers of prewar prices *within* an industry. In metallurgy, this caused wide disparities between the relative profitability of basic items, such as coke, pig iron, crude steel, and heavy rolled products and of finished manufactures such as steel constructions, castings, agricultural machinery, wire products, and hollowware produced by mills with finishing capacity. In general, the former were produced at a loss and the latter at a profit or at a smaller deficit.[16]

16. S. Stasikowski, "Podstawy urzeczywistnienia rentowności hut polskich" (Prin-

We shall see in the following chapter that this tendency for losses on heavy, basic items to be balanced against profits on finished goods has persisted up to recent years.

The basic financial reforms of August 2, 1947, were designed to replace the early postwar patchwork of economic legislation with a systematic and comprehensive code. It was intended first of all to draw a more distinct line between budget enterprises (those settling their accounts directly with the state budget) and enterprises on cost-accounting which were set up as financially independent units settling with the budget through specialized "economic accounts," to be described below. These enterprises, organized mainly under what was then the Ministry of Industry and Trade, were to have their own bank accounts, quotas of working and fixed capital, and amortization funds. The price system was rigged so as to guarantee them sufficient profits to operate without losses of working capital and without the necessity of borrowing from other firms. Such interfirm transactions were henceforth prohibited. Also, by appointing for each enterprise a normative level of working capital as well as quotas of inventories and fixed capital, the legislation aimed at bringing all the enterprise's financial operations under control: in theory, it would no longer be possible to make up capital losses by selling surplus machines or stocks left over from the German occupation ("post-German remnants"). Any sums held above the sanctioned normative were to be paid to a "working-capital account" at the National Bank of Poland from which other firms could finance their authorized requirements.

All customers were to pay the commercial centrals uniform prices for identical goods, although each producer was guaranteed an "accounting price" for his goods equal to his planned costs. Thus, "sales prices were to be stable and would remain unaffected by any rise in the accounting prices of plants, and all plants—independently of their costs—would be able to produce goods which were in demand." [17]

The "factory accounting price" received by producers from

---

ciples for putting the profitability of Polish steel mills on a realistic basis), ZG, no. 5 (1946), 136.

17. T. Chęcinski, "Rynek chemiczny w 1948 roku" (The chemical market in the year 1948), Przemysł chemiczny (Chemical industry), no. 1 (1949), 70.

their commercial central was set equal to the sum of planned variable costs, depreciation, and a profit margin usually amounting to 10 per cent of costs. Since profits were tied to the level of costs, managers were encouraged to "plan costs upward"; but this incentive was weakened by the fact that only a small share (10 per cent) of profits were given out to the staff. Profits were retained by enterprises primarily to finance their requirements for working capital. In 1947 and 1948, 80 per cent of planned profits were to be allocated to this end, together with 70 per cent of above-plan profits. The Treasury levied 10 per cent of profits in the form of an "income tax." [18]

Where several plants were organized under a trust or an enterprise, a group accounting price could be fixed for all plants "working under similar conditions." [19] The "factory accounting price" was set for one year with the approval of the central board; on the suggestion of the enterprise or trust, the board, with the agreement of the National Bank, could adjust prices during the course of the year to allow for "changes in economic or technical conditions." [20] This was rarely done.

The commercial centrals purchased goods from trusts and enterprises, which usually centralized the cost-accounting, financial, and sales functions of their subordinate plants. They paid for these goods at the differentiated "factory-accounting prices." They added to this price a small turnover tax, a provision for their administrative expenses and for those of the central board, and various small margins to finance special funds. The resulting sum made up the "accounting sales price." The uniform price paid by consumers, called the "effective price," was supposed to cover the average production costs of producers in the industry plus all the markups and taxes already mentioned. At the end of each month the sales offices of every commercial central compared the total value of their purchases and markups at "accounting sales prices" with the value of their sales at "effective prices," and settled their

18. *MP*, no. 120 (1947), *poz.* 762.

19. Circular letter FN-IV/4/17 of the Financial Department of the Ministry of Industry and Trade (October 14, 1947).

20. The source is the "Provisional instructions of the Central Board of the Metalworking Industry." In practice, "group prices" uniform for a number of plants were almost never applied. See Z. Fedak, "Cena grupowa" (The group price), *ZG*, no. 5 (1949), 204.

surplus or deficits with special "accounts of price differences" at the National Bank. The commercial central compensated the surpluses and deficits of all its sales offices, then paid over any difference into *its* account of price differences (from which it could also draw subsidies if it operated at a loss). Finally, the Ministry of Industry and Trade settled with the Treasury on the basis of the consolidated profits or losses of all the commercial centrals under its supervision.[21]

The new financial system relieved the managers of enterprises from the responsibility for earning profits. As long as costs were planned "realistically" (i.e. with a large margin of tolerance), profits were guaranteed.[22] In addition to the profits earned on standard items, for which accounting prices were fixed by higher authorities, enterprises could make money by padding their expenses on "cost-plus" contracts for special orders ("nontypical products").[23]

Until the reform of 1949 and 1950, the commercial centrals functioned as neutral buffers between producers and consumers. They registered and processed invoices, settled accounts of price differences, and organized the transfer of goods from producing plants to customers; but they had no influence whatever in inducing producers to adapt the structure of their output to the demands of the market. They were "large caldrons where the results of well-managed firms were thrown together with the adverse results of poorly-managed firms . . . They were not interested in doing away with inefficiency, nor were they competent to do so." [24] However, the centralizing of thousands of accounts and the automatic compensation of profits and losses facilitated the work of the Ministry of Finance in its task of planning the profits and losses of individual central boards and of large-scale industry as a whole. From a financial and administrative viewpoint, the system of accounting prices succeeded—but at the cost of a fundamental weakening in the traditional resource-allocating function of the price mechanism.

21. B. Blass, "Nowy system finansowy," *GP*, no. 21 (1947), 834.
22. B. Minc, "Planowanie kosztów własnych i cen" (The planning of costs and prices), *GP*, no. 6 (1952), 35.
23. Fedak, p. 204.
24. K. Szonert, "System cen fabrycznych a obowiązki aparatu zbytu" (The system of factory prices and the obligations of the marketing network), *GP*, no. 5 (1954), 34.

3. Fixed Prices

Before going on to a discussion of the present system of current prices, we shall consider the formation and the uses of "fixed prices," whose importance in planning practice, from 1949 to 1952, outweighed that of current prices.

Prewar prices began to be used for planning purposes, and particularly for computing increases in gross output, almost as soon as the war ended. Estimates of national income and investment expenditures for the years 1946 to 1949, as well as the value of production, were calculated in prewar prices.

Before fixed prices were standardized in 1949, they were either set by a central board for all its subordinate plants (usually on the basis of prewar cartel prices of 1938) or, in the case of non-cartelized goods, they were selected individually by each plant from the actual prices which it had charged in 1937 or 1938. As early as 1946, there were unified prices for coal, chemicals, and steel products. It is noteworthy that these prices did not make allowance for the legal and illegal rebates normally accorded to private customers before the war.[25]

The catalogues of fixed prices of cartelized industries were less detailed than those put out by the central boards of the textile industry and of the electro-technical industry, their group prices corresponding broadly to the industrial classification of the Chief Statistical Office. Many articles manufactured under more than one central board had different fixed prices; this made it difficult to compare the output of various branches of production.[26] These "fixed prices" were often adjusted, sometimes more than once during the course of a year, in contradiction with their established purpose.[27]

The decree of the Council of Ministers of 15 March 1949 established the legal basis for the reform and codification of the fixed prices of 1937–38. A catalogue of unified fixed prices prepared on the basis of the decree was published a few months later. It cov-

25. B. Minc, "Ceny niezmienne" (Fixed prices), *GP*, nos. 6–7 (1949), 348; W. Welfe, "Obliczanie indeksu fizycznych rozmiarów produktu globalnego" (The calculation of the physical index of gross output), *Przegląd statystyczny* (Statistical survey), no. 1–2 (1955), 102.

26. S. Róg, "Ceny niezmienne" (Fixed prices), *ZG*, no. 5, 13–14 (1949), 565.

27. Ibid.

ered 18,000 commodities, as well as railroad, train, and bus transportation (per passenger-kilometer or ton-kilometer), industrial
and administrative building (per cubic meter), and a number of
services.[28] Some branches of industry had very detailed prices
(textile machinery, lumber, and coal derivatives), while entire
groups of important products were represented by one or two
prices. All unprocessed bituminous coals, which range from nearly
worthless slurry to high-quality coking coals, had only one price
(14 zlotys per ton), as did the various grades of coke, cement, gasoline, and crude oil.

The catalogue of fixed prices was intended to correct basic shortcomings in the prewar price structure which have already been
noted. According to the law, the new prices were to correspond
not to the nominal cartelized prices of 1937–38 but to the actual
prices received by plants in those years (net of all discounts and
rebates ex-pit or ex-mill).[29] Prewar prices of cartelized steel products were reduced by an average of 15 per cent. With the exception of coal and steel, however, no significant departures from
prewar prices seem to have been introduced.[30]

It is interesting that only nonferrous metals produced in Poland
(zinc, lead, cadmium, copper, and silver) or fabricated locally from
imported materials (alloys, wire, sheets, etc.) were listed in the
catalogue. The compilers apparently intended to apply these
prices only to the measurement and planning of domestic output,
not to calculations of investment efficiency or of foreign trade
profitability, for which the prices of imported commodities would
have been necessary.

A comparison of current prices in effect in 1949 and 1950 with
the fixed prices of the catalogue shows a wide range of disparities.
By and large the fixed prices used as weights in measuring output
were completely out of line with current prices and costs.[31] This
of course set up incentives for managers to earn bonuses by breaking the stipulated assortment of output and producing items
whose ratios of current costs to fixed prewar prices were the most
favorable. The lack of differentiation of the fixed prices, grouping

28. *P.K.P.G., Katalog cen niezmiennych* (Catalogue of fixed prices), parts I and
II (Warsaw, 1949).
29. Welfe, p. 98.
30. "Producers' Prices . . . ," Table 13.
31. Ibid., Table 14.

together items with widely diverging costs, further encouraged these deviations.

New products, which were not listed in the basic catalogue of 1949, also had to have their fixed prices. This created another source of confusion. The idea was to find a product in the catalogue with a similar technological process and to set a fixed price for the new product in the same proportion as the ratio of their current costs.[32] But in practice current prices for new goods—or goods which had been reclassified as new by virtue of small changes in their specifications—were often set on the basis of their initial costs of production, without discounting the drop in costs that could be expected from the application of production methods. The fixed prices then tended to reflect these high current costs. Enterprises sought to find the most expensive "similar items" in the catalogue as a basis for calculating their fixed prices, so as to increase the value of their gross output; [33] they frequently applied for revisions in the fixed prices of their products, which revisions were "always in the interest of upward adjustments, and never the other way around." [34]

The fixed prices for quality steels recorded in one steel mill during the course of a study of the steel industry made in 1953 were found to differ markedly from those listed in the standard catalogue of 1949. These striking differences are shown in Table 7:2 below. The mill was evidently able to secure plan prices for weighting its output which made the production of the high-grade steels in which it specialized far more profitable than if it had been forced to apply the unified prices of the standard catalogue.

In 1953 when this study of prices in the steel industry was made, fixed prewar prices still served as the exclusive weighting system for aggregating the output of multiproduct enterprises (and for measuring the increases in their gross output, on which management bonuses depended). Nevertheless, their importance in the planning system had already declined, compared to what it had been at the beginning of the Six-Year Plan. By 1952 the value of marketed output was already worked out in current prices in the

32. A. Karpinski, *Plan techniczno-przemysłowo-finansowy*, part II, p. 36.
33. Welfe, pp. 100–01.
34. F. Kowalski, "System cen fabrycznych w przemyśle środków spożycia" (The system of factory prices in the consumer-goods industry), *GP*, no. 6 (1954), 37.

National Economic Plan. Prior to this time, total output had been measured only in fixed prices, so that there had been no link between the cost-reduction plan—which obviously had to be calculated in current prices—and the value of output.[35]

TABLE 7:2. *Catalogue and Actual Fixed Prices of 1937–38 for Steel Ingots and the Fulfillment of Production Plans*

Type of steel ingot	Unified catalogue prices of 1937–1938 (zlotys per ton)	Actual fixed prices of a steel mill in the Central Board for quality steels (July 1953) (zlotys per ton)	Percentage fulfillment of production plans
Ordinary open-hearth steel	179	180	n.a.
Carbon constructional steel	272	320	31
Carbon tool steel	323	551	70
Tool steel { low alloy	697	1,058	94
{ high alloy	697	2,365	95
Fast cutting steel	3,698	6,480	133
Stainless, heat-resistant steel	1,224	2,520	307

Sources. Fiszel, *Czynniki i rezerwy* . . . , pp. 161–62. Państwowa Komisja Planowania Gospodarczego, *Katalog cen niezmiennych* (Catalogue of fixed prices), Part I (1949), p. 44.

Fixed prewar prices were finally abolished in 1956, when they were superseded by a system of "comparable prices" (transfer prices of 1956, net of turnover taxes in consumer-goods industries), which eliminated the most obvious defects of the old scheme.

4. Current Prices: The Six-Year Plan

In 1949 and 1950, the Polish government put into effect a number of financial reforms, patterned after Soviet models, for the purpose of regulating the economic activity of socialized enterprises in the forthcoming Six-Year Plan. These reforms implicitly recognized that producing enterprises did not operate as technological units in an economic vacuum and that their operations were influenced to some degree by financial motives—whether for the benefit of the staff or for the general welfare of the enterprise

35. B. Minc, "Zmiany w metodologii planowania na rok 1952," (Changes in the methodology of planning for the year 1952), *GP*, no. 7 (1951), 11–15.

as an entity. Since total planning of the most minute operations was impossible, it was necessary to control these decentralized pressures and to guide them into proper channels.

For "control by the zloty" to be at all effective, it was imperative to mend the system of accounting prices, which had failed to provide enterprise managers with incentives to work economically. But before producers could be granted any reasonable measure of economic independence, a number of controls on their activities had to be perfected. In 1950 a unified plan of accounts was imposed on all enterprises on independent cost-accounting, so that planners and controllers might make comparisons of the economic results of different enterprises and branches of industry. The banking system became one of the main instruments of financial control. In 1948 exclusive responsibility for granting short-term credits had been vested in the National Bank of Poland, while investment business was concentrated in specialized banks. Henceforth, all payments within the socialized sector were to be effected by bookkeeping transfers in the National Bank. The bank was to supervise the costs and sales of enterprises, attend to their minimum needs for working capital and generally assist in carrying out the financial tasks set by the Planning Commission and by the ministries.

The legislation of April 17, 1950, which consolidated and expanded many previously issued decrees, circulars, and regulations, is fundamental to an understanding of the mechanics of the price system during the Six-Year Plan.[36] Many more enterprises were placed on full cost-accounting as a result of the reform. Most trusts were broken down into enterprises, which acquired bank accounts and were from now on responsible for filing profit-and-loss statements. In many cases, the individual plants of large enterprises were also set up on cost-accounting when they became enterprises in their own right.

Commercial enterprises, such as the sales or commercial centrals, were split into two parts: their warehouses, stores, and sales points were placed under the administration of branch or local offices, which were set up on cost-accounting, while their sales and

36. Decree of the Council of Ministers of April 17, 1950, *MP*, no. A-55 (1950), *poz*. 630, reprinted in Z. Karpiński's *Obieg pieniężny w gospodarce socjalistycznej* (Monetary circulation in the socialist economy), pp. 25–34.

procurement sections became budgetary units of the central boards of industry under which they operated. The old centrals had functioned as financial intermediaries between buyers and sellers. From this time on, suppliers were to obtain payment for goods delivered directly from purchasers by way of a bank transfer to the supplier's account.

Producers were to charge uniform transfer prices (*ceny zbytu*) to all clients including wholesalers. It was stipulated that these prices would "basically" cover unit costs of production and of distribution (including railroad delivery) together with the turnover tax (in the case of consumer goods) and planned profits.

Prices of producer goods were set free of turnover taxes, with the exception of petroleum products and natural gas. In certain industries characterized by a large spread in the costs of individual plants, producers might still receive planned-accounting prices (equal to planned costs plus profits). In that case an account of price differences would be created at the National Bank either in the name of the central board or of the sales central of the industry. This account would redistribute differences arising between the planned-accounting prices and the uniform transfer prices. Any net surplus or deficit in the account was to be settled with the central budget.

The new law was to go into effect on January 1, 1951. Its provisions on the uniformity of factory prices and on the transfer of sales functions from the sales central to the enterprise were long in taking effect. In March 1951, a regulation of the Ministry of Finance stipulated that, in case producers were not able to invoice purchasers directly for consignments delivered, this function could be taken over temporarily by a sales central in the name and account of the producing firm.[37] In early 1953 in the course of a debate on the law of value under socialism occasioned by Stalin's recent pronouncements on the subject, a critic complained that the system of factory-accounting prices had been liquidated "in name only." A mechanism of internal compensation resembling the old system had been created to protect deficit enterprises from excessive losses of working capital.[38]

37. Szonert, "System cen . . . ," p. 34.
38. Report on the "Sesja naukowa instytutu kształcenia kadr naukowych" (Scientific session of the institute for the formation of scientific cadres), *Ekonomista* (II

The cornerstone of both the old and the new system was the cost plan of the enterprise, which formerly had served to fix the level of factory-accounting prices and was now to provide the basis for drawing up the plan of profits and losses for the enterprise. Under the system of accounting prices, planned profits and losses had been proportioned to output. The new regulations specified that a fixed amount of profit or subsidy should be planned independently of the volume of output. The overfulfillment of output plans for items that did not cover costs would no longer automatically call for higher subsidies. The financing of losses in industry was made contingent on the financial performance of all the enterprises organized under the same central board. Similarly ministries were made responsible for the results of all their central boards.

The main emphasis of the financial legislation of the 1950s was to control the over-all volume of subsidies to the national economy. Most of the responsibility for offsetting surpluses and deficits within individual branches of industry came to rest on the ministries and central boards. By the end of the Six-Year Plan, as we saw in Chapter Six, the procedure for financing losses had become so loose that even above-plan losses gave the enterprise little trouble. This greatly relieved the pressure on managers to economize the resources placed at their disposal and weakened the impact of the price system on management decisions.

5. *Prices of Consumer Goods*

Before the reform of 1950, the state had collected the margin between prices charged to socialized enterprises and prices paid by the population, partly in the form of a small turnover tax, equal to a percentage of the "effective price" or of the sales volume of distributing agencies, but mainly in the form of "positive price differences." From 1951 on, the two levies were merged. At first, the turnover tax for each consumer good was set equal to the spread between a uniform transfer price and the planned cost of the good in each individual enterprise. This "sliding tax" was clearly a survival of the system of accounting prices: enterprises had little or no incentive to reduce the level of their planned costs, since the state would be the sole beneficiary of these improve-

quarter 1953), p. 236. Note that in the coal-mining industry, accounting prices were never abolished; see *MP*, no. A-38 (1951), *poz.* 459.

ments.[39] Industry-wide, uniform prices of consumer goods net of turnover taxes—the so-called "factory prices" (ceny fabryczne)—did not gain wide currency until at least the middle of 1954.

After 1950 "positive price differences" were also collected in the foreign trade centrals and in certain producer-goods industries selling a part of their output to the population. In foreign trade, the variability of purchase prices in foreign currency, which were translated into local currency at an arbitrary exchange rate, made it convenient to retain the old system and to tax import products sold to the public through the elastic instrument of price differences.[40]

The shift from price differences to turnover taxes in the revenue of the state budget can be traced in Table 7:3 below.

TABLE 7:3. *Turnover Tax Receipts and Positive Price Differences in Relation to Budget Revenue (1947 to 1951 and 1954)*

	Percentages of Total Budget Revenues					
	1947 Actual	1948 Actual	1949 Actual	1950 Budget	1951 Budget	1954 Actual
Turnover taxes from socialized enterprises	9.8	19.5 [a]	35.3	35.4	55.8	49.0
Positive price differences and profits of enterprises	19.7	30.4	19.8 [b]	35.8 [b]	23.7 [c]	19.1
TOTAL	29.5	49.9	55.1	71.2	79.5	68.1

[a] Turnover taxes from all sources.
[b] Includes amortization payments.
[c] All nontax revenues from socialized enterprises.

Sources. *RS 1949*, pp. 150, 152, 157; *WS*, nos. 7–8, pp. 28–29 (English edition); Z. Pirozynski, *System budżetowy Polski Ludowej* (The budgetary system of Peoples' Poland), p. 86; *Sprawozdanie Komisji Planu Gospodarczego i Budżetu 1950* (Report of the Commission on the Economic Plan and on the 1950 budget); Ibid., *1951*; *RS 1956*, p. 296.

Since the proportion of budgetary revenue to national income was increasing during the period, the figures in Table 7:3 give

39. F. Kowalski, p. 36.
40. The foreign trade centrals paid producers for the domestic goods they exported at uniform transfer prices—including turnover taxes until August 1953 and net of taxes after that date. See W. Metrycka, "Głos w dyskusji o cenach" (An opinion in the discussion about prices), *GP*, no. 6 (1954), 40–41.

only an imperfect idea of the growing importance of turnover taxes. Expressed as a percentage of national income in current prices, turnover taxes came to about 10 per cent in 1950; they rose to nearly 30 per cent of national income in 1954.[41] The abolition of consumer-goods rationing in January 1953 was accompanied by an increase in retail prices officially estimated at 47 per cent; [42] wages and other costs also went up but by a smaller extent; [43] the increased margins between the costs and retail prices of consumer goods account for an important part of the larger revenue collected from turnover taxes from 1953 on.

With the abolition of formal rationing in 1953 and with the price and wage increases that accompanied this measure, the government made an effort to establish a market-clearing level of retail prices. However, the failure to introduce a flexible price policy caused frequent shortages and gluts for individual commodities in subsequent years.

The Planning Commission, which had been responsible for setting retail prices during the period of rationing, could not cope with the new problem of maintaining equlibrium in thousands of separate markets. In the course of 1953, this duty devolved on a new institution, the State Price Commission.[44]

The ways of this Commission have remained mysterious to the present day. Almost nothing is known about the techniques that it uses in fixing the prices of individual commodities. One Polish specialist in internal trade recently commented that the setting of prices involves a "trial and error process, which is practical but of doubtful quality." [45] Up to 1957, in any event, the State Price Commission was hemmed in by various limitations on its activities. It was obliged, for instance, to honor an engagement taken by the government after the great rise in the level of retail prices of January 3, 1953, to bar any further price increases for any commodity whatsoever.[46] This complicated matters for the trading

41. The sources for budgetary revenue are the same as those noted for Table 7:3. For national income, they are from *Dochód narodowy Polski 1954 i 1955*, pp. 3, 47.
42. *RS 1956*, p. 245.
43. See below, Chap. 8, pp. 226–27.
44. *GP*, no. 6 (1956), 41.
45. A. Hodoły, "Analiza podaży" (The analysis of supply), *HW*, no. 6 (1956), 82.
46. W. Jampel, "Kierunki zmian w handlu polskim na tle oceny jego działalności" (Trends in Polish trade and the appraisal of its operation), *HW*, no. 3 (1957), 18.

network, since many items were perennially in short supply and
had to be rationed informally. There was no automatic reaction
on the part of producers to meet the demand for deficit commodities. Producers tended to eschew the production of staple items
whose prices had remained stable and concentrate on "new" products—old lines with a new twist, but technically unavailable at the
beginning of 1953—which they could sell at a more advantageous
price.[47]

What producers of consumer goods could get away with—despite penalties on nonfulfillment of the assortment plan—may be
illustrated in Table 7:4 based on the records of a bicycle factory,
producing five items with widely diverging cost-price relations.

TABLE 7:4. *Plan Fulfillment and Profitability*

Type of bicycle	Percentage fulfillment of the 1953 plan	Profitability (including turnover tax) as percentage of production costs
Racing	32 per cent	9 per cent
Ladies'	83 " "	39 " "
Child's	107 " "	58 " "
Sport "Torpedo"	103 " "	71 " "
Free wheeling	117 " "	98 " "

Source. H. Fiszel, "W sprawie systemu cen zbytu w gospodarce Polski Ludowej"
(On the system of transfer prices in the economy of Peoples' Poland), *Ekonomista*,
no. 4 (1954), 87.

Where enterprises sold some products at transfer prices and
others at retail prices with a substantial margin of profits and
taxes, they tended to favor the latter. In the central board of the
petroleum industry, the output plans for motor gasoline (sold far
above cost) was usually overfulfilled at the expense of typical intermediate products such as benzene whose prices were close to
production costs.[48]

The diverging rates of turnover taxes were the effect not only
of the Commission's price policy but also of the government's discrimination in favor of certain consumer goods at the expense of
others. Without prior knowledge of the market situation, one can
never be sure whether a low price and a small tax-and-profit mar-

47. Ibid., p. 19.
48. Fiszel, "W sprawie systemu cen zbytu . . . ," *Ekonomista*, no. 4 (1954), 88.

gin were justified by high output at low cost (and hence the price was just market clearing) or whether the price had been set low for reasons of social policy and the demand for the item exceeded the supply. Typical low-tax items in the clothing industry, for instance, were poor quality suits of low wool content and children's wear; on the other hand, pure wool men's suits were taxed extremely high (see Table 7:5).

TABLE 7:5. *Gross Profitability (Including Taxes) of Clothing Made in the Warsaw Garment Industry September 1953*

	Profitability (including turnover tax) as percentage of production costs
Man's suit, 100 per cent wool	31.5
Man's suit, 60 per cent wool	2.7
Man's coat, 70 per cent wool	2.0
Child's coat, 60 per cent wool	— 3.8
Child's coat, cotton	—10.2

Note. The turnover taxes levied on the garment industry represent only a part of the taxes paid by consumers: in 1956 the taxes and profits on woolen fabrics came to 70–80 per cent of the sales price or 300 to 500 per cent of costs; see *WS*, no. 1 (1957), 12. The garment industry bought these fabrics at prices including turnover taxes.

Source. Gliński, Nowicki, and Marzantowicz, p. 44.

In 1956, it was observed that children's wear was harder to find than adult clothing, but no general rule will fit all cases: many sought-after, high-priced, luxury items were bought up as soon as they hit the market and were always "out of stock" thereafter. In many instances there was no apparent reason at all for wide differences in profitability: Was it for reasons of state that large powder compacts were priced at 184 per cent of production costs while small compacts were priced at only 107 per cent of costs? [49]

The "abracadabra" of the price system, as one journalist called it, was not confined to trivial errors.[50] For years, the rents on apartments have been nominal and the allocation of space has been strictly rationed. Gas and electricity prices were so low in 1956

49. Gliński, Nowicki, and Marzantowicz, "W sprawie bodźców zainteresowania materiałowego," *GP*, no. 4 (1956), 44.
50. Cf. "Abrakadabra cen" (The abracadabra of prices), *ZG*, no. 19 (1956), 12.

that the most intensive campaigns to economize on these services met with failure. (Power cuts at peak-load and low gas pressure during meal hours were the unpleasant remedy to this anomalous situation.) Trains and tramways were so underpriced during the 1950s that only the discomfort of riding in unbelievably crowded conditions put a check on the demand for these services. The low prices on international telephone calls, stamps, and airplane tickets invited the squandering of critically scarce foreign currencies: While there was a limit on foreign travel—the issuance of passports—there was none on transatlantic calls, which cost less per minute in 1956 than a medium-price meal in a restaurant (in a country where food is relatively cheap).

The reticence of the authorities to set equilibrium prices in housing, utilities, and transportation services—traditional sectors of government interference in the West—is not surprising. The Polish authorities reasoned correctly that the population would hold the government more directly responsible for raising these prices than the prices of vegetables or furniture which had always been subject to variations under the pressure of the forces of supply and demand.

6. *Who Pays Which Prices?*

All prices free of the turnover tax are called procurement prices (*ceny zaopatrzeniowe*). There are two levels of these prices: the transfer prices already described and wholesale prices (*ceny hurtowe*) at which authorized consumers may buy from warehouses and other wholesale outlets. The wholesale markup ranged from 5 to 8 per cent of the transfer price prior to 1953; it fell to 3 per cent for steel products in 1956.[51] In the case of "drop shipments," organized by wholesale outlets but going straight from the producing mill to the consumer, a small charge of about 0.5 to 1 per cent was levied on the transaction by the wholesaler.

Market prices (*rynkowe ceny*), equivalent to the old "commercial prices," are charged in sales of producer goods to all consumers not entitled to buy at procurement prices. This category includes mainly solid fuels and building materials, which are sold in appreciable quantities to both the urban and the rural population.

51. Ministerstwo Hutnictwa, *Cennik Nr. 21/53*, (Price catalogue no. 21/53), Katowice, 1953, and *Cennik Nr. 13/Z*, 1955.

Prior to September 1952, all private individuals bought build-ing materials at retail prices, while all public bodies ("moral per-sons") were authorized to buy at procurement prices.[52] This was a simple distinction, which created few administrative problems. After this date, new regulations were applied to a number of basic materials including cement, lime, bricks, tiles, tar paper, and cer-tain types of glass. From then on, only persons or organizations specifically exempted from paying retail market prices would be authorized to purchase these materials at the lower procurement prices.[53] So exempted were budgetary organizations of the state, nationalized enterprises, all distributors of building materials ex-cept retail outlets, political organizations, trade unions, producers' cooperatives purchasing the materials for further processing or for their own investments or repairs, retail firms for their investment needs, and private industry within the allotments it received from the Ministry of Small-Scale Industry and Handicrafts.[54] This ex-tensive list ruled out cooperatives performing services, auxiliary cooperatives, and purchases made above official allotments by co-operatives and private industry.[55] This was an important restriction at a time when only state firms received quotas of materials at all commensurate with their needs. In addition to the organizations listed, certain individuals might be empowered to buy at procure-ment prices by the Planning Commission on the suggestion of the interested ministry. All such persons were charged a special markup of 10 per cent of the procurement price, "reflecting the principle of discrimination in favor of socialized entities." [56]

The regulations were so complex that there was often con-siderable doubt as to which prices ought to be paid. In 1955, for

---

52. K. Szonert, "System cen w materiałach budowlanych" (The price system for building materials), *Materiały i budownictwo* (Materials and construction), no. 4 (1954), 103.

53. Note that the divergence between the two levels was extremely high from 1953 on, and the buyers allowed to shop at lower prices were highly privileged. The transfer price of Portland cement, to cite a typical example, was 111 zlotys and its retail price was 576 zlotys per ton from 1953 to 1955.

54. *MP*, no. A-91 (1953). The "progressive" Catholic organization "Pax," which was supported by the regime, carried on certain industrial and commercial activi-ties. It is said to have received a special dispensation from the Council of Ministers to buy materials at procurement prices.

55. Cooperatives received no allotments of the following materials in 1955 and had to purchase them at retail prices: lacquers, enamels, springs, chains, furniture nails, machine-screws, drills, files, steel bars etc. (*ZG*, no. 15 (1955), 632.)

56. Szonert, 103.

example, the cost of building individual houses for Silesian miners was estimated at 45,000 zlotys (on the basis of procurement prices), and the houses were promoted at this price. But they eventually cost over 80,000 zlotys and they were sold to miners at this higher price—because retail prices had to be paid for materials.[57]

7. Calculated Prices and Prices of Small-Scale Industry

Beside the uniform procurement and market prices already described, which form the core of the Polish price system, there are special prices for investment goods produced in small quantities on clients' specifications and for the products of small-scale nationalized firms and cooperatives.

Regulations were issued in 1953 and 1954 which permitted producers to settle the prices of inexpensive made-to-order items directly with their clients. In cases of dispute, the central boards or ministries supervising the parties involved arbitrated the matter. For more expensive items (above 10,000 zlotys), prices were to be fixed by agreement between the ministries concerned, with the Planning Commission acting as supreme arbiter.[58] Since all such "nontypical" items were priced at planned cost, plus a standard profit margin, disputes concerned mainly the level of anticipated costs.

In the plants of the Ministry of Machine-building, at least 20 per cent of output was sold at cost-plus prices.[59] Many enterprises in this industry utilized loopholes in the legislation to classify their products as nontypical in order to sell them at higher prices. This practice was thought to have an appreciable influence on the financial results of central boards producing standard items at a loss.[60]

57. *ZG,* no. 6 (1955), 225.
58. Bolesław Rotsztejn, "O organach i podstawowych zasadach oraz trybie ustalania cen środków produkcji" (On the organs and on the basic principles for setting the prices of means of production), *Przegląd ustawodawstwa gospodarczego* (Survey of economic legislation), no. 4 (1955), 117.
59. Fiszel, *Prawo wartości* . . . , p. 52. In the Central Board of the Heavy Machine-building, Boilers, and Turbines Industry, only 30 per cent of output was standard in 1955. It was hoped to increase this share to 40–50 per cent in 1956; see *Z zagadnień cen środków produkcji* (Selected problems on producer goods prices), pp. 126–27.
60. From 1953 to 1955 the literature is replete with instances of inflated calculations of "costs" charged consumers under this guise. Many examples are cited by Fiszel in his article, "Jednakowe wyroby muszą posiadać jednolite ceny" (Identical goods must have identical prices), *TL,* no. 115 (April 27, 1955). According

The prices of goods manufactured by local industry and by co-operatives were higher than those of key industry,[61] which operated at lower costs. Local and cooperative plants usually worked with obsolete equipment or with primitive unmechanized methods. Many cooperatives bought a part of their material inputs on the open market at higher retail prices. Almost all these enterprises would have incurred a deficit if they had had to compete at the same prices as large-scale industry. On the other hand, the subsidization of thousands of small firms would have created an embarrassing administrative problem. From May 1951 to January 1953, the delivered prices of local industry exceeded the transfer prices of key industry only by the cost of railroad transportation to the consumer's station. In the case of bulky building materials, it was an appreciable advantage for small producers to be allowed to add the cost of delivery to their ex-factory prices. From 1953 on, bricks and other ceramic products sold by local industry were priced to include the cost of delivery; however, the new uniform prices of local-industry products were set at a higher level than prices of comparable products sold by key industry.[62] Table 7:6 shows the two price levels for typical building materials produced both in local and in key industry. Most of these indirect subsidies to local industry were eliminated by the price reform of January 1, 1956.

TABLE 7:6. *Prices of Ceramic Products in Key and in Local Industry, 1953*

	Prices	
	Key industry	Local industry
	(zlotys per thousand)	
Bricks, solid (first quality)	277.5	388.5
Ackerman cement blocks (18 cms.)	1,015.8	1,220.0
Berlin tiles	3,270.0	3,600.0

Source. H. Fiszel, "O oddziaływaniu prawa wartości . . . ," *Ekonomista*, nos. 1–2 (1954), 173.

---

to Fiszel, the Investment Bank turned up 17,000 faulty invoices in 1954, in a majority of which the prices charged did not conform to regulations.

61. "Key industry" includes all nationalized enterprises subordinate to industrial ministries (Power, Mining, Metallurgy, Machine-building etc.). It excludes enterprises organized under the Ministry of Small-Scale Industry and Handicrafts as well as enterprises of local importance attached to voivodships and to city councils.

62. *GP*, no. 7 (1954), 90.

A comprehensive law for pricing the products of small-scale industry was finally promulgated in May 1954. Only cooperatives
and dwarf plants supervised by the local Peoples' Councils remained outside its compass.

According to the new law, the basic uniformity of sales prices
for identical articles could be realized in any of the following
three ways:

1) If local industry accounted for less than 30 per cent of the
total national output, then the price fixed for key-industry plants
was to be binding for all local plants.

2) In case local industry produced between 30 and 50 per cent
of total output, the uniform price was to be equal to the "average
planned cost" (plus 5 per cent profits) of all state-run plants. This
average cost was interpreted as the average unit cost of plants producing the bulk of output.

3) In case local industry produced over 50 per cent of the output, its costs were to determine the level of uniform prices.[63]

Small production units attached to the Peoples' Councils still
had their prices set at the level of their planned unit costs plus a
5 per cent profit margin, with the exception of materials distributed centrally. All such materials, whatever their origin—even from
cooperatives—were sold at uniform procurement prices within the
state sector; accounts of prices differences were opened to compensate profits and losses, net differences being settled with the National Bank by the marketing organization in charge of buying
from the various sources.

The prices paid to cooperatives by the sales centrals were far
from uniform, since prices were set at cost plus profits, and cost
calculations were inflated. There was little or no way for the Peoples' Councils of voivodships or for the Ministry of Small-Scale
Industry and Handicrafts to verify scrupulously the thousands of
cost-price estimates that were submitted to them for approval each
year.

Table 7:7 illustrates some extreme instances of the price disparities involved.

That "nontypical" products sold by cooperatives and local
plants could find an outlet within the state sector at prices several

63. B. Rotsztejn, "Ustalanie cen środków produkcji w przemyśle drobnym" (Price-
setting for means of production in small-scale industry), in Z zagadnień cen środków
produkcji, p. 142.

times higher than those charged by large-scale industry is clear evidence of the unsatisfied demand in this sellers' market. The demand for high-price goods would not have been so great, of course, if the enterprises purchasing from these marginal sources of supply had had a strong incentive to reduce planned costs. But

TABLE 7:7. *Prices in Large-Scale State Industry and in Producers' Cooperatives in 1955*
(zlotys per unit)

	Unit	State industry	Cooperatives
Quicklime	ton	115	315
Plaster-of-Paris	ton	160	341
Tar paper	sq. meter	14.6	29.5
Sodium bichromate	ton	4,990	12,100
Barium nitrate	ton	5,045	10,897
O-chlorophenol (pure)	kg	51	483
Pitch (from coal distillation)	ton	250	700
Oxygen (gas)	m³	1.7	4
Harrow "16"	unit	74.6	187

Sources. H. Fiszel, *Prawo wartości a problematyka cen w przemyśle socjalistycznym* (The law of value and the price problem in socialist industry), p. 57; Rotsztejn, "Ustalanie cen środków produkcji . . . ," pp. 144, 145.

since these high-price purchases were rarely questioned in the cost plans submitted to higher authorities, it seemed a fairly safe way for large enterprises to secure inputs above their regular allotment.

8. *Prices of Construction Works*

Enterprises in the building industry sold their services at "standard cost-estimate prices." The investor (e.g. the industrial ministry for which a new plant was being built), called upon the project-making bureau of its ministry to estimate the cost of the project on the basis of blueprints and drafts and of an official "handbook of construction prices." The basic handbook, which remained valid until the middle of 1956, dated back to 1950.[64] The cost estimate, called *kosztorys,* was binding both on the investor and on the building contractor, not in its total sum but in its unit prices—the cost of one cubic meter of earth removed, of one square meter of brick wall, of one thousand roof tiles laid, etc.

64. ZG, no. 17 (1955), 672. The handbook is the *Cennik robót budowlanych i instalacyjnych na rok 1950.*

However, building contractors could charge cost-plus prices for "nonstandard" items in the project. They would cut their losses by finding holes in the *kosztorys* which permitted them to add special charges.[65]

A peculiar feature of the system is that *kosztorys* prices were sometimes adjusted by decree. The changes often had little relation to the actual trend in construction costs; nevertheless, contractors had to comply and sell their services at unit prices which had been fixed without their participation. Prices charged by building enterprises under the Ministry of Industrial Construction were reduced by decree in 1951 and again in 1953. The two reductions came to 21.5 per cent, while costs during the same period fell by only 15.7 per cent. The ensuing losses were in part financed from the working capital of construction firms.[66] Prices in the Ministry of Construction of Towns and Settlements were also cut by about 20 per cent between 1951 and 1953, again with consequent losses.[67]

Some sample studies were made in 1952 and 1953 to compare actual costs with cost-estimates. Twenty-eight finished buildings of various types were investigated for 1952. The cost of all additional works not covered by the standard *kosztorys* prices were subtracted. The percentage difference between actual and *kosztorys* costs for various types of works is shown below:

	Percentage difference
Materials	− 0.2
Labor	+ 51.2
Transportation	+ 25.9
Equipment	+166.9
Overhead	+ 3.7

65. The records for 1950 and 1951 showed that losses were incurred by construction firms in building standard elements (excavations, walls, roofing, etc.), while profits were realized on specialized works (installing central heating plants, water, electric works, etc.) where there were greater possibilities of manipulating the estimates. See *Finanse*, no. 5 (1954), 12.

66. C. Bąbiński, "O błędach w metodologii planowania inwestycji przemysłowych i budownictwa" (On errors in the methodology for planning industrial investments and construction), part I, *IB*, no. 2 (1955), 10; *MP*, no. A-16 (1952), *poz.* 190; Ibid., no. A-28 (1953), *poz.* 335.

67. J. Stępiński, "Ceny porównywalne i ceny niezmienne w budownictwie" (Comparable and fixed prices in construction), *GP*, no. 5 (1955), 24–26.

The discrepancies were due to inaccurate costing, to inefficiency (especially in handling equipment), and to the "lack of realism" of the decreed price cuts.[68]

The increases in the prices of building materials decreed in January 1956 compelled new changes in the coefficients relating current costs to 1950 norms. Percentage increases were applied *en bloc* to the cost-estimate prices of various central boards and trusts. "Mostostal," which carries out steel-construction jobs of national importance, had its prices raised by a flat 80 per cent, but the increase was later reduced by a special decree to 52 per cent. The construction trust in charge of building the Lenin Works in Nowa Huta was authorized to raise its prices by 43 per cent. The prices of urban housing projects were increased by 45 per cent and of most industrial construction by 25 per cent.[69] One reason for the greater rise in housing prices may have been the heavy deficit (around 750 million zlotys) that this industry suffered in 1955, whereas the Ministry for Industrial Construction had succeeded in earning a slight profit.[70]

These across-the-board increases in *kosztorys* prices of January 1956 were only a temporary expedient, pending a general overhaul in the system. New physical norms were introduced during the course of 1956. From now on, the cost-estimate was to be made up from these norms and from a special catalogue of average procurement prices of building materials, together with the authorized wage rates for building workers. It was no longer possible to read off the "price" of a standard item of construction directly from the catalogue.[71] According to a 1956 interview with an official in an enterprise working under the Ministry of Construction, the new system, although somewhat more complicated and time consuming than the old, was so much more realistic that both investors and contractors had found it a real improvement.

68. Stępiński, "Możliwości badania kosztów budownictwa a dotychczasowa praktyka" (The possibilities of investigating building costs and practices up to date), *IB*, no. 3 (1956), 16. A similar example is given by the director of a construction project; see *ZG*, no. 9 (1955), 332.

69. *MP*, no. 2 (1956), *poz.* 20.

70. *Finanse*, no. 3 (1956), 19.

71. Urząd Rady Ministrów (Biuro norm budowlano-montażowych), *Katalog scalonych norm kosztorysowych* (Catalogue of scaled cost-estimate norms), 2 vols.; and *Cennik materiałów budowlanych dla celów kosztorysowania* (Catalogue of building materials for cost estimate purposes) (Warsaw 1956).

9. *Summary and Conclusions*

The Polish price system evolved in several stages from the dual level of stabilized and fluctuating market prices of the early postwar period. At first, both consumer and producer goods were sold at official or stable prices, which served as a shield for the entire state sector, including socialized enterprises and their employees drawing rations, against the inflation and the "extortions" of private traders. It was not until the beginning of the Six-Year Plan that private consumers were dealt out of the privileged sector, which became the exclusive province of state-run enterprises. Even the abnormal rationing period of 1951 and 1952 did not fundamentally alter this separation; when rationing was abolished in January 1953, the turnover tax rose to absorb most of the increased margin between retail prices paid by households and producers' costs. At that time, in fact, the turnover tax was almost identical with this margin and varied with the cost level of each enterprise and with changes in these costs. Uniform factory prices for consumer goods, net of turnover taxes, which were to apply to transactions within the state sector and in export trade, gained wide currency only in mid-1954.

The artificial nature of the first postwar official prices based on multipliers of prewar cartel prices and the varying extent to which the inflation of market prices was allowed to impinge on the costs of producers—through the consumption of nonstandard items and through purchases of above-ration quotas on the open market—created a price and cost structure in the socialized sector that was neither a stable nor a reliable indicator of relative values. In this inflationary period, the use of fixed prices for planning purposes may have been a lesser evil than reliance on an unsound system of current prices. The growth in the importance of fixed prices coincided with the trend toward physical planning. From 1949 to 1952 or 1953, prices served to aggregate output rather than to guide the allocation decisions of planners and producers. As a result of the institutional reforms of 1949 and 1950, socialized producers in key industry, for the first time since the war, had to transfer their products at uniform sales prices, irrespective of their efficiency or location. These uniform prices should have goaded the managers of high-cost plants into special efforts to eliminate waste and reduce losses. But the willingness of the planners to mete out subsidies according to planned costs without sufficient economic discrimination impaired the reforms. Stringent regulations "on paper" were ineffective because the planners were reluctant to risk the slightest drop in the output of deficit enterprises, which usually belonged to priority industries (e.g. mining, metallurgy, and heavy chemicals).

From 1953 on, the planners directed their efforts toward the standardization of the price system. They expanded the coverage of the price lists and reduced the opportunities open to firms of earning high profits on special orders sold at cost-plus prices. The experiment with "parametric prices" in the building industry was not a success: *kosztorys* prices were so arbitrary that contracting organizations did not bestir themselves to reduce losses.

The lesson the Polish planners have drawn from their experience with price-setting in recent years is that prices must be close to costs to mobilize the initiative of managers toward improving their firms' financial position. If losses are very large, managers despair and direct all their attention toward the production bonus; on the other hand, if profits are earned too easily and then are automatically taxed off by the state, these profits invite waste and swollen costs, which will be hard for higher authorities to detect and harder still to eliminate.

CHAPTER EIGHT

The Pricing of Producer Goods

1. *General Lines of Policy*

In Chapter One, we concluded that rational prices could only be determined after an efficient allocation of resources had been established. In subsequent chapters, we found that the actual allocation of resources in Poland was far from efficient; techniques of physical allocation had to be supplemented by value calculations to keep the planners from making gross errors in foreign trade and in the distribution of their investment outlays. Since labor, along with a few materials, was not distributed by central organs, prices were also needed to guide enterprises in the selection of these inputs.

The present chapter deals with the efforts of the Planning Commission to steer its price-setting policy toward a number of objectives, which eventually proved to be incompatible. Foremost, prices had to be relatively stable to satisfy the demands of the Ministry of Finance for budgetary stability; then they had to cover production costs, or at least come close to so doing, to hold down the level of subsidies. Prices of capital goods had to be kept low to reduce the level of budget-financed investment outlays. A majority of socialized enterprises were supposed to earn a modest level of profits so as to encourage their efforts to reduce costs. Finally, prices were to be used to mitigate deficits of scarce materials by causing consumers to replace them by materials in more abundant supply.

The policy of the Planning Commission evolved as a compromise among the following goals: 1) to please the financial authorities, producers' prices were kept low and were reformed only at wide intervals; 2) whenever prices got too far out of line with costs in an entire industry, prices were raised so as to eliminate subsidies and to maintain most enterprises on the edge of profits; 3) while the sales proceeds of an industry could not exceed costs by a wide margin (except in the consumer goods sector where taxes siphoned off most of the surplus), many individual products were priced above cost to spur their production or to discourage their use as inputs; 4) "ersatz materials" were frequently priced below cost to promote their consumption.

Before describing the government's price-setting policy in the 1950s, we shall briefly dwell on the organs responsible for actually setting prices during this period.

2. Who Sets Producers' Prices?

A decree issued in June 1953 apportioned the responsibility for price-setting among various government organs. The Planning Commission was authorized to set prices, subject to the approval of the Council of Ministers, for all raw materials and investment goods, for semifabricates, export articles, rejects and by-products of industry sold on the market, for transportation, water, gas, and other tariffs, and for services rendered among socialized plants. However, the Commission could delegate the responsibility for price-setting to an individual ministry for products transferred exclusively among the plants under its supervision, for special-order goods, and for filling in gaps in the price catalogues. The Commission might also delegate to the Peoples' Councils of the voivodships the right to determine the prices of locally produced materials directly supplying the needs of local industry.[1] Finally, the Ministry of National Defense was empowered to fix prices for food staples, uniforms, and equipment bought for the use of the armed forces.

The State Price Commission set all retail prices of goods sold to the population, procurement prices in compulsory deliveries of agricultural products, prices of medicines and of printed materials.

Subsequent regulations prescribed which products might be priced by industrial ministers. For example, the Ministry of Min-

1. In the case of goods sold both to the population and to socialized enterprises (building materials, chemicals, coal, etc.), the two organs acted in consultation; but prices for these two separate markets were still set independently.

ing could set prices for materials used in backfilling, as well as prices of mining machinery, of pit props, and of certain semi-fabricates in transfers among refineries. Where prices were pegged to production costs, they were to be revised between three and seven months after their original promulgation on the basis of actual cost records.[2] In the decree regulating prices in the metal-lurgical and chemical industries a list of standard products was appended which the ministries concerned were *not* permitted to price. This list included all ferrous and nonferrous ores, scrap, nonferrous metals in ingots, pig iron, crude steel, semis, steel con-structions, soda, sulfuric acid, ammonia, and other chemicals, the pricing of which was to remain within the exclusive province of the Planning Commission.

3. *Price Reforms of the Six-Year Plan (1950–55)*

The reform of January 1950, which more than doubled the prices of iron and steel products and raised the prices of building materials by 25 to 35 per cent, closed the period of postwar recon-struction that had been marked by large-scale subsidization of heavy industry through special offsetting accounts. The legislation of April 17, 1950, by stipulating that the new transfer prices would "basically" be equal to production costs plus profit and turnover tax, reinforced the January reform. The new law seemed to clear the way for a system of prices linked to average costs and free of subsidies.[3]

Indeed, despite the wage increases authorized in 1950 (esti-mated to have averaged 20 per cent), the year closed with a deficit of only 10 per cent in coal mining and less than 5 per cent in fer-

2. *MP*, no. A-65 (1954), *poz.* 839. The prices of newly produced articles were to be interpolated into the catalogues "in an economically justified manner" by re-lating them to standard articles already priced or, in the absence of the latter, on the basis of planned costs plus profits. In practice, there were frequent complaints that prices were initially set too high—at levels corresponding to low rates of production—and then never revised.

3. The main provisions of the law were set forth in Chap. 7, Sect. 4. The deci-sion to price producer goods at cost, net of turnover taxes (i.e. below full "socially necessary costs," which include surplus product in the form of the turnover tax) was apparently made in 1951 at the time the incidence and the uses of the turn-over tax were adapted to Soviet practice. See Z. Augustowski, "Zmniejszenie kosztów własnych a obniżka cen" (The compression of costs and the reduction of prices), *GP*, no. 1 (1951), 11. On the relation between average-cost pricing and the labor theory of value, see Chap. 1, above, pp. 42–43.

rous metallurgy.[4] Profits seem to have been earned on most lines of machinery and metal manufactures, and especially on wire products.

The decree of December 30, 1950, which reduced the prices of metallurgical products, metal goods, machinery, and equipment by 7 to 30 per cent for 1951, appears to have involved a major deviation from the policy of 1949 and 1950, which had aimed at setting all socialized firms in heavy industry on a sound financial basis.[5] Even if the sanguine expectations of cost reductions planned for the next few years had eventually been realized, heavy industry, in the meantime, would have suffered large financial losses.

For example, the uniform reduction of 7 per cent decreed for the prices of iron and steel products could not possibly have been warranted by the cost reduction of 2.4 per cent planned for the whole metallurgical industry for 1951. Even if this plan had been fulfilled and there had been no wage increases, the price cut would have caused a deficit in the industry. As it turned out, when "comparable costs" rose slightly in 1951 instead of declining according to plan, and wage increases granted in the early part of the year raised labor costs, the deficit in the metallurgical industry more than doubled compared to 1950.[6] While the total net deficit of the industry remained below 15 per cent of costs, the subsidies on basic products such as pig iron and crude steel rose to an estimated 28 per cent and 37 per cent of costs respectively.[7]

Three lines of argument seem to have influenced the planners' decision to cut the prices of metallurgical products when the industry was already working at a loss:

1) It was thought desirable to concentrate losses in a few key products such as coal, pig iron, and crude steel produced in a limited number of large enterprises, so as to allow the thousands

4. The heavy deficit on pig iron and steel (over 20 per cent) was offset by profits on coke, on finished manufactures, and on castings produced in the metallurgical industry. The relatively small losses on rolled products (around 10 per cent) also tended to lower the ratio of losses to costs. See Appendix A, and pp. 434, 436 of "Producers' Prices. . . ."

5. "Producers' Prices . . . ," p. 223.

6. T. Iwański, "Próba ekonomicznej oceny realizacji Planu C.Z.P.H. w r. 1952" (An attempt at an economic appraisal of the execution of the plan for the Central Board of the Metallurgical Industry), GP, no. 2 (1953), 28.

7. "Producers' Prices . . . ," Appendix A, p. 280.

of plants processing these inputs to work at a small profit or at an erasable loss.

2) The losses created by the price reductions were believed to be temporary. The cost reductions planned for the next two years were discounted in setting prices at a level that would guarantee profits in subsequent years and in the meantime would compel plants to economize and hold down losses.[8]

3) Some officials believed that it was necessary to cut prices of semifabricates to reduce money costs in the metal-working industries, under the misapprehension that this policy would eventually reap benefits in the form of lower costs and prices for consumer goods.[9] The fact that the profits made by metal-consuming industries as a result of lower material costs would be purely nominal, corresponding neither to an improvement in productivity nor to any progress in the management of the resources placed at the disposal of producers, was lost sight of in contemporary accounts of the reform.[10]

It is an interesting reflection on the state of price theory during the Six-Year Plan that the administrative convenience of concentrating losses on fewer enterprises was thought to outweigh the disadvantage of underpricing scarce material inputs; still, it must be conceded that rationing was so tight at the time that enterprises had not much chance to purchase excessive quantities of the materials that had been underpriced.

Under the pressure of swiftly increasing deficits in mining and metallurgy, the planners were moved to introduce a new reform which went into effect in January 1, 1953. Indeed, the deficit on coal had risen to 23 per cent of costs in 1952, while pig iron and crude steel were being produced at a loss estimated at 34 per cent and 42 per cent of costs respectively.[11]

In the course of preparing the 1953 reform, higher iron and

8. According to the official text of the price-reduction decree, the Council of Ministers took into consideration in ordering price reductions "achievements in reducing production costs up to the present time as well as the future necessity for systematic efforts in furthering these achievements." See MP, No. A-1 (1951), poz. 6.

9. The decree also stated that price adjustments were necessary "to create favorable conditions for fulfilling tasks connected with the industrialization of the country . . . by an appropriate price structure." (Ibid.)

10. Cf. for example Augustowski, "Zmniejszenie kosztów własnych . . . ," p. 14.

11. "Producers' Prices . . . ," Appendix A.

steel prices were circulated to the metal-working industries to help them work out the costs of their products at these new input prices. The costs of the manufactures then served as a basis for establishing their 1953 catalogue prices. For instance, on August 4, 1952, percentage increases in the prices of metallurgical products were passed on to the Ministry of Machine-building, where their effect on the costs of the capital goods manufactured in this industry was worked out in the next few weeks.[12] These calculations formed the basis of the 1953 catalogue prices issued toward the close of 1952.[13] According to contemporary evidence, the officials of this ministry "had to carry out their tasks hurriedly on the basis of insufficient data [on the output plans for 1953] and from indexes of price changes of industrial inputs, whose effect on costs was not differentiated according to the actual consumption of individual commodities or even of groups of commodities with a similar material composition."[14] Many items of equipment retained their old prices and producers were eventually squeezed between the rising costs of materials and stable sales prices.[15]

The percentage changes circulated in August 1952 for prices of raw materials and semifabricates were final. The higher prices of machines and other fabricated products entering into the production of these basic materials, though they undoubtedly raised their costs—if only through higher depreciation charges—were not allowed to affect their prices. These feedbacks were apparently not taken into account in setting the initial percentage increases. This appears clearly from analysis of steel prices and costs. 1953 prices

12. Communiqués No. 1 and No. 2 of the Department of Costs and Prices and dated annexes. For the actual percentages, see Table 8:1 below.

13. The actual work of price-setting was split between the marketing organization of the industry (in the case of tools, electrical equipment and cable) and its central board (in the case of motorized equipment and heavy machinery, which are normally sold without the participation of the marketing organization). In the chemical industry, pricing of basic products was undertaken by the ministry in Warsaw. All prices of basic products had to be approved by the Department of Costs and Prices of the Planning Commission.

14. L. Ząbkowicz, "Organizacja prac nad zmianą cen artykułów inwestycyjnych i zaopatrzeniowych w przemyśle maszynowym" (The organization of the work on price changes for investment and procurement goods in the machine-building industry), GP, no. 11 (1954), 2.

15. See for example the recriminations on this subject by an official of an important factory producing railroad equipment: J. Zdziech, "Co dała Pafawagowi konferencja partyjno-ekonomiczna" (What Pafawag got out of the party-economic conference), ZG, no. 22 (1954), 855.

of pig iron and scrap, the chief inputs of steel, were 52 and 87 per cent respectively above their previous levels. The rise in the price of crude steel was limited to 4 per cent above its 1952 cost, an increase that could not have sufficed, even by the most optimistic forecasts of cost reductions, to absorb the higher costs of pig iron and scrap. Nevertheless, Augustowski, who had planned the reform, wrote in January 1953 that, even though the new prices of coal and metallurgical products would not at present cover costs, losses would be wiped out in the next few years as a result of expected cost reductions.[16]

The 1953 reform was far more detailed and precise than the reform of 1951. New individual prices for iron ore, scrap, rubber products, plastics, inorganic and organic chemicals, and cotton yarns were decreed. It was mainly in metallurgy and metal products, including some machinery items, that percentage changes applying uniformly to all commodities within wide groups were circulated to ministries as a basis for their new catalogues, as had been done for all industries whose prices had been altered in 1951. A sample of the price changes decreed in a series of special communiqués are shown in Table 8:1.

The failure of the 1953 price reform to erase subsidies (and its occasional creation of subsidies where profits had been earned before) [17] was due not only to mistakes in forecasting the direct and indirect effects on costs of higher input prices but also to the impact of the round of wage increases which took place in January 1953. The Department of Costs and Prices of the Planning Commission bears no responsibility for omitting the 1953 wage reform from their calculations, for its officials were told nothing about it. On January 3, 1953, two days after the new producers' prices had come into effect, the abolition of consumer-goods rationing was announced; it was accompanied by higher retail prices and wage increases, which ranged from 12 to 40 per cent (and averaged

16. Z. Augustowski, "Ceny środków produkcji" (Prices of means of production), *GP*, no. 1 (1953), 43.

17. The cement industry had been on the average profitable until 1953, when its raw material prices rose as a result of the price reforms, while its sales prices remained constant. Only a few plants could avert losses and the whole central board suffered a net deficit (*Z zagadnień cen środków produkcji*). According to information received from the Planning Commission, this reversal took place in most of the other sectors of the building-materials industry.

about 25 per cent). The entire operation had been kept a tight secret among a small number of trusted officials for fear of market panics and speculation. There were apparently too many specialists and lower-rank bureaucrats working on the revision of pro-

TABLE 8:1. *Percentage Changes in Transfer Prices, 1952–53*

	Per cent increase (+) or decrease (−)		Per cent increase (+) or decrease (−)
Metallurgy			
Conversion iron	+52	Steel plate	+40
Steel ingots	+78	Sheets—ordinary steels	+38
Carbon tool steels	+ 8	Sheets—quality steels	+36
Wire rods and strip	+35	Tin	+36
Metal products and machinery			
Hand drills	−35	Building nails	−56
Wood-working lathes	−18	Galvanized hard wire	−28
Heavy machinery and equipment	− 8	Metal and wood lathes	− 3
Electric motors	−40	Automotive equipment	− 2
Electrical machinery	−25		
Raw materials and chemicals			
(computed percentage changes)			
Coal (average)	+28	Blast-furnace coke (average)	+60
Iron ore (acid, sintered, Borek mine)	+14	Steel scrap (top grade)	+87
Iron ore (Kryvoi Rog)	−26		
Sulfuric acid	0	Acetic acid	−63
Calcium carbide	0	Zinc white paint	−44

Sources. Ministerstwo Górnictwa, *Cennik P/53;* Departament Kosztów i Cen (P.K.P.G.), *Komunikat Nr. 1 w sprawie zmian cen artykułów zaopatrzeniowych i inwestycyjnych,* (Communiqué no. 1 on price changes for procurement and investment items); Ibid., nos. 2, 4, 5, 19, 21, 27, 28, 32, 36, 40, 41, 44, 55, 56; Augustowski, "Ceny środków produkcji," pp. 44 and 45.

ducer prices to be entrusted with confidential information on the "other reform."

By the end of 1953 the average monthly wages of all workers in socialized industry had risen by 40 per cent compared to 1952, a good deal more than the scheduled 25 per cent.[18] As might have been expected, the deficit on coal, 60 per cent of whose costs was labor, grew apace. It was already 30 per cent higher by the middle of 1953 than it had been in 1952.[19]

Table 8:2 shows some of the deficits that had arisen by 1954 and 1955 in heavy industry.

TABLE 8:2. *Percentage Deficits in Heavy Industry, 1954–55*

Material	Deficit as percentage of costs
Bituminous coal (1955)	40
Machine-cut peat (1954)	11
Iron ore (Częstochowa 33% Fe) (1954)	35
Pig iron (1954)	21
Crude steel (1954)	30
Semis for rerolling (1954)	36
Heavy rolled products (1955)	18
Cement (1955)	20
Bricks (local industry) (1954)	42
Pine boards	15
Soda ash (1954)	26
Caustic soda (1954)	34
Sulfuric acid 60° Be (1955)	36 [a]
Superphosphates 18% (January to May 1954)	21 [b]
Nitrate fertilizer (January to May 1954)	42 [b]

[a] Sulfuric acid of higher concentration (66° Be) produced by the contact method was sold at a deficit of only 9 per cent. Thirty-eight per cent of total sulfuric acid was generated by the contact method; see *Chemik,* no. 1 (1956), 4.

[b] The prices of fertilizers were doubled after May 1954, and their deficits turned into sizable profits.

Methods. "Producers' Prices . . . ," Appendices A, B, C to Chap. 8.

Source. Unpublished cost statistics and price catalogues of the coal, steel, chemical, and building industries; for the deficit on lumber, *Z zagadnień cen środków produkcji,* p. 93.

The net subsidies paid out to ministries were not so high as the percentage of losses on individual commodities listed in Table 8:2 might indicate. Within each central board, losses tended to be concentrated in the "heavy items"—which are mainly represented in

18. *TL,* January 4, 1953. The average wage in 1952 was 682 zlotys per month (*RS 1956,* p. 277). Workers earning between 462 and 924 zlotys a month were to receive increases of 21.3 to 27.7 per cent.

19. Interview material.

the table—while finished products rode along at a small deficit or even earned a small profit. In the chemical industry, one official observed, "Prices of chemicals are fixed by plan in such way that raw-material products . . . may be inexpensive and may not hamper the development of industries based on these products, whereas light chemical industries have higher prices to cover the losses of deficit industries with their receipts." [20]

Administrative convenience seems to have been an important justification for the above policy. The Ministry of Finance preferred to pay subsidies into a special account for the entire coal-mining industry and to make up the deficits of twenty-four steel mills than to finance and control the losses that would have arisen in a majority of the 5,000 factories in the machine-building and metal-processing industries [21] if coal and steel prices had risen enough to cover costs.

Every producer-goods industry sold some commodities on the consumer market that were usually priced above cost and on which high rates of turnover tax were levied. In the ministries of mining, power, and machine-building and in the building-materials industry, products sold to households at higher prices did not contribute any turnover taxes to the state but earned "positive budget differences" to offset losses in these industries. This accounts in great part for the relatively small *net* losses (or relatively high net profits) registered for these ministries in the national income accounts shown in Table 8:3 below. Special-order items sold on a cost-plus basis also helped to reduce total losses.

By transfers of funds among firms and even occasionally among central boards,[22] the ministries offset losses with profits earned in profitable firms. This allowed the Ministry of Finance to reduce the sums earmarked for subsidies in the national budget. If the gross losses of deficit central boards had not been offset by profits and by budget differences from other boards,[23] their total in 1955

20. J. Korytkowski, "Efektywność ekonomiczna nakładów inwestycyjnych w przemyśle chemicznym" (The economic efficiency of investment outlays in the chemical industry), *PCh*, no. 1 (1956), 16–18.

21. *RS 1956*, p. 118. This number of enterprises includes plants and workshops of the Ministry of Communal Economy

22. See Chap. 6, Sect. 4.

23. The gross losses of deficit central boards are estimated from data in the 1955 budget speech of the Minister of Finance. See *Finanse*, no. 2 (1955), 10.

would have risen to some 11 or 12 billion zlotys (compared to a net loss of 4 to 5 billion zlotys for the deficit ministries listed in Table 8:3).

No figures have been published on the financial operations of individual central boards of industry, but from the information available it appears that many boards suffered appreciable losses, even in ministries showing profits or drawing only small subsidies. This was certainly the case for the central board of the inorganic-

TABLE 8:3. *Subsidies and Turnover Taxes in Producer Goods Industries, 1954 and 1955*

Ministry	Subsidies (−) or profits (+) (millions of zlotys)		Turnover taxes (millions of zlotys)		Subsidies (−) or profits (+) as percent of total costs	
	1954	*1955*	*1954*	*1955*	*1954*	*1955*
Metallurgy	−1,728	−1,533	11	550	−9.6	−8.5
Mining	−1,008	−2,746	—	—	−8.2	−19.7
Power industry	−27	+108	1	1	−1.2	+4.4
Metal-processing Industries a	−165	+692	338	248	−1.0	+8.9
Chemical Industry	+264	+242	1,202	1,377	+4.1	+3.2
Building Materials	−139	−229	5	66	−5.2	−7.5
Lumber and Paper Industries	+72	+170	661	728	+2.1	+4.6
Central Administration of Petroleum Industry	+13	+16	807	881	+2.0	+2.5

a Ministries of Machine-building and Automotive Industries. Besides armaments, include hollowware, wire, and other metal-consuming industries which sold a large share of their production on the consumer market.

Source. *Dochód Narodowy Polski 1954 i 1955*, pp. 8–9.

products industry and for the board of the sulfuric-acid and fertilizers industry in the generally profitable chemical industry. Steel mills organized under the central board of the metallurgical industry (C.Z.P.H.), incurred a deficit amounting to an average of 15 to 20 per cent of costs, compared to only 8.5 per cent for the whole ministry.[24]

Although the total financial burden of losses from 1953 to 1955 was not very onerous, the structure of costs was completely distorted by the systematic subsidization of semifabricated products.

24. "Producers' Prices . . . ," p. 238.

The Planning Commission, aware of the errors that this distortion might lead to at a time when the role of the price system in economic calculation was being revived, resolved, as far back as the last months of 1953, to embark on a new round of price increases.[25]

4. *The 1956 Reform*

a. *Average-Cost Pricing.* The 1956 reform was the most comprehensive since 1945; for the first time it ranged over the whole field of producer goods, including imports. We shall dwell at some length on this reform, about which a good deal is now known. We shall first see how prices were set to cover the average level of production costs in each industry. In the next section we shall consider how the prices of individual goods were allowed to deviate from cost.

A decree of December 9, 1953, defined with greater precision than in the past the meaning of average-cost pricing. It stipulated that the price of each product should cover the average of the planned costs of individual producers—plus a profit margin not to exceed 5 per cent of costs.[26] In case at least 60 per cent of the output of a given article or group of articles was produced by enterprises of one or more central boards of industry under the same ministry,[27] the transfer price must cover the planned costs of these enterprises (together with the appropriate profit margin), even if they exceeded the average cost for all producers.

The first step in preparing the 1956 reform was to compute the price increases needed to cover costs and cancel subsidies in basic branches of industry and transportation; the next step was to gauge very roughly the secondary effects of increased input prices on these industries.[28] This work was carried out in the Planning

25. Joseph Stalin's *Economic Problems of Socialism in the U.S.S.R.*, published in 1952, had taught that the law of value must "influence," though it must not "govern," the allocation of producer goods. This document, which was widely publicized in Poland, served as a justification for the wider application of costs-and-returns calculations. The latter, in order to be meaningful, required a more rational price system than the one in effect hitherto.

26. Except where prices of specific goods were set higher than costs to induce their economy.

27. This regulation affected only large and medium-scale industry, not the Ministry of Small-Scale Industry and Handicrafts.

28. For the theory of this iterative procedure, see the concluding section of this chapter.

Commission in early 1954, the intention at that time being to put the reform into effect on January 1, 1955. During these first two or three months, working balances were prepared that equilibrated price increases for major groups of commodities, beginning with raw materials and going on to key manufactures and back to the inputs that raised the costs and prices of raw materials. All this was done before any preliminary percentage increases of basic materials were turned over for detailed computations to organizations outside the Planning Commission.

In the second of these versions, the prices of steam coals were increased by 45 per cent, the prices of coking coals by 60 per cent, and freight rates by 15 per cent. The following version, which was eventually passed on to the Ministry of Metallurgy to calculate iron and steel prices, already foresaw a rise of 80 per cent in all types of coals and of 30 per cent in freight charges. These higher increases were due in part to an estimation of the feedback effects that price changes in the industries selling inputs to these basic sectors would exercise on the latter's costs. But they were also precipitated by the rising level of subsidies in the raw material industries in 1954 and 1955 in the wake of the wage inflation.

One limiting factor in juggling these preliminary balances was the official decision to maintain the market prices of consumer goods at their previous level. Higher prices of raw materials and semifabricates were not supposed to raise the costs of manufactures above their retail price (net of trading margins). This was not so cramping a limitation in pricing textiles and shoes, which had sizable margins that could be whittled away, but it set a low ceiling on increases in the prices of metallurgical products, and especially of sheet metals used in the manufacture of household hollowware. Factory prices, net of turnover taxes, of metal containers, including pots, pans, and buckets,[29] went up 60 per cent from 1953–55 to January 1956, as a result mainly of increases in the prices of steel and galvanized sheets. This left a taxable margin of only 20 to 25 per cent of the final price, compared to 50 to 60 per cent before the reform. This new margin afforded just enough leeway to cover possible wage increases or errors in estimating the effect of

29. These consumer goods pay a turnover tax and therefore have both a factory price and a transfer price (including the tax) at which the goods are sold to the wholesale network.

increased raw material prices on the costs of the final products.[30]

By the beginning of May 1954, the Department of Costs and Price Policy of the Planning Commission had completed this first phase of the work and settled on price increases that were expected to eliminate subsidies in the producer-goods sector without creating new deficits in the production of consumer goods. These tentative indexes of price changes (shown in detail in Table 8:4) included freight charges (to be raised by 30 per cent), amortization (100 per cent increase), electricity (200 per cent increase), steel (70 per cent increase for commercial grades), sulfuric acid (50 per cent increase), and eleven other individual products. Metal goods as a group were to rise 60 per cent, lumber 80 per cent, metal scraps 110 per cent, ores 35 per cent, chemicals 60 per cent, and ferroalloys 135 per cent.

On May 6, 1954, these percentages were passed on to a committee made up of costs and price specialists from the Ministry of Metallurgy in Warsaw and from representatives of the marketing organizations. Their task was to compute the impact of the proposed price increases on the costs of metallurgical products. The first part of this assignment consisted in recalculating the exact production costs of all steel mills under the ministry for the first four months of 1954 as if these new input prices had been in effect at the time. This was the starting point for setting the final prices of iron and steel products. After that the committee working in collaboration with price specialists in the Planning Commission still had to set steel prices in correct relation to each other, starting from the over-all level indicated by the rise in costs.[31]

At a conference on price policy which took place in October 1955 Professor Ignacy Haendel, one of the officials of the Ministry of Metallurgy who participated in the discussions of the committee, decried the pace at which the work had been hurried through ("often with deadlines 'for yesterday' ") and criticized the Planning Commission's indices of price changes which covered an excessively wide range of commodities and services. His ministry had been informed that coal prices would rise by 80 per cent, but in fact coking coals (the prices of which influenced pig iron costs) eventually doubled. Railroad tariffs were to go up by 30 per cent,

30. Information based on interviews in the Planning Commission.
31. See below, Sect. 4b.

TABLE 8:4. *Four Steps in the Price Reform for Metallurgical Products, 1954–56 (Percentage Increases)*

I. Early draft.
II. Price increases based on I. and on actual
    costs in the metallurgical industry.
III. Indices circulated to the ministries.
IV. Average of actual price increases.

	I First quarter 1954	II June 1954	III August 1954	IV Final 1956 reform
Coke	40	62.1	65	70
Coke gas	60	..	100	110
Pig iron	..	64.1	68	75
Ferroalloys:				
Chrome .... } 135		72.8 { ..	43	35
Silica .... }		{ ..	118	239
Tungsten, molybdenum, titanium	..	187.8	220	..
Silicomanganese	..	45.3	63	60
Ordinary carbon steels	..	82.7	89	90
Quality steels:				
Class 1 (Constructional carbon)	70	56.1	146	66
Class 2 (Tool carbon)	20	55.7	84	60
Class 3 (Constructional alloy without nickel)	56 to 76	78.5	93	94
Class 4 (Constructional alloy with nickel)	117 to 180	119.9	60	126
Class 5 (Low-alloy tool)	17 to 80	51.6	126	71
Class 6 (High-alloy tool)	1 to 69	99.5	96	140
Class 7 (Fast-cutting)	41 to 54	52.9	83	72
Class 8 (Stainless, heat-resistant)	32 to 63	188.6	114	177
Class 9 (Special)	40 to 50	85.7	136	186
Blooming mill products (semis)	..	97.7	108	108
Tin plate	..	87.9	95	67 to 121
Galvanized sheets	..	88.8	25	40
Zinc (99.99%)	70	..	80	80
Tin (99.9%)	70	..	267	267

Methods. "Producers' Prices . . . ," Appendix C.

Sources. Indices of price changes and other material of the Department of Costs and Price Policy of the State Planning Commission.

but this was only an average, and, as it turned out, freight charges on short hauls in the Silesian complex—where most of the steel is transported—increased as much as 120 per cent.[32]

Table 8:4 presents a comparison of the changes proposed by the Planning Commission with the percentage increases for basic products of the industry calculated by the price committee working in the Ministry of Metallurgy, and with the finally approved price increases that were circulated to the central board of the machine-building industry. The fourth column shows estimated average increases based on the prices actually listed in the published catalogues.

The final increases in the table above diverged significantly from those first derived by the committee from cost estimates. Not only did they average out higher but there were also basic changes in structure which reflected the work of the committee in setting steel prices in appropriate relation to each other.

At the end of August 1954 when the prices of most metallurgical products had been approved, a list of price increases was sent to the Ministry of Machine-building to permit the various boards to compute new prices for their products which would offset the higher costs of their inputs. It was also about this time that the building-materials and the chemical industries received *their* "indices of price changes" (*wskaźniki zmian cen*). The new prices were generally prepared from these indices and from actual costs incurred in 1954, reworked with higher prices of inputs. Alternatively, some central boards worked with planned costs of 1955 computed from both 1953–55 prices and the revised prices of materials. Prices of chemicals and machinery products were pegged to average costs without any allowance for profits (normally up to 5 per cent of average costs), in view of the great possibilities for cost reductions in these industries.[33]

32. *Z zagadnień cen środków produkcji*, p. 66. An official in the central board of the cement industry, where the new prices were hammered out on the basis of similar indices, complained that the new electricity tariff paid by the cement industry was significantly higher than the personnel of the central board had been led to anticipate. (Ibid., p. 57.)

33. T. Krajewski, "O zmianach cen środków produkcji i towarowej taryfy kolejowej" (On changes in producer goods prices and in railway shipping rates for merchandise), *Przegląd kolejowy* (Railroad survey), no. 1 (1956), 7.

It is not possible to make the same type of detailed comparisons as in Table 8:4 for the metal-working industries, partly for lack of data but mainly because, along with adjustments in the price levels of individual products, the successive approximations to the final prices entailed a good deal of disaggregation of groups, each set of indices being more detailed and accurate than the last.[34]

The successive price levels may be compared for a few of the basic products of the chemical industry. Prices of caustic soda and sulfuric acid were first raised by 50 per cent; they both eventually doubled. Coal derivatives were to go up by 65 per cent; by November 1954, they had risen by 119 per cent. A few products such as liquid ammonia and arsenic-free hydrochloric acid went up less than had been forecast in the preliminary estimates.[35]

How could industries manufacturing highly finished products prepare their cost estimates from indices that were constantly being revised? At least in the Ministry of Metallurgy, which bought products whose nomenclature alone filled three volumes, it proved impossible to recalculate production costs each time any of the suppliers revised its tentative prices.[36] We should not be surprised to learn therefore that there was a wide discrepancy between the total material costs planned for 1956 by industrial consumers on the basis of tentative 1956 prices and suppliers' estimates of total receipts from the sales of these same materials at what were supposed to be the same prices. According to officials interviewed in the Planning Commission, this gap amounted to thirteen billion zlotys, in the order of 5 to 10 per cent of total material costs in all industry in 1956. In metallurgy, the expected receipts from sales of iron and steel products to metal consumers came to 1.5 billion zlotys less than the planned disbursements of consumers for these products. The gap may be estimated at roughly 5 per cent of the

34. We may note in passing that the price increase of 60 per cent proposed in the second version for a whole group of metal goods comprising wire, cables, and wire products was later broken down (in the circulated version) into the following indices: bare iron wire 100, galvanized wire 68, special steel wires 80, barbed wire 43, building nails 90, and screws 70. Although we do not have the output weights to average out these percentages, a rough calculation shows that the average would be at least 15 points above the originally proposed 60 per cent increase. The actual increases built into the price catalogues by the metal industry ranged from 16 per cent for barbed wire to 150 per cent for ordinary iron wire.

35. "Producers' Prices . . . ," p. 250.

36. *Z zagadnien cen środków produkcji,* p. 66.

steel mills' receipts. There was a marked tendency for suppliers to underestimate their average proceeds by picking excessively low prices to make up their averages, while their consumers behaved in an opposite manner, being unduly pessimistic about their average costs. It turned out that the steel industry in 1956 sold its output for 0.5 billion zlotys more than had been anticipated, mainly by virtue of higher-than-planned average transfer prices. This was a contributing factor in the industry's ability to earn a profit of about 3 per cent in 1956.[37]

At the conference on price formation that took place in October 1955, several representatives of central boards warned that the new prices approved by the Department of Costs and Price Policy of the Planning Commission would fall short of covering their costs and that their branches of industry were likely to require subsidies. Józef Marzec, chief of the Costs Department of the Central Board of the Tool Industry, claimed that the new prices would wipe out the net profits of the central board, estimated at 44 million zlotys in 1955, and create a deficit of 33 million zlotys in 1956. Marzec forecast losses for every one of the enterprises organized under his central board.[38]

It is not possible to judge whether the Planning Commission had been correct in holding down prices and cost limits below the demands made in the field. For one thing the deficits that actually occurred may have been due to the rise in wages that took place in 1956 and not to inflated material costs. Wages actually rose by 8 per cent during the course of 1956. However, about half of this increase was bunched in the last quarter of the year;[39] it is improbable, therefore, that the subsidy to the cement industry, which already exceeded 15 per cent of costs in the first quarter of 1956, should have been caused mainly by higher wages.[40]

During this same quarter, a deficit of 7 per cent developed in the production of sulfuric acid and of 5 per cent in the production

37. Profits on finished steels and on coke still made up losses on basic iron and steel products: it was reported at the beginning of 1957 that the loss on steel ingots was of the order of 200 zlotys per ton or about 12 per cent of costs. See *Wiadomości hutnicze*, no. 5 (1957), 158.

38. *Z zagadnien cen środków produkcji*, p. 69.

39. Główny Urząd Statystyczny (Chief Statistical Office), *Biuletyn statystyczny 1956*, no. 1, p. 29; no. 2, p. 25.

40. The cost of Portland cement (grade "250") in the first quarter of 1956 was 203 zlotys per ton and its transfer price 170 zlotys (unpublished cost statistics).

of hydrochloric acid.[41] Soda ash and caustic soda were also produced at a loss almost as soon as the new prices had been put into effect. Nevertheless, the net subsidy received by the Central Board of Inorganic Industry remained small, owing to the sizable profits earned on fertilizers and other fabricated products which helped make up losses on the basic products.[42]

In the year preceding the reform, losses in bituminous coal had been heavier than in any other industry. In the entire Ministry of Coal Mining, which included a number of plants producing mining machinery, pit props, and spare parts at a profit, losses came to 36.9 per cent of total costs in 1955. Out of 119 enterprises (mainly coal mines) supervised by the ministry, 92 were operated at a deficit.[43] In one of the early balances of price changes, it had been proposed to raise the prices of steam coals by 45 per cent and of coking coals by 60 or 61 per cent. With doubled amortization, a 15 per cent increase in freight tariffs, and higher material costs in mining, the proposed increase would have been barely enough to cover the new level of mining costs. In mid-1954, under the pressure of rising costs, the State Planning Commission circulated "indices of price changes" to coal consumers which averaged out to

TABLE 8:5. *Percentage Increases in Coal Prices*

	Circulated indices 1955	*Actual percentage increases 1956*
Large coals	65	75
Medium-sized	98	103
Slack	108	93
Gangue stone (carboniferous)	190	157
Average, all coals	82	85

Sources and Methods. Detailed data on the breakdown of coal output by sizes of coal in 1955 were published in B. Dąbczak's "Zagadnienie sortymentów w węglu energetycznym na tle produkcji w latach 1950 do 1955" (The problem of the size and quality of steam coals in the light of output in the years 1950 to 1955), *Gospodarka węglem*, no. 1 (1957), 22, 24. This source also provides average prices for each size of coal, taking into account the ranking of coals by class (determined mainly by ash content). These data yielded exact estimates of average prices for the four general categories listed in the table.

41. The subsidy to the sulfuric acid industry was exclusively for the large, high-cost Wizow plant, which pulled up the average cost of the industry above its sales price.

42. See "Producers' Prices . . . ," Appendix D, Chap. 7.

43. Z. Madej, "Ceny i rentowność w państwowych przedsiębiorstwach przemysłowych" (Prices and profitability in state industrial enterprises) *GP*, no. 12 (1957), 2–3.

an 80 per cent increase. Finally, on August 25, 1955, the price indices listed in Table 8:5 were circulated, which are shown together with estimated increases in actual catalogue prices.

Before the end of 1955, however, mining costs had already risen to 120 zlotys per ton. An increase of 65 to 70 per cent would have been necessary merely to cover costs at the old level of amortization, transportation, and material costs. The new input costs of steel and lumber pit props (up to 80 per cent), doubled amortization charges and a one-third rise in freight costs [44] would have boosted average costs per ton up to nearly 150 zlotys, or over 110 per cent above the average price prevailing in 1953–55. The new schedule of coal prices, which averaged 80 to 85 per cent above previous levels, fell short of the mark before it had even been put into effect.

Since prices of coal and coke have a decisive influence on the cost level of many basic industrial products, the Department of Costs and Price Policy could not circulate new price increases for fuels every time mining costs rose by a few per cent. This would have meant starting all over again the process of mutual adjustments of prices and costs. By mid-1955, there had already been about eight of these "paper cycles," which had already taken up considerable time in the Planning Commission and in the central boards of industry; this was considered quite enough.

An industry-wide survey was made by the Chief Statistical Office at the end of 1956 to assess the financial results of the 1956 price reform.[45] It was discovered that only the metallurgical industry, of all the industries that had been sustaining losses in 1955, had managed to register a profit in 1956. A small decrease in the total number of deficit enterprises and in the proportion of losses to total costs in most ministries was all there was to show for more than two years of work.[46]

44. On the basis of an average 300 kilometers haul; see Ministertwo Kolei, *Taryfa Polskich Kolei Państwowych* (Polish State Railways Tariff), for January 1954 and ibid. for January 1956.

45. Altogether, the enterprises covered by the survey contributed 93 per cent of the total turnover taxes and 73 per cent of the total profits paid by state-run enterprises in 1956. The survey apparently embraced all large deficit enterprises in heavy industry (Madej, pp. 1–3).

46. Madej, p. 2. All the statistics in the following paragraph are from Madej's report on the results of the 1955 and 1956 surveys.

The proportion of enterprises incurring losses exceeding 20 per cent of costs declined from 14.6 in 1955 to 11.3 per cent in 1956. The deficit in the coal mining industry fell from 36.9 per cent of costs in 1955 to 18.7 per cent in 1956; losses in the building materials industry were almost as large in 1956 as they had been in 1955 (9.2 against 9.5 per cent). The number of deficit enterprises in the machine-building industry was 43 per cent in 1955; it was still 40 per cent in 1956. Net profits rose in the power and petroleum industries. In the chemical industry, however, there was an increase of 28 per cent in the number of deficit enterprises.

In short, in the first year of the reform, there was moderate improvement in the financial condition of producer goods industries compared to 1955, but the failure to wipe out losses balked the high expectations that had been placed in the reform.

Up to the 1957 reform of building materials prices, which already belongs to the Gomulka era,[47] the main concern of the price-fixers had been to match prices and costs and eliminate subsidies. This principle was so well ingrained that they made little or no effort to discount adjustments of industrial consumers to the price structure. Actually, there was really no way such adjustments could be predicted. When officials of the Department of Costs and Price Policy were asked in 1956 whether cost savings from decentralized attempts by consumers to buy relatively cheaper materials were ever anticipated in working out the new price levels, they answered that cost limits were always prepared as a *resultant* of physical planning and not as a *determinant* of inputs or outputs, but when scarce materials were priced high, their consumption was discouraged and the cost limits imposed on enterprises reflected the planners' policy with respect to input-mixes. As we saw, cost limits were set lower than the representatives of industry thought adequate in the hope that tight plans would spur producing plants to stringent material economies. In the next section, we shall study the efforts the planners made in the 1956 reform to use price policy to support the allocation decisions of the Planning Commission, to induce managers to economize materials in short supply and to direct their efforts toward producing more of the critically needed products.

47. See below, Chap. 9, p. 280.

b. *Deviations from Average-Cost Pricing.* Prior to 1953, price catalogues did not always literally follow the average-cost pricing
principle. For one thing, it was impossible to stick to this rule in
the case of jointly-produced materials, whose costs could not be
segregated with the accounting methods in vogue.[48] For another,
it would have been sheer nonsense to price low-quality above high-
quality materials simply because the former happened to have
been produced mainly in high-cost plants. Electrolytic zinc in the
price reforms of 1948 and 1949 was already priced above metallurgical zinc even though its average cost of production was nominally lower.[49] Lime which cost more than cement was priced below cement to encourage its substitution wherever possible. Prices
for the various grades of coal—whose costs cannot be determined
from supply relations alone—were set in all postwar years with
some regard for the relative demand of the "market" for different
grades.

Prior to 1950, ministries and central boards responsible for
pricing products by grades and types frequently relied on past
commercial tradition or on the catalogues of foreign countries
rather than on Marxist principles to execute in detail the general
directives of the Planning Commission. The reforms of 1950 and
mid-1951 (when coal prices were adjusted) occurred at the high
point of the trend toward centralization and technological planning: they marked the regression of demand-oriented pricing. In
1951 the relative prices of large coals were reduced from four times
the price of finely divided coal-slack to 2.5 times this ratio. This
was done in order to value the different sizes of coal in closer accord with their calorific content, in disregard of the fact that about
three quarters of the nation's furnaces were unable to fire small-
size coals without an enormous loss in efficiency.[50] The 1953 reform reversed this tendency: it widened the spread between large

48. For a discussion of these techniques, see "Producers' Prices . . . ," Chap. 8.
49. Zjednoczone zakłady metali nieżelaznych, *Cennik* (in effect from May 15, 1948),
p. 5. Ministerstwo Przemysłu Ciężkiego, *Cennik Nr. 31,* p. 5; J. Borysiewicz, *System
cen środków produkcji w przemyśle na przykładzie hutnictwa* (The system of producer goods prices in industry with special reference to metallurgy), p. 106.
50. Cf. Olczakowski, ed., *Gospodarka węglem w przemyśle,* p. 126. Note that up
to 1950 the sales central distributing coal had been responsible for setting coal prices.
The new policy corresponded to the transfer of price-setting powers to the Planning
Commission.

and small coals back to 1949 levels. Moreover, the Planning Commission, conscious of the growing deficit of coking coals due to the demand for high-quality cokes on the part of the rapidly expanding metallurgical industry, resolved to increase the spread between coking coals and the best grades of steam coals from 10 to 50 per cent to promote the economy of the best coking coals and to encourage their segregation in the output of mines producing different types of coal.[51]

The price reform of 1953 and particularly the lengthy preparations for the 1956 reform departed from previous practice in that the proper "relationing" of producers' prices was now encompassed in theory, to some extent systematized, and applied to a wider group of substitutes than merely grades of the same product, imports, or jointly supplied commodities.

The first comprehensive statement on when and why prices should diverge from costs dates back to January 1953. In an article published in *Gospodarka planowa,* the semi-official organ of the Planning Commission, Zbigniew Augustowski, the director of the Department of Costs and Price Policy, explained the principles underlying the reform of producer goods which he had directed and organized. While laying due stress on the need for doing away with subsidies and for pricing at cost, he singled out a number of important exceptions to the rule, distinguishing systematically between exceptions applying to "instruments of production" (capital goods) and "objects of production" (material inputs).[52] He justified this distinction by arguing that material inputs can often be substituted for each other in different production processes while alternative uses for machinery, equipment, and tools are relatively rare.[53] Still, even in the latter case, there might be circumstances which might justify deviations from average-cost pricing:

1) Where alternative employment is available, the machine or tool should be priced with due regard for its relative "utility" (i.e. for its productivity).

2) "In certain rather isolated instances," it may be advisable to detach prices from costs because two or more instruments of

51. "Producers' Prices . . . ," pp. 445, 485, 488.
52. Augustowski, "Ceny środków produkcji," *GP,* no. 1 (1953), 42–43.
53. Ibid., p. 44.

production (which may be applied in a given process) are made from materials differing in scarcity, and their consumption must be promoted or restricted according as the materials happen to be in abundant or short supply.

3) Products of new processes must not be priced at their high initial cost but at the cost anticipated after the process has been mastered.

4) To promote the consumption of standardized products (and to eliminate the production of special-order items), prices of mass-produced, standardized products may be set somewhat lower than the relative costs of the two types of products might justify.[54]

5) In all cases, prices may diverge from costs by a profit margin, whenever such profits would make for improved financial or economic management of the firm.

6) Quality discounts for products failing to meet contract or standard specifications should be larger than any savings in costs that might arise from this deterioration.

In describing the most recent price reform (1953), Augustowski pointed out that across-the-board percentage changes had been applied to whole groups of machines, equipment, and tools, so as to bring prices generally in line with costs—except where evident errors had been uncovered in the reciprocal relations of prices within the group. Generally speaking, prices of instruments of production should not deviate from planned costs (plus a fixed profit) except for "evident and unequivocal reason." [55]

The prices of "objects of production" might differ from average costs on more general grounds. For this group of factors, Augustowski lay down the broad principle that "prices might differ from planned costs plus profits wherever such a policy might complement and reinforce existing regulations for the most effective utilization of the resources placed at the disposal of the State." [56] Within this broad framework, he listed a number of specific in-

54. Augustowski does not make clear whether standardized articles should be priced below (long-run) cost or whether nonstandardized articles should be priced above cost. In either case, producers would lose any incentive to standardize their production. Concentration on a few lines of production, if it reduces unit costs and prices, should call forth a sufficient increase in consumption to make standardization profitable without the need for any superimposed incentive.

55. Ibid., pp. 43–44.

56. Ibid., p. 45.

stances where deviations were clearly called for. Among these he mentioned (1) joint costs, such as coal lumps and slack, which, he reasoned, have equal costs but a different degree of "utility"; (2) "substitute materials," (e.g. waste paper for wood pulp in the manufacture of newsprint, or crushed glass to replace soda in glass making), whose prices must be set low enough—if necessary below cost—to induce industry to consume them in preference to "full-valued materials"; and (3) various groups of close substitutes (e.g. cement and lime, steel scrap and pig iron, copper and aluminum electric wire) whose prices must be set in proper relation to each other to induce the economy of the scarcer products. Iron ore prices must be so worked out that no steel mill would be penalized by increased costs for consuming low-grade ore (as would be the case if the prices of inferior ores were too high relative to the better ores).[57]

The only constraint on this "relationing" was that the "sum of the prices" (i.e. the total value) of all material inputs—and even of particular groups of materials—should come as close as possible to total costs or to group costs.[58]

Although this detailed exposition of government policy in the sphere of producers' prices was written as a commentary to the price reform of 1953, it was more an expression of the aims and of the evolving thought of the officials responsible for price-setting than a faithful description of the methods utilized in fixing 1953 prices.

Augustowski's principles were incorporated into a decree of December 1953, which supplied the legal basis for the price reform of 1956. The decree explicitly sanctioned prices deviating from costs wherever these prices might "create an incentive to economize on the means of production." [59]

Since the 1953 decree was no more detailed than Augustowski's article, we should have remained in the dark as to how all these principles were to be translated into practice if it had not been for a highly instructive commentary written by another official of the Department of Costs and Price Policy on the methods applied

57. "Producers' Prices . . . ," pp. 384–85.
58. Augustowski, "Ceny środków produkcji," p. 45.
59. *MP*, A-63 (1954), *poz.* 823.

in setting prices in the metallurgical industry.[60] The range of products in this industry being very wide—from foundry coke and mineral ores to nonferrous sheets and bars—Jerzy Borysiewicz, the author of this study, was able to illustrate every essential point of the new pricing policy.

Pricing policies in Borysiewicz's scheme fall into two basic categories: (1) a policy for pricing producer goods rationed out to consumers exerting no appreciable influence on the product-mix of suppliers; (2) a policy for pricing goods whose output is determined by the pattern of consumer demand (that is, with the costs of suppliers having little or no influence on the relative outputs of the products they are prepared to sell). The output of the first group of goods may be thought of as "supply determined"; the second as "demand determined." Other cases may fall somewhere between these poles, "depending on whether the producer or the consumer has the greater influence on the product-mix." [61]

In general, products whose output is demand determined should be priced at average cost or close to that level; while prices of supply-determined goods should be related according to their "utility" (that is, their productivity in the production function of industrial consumers) or to their scarcity.

The rationale behind this method of price-setting appears to be as follows: If consumers are free to choose between materials whose relative output can easily be shifted within the producing industry according to market demand, then they will buy those materials whose average-cost prices are low relative to their productivity; and consumer demand will cause the most desirable structure of output to be produced. If, on the other hand, materials are in short supply and consumers can exert no influence on their allocation, then the relative average costs of production of the different materials will not reflect their scarcity; it will be necessary to set a higher price for scarcer materials than their average costs would warrant. Borysiewicz describes three methods

60. Borysiewicz, *System cen środków produkcji* . . . The material in the following pages is reproduced with the kind permission of the University of California Press from the author's article "Producers' Prices in a Centrally Planned Economy: The Polish Discussion," in *Value and Plan: Economic Calculation and Organization in Eastern Europe*, ed. by Gregory Grossman, pp. 52–57.

61. Ibid., p. 91.

("relations") of price setting for materials: 1) the "simple relation," expressing the price of an item as a proportion of its average
cost; 2) the "compound relation" (*relacja złożona*), equating the
price of a material to its average cost adjusted for any added expenditure that a typical consumer would incur as a result of using
this material instead of some specified standard material; 3) the
"equivalent relation" proportioning the prices of inputs to their
average productivity in a given process or relating prices of inputs
according to their scarcity.

These relations will now be outlined and a few of their applications illustrated. In the next section, some comments will be made
on their suitability for the purposes for which they were designed.

1) The selection of an "average-cost" basis and of an appropriate profit margin are the only decisions requiring economic judgment in applying the "simple relation." Borysiewicz informs us
that the weighted average of the unit costs of all enterprises in a
centrally planned industry was usually chosen as a basis for building up "average-cost prices." He himself felt that it would be better to set the prices of related products turned out in the same industry at the cost level of a large multiproduct plant, as long as
the costs of this plant did not diverge markedly from the weighted
average cost of the entire industry. At least one plant would then
have no incentive to break its assortment plan, because the prices
of all its products would bear the same relation to their full cost.[62]

Profit levels were to reflect the possibilities of cost reduction in
the period between price reforms. If rapid technical progress was
expected to cut costs in a given industry in the next two or three
years, prices could be made equal to the average cost planned in
the initial year of the reform without any profit margin.[63]

2) The compound relation may be illustrated by reference to
the pricing of the various grades of pig iron.

A typical, widely used grade of pig iron is selected and priced
at cost. From empirical data in a "typical plant," specialists compute the cost of steel from this grade of pig iron and the additional
cost (or cost reduction) that would result from substituting the

62. Ibid., pp. 35–36.
63. For the 1956 reform, prices were generally based on actual 1954 costs or
on 1955 planned costs. It should be recalled that the price reform was originally
scheduled to go into effect on January 1, 1955.

actual grade whose price is to be computed. Letting K_0 stand for the cost of steel made with a typical grade of pig iron (priced at P_0) and E_1 for the incremental cost of steel made with grade 1 iron, whose price will be P_1, then:

$$\frac{P_1}{P_0} = \frac{K_0 + E_1}{K_0}$$

Note that the sign of E_1 is made positive if costs are reduced and negative if costs are raised by the substitution of grade 1 for grade 0.

3) The equivalent relation may be demonstrated by an example for setting the prices of steel scrap. If P is the price of a grade of scrap (to be computed), P_c the price of pig iron to which scrap is to be related, and Q the "index of equivalence," expressing the ratio of the "use value" (*wartość użytkowa*) of pig iron to the "use value of this scrap," [64] then the index of the equivalent relation S_e is defined as $P/(P_c \times Q)$. Hence, the desired price of scrap P equals $S_e (P_c \times Q)$.

We learn that the relation S_e depends on "the fundamental assumption particular to a given stage of economic development." [65] Thus, the index of the equivalent relation for scrap was raised from 0.7 in 1953–55 to 1.0 in 1956 in view of an anticipated shortage of scrap. Unfortunately, Borysiewicz weakens his case when he asserts that scrap prices set by this index will insulate the cost of steel from changes in the ratio of scrap to pig iron in the open-hearth burden. The index must then be "all things to all men": It must reflect the growing scarcity of scrap; it must relate average productivities; and it must insulate the costs of steel from changes in its inputs.

Toward the end of his book, Borysiewicz reaffirms his stand on the use of "relationing" as a flexible instrument of price policy. After suggesting that the relative "utility" of aluminum and copper could be measured by comparing their electrical conduc-

64. The "use values" refer in this case to the relative "metallurgical values" of scrap and pig iron. "Utility" in the equivalent relation usually corresponds to average productivity in a typical plant.

65. Borysiewicz, p. 23. Note that Q is strictly technical, corresponding essentially to the average productivity of inputs in physical units. S_e, so far as it reflects "scarcity," may be thought of as a very rough ratio of marginal to average productivity for the entire industry.

tivities (adjusted for differences in the weight of metal per meter of cable), he goes on to warn that if copper is in greater deficit than aluminum, the ratio of their prices must be larger than would appear from this comparison. He confesses, however, that it was found expedient in working out the price catalogue for nonferrous metals in 1956 to base the relations among the prices of metals neither on costs nor on relative productivities, but on the ratios of metal prices to the price of zinc in the Soviet Union "after adjustment to local conditions." [66]

A comparison of the structure of nonferrous metal prices in Poland, in the U.S.S.R., and in the United Kingdom (Table 8:6) reveals that price spreads were much wider in the Soviet Union

TABLE 8:6. *Price Relatives of Nonferrous Metals in Poland, U.S.S.R., and U.K.*
(Price of zinc = 1)

Metal Ingot	Purity (Polish standard) (in %)	Price Relatives		
		Poland 1956	U.S.S.R. 1954	U.K. Jan.–Feb. 1956
Zinc	97.5	1.0	1.0	1.0
Lead	99.97	1.7	2.2	1.2
Aluminum	99.5	4.0	2.2	1.8 [a]
Electrolytic copper	99.9	5.0	2.2	4.0
Nickel	99.8	17.5	8.9	5.0 [b]
Magnesium	99.7	5.5	4.0	2.6
Chromium	98.0	20.0	..	8.0
Tin	99.9	33.0	33.0	7.9
Cadmium	99.9	75.0	75.0	12.9
Cobalt	..	100.0	99.0	23.0
Titanium	99.0	400.0	..	26.4 [a]

[a] Based on New York price.
[b] F.o.b. Port Colborne, Canada.
Note. With the exception of magnesium, the Soviet price relatives in the table are taken directly from a Polish source. Recalculations on actual Soviet data show some discrepancies, possibly due to the choice of grades (e.g., tin: Polish source, 33; Soviet price data, 38 to 40, depending on purity).

Sources. Fiszel, *Prawo wartości a problematyka cen w przemyśle socjalistycznym*, p. 147; Ministerstwo Przemysłu Ciężkiego, *Cennik Nr. 31* (1951); Ministerstwo Hutnictwa, *Cennik Nr. 15* (1956); *Quin's Metal Handbook 1955* (London, 1956); *Metal and Mineral Markets*, 27 (London, Feb. 1956); *American Metal Market* (New York, Feb. 1956); *Materialy i oborudovanie primeniaemye v ugol'noi promyshlennosti* (Materials and equipment used in the coal industry), *1*, 286–91.

66. Borysiewicz, pp. 113–15.

than on the world market and were made wider still in Poland after January 1956. Such adjustments as the Polish planners made in adapting Soviet prices to "local conditions" were in the direction of raising the "price barrier" erected to deter consumers from ordering the scarcer metals.

As for the few other groups of close substitutes whose prices were systematically related (the various grades of coal and coke as well as certain ferroalloys), a similar tendency could be observed: the relative prices of the scarcer materials were increased out of proportion with world market relations.

Consider, for example, the pricing of coke. In Poland, foundry cokes were worth two and a half times the price of high-grade coking coals; the ratio of these two prices in Germany and Sweden was about 1.4. The Polish price of these same foundry cokes was sevenfold as high in 1953 as the price of finely granulated coke used for fuel; in the Ruhr the corresponding ratio was a little over twofold.[67]

Before trying to explain why the prices of substitutes fanned out to such an extent, we may comment briefly on the "complex relation." It has already been mentioned that prices of material inputs set according to this formula were supposed to compensate consumers for the uneven quality of deliveries and to leave them indifferent as to which grades of materials they received from the rationing organization. The way to do this was to pick out some standard type of equipment and to measure the differential effect of various grades of materials on its productivity.

This method suffers from serious limitations and shortcomings:

1) The basic aim of the method cannot be achieved unless all production functions of consumers are identical. If they are not, then the cost increment due to the consumption of a given material will differ according to the type of equipment used, and it will not be possible to safeguard the costs of consumers from vicissitudes in the rationing process.

2) It is doubtful whether the costs of producers *should* be made independent of variations in the quality of materials consumed, even if these producers have no say in the selection of their inputs. For the purpose of allocating material inputs efficiently, the cost

67. Official price catalogues of the Planning Commission; *Kohlwirschaftszeitung*, nos. 6, 7 (1954); *Kommersiella Meddelanden*, no. 1 (1957).

records of steel mills are at least as useful to the organizations distributing cokes and iron ores as the technical information at their disposal. They will do a better job of allocation if they can check the effect on a mill's costs of changes in the composition of its coke intake or of its ore burden.

In essence, the complex relation rests on the assumption that administrative rationing, based on material balances unaided by price and cost comparisions, can be carried out in such way that every consuming enterprise will receive those inputs which it is best adapted to consume. Although designed to facilitate centralized control of management efficiency (by widening the scope of cost comparisons), the complex relation, with its emphasis on the formal-accounting properties of prices and costs, hindered the planners from broadening the allocative functions of the price system.

The equivalent relation (emphasizing demand elements in price setting) was at least in the spirit of price-guided decentralization. If it failed as a planning tool, as we believe it did, the reason is to be found not in the technique itself but in the institutional conditions governing the demand of socialized enterprises for material inputs.

5. *Theoretical Conclusions*

Prior to the 1956 reform, average-cost pricing was rudimentary: the secondary effects of price changes were hardly taken into account. For the 1956 reform, the Planning Commission, with the help of economists and accountants in the field, sought to eliminate all subsidies by tracing through several cycles of price increases until the final estimated prices just matched costs for the principal products taken into consideration. This procedure, as we shall show below, was theoretically sound (within the limits of average-cost pricing); if the reform eventually failed, in the sense that the cost inflation soon caused renewed financial losses in key industries such as coal mining, the fault was not in the iterative process itself but in the inordinate length of time it took to carry it out and in the inability of the planners to start the "paper cycles" over again each time the costs of basic raw materials went up.

The algebraic solution to the average-cost pricing problem will first be outlined; then it will be shown that this solution would in fact be attained by the iterative procedure described for the 1956 reform.

We shall let a_{ij} stand for the technical coefficients relating the input of good i to a unit of output of good j (both input and output being measured in physical terms). There are n goods ($j = 1, 2, \ldots, n$). The symbol a_{oj} will denote the value added (wages, depreciation, and profits) per unit of output of every good j.[68]

If the prices $(p_1, p_2, \ldots, p_n)$ of the goods produced just covered average costs, then:

1)
$$p_1 = a_{11}\, p_1 + a_{21}\, p_2 \ldots + a_{n1}\, p_n + a_{o1}$$
$$p_2 = a_{12}\, p_2 + a_{22}\, p_2 \ldots + a_{n2}\, p_n + a_{o2}$$

$$p_n = a_{1n}\, p_1 + a_{2n}\, p_2 \ldots + a_{nn}\, p_n + a_{on}$$

or, multiplying both sides by -1 and transposing terms:

2)
$$a_{o1} = (1 - a_{11})\, p_1 - a_{21}\, p_2 \ldots - a_{n1}\, p_n$$
$$a_{o2} = - a_{12}\, p_1 + (1 - a_{22})\, p_2 \ldots - a_{n2}\, p_n$$

$$a_{on} = - a_{1n}\, p_1 - a_{2n}\, p_2 \ldots + (1 - a_{nn})\, p_n$$

Denoting the vector of "value added per unit of output" by $\overline{a_{oj}}$ and the column vector of prices $(p_1, \ldots, p_n)'$ by p we may write 2) in matrix notation:

3)
$$[\mathbf{I} - \mathbf{A}]'\, p = \overline{a_{oj}}$$

68. For our scheme to work, wages, depreciation, and profits must be independent of the value of material costs. In Polish practice, profits are usually tacked on as a percentage of production costs. But the resulting error will be small since profits make up at most 3 or 4 per cent of costs. The depreciation problem could be more troublesome since, technically, prices of equipment should be significantly affected by every round of price increase of materials, and depreciation allowances should rise *pari passu*. In the 1956 reform, however, depreciation allowances were based on a multiple (usually doubling) of past allowances, without regard to the exact effect of the new prices on the cost of equipment.

where $[\mathbf{I} - \mathbf{A}]'$ is the transpose of the Leontief matrix of technical coefficients.[69]

To solve the above expression for the price vector $\bar{p}$ we need only pre-multiply both sides of 3) by the inverse of the transposed matrix:

4) $$\left[[\mathbf{I} - \mathbf{A}]'\right]^{-1} [\mathbf{I} - \mathbf{A}]'\, \bar{p} = \bar{p} = \left[[\mathbf{I} - \mathbf{A}]'\right]^{-1} \overline{a_{oj}}$$

After expanding the last expression on the right we obtain:

5) $$\bar{p} = \left[\mathbf{I} + \mathbf{A}' + [\mathbf{A}']^2 + \ldots [\mathbf{A}']^m\right] \overline{a_{oj}}$$

The exponent m in the above expressions corresponds to the number of iterations needed to reduce $\mathbf{A}^m$ to an array of negligibly small numbers.

Let us now follow through the algebra of the iterative procedure used in Polish planning. We start with a given price level $\bar{p}^{(0)}$ (an n-dimensional vector), which may be chosen arbitrarily but which in practice will actually equal the level of prereform prices. Our first estimate $\bar{p}^{(0)}$ of the new prices just covers costs at the old price level (including the invariant value-added costs $\overline{a_{oj}}$):

$$p_1^{(1)} = a_{11}\, p_1^{(0)} + a_{21}\, p_2^{(0)} \ldots + a_{n1}\, p_n^{(0)} + a_{o1}$$
$$p_2^{(1)} = a_{12}\, p_1^{(0)} + a_{22}\, p_2^{(0)} \ldots + a_{n2}\, p_n^{(0)} + a_{o2}$$

$$p_n^{(1)} = a_{1n}\, p_1^{(0)} + a_{2n}\, p_2^{(0)} \ldots a_{nn}\, p_n^{(0)} + a_{on}$$

In matrix terms, the above system of equations reduces to:

6) $$\bar{p}^{(1)} = \mathbf{A}'\, \bar{p}^{(0)} + \overline{a_{oj}}$$

where $\mathbf{A}'$ is the transpose of the matrix of technical coefficients $\mathbf{A}$.

In the second round, costs are just covered at the prices obtained in the first round:

7) $$\bar{p}^{(2)} = \mathbf{A}'\, \bar{p}^{(1)} + \overline{a_{oj}} = [\mathbf{A}']^2\, \bar{p}^{(0)} + \mathbf{A}'\, \overline{a_{oj}} + \overline{a_{oj}}$$

69. For the Leontief matrix, see Appendix A, Sects. 1–3. In the transposed matrix $[\mathbf{I} - \mathbf{A}]'$, the rows and columns of the Leontief matrix $[\mathbf{I} - \mathbf{A}]$ are interchanged, i.e. every element a_{ij} in the original matrix becomes the element a_{ji} in the transposed matrix. The diagonal elements remain unchanged.

For the $(m + 1)$'th round we have:

8) $\qquad \bar{p}^{(m + 1)} = \mathbf{A}' \, \bar{p}^{(m)} + \overline{a_{oj}} = [\mathbf{A}']^{m + 1} \, \bar{p}^{(0)} +$
$\qquad\qquad \left[\mathbf{I} + \mathbf{A}' + [\mathbf{A}']^2 + \cdots [\mathbf{A}']^m \right] \overline{a_{oj}}$

If the number of iterations is large enough the term $[\mathbf{A}']^{m + 1} \, \bar{p}^{(0)}$ will vanish, on the assumption that the largest characteristic root of the matrix $\mathbf{A}$ is smaller than one.[70] This will be the case if the system is indecomposable and if the economy thus represented is capable of generating any net output whatsoever.[71]

This last result is then identical with that obtained by the simultaneous solution of the system of equations summarized in expressions 4) and 5).[72]

We may conclude that if the matrix of technical coefficients is such that a consistent set of material balances can be reached by iteration, then a system of average-cost prices can also be found by iteration. *Mutatis mutandis,* if a system of prices can be found such that it just covers production costs including invariant labor costs, depreciation allowances, and profits, a consistent set of material balances can be approximated by an iterative procedure. The essential difference between the two types of iteration is this: in planning practice, the "control figures" or plan directives, issued at the beginning of the planning period, provide a first approximation of the gross outputs: the initial error need not be very large and it may be reduced to a satisfactory level in a very few iterations. Whereas the procedure followed in setting prices is to start with the old set of prices which, if the cost inflation has been severe, may be 50 per cent or less of the price level that will eventually be necessary to cover all costs simultaneously. It should therefore normally take at least four or five rounds to achieve a convergent level of prices or a reasonable approximation to this goal. This is perhaps the main reason why many officials of the

70. The characteristic roots of a transposed matrix are identical with the roots of the original matrix.

71. See Appendix A, Sect. 3.

72. After completing this analysis, we came upon a similar iterative process and an equivalent proof of convergence in a paper by the Soviet mathematical economist A. Boyarski entitled "Sebestoimost' i stoimost'" (Cost and value), published in *Voprosy ekonomiki planirovania i statistiki* (Problems of economics, planning, and statistics), pp. 72–82.

Planning Commission, though they were quite aware of the feedback effects (*powtórne wpływy*) of raising the prices of materials, failed to perceive or to understand the nature of these repercussions when interdependent material balances were being consecutively adjusted.

Once prices have been set at a level permitting all branches of industry to cover their production costs, the next task is to differentiate the prices of materials so as to induce desirable substitution reactions on the part of producers and investors. We have seen that the price spreads between substitutes that the planners deemed necessary to bring about these reactions were very wide in practice, wider actually than the corresponding spreads prevailing on world markets.

Two explanations suggest themselves, which will be discussed in turn: first, the institutional framework of planning makes firms insensitive to increases in costs due to price changes; second, the rationing of materials blunts the effect of the state's price policy. In either case, a larger spread will be required to achieve a given substitution reaction than if the materials were available at market-clearing prices.

1) If the resources placed at the disposal of the enterprise are fixed, managers, whether they are trying to maximize profits or to earn a bonus based on increases in output, cost reductions, or both, will find it advantageous to minimize the costs of the output for which they choose to target. None of the bonus systems described in Chapter Six should induce managers to produce inefficiently, i.e. inside the production possibilities surface determined by the fixed amount of resources available to them. Supposing that managers were free to choose among inputs at parametric (fixed) prices and that the total production costs of the enterprise could not exceed a certain sum of money per period of time, then it would be rational for managers to consume any two materials in such a way as to equalize the ratio of their marginal productivities (in producing any product) with the ratio of their prices. If one of the inputs were rationed while the others were not, then production possibilities would not be confined to a "simplex" (e.g. in two dimensions by a triangle with its apex at the origin) but by a polyhedron. This is illustrated in two dimensions in Diagram 8:1 below: If both inputs A and B are obtainable at parametric prices,

the production-possibilities surface can be represented by the triangle *a b o*, production will take place at *p*, and output will be equal to x_3 units. If the consumption of material *I* cannot exceed *o d*, then *a c d o* is the limiting polyhedron and *c* is the best possible point, whatever bonus system may be in force.

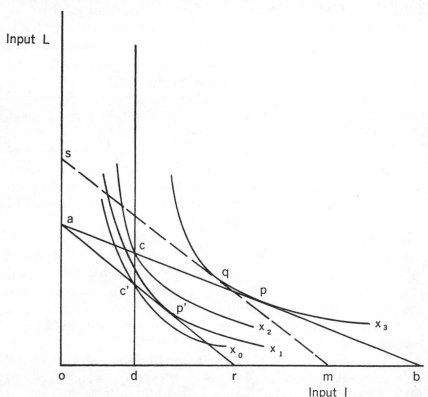

DIAGRAM 8:1. *The Consumption of Inputs under Fixed and Flexible Cost Budgets*

Under these conditions a change in the relative prices of inputs *L* and *I* must provoke a change in their relative consumption (unless both goods are rationed). Assuming the price of *I* increases, the two new equilibria—one corresponding to the free purchase of both inputs *L* and *I*, the other to the rationing of input *I*—are indicated in Diagram 8:1 by the points *p'* and *c'* respectively.

But no such change need come about if the authorities supervising the enterprise are willing to condone a higher level of planned costs after the relative increase in the price of input *I*.

They may, for instance, approve costs equal to *os* in terms of (un-rationed) input *L,* which would make it possible for the firm, if both inputs were freely available, to achieve the same output x_3 as before the rise in the price of *I*. There would then be some substitution of *L* for *I*, but far less than if the original cost ceiling had been maintained. Assuming a similar policy in the case where input *I* were rationed (limited to *o d*), the new cost line, which has not been sketched, would be parallel to *a r* and would go through point *c* (to enable the firm to produce the old output x_2); there would be no change at all in the relative consumption of inputs *L* and *I*, compared to the situation before the price increase.

Notice, however, that if the enterprise sets its own restraints—if managers can somehow be induced to cut costs even at the expense of output gains—price movements may cause the substitution of inputs even in the absence of restrictive cost plans. The evidence presented in Chapter Six pointing to the overwhelming impact of output bonuses suggests that self-restraint on the part of managers is not likely to take the place of externally imposed resource limitations.

In general we may conclude that as long as the officials supervising the cost plans of enterprises are willing to pass approval on cost budgets that more or less mechanically incorporate price increases, then the impact of these changes must remain small; or equivalently a large change is necessary to bring about a desired effect.

2) The rationing of inputs also tended to diminish the impact on consumption decisions of the price spreads between substitutable materials fixed by the Planning Commission. It is clear that if all inputs were rationed, prices could have no influence whatever on consumption decisions. In order to induce the substitution of one rationed input by another in more abundant supply through the agency of the price mechanism, there must be some freely available inputs whose purchase can be increased or curtailed as a result of price changes. In Soviet-type economies, labor is the principal factor of production whose allocation is decentralized. An increase in the price of a rationed material will leave less funds available to hire labor (unless of course the supervising central board is willing to authorize an increase in the cost plan offsetting the rise in price). If the threatened reduction in the wage bill is

large enough, the director of an enterprise may prefer to replace the input whose price has risen by an ersatz material, which, though inferior in productivity, will leave sufficient funds to maintain an adequate labor force. This situation is illustrated in Diagram 8:2, where the two horizontal axes represent the consumption of materials A and B and the vertical axis represents the consumption of labor. Only one product, whose level of output is shown by the x-isoquants, is produced by this hypothetical enterprise.

First consider point p which is located on an isoquant corresponding to a production of 100.

This point can be attained by using only two inputs: labor and material A. If material A could be acquired in unlimited quantities at the price indicated by the slope of $st,$ a higher output than 100 would become feasible by substituting material A for labor. But only oa units of A are rationed out to the firm, which cannot do better than point p with these two inputs. We shall suppose that the firm may also apply for material B instead of A (mixtures of A and B are excluded) at the price $sv,$ but in the limited amount ob. The shift from A to B would in this case be disadvantageous since at the optimum point q the index of output of x is only 90. Maintaining the rations of A and B as they are, we may ask, how much should the price of material B be lowered to induce the firm to shift its orders from material A to material B? At the price sw the price line crosses the vertical line drawn from b at an x-isoquant just larger than 100. Assuming no inertia or friction, this drop in the relative price of B will be sufficient to bring about the substitution of B for $A,$ and q' will be the new equilibrium.

But if material B is in ample enough supply to warrant its being placed on unlimited sale, then its price need only be lowered to sy to cause the shift: the equilibrium will be at q'', and the consumption of B will exceed ob.

When both materials are rationed, the only possibility of reaching a higher isoquant through a lower price of one of the materials is to intensify the consumption of the freely available complementary factor (labor in our example), more of which can be purchased as a result of the cost-reduction associated with the price cut. The substitution effect can be induced by means of a less radical price adjustment if the inferior material, whose consumption is to be

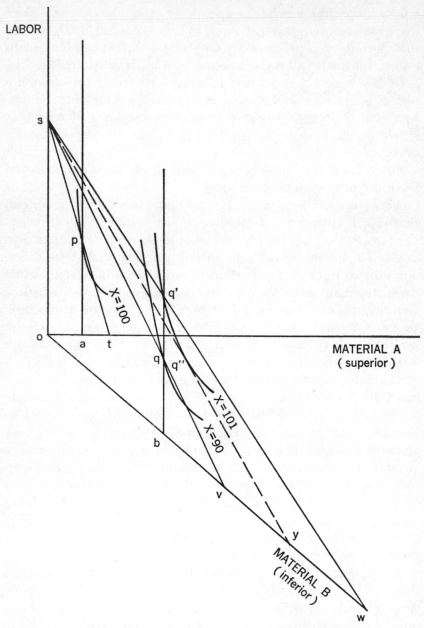

LABOR

MATERIAL A
(superior)

X=100

X=101

X=90

MATERIAL B
(inferior)

DIAGRAM 8:2. *The Impact of Prices under Conditions of Materials Rationing*
(Fixed Cost Budget)

encouraged, can be purchased in unlimited quantities; for then more labor *and* more of the material can be had than before the price cut.[73] Basically, the elasticity of substitution of unrationed for rationed inputs is the main determinant of the effectiveness of price policy when one or more materials are rationed. If, for example, it is sufficient to assign more labor (stokers) to tend furnaces fired with inferior coals to obtain the desired steam pressure then a moderate price discount will be sufficient to cause the shift. But if most of the furnaces of coal consumers are fed automatically, inferior coals may be given away free and still fail to attract clients.

This applies mainly in the short run. In the long run there are possibilities of converting or adapting the equipment to burn the cheaper fuel; if this can be done at a reasonable investment cost, the discounts will be attractive to consumers who cannot take immediate advantage of the lower price. Many of these minor investment outlays being decentralized, the long-run demand for inferior fuels is appreciably more price-elastic than in the short run. If the Planning Commission wishes to encourage innovations and decentralized investments tending to diminish the consumption of the scarcest materials, it must set prices that will reward these efforts financially, and, in particular, will enable firms to recoup their outlays in less than the prescribed period (one year for most projects prior to 1956).

The forces so far described have all conspired to widen the price spreads between materials which the Planning Commission must establish if it wishes to harmonize its directives with respect to the allocation of scarce materials with the applications for these materials and with the investment policy of socialized enterprises. There is one factor, nevertheless, that would tend to narrow price spreads among substitutes in the conditions of the Polish economy: the built-in bias in favor of output gains at any cost tends to put heavy pressure on the demand for high-productivity inputs

73. Each of the successive isoquants crossed by the vertical line originating at *b* should be steeper because more labor is being consumed with a fixed amount of the cooperant factor *B* and the marginal productivity of labor must be decreasing. Hence the lower the price of *B*, the larger the contribution a small extra amount above the *ob* ration can make toward increasing output. If *ob* is fixed, there may come a point where its further cheapening will have no effect on the output index, as the marginal productivity of labor will have dropped to zero. From that point on, a negative price of *B* would be required to induce a shift from *A* to *B*: consumers of *B* would have to be paid to consume the ersatz material.

(e.g. on the best coals). The unsatisfied demand at prevailing prices for these inputs is larger than for other rationed substitutes.[74] If equilibrium prices were to be set for all inputs, the prices of the superior materials would rise more than the others, especially if the financial authorities were willing to authorize the larger cost budgets necessary to translate this potential into effective demand. The "equilibrium" price spreads would probably be wider than under profit-maximizing conditions where a decrease in costs would be given the same attention and effort as an increase in sales of the same magnitude. As the statistical comparisons we made were with prices prevailing in world markets, not with the prices that would have prevailed in Poland if the materials had been auctioned off to managers of firms bent on achieving their output bonuses, all we can do is to suggest reasons why the prices of substitutes should fan out to an abnormal extent wherever we observe this trend.

Taking for granted that price spreads among pairs of substitutes must be unusually large to be effective, we may still ask whether the planners can set the prices of entire chains of substitutable materials in such a way as to reinforce their allocation decisions in consistent fashion. This might be possible if the Planning Commission, freed of doctrinal prejudices, could systematically sever the link between prices and production costs (leaving the Ministry of Finance the responsibility for juggling the profits and subsidies that would result from such a policy). Unless this was done, there would always be some substitute priced at average cost which would be out of line with the others. Take, for example, the case of solid fuels, which form one long chain of substitutes. Let the prices of the various sizes and grades of bituminous coal be differentiated around an average approximately equal to production costs (so as to permit the entire industry to operate at a small profit margin). Low-calorie coals, such as slack and slurry residues, will have to be assigned near-zero prices to attract consumers. These low prices will run against the government's policy to replace bituminous coal—including the inferior grades—by lignite and

74. This was made clear in discussions with officials familiar with the marketing of coals to the socialized sector and in interviews with the personnel of sales centrals dealing with other commodities.

peat, which are produced at a relatively high cost (lower than the average for coal but higher than the prices of slack and slurry determined in this manner). Similarly, copper prices must be set low relative to imported nickel and tin, but high relative to zinc, which is domestically produced and must cover production costs. If zinc is priced below cost, this will spur the substitution of zinc for cast iron in keys, locks, and other hardware (as actually occurred in the early 1950s) unless steel itself is priced at a loss. But if steel is priced too low, this would upset the plans for the bakelite industry which produces plastic sheets competing with steel in many uses: a policy promoting the consumption of bakelite but making it profitable for enterprises to order steel sheets will run up against the bad will of consumers, who would be likely to try and bypass official allocations, thereby disrupting the distribution system. If on the other hand bakelite is priced at cost, it must be "protected" from the competition of steel, zinc, copper, and nickel by extra large spreads; these metals, particularly the higher members of the chain, will then have to be priced way above cost. Not only would this be in conflict with the official prescriptions about average-cost pricing but it might also lead to concrete errors in investment policy: if nickel were priced too high, any calculations of the costs and returns of mining or beneficiating low-yield nickel ores would be distorted, and uneconomic investments in these lines would result.

Prices are delicate instruments. The desirable effects they produce in the short run may be disastrous in the long run if they cause malinvestments; they may help unload a material in surplus, yet cause the waste of complementary inputs. Prices may be set just right to support the policy of a marketing organization distributing substitutes, but they may cause the wrong reaction on the part of the producers of these materials.

In Chapter One where we discussed the essential interdependence of rational prices and outputs, we found that even marginal-cost pricing would not generate rational prices if the underlying allocation determining these costs was not fully efficient. When this last obstacle is added to those already analyzed, we can see what difficulties the price-planners were up against. It is ironic that they never realized the nature of these dilemmas. Because they did not venture very far from the safe premises of average-cost pricing, they never faced the contradictions that a more forceful policy would have exposed.

In Chapter Nine, devoted to an analysis of the economic policies of the Gomulka regime, we shall study the price policy behind the price reforms of 1957 and July 1960. We shall find that the responsible officials, ill-equipped with theory, dodged by compromises, also failed to test the limitations of price-setting policy in a materials-rationing system.

CHAPTER NINE

The Polish Model: 1956-60

1. *The Thaw: March to September 1956*

Overcentralization and defective planning methods had not been immune from criticism prior to 1956, but this criticism had been confided to the relative obscurity of specialized journals; it touched on localized sores rather than on general ills.[1] Following the Twentieth Congress of the Communist Party of the U.S.S.R. in February 1956, the death in March of Bolesław Bierut, the First Party Secretary, and his replacement by Edward Ochab, who favored political "decompression," economic problems were subjected to much more searching analysis; after a few months the system itself—though not its socialist framework—came under attack, not only in the specialized journals but also in the glare of the daily press.

Ironically, it fell to Bronisław Minc, the brother of Hilary Minc, to wage the first determined assault on the bureaucratic practices of the Planning Commission and on its excessively centralized management of the economy. It was this same Minc who, as chief of the Coordinating Department of the Commission in the early 1950s, had taken a vigorous part in remolding the Polish system in the Soviet image and in instituting some of the practices that he now condemned. Minc did not restrict himself to a few sarcastic remarks on the planning of cucumbers and hares:[2] he called for "essential reforms," in contrast with the minor revisions made each year in the official books of instructions for making up the plans. "First of all," Minc wrote, "we must substantially restrict

1. See for example *IB* and *GM* for 1954 and 1955. Some adverse comments taken from these journals were cited in previous chapters
2. See Chap. 3, p. 90.

the scope of directives laid down by the central authorities and accord a much wider measure of independence to enterprises and local organs." [3] He also pointed out that the elimination of routine duties would enable the planners to concentrate on long-range problems (e.g. on maintaining optimal proportions in the economic development of the country), on synthetic balances, on economic calculation in the field of investments and foreign trade, on price-setting, and on the elaboration of more effective material incentives for enterprises and their staff.

These recommendations set the official tone of the reforms which were carried out in the next four years. Less than a month later, the first decree extending the rights of the directors of state industrial enterprises was promulgated. The decree revealed how little power directors had come to exercise after years of growing intrusion and encroachment on the part of superior authorities. For the first time, the director of an enterprise was to become the ultimate authority on the enterprise's technical-industrial-financial plan. All that was required of such a plan was that it should conform to the "basic directives" in the yearly plans forwarded to the enterprise by its central board. This was an important step forward, since, as hard-to-fulfill and numerous as centrally assigned tasks might be, it was advantageous to be able to choose the best way to execute them. Henceforth the director could take on orders from customers not included in the plan, as long as this did not disrupt the fulfillment of his other targets. He could introduce minor technical changes designed to reduce costs or improve quality without requesting the permission of his superiors. He could apply for bank credits to finance small investment projects. He was granted more latitude in the use of his depreciation fund (for example in choosing to replace a machine rather than to overhaul it). If he kept within his wage-fund limit (one of the basic directives), he was permitted to adjust the average wage planned for the different categories of workers on his staff. In case new machines or improved technologies had been introduced, he was empowered to set temporary piece-rates for his workers until new norms had been worked out by specialists from the ministry appointed for this purpose.[4]

3. B. Minc, "W sprawie metod planowania" (On planning methods), *TL*, March 20, 1956.

4. *TL*, April 12, 1956.

On April 12, 1956, an animated session took place in the Polish *Sejm*, which, after many years of supine acquiescence to any and all legislative proposals by the Party, was now resuming its normal activities and questioning government representatives on the performance of their functions. Minister Eugeniusz Szyr, the head of the Planning Commission, was asked to report on the progress made toward decentralization. He told the delegates that the Central Board of Machine Economy, which functioned as the marketing organization for the machine-building industry, had been moved out of the Planning Commission and its activities divided between the Ministry of Metallurgy and the Ministry of Foreign Trade. The Planning Commission had also succeeded in unloading the organization in charge of collecting and delivering scrap, rejects, and remnants (*Centrala odpadkowa*) on the Ministry of Metallurgy. Szyr alleged that the provincial planning commissions [5] and the local peoples' councils had been granted more leeway in preparing their plans.[6] The economic leadership was already on the defensive.

During the late spring and early summer, *Trybuna Ludu*, the official Party newspaper, ran a series of articles written by contributors in the field—plant managers, officials in the economic administration, and minor party leaders—on the economic system and on the need for its reform. At first, proposals for improvement touched only on the administrative arrangements: no one pressed for a radical dismantling of the central apparatus or for a revival of markets. One writer proposed the liquidation of the central boards of industry and the concentration of their most highly qualified personnel in the specialized departments of the ministries, which were capable of supervising their subordinate enterprises without intervening links.[7] Another was of contrary opinion, arguing that the powers of the central boards should be increased, while the departments of ministries should be eliminated.[8] A few days later, in an article with the significant title

5. On the atrophy of their functions prior to this date, see Chap. 3, Sect. 1.

6. *TL*, April 13, 1960.

7. He pointed out that there were 141 central boards of industry, with 19,000 employees in addition to 159 "functional central boards" (mainly market and procurement organizations) with 13,500 employees. See L. Guz, "Centralne zarządy czy departamenty branżowe" (Central boards or branch departments), *TL*, May 31, 1956.

8. A. Kawecki, "Rozszerzyć kompetencje C.Z." (Widen the competence of the central boards), *TL*, May 31, 1956.

"Half-way measures will not help," an engineer decried the petty interference of the Planning Commission, of the National Bank, and of the Ministry of Finance in the affairs of producers. He outdid his predecessors in his suggestion that the Planning Commission be restricted to three functions: (1) the elaboration of mutually consistent plans for the development of the different sectors of the national economy; (2) the balancing and distribution of critical products; (3) price-setting and the allocation of profits.[9] At about the same time, in *Nowe Drogi,* the official journal of the United Workers' Party, Henryk Fiszel published an interesting theoretical article, where he sought to rally Party economists to the idea of charging interest on the fixed assets placed at the disposal of socialized enterprises. This might be a good way, he argued, of encouraging managers to rationalize the use of plant and equipment.[10] The suggestion was manifestly unorthodox, at least by Marxist-Soviet standards.

The pitch of the discussion rose with the Second Congress of Economists which took place June 7–10, 1956. The congress was attended by 800 university economists, plant managers, officials in the economic administration, and other amalgamated members of the profession, representing every part of the country. *Trybuna Ludu* captured the essential significance of the congress in an editorial comment preceding the debates: "In the present period of animated discussion on economic matters, there is an acute need for a theoretical analysis of the principles on which the economy functions and on the methods used to direct it." [11] For the last few months, specific malfunctions in the centrally planned system had been detected and exposed; it was now up to the theorists to reveal the etiology of these disorders and to place them in their proper analytical context.

Many of the participants had hoped that Oskar Lange, who was scheduled to be the first speaker at the congress, would lead the way. They were disappointed. Lange dwelled at length on the successes of the Six-Year Plan and on the development of Marxist economics in Poland since 1949. He did point out that "political economy" had been wrongfully displaced by "moral-political ap-

9. J. Jesionowski in *TL,* June 4, 1956.

10. H. Fiszel, "O prawdziwy rachunek ekonomiczny" (For a correct economic calculation), *ND,* no. 5 (1956), 45–46.

11. *TL,* June 8, 1956.

peals and administrative orders," [12] but he had nothing new to offer along theoretical lines. His concrete suggestions were stereotyped. Prices of both producer and consumer goods must be set "in accord with the law of value"; the material interests of the staff of socialized enterprises must be more closely geared to their financial results; investment calculations must be perfected, and so forth. The speech was not in the spirit of the gathering. The public desired more potent medicine. Subsequently, Lange's apology for the system (or what was regarded as such) came under attack by younger economists. Stefan Kurowski, in particular, argued that theoretical economics was not flourishing at all but had been impoverished in recent years by "dogmatism, exegesis, an uncritical attitude toward Soviet science, and the lack of free scientific discussion." [13]

Edward Lipiński, the dean of Warsaw economists, ventured further in his conclusions than Lange. In his view, central planning was "an impediment to economic development"; it was necessary therefore to decentralize the economy and to grant greater autonomy and initiative to socialized enterprises.[14]

Bronisław Minc cast his stone at Stalin's "law of socialist development," formerly held immune from criticism, according to which the capital-goods industries (sector I of the economy in Marx's reproduction scheme) must necessarily grow faster than consumer-goods industries (sector II). This faster rise, in Minc's opinion, was nothing more than a historical phenomenon in the development of the Soviet Union. By implication, this law need not apply to Poland where other conditions prevailed.[15]

Włodzimierz Brus, a professor at the University of Warsaw and a high official of the Planning Commission, made what was perhaps the most important speech at the congress. Its significance was heightened by the fact that Brus had once been one of the most orthodox Marxists in Poland and a trusted protégé of the Party. This was the gist of his contribution:

> In a socialist economy it is inconceivable that production should be severed from market conditions. If products are transferred to consumers through the market, this means that

12. *Ekonomista*, no. 5 (1956), 9.
13. *TL*, June 8, 1956.
14. Ibid.
15. *TL*, June 9, 1956.

the reverse process of adjusting the structure of production to consumer demand must take place through the transmission of market impulses to the productive sphere. The planned targets should be implemented by economic means, which would induce enterprises to choose the kinds of products and the levels of output which have been laid down in the balances . . . If prices are set correctly, the financial results of enterprises can become the main criterion of their economic activities.[16]

At a later point in his speech, Brus linked together "decentralization and democratization." This introduced a new political element in the discussion, which for many Poles overshadowed all theoretical issues in the turbulent months that lay ahead.

In his closing address to the congress, Lange caught up with his audience. He conceded that all was not well with the state of Polish economic science which had "gradually slipped toward apologetic functions." Decentralization in the planning and management of the economy was indeed necessary, and so was a fully efficient economic calculus.[17]

Once those who had preached Marxist theory and proclaimed the benefits of central planning for the last decade had themselves cast doubt on some of the most sacred tenets of the faith, it was too much to expect that the uninitiated, the lumpen-intellectuals, would refrain from adverse comment. In the months that followed the congress, journalists, writers, poets, and jokesters outdid each other in their attacks on central planning.[18]

On June 28, the workers of a large locomotive factory in Poznan, who had gone on strike to protest against high norms and low wages, marched in the streets calling for "bread and freedom." They were joined by thousands of irate citizens. The demonstration soon became political in character. The marchers clashed with the security police (U.B.). Regular troops and tanks had to be summoned to quell the disorder. At the official count 53 persons lost their lives in the fray.[19] Less than three weeks later the

16. *TL,* June 10, 1956.
17. Ibid.
18. See, for example, the satirical journal *Szpilki* (Pins and needles), for April, May, and June, 1956.
19. Dziewanowski, *The Communist Party of Poland,* p. 265.

Central Committee of the United Workers' Party convened in plenary session. The deliberations of this Seventh Plenum turned on the causes and consequences of the "Poznań events." Edward Ochab, the recently appointed First Party Secretary, devoted a good part of his keynote speech to the economic background of the crisis. He pointed out that 75 per cent of the workers at the *Zispo* factory where the strike had originated had suffered a pay cut after progressive piece-rates for the overfulfillment of norms had been eliminated in the fall of 1955. This situation had been "corrected" in November but the arrears that had been promised to compensate workers for their foregone earnings had not been paid. Another complaint rooted deep in the system was that workers received only a part of their normal pay when production breakdowns, due to materials shortages, forced them to lie idle. Passing to the more general sources of disaffection, he pinned most of the blame for low real wages—or for their failure to rise according to expectation—on the hasty build up of defense industries which had not been envisaged in the officially approved version of the Six-Year Plan. He also castigated the excessive centralization of planning and management which had developed concurrently with the revisions in the plans. "As a consequence of this system, mistakes, once made, were magnified and became impacted . . . Local initiative—the initiative of the staff and management of factories—was paralyzed." [20]

The resolutions of the Seventh Plenum called for the liquidation of excessive centralization in the planning and administration of the economy and a reduction in the number of the central directives binding on industrial enterprises. Managers of enterprises were promised more autonomy; central powers were to be delegated to provincial authorities, who were expected to transfer some of *their* powers to local organs. Henceforth incentive schemes for management would be designed to encourage the elimination of waste, the compression of costs, and the improvement in the quality of goods produced, instead of just stimulating indiscriminate increases in output. The enterprise fund should be reinforced by larger deductions from profits. Finally, a new policy was announced designed to ease the supply situation of industrial enterprises: production plans would from now on be based on "realistic

20. *TL*, July 20, 1956.

estimates" of the supplies of materials necessary to fulfill the plans, and sufficient inventories of raw materials and semifabricates would be assigned to plants to permit them to work "rhythmically" (i.e. without production breakdowns).[21] In later sections we shall see how these resolutions were translated into decrees and ordinances which modified the old system and laid the basis for what later became known as the "Polish model."

Toward the end of the summer a new institution made its appearance, as if by spontaneous generation. This was the workers' councils, many of which were set up in parallel with, and often in opposition to, the plant councils (rady zakładowe) representing the trade union organization at the factory level. The trade union movement had acted for so long as an instrument of the state for enforcing labor discipline and tightening up work-norms that the belated efforts made at the Seventh Plenum and at the Trade Union Congress in August to regain the workers' confidence by increasing the autonomy of the plant councils had fallen flat.[22] The plant councils, being dominated by representatives of the Party and of management, remained unpopular among the rank-and-file workers.

The visit of high Party officials to Yugoslavia where they observed the workers' councils in action had apparently been influential in determining a tolerant, if not a patronizing, attitude toward the newly formed councils in a few Polish factories.[23] The councils received official Party sanction in the resolutions of the Eighth Plenum in October 1956, which hailed the initiative of workers in creating their own organs of self-management. The extension of the prerogatives of the plant councils which had taken place after the Seventh Plenum no longer "answered the aspira-

21. TL, July 31, 1956.

22. Wiktor Kłosiewicz, the chairman of the Central Council of the Trade Unions, was associated with the Stalinist or "Natolin" group of the Party. He was so disliked by the workers that until he was dismissed from his post, shortly after the Eighth Plenum in October, nothing could be done to assuage the distrust in which the organization was commonly held. Kłosiewicz at the Eighth Plenum denounced the head of the Party organization at the Zeran works who had dared to call the trade unions "an open sore on the healthy organism of the working class." See ND, no. 10 (1956), 83.

23. Tadeusz Daniszewski reported favorably on the visit of the Party delegation to Yugoslavia and on the Yugoslav workers' councils in his speech to the Eighth Plenum. See ND, no. 10 (1956), 100.

tions of the most active part of the working class." [24] Workers' self-management, representing the entire staff, was to participate in the management of the enterprise, that is, in setting production plans, in deciding questions of norms and wages, in apportioning funds left at the disposal of the plant, and in other functions. The new organs would be privileged "to take a direct part in the appointment and removal of the director." [25]

Besides the resolutions on the workers' councils, the Eighth Plenum had little to offer in the way of institutional reforms in the nationalized sector. The government still had not caught up with the reforms proposed by the Seventh Plenum; many decrees and ordinances remained to be drafted before the plenum's resolutions were to be realized. The Eighth Plenum had more important work to do. It had to thrash out all the political questions that had been raised but had not been settled at the last two plenums: the sovereignty of Poland and her relation to the Soviet Union; anti-Semitism in the Party; the cult of personality and the abrogation of Party democracy; police terror during the Stalinist years; the personal responsibility of top leaders such as Jakub Berman and Hilary Minc for "the errors of the past"; and perhaps most important the personnel changes that were necessary to correct previous abuses and to restore a measure of popular confidence in the Party. The reinstatement of Władysław Gomulka as First Party Secretary, the post he had held until 1948, and the elimination of a number of Stalinist die-hards from the Politbureau and from the Central Committee were the most widely hailed results of the plenum. The vehement opposition of Khrushchev and of the other members of the Soviet delegation who had flown to Warsaw to negotiate with the Central Committee on the contemplated shake-up in its top leadership rallied public opinion to the Party and shored up Gomulka's reputation as a Communist patriot.

Gomulka's popularity upon his accession to power was reinforced by several measures indicating his intention to rule by consent rather than by fear. The security police was curbed, as were the arbitrary powers of provincial party bosses.[26] As soon as the

24. *ND*, no. 10 (1956), 6.
25. Ibid.
26. The present writer, who was in Warsaw when these events were taking place,

government vouchsafed freedom from interference in the affairs of collective farms and guaranteed their right to break up into private farms, their members began to desert in droves.[27] By the end of 1956, about 8,500 out of a total of 10,500 collectives registered in September had been dissolved; membership had fallen from 165,000 families in 1955 to 21,000 families. In December the collectives were left with only 1.4 per cent of the country's farm land, as against 11.2 per cent in June.[28] Another popular measure was the dissolution of the Village Machine Centers (G.O.M.) and the sale of most of their equipment to individual farmers and to voluntary peasant associations during the last two months of 1956 and in the first half of 1957.[29]

2. *Theoretical Discussions of the Polish Model after October*

In this brief survey, justice cannot be done to the numerous conceptions and schemes spawned in the months of active discussion after October. We shall single out three basic approaches to the "new model," which entered into the compromise plan finally hammered out by the newly created Economic Council attached to the Council of Ministers.[30]

First, there were the views of the extreme "value-men" (*wartościowscy*) who believed in consumers' sovereignty and in the use of the market mechanism, untrammeled by administrative controls, to bring about the allocation of resources corresponding to

---

sensed a tremendous release of tension immediately after the October Plenum. Up to mid-October, the security police and its informers still lurked in the background and made their presence felt, despite the gradual liberalization of the regime in recent months (particularly noticeable in the easing of censorship).

27. The resolutions of the Eighth Plenum had declared that it was necessary to dissolve weak collectives. Nevertheless they reaffirmed the necessity of collectivizing the countryside (to eliminate all forms of exploitation of man by man, to mechanize farm production, etc.). See *ND*, no. 10 (1956), 11.

28. *RS 1957*, pp. 137–39.

29. For detailed data see *RS 1957*, p. 144.

30. The Economic Council, which was founded soon after the Eighth Plenum, was to advise the government on economic legislation and on current planning problems. Oskar Lange was appointed as chairman and Czesław Bobrowski as vice-chairman. Bobrowski, the former head of the Central Planning Office, was (and still is) its moving spirit and promoter. In 1957, the membership of the Economic Council included the most prominent Warsaw economists (including, besides Lange and Bobrowski, M. Kalecki, W. Brus, J. Drewnowski, J. Pajestka, E. Lipinski, L. Horowitz, etc.).

consumers' demand. They wished to confine central planning to indirect—monetary and fiscal—pressures to prod the economy along a steady path of development (again compatible with the evolution of market demand). Certain key investment decisions might be made centrally, but only as long as the sovereignty of consumers was observed. The foremost proponent of these views was Stefan Kurowski, a young Warsaw economist who had specialized in the problems of the building industry. Kurowski in his article on "The model and the ends" argued that the planners, by imposing a pattern of allocation during the Stalinist era that was in flagrant conflict with the preferences of consumers, had been forced to rely on centralized controls. The ends, the armament build-up and the rapid expansion of heavy industry to support it, had determined the means, administration of the economy by *fiat* and the relegation of the price system to cost-accounting and record-keeping. Moreover,

> the creation of an apparatus of administrators was not sufficient in itself to guarantee the functioning of the system, which . . . , in order to attain its strategic ends, had to overcome the resistance of society. A separate apparatus, which we shall call an apparatus of "stabilization," was founded to overcome this resistance, to maintain the system, to execute administrative orders and control their fulfillment, and to defend the privileges of the bureaucracy. It is more than certain that a system of central administration of the economy in conflict with consumers' preferences would not last a month if it were not for the presence of this apparatus of stabilization.[31]

This link between political repression ("the apparatus of stabilization") and centralized planning was central to Kurowski's thinking. For Kurowski, as for F. von Hayek and W. Röpke who influenced him in this respect, economic decentralization, democracy, and consumers' sovereignty were inseparable.[32] One of his

31. S. Kurowski, "Model a cele gospodarki narodowej" (The model and the ends of the national economy), *ZG*, no. 7 (1957), 2.

32. Another advocate of consumer's sovereignty, Józef Popkiewicz, concentrated on the revival of markets and on price policy rather than on the political aspects of the problem; see "Prawdziwa rentowność" (True profitability), *TL*, January 6, 1957.

opponents correctly pointed out that this belief ignored the Yugo-slav experience with decentralized planning under conditions of planners' sovereignty.[33]

Oskar Lange, whose views on most points diverged from Kurow-ski's, shared the latter's distrust of planners' preferences, insofar as they tended to shunt Poland's development along autarkic lines:

> The Stalinist scheme of industrialization . . . was not suited to a mechanical transfer to Poland, a country of entirely dif-ferent economic and geographic conditions . . . A miniature of Soviet industrialization was forced on the country. This miniature imitated the autarky of the Soviet Union.[34]

In his contributions to the "debate on the model," Włodzimierz Brus expressed more moderate views than Kurowski. In the welter of ideas circulating at the time, Brus came as close as any one to reflecting a consensus of academic opinion. He appealed to a large number of university economists professing Marxist views who wished to substitute decentralized incentives and guidance by the price system for the old administrative orders and controls but at the same time favored the maintenance of a vigorous development policy, whether or not this policy squared with the immediate de-sires of consumers. Brus recognized the distinctions made by Stalin between profitability to the enterprise and profitability to the economy, although he admitted it had been stretched too far in the past. Given this higher criterion of social profitability, it would be wrong to let the economy ride on market forces. The presence of external economies—benefits to society that cannot be appro-priated by the firm—militates against total decentralization, par-ticularly of investment programming. "The decision whether and how much to invest in coal mining, in the chemical industry or in ship-building cannot, and should not, depend on an economic

33. M. Mieszczańkowski, "Koncepcja Kurowskiego a rzeczywistość" (Kurowski's con-cept and reality), ZG, no. 12 (1957), 5. The gradual curtailment of the role of the market in shaping prices in Yugoslavia since the high point of decentralization in 1954 suggests that, while there may be no incompatibility between centralized political power and planners' sovereignty on the one hand and decentralization on the other, the leaders must exercise constant care to check any trend toward the resurgence of bureaucratic controls (cf. J. M. Montias, "Economic Reform and Retreat in Yugoslavia," Foreign Affairs, January 1959).

34. TL, December 5, 1956; source quoted in Z. Brzezinski's The Soviet Bloc: Unity and Conflict, p. 345.

calculus based on the profitability of these individual branches of industry at a given moment." [35] These crucial reservations aside, Brus was eager to dismantle administrative controls, grant socialized enterprises full autonomy, and guide their activities through the price system. He favored the extension of wide powers to the workers' councils, partly as a guarantee of the democratization of the economy. Finally, Brus argued that, if profits were going to be the primary criterion for assessing an enterprise's management and the chief impulse for adapting its operations to market pressures, incentives to managers and workers must be geared to financial results and not to above-plan output or cost reduction.

A third group of participants in the debate, consisting mainly of experienced practitioners in planning stood in sharp opposition to the "value-men" in the first two groups. They agreed with their opponents on the need for a fundamental reform of producers' prices, which might be used more effectively than in the past for guiding the allocation of resources, but they warned that prices could not possibly supplant the work of a central administration in coordinating the plans. Some, like Adam Wang, one of the highest planning officials, were apprehensive of the violent price fluctuations—dominated by an upward trend—which would follow if prices were allowed free play.[36] Others, having observed that the removal of the pressures formerly exerted by the Planning Commission on the ministries and by the ministries on lower organs was creating slack in the economy at a time when there was a critical need to take advantage of every "reserve" in production to improve living standards, advised against wrecking the old planning machinery before satisfactory new methods had been worked out.[37] Michał Kalecki was most explicit in his rejection of the "automatism" of prices: he predicted that price manipulations would not have a sufficient impact on socialized enterprises to effect the sweeping changes in resource allocation that frequently had to be

35. W. Brus, "Spór o rolę planu centralnego" (Controversy on the role of the central plan), ZG, no. 12 (1957), 4; and "Październik, model Październikowy" (October, the October model), ZG, no. 42 (1957), 1.

36. A. Wang, "Co zmienić w systemie cen" (What should be changed in the price system), TL, no. 348 (1956).

37. S. Hatt and A. Karpinski, "Palące problemy planowania" (Urgent planning problems), ZG, no. 6 (1957), 6; B. Warzecha, "Reforma cen bez wstrząsów" (A price reform without shocks), ZG, no. 30 (1957), 1.

made in the periods of stress accompanying rapid economic development. Without administrative orders to reinforce the financial pressures transmitted through the price mechanism, it would take too long to curb the consumption of materials or of other factors that had suddenly become critically scarce. In the meantime the inventories of priority consumers would "melt," with possible production breakdowns as a consequence.[38]

The Commission on the Economic Model of the Economic Council examined the foregoing and many other arguments in the spring of 1957. Out of those deliberations there finally emerged a number of "Theses," upon which the members of the Commission, who were drawn from all parties to the controversy, had found it possible to agree. A number of these Theses eventually found their way into the decrees and ordinances promulgated in the next two years. We shall now summarize only those recommendations that bore directly on the reform of the model; other recommendations dealing with long-term planning, investment, and foreign-trade calculations reflected trends already established in Planning Commission practice since mid-1956.[39]

Characteristically, the Theses opened on a note reaffirming the principle of central planning: "One of the principal conditions for the correct development of our economy consists in the deepening of central planning and in raising it to a higher level." This was to be achieved, however, neither by increasing the number of directives nor by breaking down the balances into finer detail, but by more exhaustive economic analysis. In order to realize the plans laid down for the development of industry, central organs should rely "in the first place on economic instruments" (i.e. financial inducements) and secondarily on administrative means, but only insofar as the latter proved "indispensable to the correct conduct of operations." These were some of the more specific recommendations:

1) Plans drawn up at the central level should stipulate the value of marketed output for each branch of industry as well as its net output (value added). In addition, physical output targets should be set for basic materials.

38. M. Kalecki, "Rady robotnicze a centralne planowanie" (Workers' councils and central planning), *ND*, no. 12 (1956), 41–42.
39. See Chap. 5, Sects. 5 and 6.

2) The output-mix of the enterprise (its assortment plan) should only be fixed centrally in "justified instances," e.g. where the entire output was subject to centralized distribution, or where the enterprise's basic material input was rationed. In general "the scope of autonomy of the enterprise should comprehend production planning, based on an appraisal of marketing and supply possibilities, subject to the obligation of complying to plan directives wherever they may occur."

3) The scope of material rationing should be steadily curtailed. "Rationing may be applied only to basic materials which are manifestly in deficit supply."

4) The enterprise is guided in its activity by profitability considerations, but must take into account the orders it receives from administrative superiors, wherever such orders have been issued to reinforce economic "instruments." In no cases should orders and incentives act at cross purposes.

5) Organizations in charge of enterprises should be set up on cost accounting in such a way as to give them a financial incentive in supervising the activities of their subordinate enterprises.

6) The incentive system of the enterprise should no longer be tied to its performance in carrying out its production plans. A fund of material inducement should be established which would provide longer-run incentives than those at present in force.

7) Investments in industry should be financed by nonreimbursible grants, on which recipient enterprises would be expected to pay interest.

8) All major repairs should be financed by the enterprise, which should have command over its depreciation allowances "with due regard for possible planned deductions from these funds or for their immobilization for general reasons of investment policy."

9) If the wage fund should be fixed by higher authorities, the enterprise should be allowed to dispose of it as it wishes "within the confines of official regulations." Corrections in the wage fund made during the course of execution of the plans should be determined by the volume of the enterprise's net output, not by its gross output as heretofore.

10) Since enterprises would be called upon to make important economic decisions and since profits would play a major role in their complex of material incentives, special attention must be

paid to correct price-setting. The two-tier system of widely divergent producers' and consumers' prices, "which makes it impossible to employ the zloty as a unique measure of value and distorts national-income accounting," should be liquidated. A new reform of producers' prices must be carried out, by the end of 1958 at the latest, which would take into consideration: (a) realistic unit-cost calculations, (b) the absolute level of world prices and their reciprocal relation, and (c) the level of costs incurred by the most important producers of each good. The new prices should eliminate all "plan-deficit enterprises"; if by chance "for objective reasons" it happened that an item had to be priced below cost and if an enterprise received an administrative order to produce it, the item must be assigned a profitable "factory price": negative differences would be settled at a higher level.

11) The Theses rejected the notion that prices should be formed spontaneously (i.e. on unregulated markets). But the impact of the state on prices need not be limited to centralized price-fixing; it could also be effected by "indirect regulation," that is, by influencing production and the market.[40]

It should be evident from this detailed summary that the Theses were hammered out by compromise. Although obeisance had been done to the principles of decentralization, the partisans of the *status quo ante* had little cause for alarm.[41] Most of the recommendations were set forth in vague terms or allowed broad exceptions; they were open to almost any interpretation. The "conservatives" could always make their opposition felt when the time came to translate the recommendations into concrete legislation or, better yet, into circulars and other unpublished instructions which were likely to be drafted by officials committed to similar views.

Before we trace the course of administrative decentralization and compare practice with the reforms advocated by the Theses,

40. "Tezy Rady Ekonomicznej w sprawie niektórych kierunków zmian modelu gospodarczego" (Theses of the Economic Council concerning some changes in the economic model), ZG, no. 22 (1957), 1–2.

41. According to Brzezinski (p. 351) "in February 1958 a Party commission rejected the key recommendations of the Economic Council, namely, the transfer of direct authority (to fix annual plans, to approve investments, and to make the decisions on new productions) to the factory or enterprise." The rejection is essentially correct, but the recommendations, at least insofar as they were published, were milder and more ambiguous than Brzezinski implies.

we shall first examine the background and then the execution of the most recent price reform which, back in 1957, was considered "the essential condition for realizing any of the more profound changes in the economy of the enterprise." [42]

3. Producers' Prices (October 1956–July 1960)

Throughout 1956 there had been some discussion of official price-setting policy for producer goods, but it was not until after October that original suggestions for rehauling the old system began to appear. In November, J. Borysiewicz and B. Jakubowski, both of the Department of Costs and Price Policy of the Planning Commission, urged a return to a modified version of the multiple-price system that had been in force from 1947 to 1949.[43] According to their scheme, each good produced in an enterprise would be assigned a price covering the actual cost per unit in the previous period. The good would then be sold to other socialized enterprises at a uniform price. This would leave the planners free to stimulate the consumption of goods in relative surplus by lowering their transfer price or to induce the economy of goods in short supply by raising their price, without having to worry about the effect of these price manipulations on the finances of suppliers. The obvious defect of the proposal was that suppliers, insulated from consumers' demand, would have no incentive to produce goods in heavy demand. Administrative pressure would have to be applied to induce them to concentrate their efforts on deficit items.

In December 1956, Jerzy Zachariasz, who was soon to become director of the Department of Costs and Price Policy, introduced the idea that the relations among prices of raw materials traded by Poland, such as coal, iron ore, nonferrous metals, sulfur, and grain, should be patterned as far as possible after the structure of world prices.[44] The new prices of raw materials, together with wages and depreciation, would determine the costs of semifabricates and manufactures, which would then be priced at average cost.

42. "Tezy Rady Ekonomicznej . . . ," p. 2.
43. J. Borysiewicz and B. Jakubowski, "Usamodzielnienie przedsiębiorstw a problematyka cen" (The autonomy of enterprises and the price problem), ZG, no. 22 (1956), 1.
44. J. Zachariasz, "O własciwą politykę cen surowców" (For a correct price policy for raw materials) Finanse, no. 6 (1956), 39.

A partial reform, limited to the prices of building materials was decreed on January 1, 1957. The new prices were quite in keeping with the "relationing principles" of the January 1956 reform, but they were marked by more radical departures from average-cost pricing. Prices of lumber, cement, and bricks were set in closer relation to world prices than they had been hitherto.[45] The Planning Commission raised prices of the different grades of lumber two to threefold with the unequivocal aim of discouraging its consumption. Many reports in the press had complained that lumber was wasted on construction sites because it did not pay building enterprises to try and save scaffolding material, crates, and other used lumber.[46] With the new prices of virgin lumber, builders would have a strong inducement to substitute steel for lumber in scaffolding and in other uses, since steel prices had not risen at all. Interestingly enough, the ratio of the prices of steel bars and plane boards in Poland, which had been about the same as in Sweden in 1956 (a little more than 3 to 1), was now reduced to 1.5 to 1. The point is not that lumber had become too expensive but that steel had become too cheap. Lumber prices had to be raised with respect to labor costs, otherwise the expenditure of labor required to save on lumber would not have paid off. This one-sided price adjustment now called forth a new complaint: that it distorted investment calculations. One specialist in engineering works carped that the new prices of lumber had artificially reduced the advantage of building a cable bridge over the Vistula as compared to the alternative of spanning the river with a steel bridge. At European prices expressed in dollars, the material costs of the cable bridge would come to 59 per cent of the steel bridge's; the corresponding relation would be 62 per cent at Polish prices of 1956 and 73 per cent at the newly promulgated prices of 1957. Since, according to this author, price relationships on capitalist markets "reflect socially necessary costs to a greater extent than under [Polish] conditions, it would have been better to pattern Polish prices more closely to prices prevailing in the West." [47]

45. J. M. Montias, "Producers' Prices . . . ," pp. 410–12.
46. For instance, J. Kreisberg, "Drewno jest za tanie" (Lumber is too cheap), ZG, no. 14 (1956).
47. S. Michotek, "Uwagi w sprawie kosztów budowy mostów kablobetonowych" (Remarks on the construction costs of cable-concrete bridges), IB, no. 8 (1957), 17.

By no means all Polish economists went along with the views of Zachariasz on the need to adapt the Polish price structure to world relations. Ignacy Rzędowski and Henryk Fiszel [48] advanced similar arguments to the effect that, as long as the domestic allocation of resources was shaped by the government's industrialization policy which only took limited advantage of the international division of labor, it would be irrational to equalize domestic with world-price relations. This was how Rzędowski put the matter:

> Given the present structure of world prices and domestic costs, our comparative advantages lies—generally speaking— in raw materials rather than in fabricated products . . . This testifies to the relative weakness of our transformation industry; it proves that we are still very backward in this sector . . . The greater profitability of exporting raw materials arises not only from the fact that it enables us to realize an economic rent but because, in this sector, differences in labor productivity between us and the developed countries are relatively least . . . If we were to be guided strictly by profitability considerations . . . we should increase the share of raw materials in our export at the expense of finished products . . . This would be contrary to the long-run interests of our economic development.[49]

Rzędowski also observed that if prices of raw materials were set high enough to release raw materials for export, this would stimulate material-saving instead of labor-saving investments—which would tend to perpetuate the technical backwardness of Polish transformation industries. Rzędowski concluded that

> though at present it may be more advantageous in the short run to export raw materials, in the perspective of the long run the complex development of our economy should lead to such a strengthening of our transformation industry that it will attain the world level of labor productivity, and then,

48. I. Rzędowski, "Czy zrównać ceny krajowe ze światowymi?" (Should domestic prices be equalized with world prices?), ZG, no. 38 (1957); H. Fiszel, "Ceny surowców podstawowych" (Prices of basic raw materials), Ekonomista, no. 6 (1957). Both articles were reprinted in a collection entitled Spór o ceny (The price controversy). The page numbers cited below refer to this volume.

49. Rzędowski, pp. 182–83.

clearly, the relatively low profitability of exporting fabricates compared to raw materials will be eliminated.[50]

The rebuttals that followed cleared up technical errors Rzędowski and Fiszel had made in their presentation,[51] but for the most part skirted the central issue of industrial protection. Stanislaw Polaczek of the Planning Commission did make one telling point: Pricing exportable raw materials at the relatively low level of their domestic costs promotes their consumption at home and discourages the import of potentially more efficient materials—which could be purchased advantageously in exchange for these same exportables. To follow such a policy would result in a kind of autarky which would, if anything, hold back the course of industrial expansion.[52] Polaczek might have put forward the example of coal and petroleum. If investment calculations in Poland were based on the domestic prices of these two fuels, they would make investments in coal-intensive industries appear profitable; the substitution of petroleum for coal in competing uses would appear uneconomical. But actually the country might be better off exporting coal and importing diesel oil and gasoline. This barter would in no way detract from the protection of infant manufacturing industries.

After the Theses had been published, a subcommittee of the Commission on the Economic Model was charged with the elaboration of detailed suggestions to guide the forthcoming price reform. The members of the subcommittee met and deliberated during the summer and fall of 1957. There was a sharp division of views within the group. Some members, such as Jan Lipinski and Jan Drewnowski, wished to set prices at marginal cost, or at a reasonable approximation thereto, while others, such as H. Fiszel, held out for average-cost pricing. Nonetheless, the subcommittee succeeded in getting together on a number of recommendations which they finally transmitted to the Economic Council in December. These became known as the "Theses of the Economic

50. Ibid., p. 184.

51. See especially M. Kalecki, "O cenach surowców podstawowych" (On the prices of basic raw materials), *Ekonomista*, no. 3 (1958), also reprinted in *Spór o ceny*.

52. S. Polaczek, "Spór o ceny surowców podstawowych" (The controversy over the prices of basic raw materials), *ZG*, no. 15 (1958), reprinted in *Spór o ceny*, p. 280.

Council on principles of price formation," [53] although they were never officially approved by the Council.

These were the key points made in the Theses:

1) Prices must stay constant for several years at a time. (This was a concession to economists who stressed the necessity for financial stability and advocated stable prices as instruments of control.)

2) Domestic price relations must, to a greater extent than in the past, conform to the structure of world prices, but without adjusting to temporary fluctuations in world-market quotations.

3) With the exception of raw-material prices, the point of departure for setting prices of both producer and consumer goods should be the level of their domestic costs. The first estimate of the final price must approximate the variable costs of "expensive" plants, accounting for a significant share of production. To these variable costs must be added a percentage markup, uniform for all industry, which should be high enough to cover overhead costs, together with interest charges on the fixed assets and the working capital employed in industry, and profits. The initial prices so constructed should stand in constant proportion to the variable costs of expensive plants.[54] Recognizing the impossibility of basing prices on an exact computation of marginal costs, the authors of the Theses on price formation thus settled for "the average variable cost of 'expensive' plants, [which] is a practical approximation to the category of marginal costs, adequate for the requirements of price policy." [55]

Prices of producer goods, with the aforesaid exception of raw

53. "Tezy Rady Ekonomicznej w sprawie zasad kształtowania cen" (The Theses of the Economic Council on principles of price formation), in *Spór o ceny*, pp. 9–26.

54. This was commonly interpreted to mean that the price p of a product must equal the variable cost k of making this product in a group of the industry's most expensive plants plus a percentage of k equal to the ratio r of total overhead to variable costs summed over all branches of industry. In symbols, $p = k + rk$. Hence the ratio of the prices p_1 and p_2 of any two products sold by the same industry would be equal to the ratio of their costs of production k_1 and k_2 in expensive plants:

$$\frac{p_1}{p_2} = \frac{k_1 + rk_1}{k_2 + rk_2} = \frac{k_1}{k_2}$$

55. "Tezy . . . ," in *Spór o ceny*, p. 13.

materials, were to be set at the level of the initial, or "point-of-departure," prices; but this equality, it was enjoined, should not be mechanically enforced; deviations might be justified in cases where "the element of scarcity had to be taken into account." If, for example, bottlenecks arose, prices might be raised above the norm to restrain consumption. Generally, the planners should strive to maintain equilibrium on both the markets for consumer and for producer goods, but, to preserve price stability, measures should be taken to alter the underlying supply-and-demand relations before prices were allowed to vary. The prices so far described were primarily designed as indicators of available alternatives to be used in short-run economic decisions; it was conceded that they were not entirely satisfactory for the economic calculation of investments, yet the Theses had nothing of a constructive nature to offer on the subject. (This was clearly a point of some importance since labor productivity tended to rise at widely diverging rates in different industries [56] and prices based on an approximation to present-day marginal costs might not even come close to reflecting relative scarcities two or three years hence.) [57]

4) A concession was also made to the partisans of financial stability who wanted prices to be set as close as possible to the average costs of individual producers. If transfer prices, which were to be uniform for all socialized consumers, did not induce producers to undertake "correct" output decisions, special prices might be established either for groups of producers or for individual firms. This might occur, when transfer prices had been set at a level covering the costs of the most inefficient enterprises, if there was no convenient way to siphon off the rents and profits accruing to more productive units in the industry; or, alternatively, when transfer prices had been set *below* the cost level of inefficient enterprises, special "accounting prices" might be granted to these high-cost enterprises to keep them from sustaining losses.[58]

With the Theses on price formation, the value-men won their Pyrrhic victory. To foist on their opponents the principle of marginal-cost pricing, they had to compromise on price flexibility and on the special accounting prices to producers. The Theses were

56. "Producers' Prices . . . ," Table 23.
57. Cf. the "Comment" by A. Erlich in *Value and Plan*, p. 67.
58. Cf. the proposals of Borysiewicz and Jakubowski discussed above.

full of holes, and their adversaries were quick to detect them. It would have taken the authority of Oskar Lange to hold the front, but Lange was away and did not take part in the decisive "Conference on Price Theory" of March 1958, which pitted together the most eminent representatives of the contending parties.[59]

Bronisław Minc, who made the opening and closing speeches at the conference, was the leader and the most vehement representative of the group opposed to the recommendations on marginal-cost pricing in the Theses. Much of what he said would seem irrelevant or merely doctrinal to a Western economist, but a few of his shafts drove home:

> Prices based on marginal costs would lead to irrational and fortuitous economic decisions. The decision whether to employ one or more of several alternative means of production is made principally in the preparation of investment projects, that is, under dynamic circumstances and in the long run. A price based on marginal cost is a short-run price. . . . It is then obvious that the use of a short-run price, based on present marginal costs, may, and even must, lead to substantial errors in long-run investment calculations.[60]

One could always rejoin, as Brus did, that more short-run decisions would be subject to the influence of prices once enterprises were granted the autonomy they had been promised, and that, even if enterprises had no choice at all in ordering their inputs, they still had to have correct indicators of relative scarcity to guide their efforts at economizing materials and other factors,[61] but this did not solve the problem raised by Minc: Unless the entire system was drastically rehauled, the more important price-oriented decisions would still remain in the investment sector, and this was where pricing mistakes would be most dangerous. Jan Lipiński, who made the principal report in defense of the Theses (that he had helped to draft) conceded Minc's point: "If this proved technically possible, certain means of production should be assigned different prices, strictly for purposes of calculation, which would

59. Lengthy summaries of the speeches made at the conference were published in *Ekonomista*, no. 3 (1958) by Jerzy Lisikiewicz and reprinted in *Spór o Ceny*. All citations refer to the latter source.

60. *Spór o Ceny*, p. 312.

61. Ibid., p. 343.

be founded on long-range substitution relations." [62] But even then, considering the very uneven pace of technical progress, would not long-range calculations made three or four years after a reform be distorted if they relied on prices rigged to a level of marginal costs that had long since ceased to prevail?

Several of the speakers, on both sides of the fence, expressed misgivings about the nature of "marginal cost" in the sense these words were used in the Theses. One speaker (J. Zagórski) aptly remarked that marginal cost so defined was nothing but the "average cost of marginal producers." [63] Would it necessarily reflect the supply cost of producing an incremental amount of the product? Bronisław Minc thought not. Most high-cost plants, he said, are just as fully booked up with production orders as the most efficient producers. If "reserves" exist, they are to be found mainly in the new factories, which have trouble organizing full-scale production. [64]

No one seems to have seen through another important weakness in the proposal to tie prices to the costs of marginal producers. If the proposal were adopted, there would be no way to locate the economic margin of production (except with the crude apparatus of the physical balances). When should an obsolete plant be scrapped? Supposing the industry's price had initially been based on costs in an inefficient plant and this price still covered current costs, should this inefficient plant still be maintained in operation even though modern plants which made better use of the available inputs had been constructed in the meantime? The assumption implicit in the Theses, just as in much of the theorizing of Augustowski and Borysiewicz examined in the last chapter, [65] was that the state's production targets were rational and efficient; thus they expressed a correct level of demand which might be used to shape prices. In other words, since it was thought possible to determine efficient outputs in the absence of prices, current outputs could serve as a rational basis for price-setting. This is a most doubtful proposition, if only for the theoretical reasons exposed in the first chapter. [66]

The uniform percentage markup which, according to the

62. Ibid., p. 325.
63. Ibid., p. 354.
64. Ibid., p. 364. This point was also stressed by Z. Wyrozembski, p. 272.
65. Chap. 8, Sect. 5.
66. Chap. 1, Sect. 4.

Theses, was to be added to the variable costs of "expensive" producers to cover industrial overhead, interest, and profits, also came in for some justified criticism. Prices set in this manner would be completely severed from individual producers' costs, since the latter would include depreciation and capital charges computed on the basis of the producer's own assets, while the overhead margin, on prices was computed from industry-wide data. Capital-intensive branches of industry with a small range of costs among plants, such as metallurgy, would certainly be penalized by the scheme. The variable costs of their most inefficient plants would only amount to a fraction of the total average costs of most producers; the addition to these initial costs of a percentage markup calculated from an average capital intensity for all industry would probably fail to cover their total average costs.

J. Wyrozembski attacked marginal-cost pricing on different grounds. His concern was not so much for the errors in allocation that might result from faulty pricing but for keeping the accounting and control functions of the price system in good order. In his opinion, the correct price of a good must incorporate the actual expenditure incurred in making the good. Any other price would distort economic calculation.[67] Insofar as the planners might desire to use prices as constant weights for aggregating physical inputs— to facilitate appraisal and control of enterprise performance— there might be an advantage to average-cost pricing, particularly in the case of materials undergoing several stages of manufacture where the prices of the successive products could serve as a norm of "congealed" labor content, against which costs actually incurred could be compared. Of course, as Wyrozembski readily observed, producers' prices had been so out of line with average costs in the past that they had not been able to perform correctly either as guidelines to decentralized decisions or as instruments of direct control.[68]

In his concluding remarks at the end of the conference, Bronisław Minc reiterated his stand against marginal cost-pricing, "a conception which is totally unrealistic and impossible to carry out in practice." [69] The decision to close the discussion and maintain the status quo in pricing methods may already have been taken by

67. *Spór o ceny*, pp. 266, 338.
68. Ibid., p. 254.
69. Ibid., p. 362.

the Party before the conference. But the Party could guarantee Minc only an administrative ascendancy. The compromises made by the value-men in drafting the Theses and their failure to redeem themselves by sufficiently powerful theoretical oratory kept them from gaining a clear intellectual advantage.

After the conference the interest in price formation died down; the task of preparing the next price reform was left to the discretion of the Planning Commission and of its Department of Coordination of Price Policy, which had inherited some of the price-setting functions of the former Department of Costs and Price Policy. The members of the department favored a pragmatic approach to price-setting problems. They were committed to neither side in the recent controversy. Without any strong theoretical preconceptions, they were willing to experiment, at least on paper, with the notion of linking prices to the costs of marginal producers. Since Zachariasz, the new director, had been the first to speak out in 1956 for a rapprochement between domestic and world prices, there was no resistance in the department to carrying out the recommendations of the July 1957 Theses of the Economic Council on the subject. This restricted the field of experimentation to the prices of manufactures. But, as the department soon found out, the range of variable costs among manufacturing plants was not nearly so large as among raw-material producers. The cost of "expensive" producers, if by these were meant, as was commonly assumed, the group of enterprises accounting for one-third of output with the highest production costs,[70] did not diverge very much from the costs of "average" producers. Moreover, there was an appreciable margin of error in estimating the successive rounds of price increases for interdependent industries.[71] The difference between marginal and average costs sometimes nestled within this error. After some experimentation, it was apparently decided to stick to average-cost pricing, except for rough upward adjustments in the direction of high-cost producers where the latter were responsible for an important part of the industry's output. This was the only concrete result of the long drawn out debate on marginal-cost pricing.

70. This was how a number of speakers interpreted the marginal-cost notion of the Theses at the March 1958 Conference.

71. Above, Chap 8, Sect. 4.

The reform as a whole was delayed until July 1, 1960, although as early as January 1, 1959, the prices of coal were raised for a few important consumers, who were compensated for the increase by a special subsidy paid by the coal industry! [72]

The report by Zachariasz on the conduct of the reform was distinguished by common sense and by a more candid acknowledgement than in the official commentaries to past reforms [73] of the difficulties encountered in the course of the department's work. "We must point out," he wrote,

> that as a result of the radical increases in the prices of basic products (fuels and raw materials) and of the complicated reciprocal effects of price changes, the calculation of a majority of the new prices could only be made within a certain degree of approximation. Moreover, the accuracy of these calculations was lowered because of the absence of data on the real magnitude of depreciation allowances. This was linked with the lack of a correct estimation of the value of fixed assets and correct depreciation norms . . . The future magnitude of depreciation allowances—after the reevaluation of fixed assets and the introduction of the norms now in preparation—could only be approximately estimated in setting the new prices.[74]

Zachariasz was also less sanguine than his predecessors had been about the prospects for totally eliminating undesirable discrepancies between costs and prices in the course of the four or five years during which the new prices were scheduled to remain in effect. Such discrepancies might well arise, owing to the divergent evolution of labor-productivity gains in various industries, but it was hoped that they would not prove to be as serious as they had been in recent years.[75]

A key feature of the reform was the policy to price raw materials and semifabricates in greater conformity with world-market prices, especially where these materials entered in Poland's foreign trade. Some differences between foreign and domestic price ratios might

72. J. Zachariasz, "Niektóre zagadnienia rewizji cen zaopatrzeniowych" (A few problems in the revision of procurement prices), *GP*, no. 6 (1960), 2.

73. Chap. 8, p. 226.

74. Zachariasz, p. 4.

75. Ibid., p. 5.

persist, but there would be no place in the reformed system for gaps of up to 2.5 to 1, such as were commonly encountered in the past.[76]

The new prices of nonferrous metals are a case in point. We saw in the last chapter that the 1956 prices of the scarcer metals had been set out of all proportion with world prices. The idea was that high prices would form a barrier to restrain the consumption of these metals. A consequence of this policy was that, in order to conserve copper, nickel, and tin, whose prices were inordinately high, industrial consumers and project-making organizations had been compelled to use up more electricity, labor, and other less expensive materials than the saving justified. To compute the absolute level of prices for nonferrous metals, the officials preparing the reform selected a zloty-to-dollar ratio, or effective exchange rate, close to the upper limit above which it was no longer considered profitable to export a commodity.[77] The rate used in the case of zinc was approximately 35 zlotys to the dollar, as against 14 zlotys to the dollar prior to the reform. For the first time a serious attempt was made to relate the prices of nonferrous metals to the prices of plastic substitutes, which now became relatively less expensive. Table 9:1 below, modeled after Table 8:6, shows the old and the new relations between zinc and other metal prices, as well as price relatives for two of the most important plastics.

TABLE 9:1. *Price Relatives in Poland and on the World Market 1959–60* (Price of Zinc = 1)

	Poland (1956–June 1960)	Poland (July 1, 1960)	"World Prices" (1959–60)
Zinc	1	1	1
Lead	1.7	1.2	0.95
Aluminum	4.0	2.0	2.4
Copper	5.0	3.5	2.8
Nickel	17.5	12.0	5.0
Tin	33.0	13.0	8.0
Vinyl polychloride	4.75	1.4	1.6
Polystyrene (colorless)	13.75	4.3	2.0

Sources. M. Hładyj, "Nowe ceny i nowe warunki sprzedaży metali nieżelaznych" (New prices and new sales conditions for nonferrous metals), *GM*, no. 15 (1960) and Table 8:6.

76. Ibid.
77. On these rates, see Chap. 5, Sect. 5 and Table 5:1, p. 167.

Although nickel and tin remained relatively more expensive than they were abroad, their prices were no longer as prohibitive as they were before the reform. It is only fair to recall that, prior to 1956, the controls of the Western allies over the export of strategic materials, including nonferrous metals, were still stringent; the case for adjusting Polish prices to world-market relations at that time was not as strong as in more recent years when these controls were relaxed. Yet, it may be argued that, since the Soviet bloc continued to trade at prices closely tied to world-market relations throughout the 1950s, the latter continued to represent Poland's opportunity costs—at least within the quotas she could obtain from her allies and neighbors. Whatever difficulty Poland might have had in buying at world-market prices the quantities of copper, tin, and nickel she needed, this was still no reason to pattern the domestic prices of these metals after the Soviet internal price structure, which had nothing to do with the alternatives involved (cf. Table 8:6).

Coal prices were raised to an average of 321 zlotys a ton, which covered the costs of the coal-mining industry (including higher material costs at the new input prices) with a small profit. The July 1960 coal prices were 10 to 20 per cent lower than the temporary prices introduced in January 1959, but 142 per cent above the old 1956–58 prices.[78] This was the first time since at least 1950 that newly decreed prices of coal products covered the post-reform level of their costs. It is also significant that the zloty-to-dollar ratio for coal was now in the range of 30 to 35, as against 8 to 10 zlotys to the dollar in 1956 when world prices of bituminous coals had been about 50 per cent higher. Since the effective rates for other commodities rose less after the reform, this narrowed the abnormal spreads between high and low rates typical of the 1956–59 period.

The rise in coal prices entrained higher prices of electric energy (60 to 75 per cent increase), railroad tariffs (78 per cent increase), and steel (55 per cent increase), which in turn raised prices of metal products by 20 to 40 per cent and of machinery by an aver-

78. Zachariasz, "Niektóre zagadnienia . . . ," p. 3, and S. Majewski, "Po wprowadzeniu reformy cen artykułów zaopatrzeniowych i inwestycyjnych" (After the introduction of the reform of prices for procurement and investment goods), *Finanse*, no. 9 (1960), 2.

age of 25 per cent.[79] Zachariasz attributed the relatively modest increases in the prices of fabricated metals and machinery to the above-average gains in labor productivity recorded in these branches in the last few years. (Price increases for metalware and machinery had to absorb 40 per cent higher wage costs—compared to 1956—as well as the scheduled increases in steel, fuel, power, and transportation prices.) [80] As a result of the reform, prices of equipment and machinery tended to fall in comparison with labor costs. This, according to Zachariasz, had nothing in common with the old policy of setting artificially low prices for investment goods. It followed from a real change in comparative costs.[81]

The costs of metal goods produced for the consumer market, despite productivity increases, could not help but rise under the upward pressure of higher input prices. The 1956 reform, as we observed in Chapter Eight, had left relatively small margins to absorb the cost increases. Retail prices of a few metal-goods were raised in April and May 1960 in anticipation of the forthcoming reform of producers' prices. (Coordination in setting prices for consumer and for producer goods was much improved since the State Price Commission had to ratify price changes for all goods, not just for the consumer market as before 1956.) In some instances, turnover taxes were lowered to absorb the cost increases. Finally, where nothing else availed, the government had to subsidize consumer goods whose prices no longer covered production costs. The reform was said to present a grave problem for thousands of producers' cooperatives which were not permitted to adjust the retail prices of their products to keep up with the higher level of their input prices.[82]

By no means all producer-goods industries were slated to become profitable. Copper mining, for instance, would continue to be subsidized. The rationale for this policy was that copper prices could not be raised to cover costs without distorting economic calculation (since they would be completely out of line with world prices); yet domestic copper resources had to be developed, even at a high cost, for strategic and national reasons. The subsidy may

79. L. Siemiątkowski, "Reforma cen artykułów zaopatrzeniowych" (The price reform for procurement items), *WNBP*, no. 6 (1960), 254.

80. Zachariasz, p. 3.

81. Ibid.

82. Siemiątkowski, p. 255.

be considered a measure of the economic loss sustained to further these autarkic aims. The inorganic-chemicals industry, it was forecast, would suffer a larger deficit than before the reform. This deficit would be mainly accounted for by the production of fertilizers, whose retail prices had been maintained at previous levels. Similarly, the artificial-fibers industry would have to be subsidized to preserve correct relations between rayon and nylon prices on the one hand and cotton and wool prices on the other. (Prices of natural fibers could not be raised for fear of cutting too deeply into present tax and profit margins.) Altogether, it was anticipated that "a few thousand products" would be produced at a deficit after the reform, although some of the losses would soon be wiped out if labor-productivity increases developed on schedule.[83]

It was too early at the time these pages were written to appraise the results of the reform. From the viewpoint of the Polish planners, the reform will be judged successful if the level of costs planned for 1960 and 1961 is not exceeded and if subsidies are held down to budgeted estimates. One important condition in meeting this test will be the ability of the planners to restrain wage increases. We shall find in the concluding section of this chapter that this will be a difficult assignment in the years of rapid expansion and strained investment plans that lie ahead.

One thing appears certain: the main benefit of the reform will lie in the improvement of investment calculations. Raw material prices will now be in closer harmony with world prices, and the prices of most fabricated products will be closer to production costs than they were before. Nevertheless, the new prices will not be much better guides to the short-run input and output decisions of producers than the old. They still do not express the relative scarcity of goods at any given time. Even world-price relations will not help because output targets and the allocation of output between domestic consumption and exports will be influenced by autarkic considerations as well as by goals of economic efficiency. Still, we should not exaggerate the seriousness of irrationalities in the price system: As long as administrative rationing of resources continues to prevail, prices should not have enough influence on short-run decisions to cause any essential misallocations.

83. Majewski, p. 3.

4. *Administrative Decentralization: 1956–59*

At the beginning of this chapter brief mention was made of the first decree aimed at loosening the bonds restricting the autonomy and the initiative of socialized enterprises. Soon after the promulgation of this decree in April 1956, the central boards of industry were also granted wider powers. By the decree of August 17, 1956, the directors of central boards were made responsible for approving all norms of material consumption, with the exception of those already entrusted to the enterprise.[84] In the course of further decentralization, liberal instructions were issued by the ministries, which permitted the central boards to unload the greater part of their norm-setting duties on the enterprises themselves.[85] The idea behind these liberal reforms was that managers would exercise a proper degree of self-control in ordering materials, partly out of patriotic motives, partly because the new incentive systems under consideration at the time would make it worth their while to do so. In effect, for the next four years, the material norms in most branches of industry were only perfunctorily controlled by superior organs. Since the new incentives were never made powerful enough to cause managers to economize on their inputs,[86] excessive demands for materials were allowed to percolate up to the Planning Commission. The Planning Commission had to rely increasingly on statistical norms (based on actual performance in previous years) to perform its allocation tasks. This contributed to the dissatisfaction of planning officials and Party executives with the results of the decentralization measures and eventually helped bring about the policy reversal and recentralization of 1959–60.

On November 10, 1956, three weeks after the fateful Party plenum of October 1956, socialized industrial enterprises received their most far-reaching bill of rights. Earlier in the year they had been granted a few specific and narrowly circumscribed privileges. This time the law, after stipulating their duties and obligations, restrained the powers of superior authorities to order them about.

84. *MP*, no. 83 (1956), *poz.* 975.

85. J. Szymańczyk, "Progresywne normy zużycia—to ważne zadanie dle przedsiębiorstwa" (Progressive consumption norms are an important assignment for the enterprise), *GM*, no. 18 (1960), 617.

86. Ibid., p. 618.

Instead of having to fulfill an arbitrary number of "directives" at the discretion of the ministry or central board, the enterprise would now receive eight "annual plan indices" in all from its superiors. These eight indices would specify:

1) The gross value of output planned for the enterprise, including the share to be marketed.

2) Production targets for the most important goods, as laid down by the central board or other supervising entity after making sure that a sufficient supply of centrally distributed materials would be available to fulfill these plans.

3) The enterprise's total wage fund.

4) Planned profits or losses.

5) The amount of profits to be paid into the state budget (or the subsidies to be received to cover losses).

6) The maximum value of investment expenditures permitted out of centrally controlled funds ("investment limit"), with separate ceilings for construction and equipment outlays; the budgetary funds available for investments and the allowance from the amortization fund must be separately itemized.

7) Maximum outlays on major repairs.

8) The enterprise's "sum total of normalized liquid assets" (the combined value of inventories, cash, and other short-term assets whose level is regulated by centralized norms).[87]

A few of the newly sanctioned privileges may be worth mentioning. The enterprise was encouraged to launch the "sideline production" of articles for the consumer market and to set its own prices for these products; all profits from sideline production were to be turned over to the Enterprise Fund. It was permitted to make small investments in the mechanization, modernization, and rationalization of production or for expanding the production of articles of general consumption. These investments were to be financed by reimbursible credits extended by the banks normally financing the enterprise's productive activities. The enterprise was free to carry out investments and major repairs out of its own

87. *MP*, no. 94 (1956), *poz.* 1047. The quotation is from an English translation by the Polish Institute of International Affairs, "System of Planning and Administration of the Polish National Economy 1956–58," *Legislation of Poland*, no. 6 (1959), p. 33.

resources or entrust their execution to employees on the staff working on their own time. It could also conclude agreements with producers' cooperatives or independent artisans for various services; it could purchase from cooperatives, nonsocialized enterprises, and private individuals in "economically justified cases." Finally, it was given the right of effecting payments in cash up to 3,000 zlotys at a time to private individuals for the delivery of goods and services. (This sum was approximately equal to two months' wages for a rank-and-file worker.) The decree of November 10 also confirmed the concessions granted to socialized enterprises in April 1956.[88]

To consolidate the transfer of powers from higher organs to the enterprise, the Planning Commission was to be deprived of the "quasi-legislative and managerial functions" that it had accumulated in the course of the preceding eight years.[89] On November 28 the *Sejm* passed a statute reorganizing the Commission: The new organ, renamed Planning Commission of the Council of Ministers, was still charged with the preparation of over-all plans in cooperation with ministries and other economic agencies, but it was shorn of most of its direct executive powers. Its staff was cut from 1,800 to 900 employees.[90]

The main duties of the reformed Commission according to the Statute of November 28 were:

1) To prepare and to submit to the Council of Ministers suggestions concerning the main lines of the state's economic policy.

2) To draft "projects" for yearly and perspective plans.

3) To analyze the performance of the economy in carrying out the plans and to propose to the Council of Ministers ways and means of safeguarding their fulfillment.

4) To elaborate procedures and methods for making up economic plans.

5) To deal with other questions as ordered by law or as instructed by the Council of Ministers.[91]

88. Ibid., pp. 32–38.
89. United Nations, Economic Commission for Europe, *Economic Survey of Europe in 1956*, p. 39.
90. Ibid. Most of the employees laid off found work in the ministries and central boards; a few ended up on the managing staff of industrial enterprises.
91. *Dziennik Ustaw*, no. 54 (1956), *poz.* 244.

In his semi-official commentary on the reform, Minister Secomski placed special emphasis on the curtailment of the Commission's
powers: [92]

> (1) The Planning Commission *does not possess the right
> of decision:* the Commission along with its component organ-
> izations is only a consultative and advisory staff organ . . .
> The right of decision-making belongs to the Council of Min-
> isters in the realm of economic policy . . . and to the compe-
> tent ministries or to the peoples' councils in the realm of cur-
> rent problems.
>
> (2) The Planning Commission no longer occupies itself
> with a mass of operational questions . . . in particular it is
> no longer competent to take action on *ad hoc* problems of
> materials distribution and supply . . .
>
> (3) The Planning Commission is divested of all activities
> in the nature of direct management . . .
>
> (4) The work of the Planning Commission must not over-
> lap with or tend to replace the work of the ministries and of
> the peoples' councils; this applies especially to the elaboration
> of draft-projects for the economic plans (for which however
> the Commission must draft initial directives). Each ministry
> and each peoples' council prepares and is responsible for its
> own plan-project. The Commission is expected to analyze and
> to appraise the plans submitted, with particular regard to
> their mutual consistency and to the coordination of targets,
> and to prepare an overall plan-project.

The official instructions for making up the 1957 plans helped to
give effect to the administrative reform by parceling out some of
the Commission's balancing and distributing functions among the
ministries and the marketing organizations. The number of physical targets, of centrally rationed commodities, and of technological coefficients subject to approval by the central authorities was
drastically reduced: [93]

---

92. K. Secomski, "O zasadzie planowania centralnego i o roli nowej Komisji
Planowania" (On the foundation of central planning and on the role of the new
Planning Commission), *GP,* no. 1 (1957), 5.

93. *Economic Survey of Europe in 1956,* p. 39.

	1956	1957
Specific production targets	1,406	768
Centrally rationed commodities	1,411	1,150
Technical coefficients	587	230

The number of centrally rationed commodities fell from 1,800 in 1955 to some 400 in 1958.[94] Actually the deconcentration of planning was not quite as great as it was made out to be, since the reduction in the number of centrally planned targets may be laid in part to the aggregation of commodities that were formerly itemized separately. Nonetheless, some real progress was achieved in 1957 and in the following two years in alleviating the Planning Commission's workload. We shall go into more specific details on this matter when we examine the 1960 plans, which marked a certain retrogression from the policy inaugurated in 1956.

The administration understood that if decentralization was going to take root, it must proceed along both geographic and functional lines. The peoples' councils—at the county and the voivodship level—were chosen as the vehicle for decentralizing the administration of the economy on a territorial basis. According to the law of January 25, 1958, which set the framework for the activities of the Peoples' Councils, the councils "within the scope defined by the present law or by special regulations shall have the right to control and coordinate the activity of state administration bodies, institutions and economic units not subordinated to them." [95] The new law gave the voivodship councils a broad mandate to acquaint themselves with the plans and with the performance of centrally administered (key) industry and to coordinate the production and supply of the latter with the local industry and handicrafts which they supervised directly. The localization of key industry could no longer be decided upon—as it often was in the past—without the participation of the voivodship councils. Basic changes in the production profile of enterprises had to be approved by the presidia of the voivodship councils if "these changes exercised a decisive influence on the utilization of local sources of raw materials or power, on employment conditions, or on health conditions in the territory." [96] In the next two years a

94. ZG, no. 3 (1959), 1.
95. "System of planning . . . ," p. 54.
96. RPG 1958, p. 175.

considerable number of construction and industrial enterprises employing fewer than one hundred persons were transferred under the direct control of the voivodship and, in the case of very small works, to county and city councils. An expression of the growing economic potential of the councils is the recent rise in their financial importance. From 1956 to 1959, the aggregate expenditure of local budgets increased by 115 per cent, more than three times as much as the consolidated state budget. The share of the local budgets in the total state budget went up from 16 to 25 per cent. These results notwithstanding, progress toward local autonomy has been hampered by continued reliance of the voivodship councils and of most city councils on central subsidies for the bulk of their revenue: in 1959 only 31 per cent of total expenditures of the voivodship councils was covered from their own sources of revenue. Local councils as a whole derived less than 15 per cent of their total revenue from socialized enterprises.[97]

The elimination of the central boards of industry and their replacement by autonomous associations of enterprises had been under consideration ever since the spring of 1956; yet after the Economic Council recommended this reform in its June 1957 Theses, it still took nearly a year before the Council of Ministers issued its directives on the reorganization of industry.[98]

The new associations [99] (*zjednoczenia*) created by the directives were set up as independent legal entities, unlike the central boards which were technically a part of their ministry. They were to be financed by their constituent enterprises, in order to give the managing staff a material interest in the financial performance of their wards.[100]

In addition to a number of industrial enterprises, an association

97. A. W. Zawadzki, "Niektóre zagadnienia finansowe w gospodarce Rad Narodowych" (A few financial questions in the economy of the peoples' councils), *GP*, no. 9 (1959), 41, 44; *RS 1960*, 414, 422. The share of the councils in total state expenditures has been approximately constant from 1959 to 1961. (See *ZG*, nos. 52–53 (1961), 11.)

98. The directives were drafted by a commission appointed by the Central Committee of the Polish United Workers' Party. The final version was prepared jointly by this commission and by the Economic Council. The directives appeared as an annex to a resolution of the Council of Ministers on April 18, 1958.

99. The *zjednoczenie* is called "Union" in the translation of the directives published by the Polish Institute of International Affairs. The term association gives a better indication of the organization's character.

100. "System of Planning . . . ," p. 88.

could also comprise one or more marketing or supply organizations, servicing and repair establishments, project-making offices, research institutes, and specialized laboratories. The central marketing boards, which, ever since 1950, had functioned as sales organizations for particular ministries, were now detached from the ministries and amalgamated with the *zjednoczenia*.

A significant innovation of the new system was that, by order of the ministry concerned, "the powers of an association grouping together the predominant enterprises in a given branch of industry might be extended to cover specific spheres of activity in other associations and enterprises working in the same line of production." [101] This was interpreted to mean that a virtual monopoly of sales and transfers for the entire output of certain products might be conferred on a marketing organization under an association, even though a part of the output of these products was produced in enterprises not affiliated with the association concerned. In this way, the demands of all socialized enterprises for a given material would be made to converge on a unique administrative point. This would avoid the duplication of market research and the divided responsibility associated with a multiplicity of supply sources.

Since the associations were supposed to represent the interests of their members (unlike the central boards which merely transmitted and parceled out to subordinate enterprises the orders of the Planning Commission and of the ministries), the directors of all affiliated enterprises were made *ex officio* members of the collegium of the association, an advisory and consultative body with powers to decide in specific matters including the initiation of common-investment ventures and the redistribution of financial assets among members. However, the director and the vice-directors of the association, who were also members of the collegium, were to be appointed by the minister of the industry concerned. The director was expected to manage the association "according to the principle of one-man management" and to be answerable for its activity.[102]

The directives recommended that the organizational structure and the scope of activity of the individual associations should be

101. Ibid., p. 89.
102. Ibid.

adapted to the character of each branch of industry. For instance, alternative marketing and supply arrangements might be evolved; research and development work could also be organized differently in the various associations.

The directives further extended the bill of rights accorded to enterprises in 1956 and 1957. The enterprise, for the first time, was officially permitted to set work norms, piece-rates, and bonus-incentive schemes for its workers (within the limit imposed by the wage fund).[103] Perhaps more important in the light of future events was the decision to place the amortization funds of enterprises at their disposal for meeting expenditures for major repairs, for the replacement of worn-out assets, and for other decentralized investments. This was subject to restriction only if the superior authorities issued an order, within the framework of the yearly plan, blocking the use of a portion of this fund or ordering a partial transfer to fill the needs of other enterprises.[104] (We shall find that this escape clause was promptly seized upon when the authorities decided to trim decentralized investments.) Proceeds from the sale of surplus equipment and other assets "sold in conformity with existing regulations," together with the long-term credits extended by the National Bank for streamlining production and with the profits left at the disposal of the enterprise, supplied managers with important sources of finance, which helped to build up their real autonomy.

A word should be said at this point on the new role played by the Enterprise Fund (*fundusz zakładowy*) in the new system of management. Up to the end of the Six-Year Plan, the Enterprise Fund had accumulated only very small sums from profits; the allocation of the fund was strictly regulated by the authorities who sought to direct most of the proceeds to housing and to rewarding socialist emulation; only a minimal part of total profits was directly paid out to the workers and staff as bonuses.[105] In 1957 more liberal provisions were put into effect which removed previously existing limits on the yearly accruals to the fund and maintained a ceiling only on actual payments made from the fund to individ-

103. According to regulations in effect in 1957, the enterprise could only set temporary work-norms for newly launched production.
104. "System of Planning . . . ," p. 78.
105. Above, Chap. 6, Sect. 3.

ual workers; payments could not exceed 8.5 per cent of total yearly wages; but this was still generous considering that the entire fund for 1956, most of which had gone to finance housing and social amenities, had amounted to only 1.8 per cent of total wages or 675 million zlotys in all. In 1958 deductions from profits paid into the Enterprise Fund were set on the basis of actual year-to-year increases in profits earned instead of on planned and above-plan profits as in preceding years. The financial results of the revised scheme were almost exactly equal to those of 1957. However, a restriction was again imposed on the utilization of the sums paid into the fund: at least 25 per cent now had to be allotted to the construction of housing for factory personnel.[106] In 1958, about 30 per cent of the total fund was actually spent on housing and other social investments. A little less than 70 per cent went to individual workers and employees, a much larger proportion out of a total fund which now amounted to nearly six billion zlotys, or five times as much as in 1956. In 1959, the fund remained at approximately the same level as the previous year, but the proportion spent on cash awards fell to 58 per cent.[107]

In late October 1958 the Council of Ministers passed a resolution creating a new source of finance for the enterprise. This was the Development Fund which was to help finance increases in working capital and decentralized investments and, if the need arose, to make up shortages in short-term assets due to above-plan losses. A fixed share of planned profits and a declining share of above-plan profits were to accrue to the Development Fund. It already spent 6.1 billion zlotys in 1959—3.4 billion zlotys to build up working capital (mainly in heavy industry) and 2.7 billion zlotys on investments.[108] The fund is frequently mentioned as an essential component of the decentralized demand for equipment and other means of investment. Of late this demand has been held in check by the practice of the associations of fixing the quotas allotted to the Development Fund ahead of time, independently of the actual profits earned by enterprises. Only above-plan profits,

106. *Prace i materiały zakładu badań ekonomicznych*, no. 17 (1959), 109, 110–29.
107. Z. Madej, "Bodźce ekonomiczne oparte na zysku" (Economic incentives based on profits), *Finanse*, no. 8 (1960), 14, 20; *RS 1960*, p. 433.
108. "System of Planning . . . ," p. 113, 114; *RGP 1958*, p. 746; *RS 1960*, p. 434.

which seem to be immune from these controls, can be said to contribute to the unplanned expansion of investment funds.[109]

Parallel with the wider autonomy granted to the enterprises, the administration held out a new system of incentives to their managers, which was geared not only to the fulfillment of production and cost-reduction plans, as all previous bonus schemes had been, but also in large part to the profits earned by the enterprise. The key ordinance of the Council of Ministers on the subject, which appeared only at the beginning of 1960, stipulated that the bonus fund should be made up of two parts:

1) A basic fund, to which an enterprise was to be entitled "if it planned and realized in the given year an economic result at least equivalent to the result of the preceding year." [110] (The enterprise "plans an economic result," in the context of the ordinance, if it incorporates into its technical-industrial-financial plan a target at least as "mobilizing" as the directives received from its superior authority in the frame of the national economic plan.) The basic bonus fund, whose exact size was to be fixed by the ministry in charge of the enterprise in consultation with the Ministry of Finance, was to amount to somewhere between 10 and 30 per cent of the wage fund of the managing staff.[111]

2) An "additional bonus fund," accumulated from the increase in profits or the decrease in losses, actually realized between one year and the next, was to be disbursed according to percentage tables prepared by the responsible ministry. These tables related the percentage of the wage fund of the managing staff that might be earned from the bonus fund to the *planned* improvement in the profitability of the enterprise during the period. The actual percentages were to be set with due regard to the comparative difficulty of fulfilling the directives laid down by higher authorities and the plans the enterprise finally committed itself to execute.

The principle behind the additional bonus fund was simultaneously to encourage the staff to plan as high a profit as possible—in order to raise the proportion of permissible bonus awards to the

109. M. Misiak, "Samodzielność przedsiębiorstwa w uchwałach i praktyce" (The autonomy of the enterprise in decrees and in practice), ZG, no. 10 (1959), 3.

110. MP, no. 9 (1960), poz. 43.

111. The expression "managing staff" as used here embraces the broad category of white-collar workers (pracownicy umysłowi).

wage fund—and to provide a strong incentive to fulfill the plan so that the actual increase in profits should be sufficient to pay out the sums authorized.

No awards were to be made from either the basic or the additional bonus funds in case the production plan had not been fulfilled or planned wage outlays had been exceeded without prior authorization.

All we have done so far is to describe the formal content of the reforms in the administration of the economy. How did they work out in practice? Were they merely new window dressing, as some Polish economists were prompt to claim, or did they give the signal for gradual but profound changes?

On many points the directives were vague and diffuse. Hardly any of the financial and administrative practices of the old regime were categorically ruled out in the new scheme. It was evident from the first that the reorganization would only be effective in widening the base of economic power if the bureaucrats in the intermediate ranks of the hierarchy were willing to go along with the reforms. The permissive clauses in the directives gave them every opportunity for scuttling the decentralization if they so desired.

The record for the years 1957–59 reveals that the reforms were gradually eroded by the central bureaucracy; this trend was merely accelerated by the economic crisis of the summer of 1959 which impelled the government to retract some of the concessions granted in the preceding years.

Let us start with the functions and the prerogatives of industrial enterprises. We have seen that according to the law of November 1956 the enterprise was to be bound by a maximum number of eight directives. As early as May 1957 a new directive on the wage fund was superimposed on the old: in addition to the over-all limit on the wage fund, a special ceiling was placed on the total wages that the enterprise might pay to its white-collar staff. Later on restrictions were placed on the freedom of the enterprise to apportion the profits left at its disposal among different "funds" (housing, decentralized investments, and so on). About the same time, in order to combat the waste of manpower at the plant level, the state imposed separate limits on the employment of industrial workers, of engineering personnel, and of two other categories of employees in each nationalized enterprise. Special import and export directives were added in late 1958 and 1959. The original set of eight directives specified by the 1956 legislation had proliferated to nineteen by mid-1959. There were still other directives in most industries, which, though they did not have the strength of law, could be enforced fairly effectively by the ministries. A survey showed that two associations in the engineering industry, had received twenty-six directives each.[112]

The formal number of directives issued did not matter so much, since the original set of eight were broad enough "to cover almost all the directives which were supposed to have been eliminated." [113] The clause empowering the supervisors to set production targets for the most important products, as long as supplies of material inputs were adequate to fill these plans, served to justify the imposition of detailed targets covering the entire production of enterprises in many branches of industry; this clause also justified the rationing of available supplies of raw materials. Producers, instead of constructing their own quarterly and monthly operational plans on the basis of approved yearly plans and of the orders received from their clients, had to accommodate their program to the directives they received from their superiors; they could, however, exercise more initative than they did before the reorganization in filling new orders submitted by clients in the course of the plan-year.

Although the financial autonomy of the enterprise is still hedged in by a good many restrictions, relaxation of controls in this domain has been far more perceptible than in matters of current planning. A report of late 1959 on "The autonomy of the enterprise in law and practice" concluded that

> enterprises have gained a measure of independence from their superior authorities in dealing with other enterprises, particularly with commercial enterprises and with the banks, despite the fact that the system of planning production in most branches of industry has remained nearly unchanged.

112. T. Gradowski and A. Kiernożycki, "Wskaźniki dyrektywne planu a samodzielność przedsiębiorstwa" (Plan directives and enterprise autonomy), *GP*, no. 10 (1959), 14.

113. M. Misiak, "Bodźce napiętego planowania?" (Incentives for taut planning?), *ZG*, no. 1 (1961), 5.

In the opinion of the authors of this report the conflict between managerial decisions motivated by profit incentives and direct orders handed down by the association and the ministry still tends to be resolved in favor of the latter. When managers raise objections to the poorly conceived plans foisted on them by their superiors, discussion is often throttled by the dogmatic standpoint taken by higher ups, who do not permit criticism of the plans.[114]

Retrogressive trends may also be discerned in the evolution of the new associations of industrial enterprises: (1) the associations have taken over many of the operational duties which the ministries exercised prior to 1956 (and which in many cases had already devolved on the central boards before the 1958 reform); (2) the ministries have begun to encroach on the prerogatives of the associations and of their enterprises: the statutes of the Ministry of Light Industry, for example, make it mandatory for the ministry to issue regulations bearing on all detailed aspects of the operations of enterprises, including many which should normally have been left to the associations or to the enterprises themselves; (3) the associations are acting increasingly as agencies of the government representing "the national interest," instead of mediating between the enterprise and its ministry.[115]

After a year's operation, the way the associations were running the bonus system also came in for strong criticism. In practice most of the associations earmarked a uniform fraction of management salaries for the additional bonus fund whether the plan of an enterprise called for a small and easy-to-fulfill increase in profits or for a very challenging improvement.

The directives issued by the associations concerning the bonus funds reached the enterprises in the second quarter of the planyear, some time after their industrial-technical-financial plans had been confirmed when it was already too late for them to have any incentive effect on these plans. Despite some improvement compared to preceding years, profit incentives, it was argued, were still in the experimental stage.[116]

We conclude from our survey of recent developments that the

114. Gradowski and Kiernożycki, p. 14.

115. B. Gliński. "W rok po reorganizacji systemu zarządzania" (A year after the reorganization of the administrative system), *GP*, no. 10 (1959), 5–6.

116. Misiak, "Bodźce . . . ," p. 5.

autonomy of the enterprise is not so much constrained by law as it is hemmed in by the discretionary powers still residing in higher organs. Each unit, from the enterprise up, still depends on the good will of its immediate superior for its material allotments and investment quotas. As long as the bureaucracy retains these essential rationing functions, the reform of the model must remain skin-deep. This was recognized as early as March 1957 by Stefan Kurowski, whose liberal ideas on democratic socialism were summarized earlier in this chapter. In his opinion, it was enough to observe the manner in which the bureaucracy was carrying out the new regulations extending the powers of the directors of enterprises to realize that the vested interests had only made halfway concessions to the new system. This was so "because the most important attributes of the old system, namely the decisions as to what and how much to produce and the administrative character of these decisions, remain unchanged." [117]

5. The Workers' Councils (October 1956 to 1960)

The law establishing the workers' councils in November 1956 sanctified "the initiative of the working class in taking a direct part in the management of enterprises." [118] The sphere of activity of the councils was only sketched out. They were to examine, review, appraise, and, whenever necessary, approve the enterprise's operational plans, its future course of development, its organization, its structure, and its financial performance. But the law did not stipulate the manner in which conflicts between the council and management or higher authorities would be settled concerning these matters. The councils were given a few unequivocal, if less essential, rights: [119] (1) with due regard for the director's opinion, they could adopt decisions concerning the sale of surplus machines and installations; (2) they were entitled to settle the distribution of the Enterprise Fund or of the share of profits due to be paid to employees; and (3) they were to work out the internal regulations of the enterprise. The councils' power to determine work norms, wage tariffs, and rules for the granting of bonuses was

117. S. Kurowski, "Model a cele . . . ," *ZG*, no. 12 (1957), p. 4.
118. Preamble to the Law of November 19, 1956, *Dziennik Ustaw*, no. 53, *poz.* 238.
119. Quoted from the translation of the law in Polish Institute of International Affairs, "System of Planning . . . ," p. 39.

not so clear-cut. Decisions had to be made in consultation with the factory councils, on which management and the Party were heavily represented; they were also supposed to conform to the collective agreement signed by workers and management as well as to the (undefined) "rights of the enterprise." The director, who was an *ex officio* member of the council, was to be appointed and re-called "by the appropriate state organization" in consultation with the workers' council. The latter was free, however, to put forward motions bearing on the appointment or dismissal of the enter-prise's chief executives.[120]

The number of workers' councils rose rapidly after October 1956. In May 1957, 3,327 councils had already been set up; by the end of the year there were 5,619 councils, representing workers in the great majority of the medium- and large-scale enterprises in-dustry. (There were 15,866 state-run plants operating in 1956, but, of this total, only about 4,600 plants employed over ten per-sons.) [121]

Many workers' councils, in the beginning of their existence, seem to have displayed what were later called "syndicalist-anar-chic" tendencies and evinced little concern for production prob-lems. Wages, piece-rates, bonuses, housing conditions, and profit-sharing schemes were at the center of their attention. They sought to control the activities of the director and his staff mainly on matters pertaining to the workers' interest. A provincial party leader, addressing the Third Party Congress in 1959, reminded his listeners:

> If at first the workers' councils did not show any remarkable achievements, this was due to the dissipation of forces and even sometimes to the attempts of the councils to set them-selves up in opposition to party organizations and to elimi-nate workers and party members from their ranks.[122]

The Party lost no time in correcting this state of affairs. First, a concentrated effort was made to infiltrate the workers' councils with active Communists and to gain control of them. Second, the Party, after removing some of the more unpopular leaders of the

120. Ibid., pp. 39–41.
121. *RS* 1959, p. 120.
122. Report of W. Kozdra to the Third Party Congress, *ND*, no. 4 (1959), 196.

trade unions, sought to reinforce the participation of the unions in plant affairs by bringing the workers' councils under their general supervision. Already in 1957 the arbitrage commissions, established to settle disputes between the councils and higher administrative authorities,[123] were instructed to act in close harmony with the unions, "who were assured a measure of influence in the nomination of the president of the commission." [124]

In April 1958, the Central Congress of Trade Unions resolved that the councils should be subordinated in each enterprise to "conferences of workers' self-management," which would be run jointly by representatives of the councils, of the trade unions, of the party, and of the factory council. This resolution was put into effect shortly thereafter, even though several months elapsed before legislation calling the conferences into existence was issued. There had been—as a report to the Third Party Congress stated —some opposition on the part of "elements aiming at plant anarchy, who attacked the statute of workers' self-management as an infringement of workers' rights," but it was quickly squelched.[125]

The division of power between party and trade-union representatives in the conferences is still not quite clear-cut,[126] but the main objective of the reform has been achieved: The councils have been stripped of most of their management and control functions. The effect of these changes on the grass roots popularity of the councils are just those we should have expected. At the 1959 elections for membership in the workers' councils, only one-half

123. Any disputes arising between the council and the director of its enterprise were settled by the minister of the industry to which the enterprise was assigned.

124. J. S., "Rozjemstwo" (Arbitration), *GP*, no. 11 (1957), 53.

125. Report of Ewa Lipińska to the Third Congress, *ND*, no. 4 (1959), 423.

126. According to the decree on workers' self-management of December 1958, "the Central Council of Trade Unions and the relevant trade unions supervise the proper functioning of workers' management and coordinate its activity at the level of the nation and of individual branches of the national economy." See *Dziennik Ustaw*, no. 77 (1958), p. 387. On the other hand, according to the Party secretary of a large enterprise, "the Party organization was and is the motor of the conference on workers' self-management." See *ND*, no. 4 (1959), 191. An essential change in Article 50 of the statutes of the United Workers' Party is relevant in this connection: The Party committee may no longer exercise direct control over the activities of an enterprise; it must henceforth carry out its control and political functions "through participations in the activities of workers' self-management, insuring the proper conjunction of the interests of employees with the interests of the nation as a whole." (Ibid., p. 758.)

to three-quarters of the employees took part in the voting (25 to 30 per cent in Warsaw). Less than a quarter of the members of the old councils were re-elected, some of the latter withdrawing "because they saw no opportunity for effective action." The proportion of party members in the councils rose from 30 to 38 per cent. The most notable aspect of recent developments, according to the source of this information, is "the fall in the employees' interest in the activities of workers' self-management." [127]

127. J. L. Toeplitz, "KSR po roku" (Conferences of workers' self-management after a year), ZG, no. 28 (1959), 1, 3.

CHAPTER TEN

Counterreforms

1. *Economic Developments: 1956–60*

The Polish government's policy in regard to institutional reform and to the new "economic model" cannot be understood in recent years except in the light of changing economic conditions. The achievements and the windfalls of 1956 and 1957—the foreign loans that alleviated pressure on the balance of payments, the more modest investment rate that left room for raising depleted inventories in industry, the gains in real wages, the peasants' efforts to increase their production of foodstuffs—all this made for a hospitable climate in which the decentralization of the economy could be pressed forward without too much opposition from entrenched bureaucrats and dogmatic Marxists. The inflationary pressures generated from 1958 on by an accelerated tempo of investment, the failure to raise farm production according to plan, and the decline in real wages which occurred in the second half of 1959 and in early 1960 offered the opponents of decentralization a splendid opportunity to attack the liberal measures taken since 1956. Their arguments did not fall on deaf ears.

Let us go back a moment to the hiatus between the Second Party Congress in March 1954 and Gomulka's access to power in October 1956. These years had given the economy a breathing spell during which the gains chalked up in the frantic industrialization drive of 1949–53 could be consolidated. The total volume of fixed investment outlays kept on rising but at the leisurely pace of 3 to 5 per cent per year. Most of this increase went to agriculture and to the construction of new housing. Investments in other branches of the economy, including industry, either stagnated or declined. The new Five-Year Plan scheduled to run from 1956–60 was expected to drive the economy forward with a higher momentum. The original version of the plan, which was circulated some time before the Poznan riots, was too austere for the rebellious mood of the country. Its investment program was trimmed at the July 1956 plenum of the Party. The resolutions of the plenum called for fixed investment outlays of 318 billion zlotys (at 1956 prices) for the period 1956–60, or about 50 per cent more than the actual volume of these investments from 1951 to 1955. Industry stood to receive 48.5 per cent of this total, a slightly larger share than in the previous period.[1] As the political situation became increasingly tense in the months preceding October, it seemed increasingly evident that the July version was still too ambitious. Higher and more certain improvements in living standards would have to be held out to the masses to ward off popular discontent. Just before the October plenum investments were trimmed again, this time by 16 billion zlotys, or 5 per cent of the sum formerly planned for the period 1956–60. The share earmarked for agriculture, housing, and social amenities went up from 32 per cent in the July version to 41 per cent in this latest draft.[2] The 1960 target for coal output was cut from 110 to 104 million tons, the steel target from 7.2 to 7.0 million tons, sulfuric acid from 795,000 to 723,000 tons, and electric power from approximately 30 to 28 billion kilowatt-hours. Curiously enough, the same increase in real wages—30 per cent over the five-year period—was planned in both versions. (The regime had good reasons to hold down its commitments: the population was still seething over the failure of the Party to make good on the promises of the Six-Year Plan.) Total investments, including inventory accumulation, for the years 1956 to 1958 were now planned at 19 to 21 per cent of national income, computed according to official precepts, and at about 23 per cent for 1959 and 1960. This was on a par with 1954–1955, but definitely less than in 1953 when 27.1 per cent of national income had been invested. The absolute level of investments was to rise slowly at first—by 2.4 per cent in 1956 and 6 per cent in 1957—and quite rapidly thereafter: increases over the preceding year of 12.8, 11, and 9 per cent were scheduled for

1. Statistics on the July version of the plan are cited from *GP*, no. 10 (1956), 1–8.
2. Data for the October version of the plan are from K. Secomski, "Z problematyki planu 5-letniego" (Selected problems of the Five-Year Plan), *GP*, no. 9 (1957), 1–10.

1958, 1959, and 1960 respectively. This sudden acceleration in the development pace would also be reflected in the targeted increases in gross output in producer goods (sector A) and in consumer goods (sector B); in 1957 output would rise by 5.3 per cent in sector B and only 2.1 per cent in sector A; but producer goods increases of the order of 10 to 11 per cent were scheduled from 1958 on, while sector B was expected to maintain a growth rate of 8 to 9 per cent per year.[3]

Targets for 1957 in the Five-Year Plan were set at easily attainable levels. Most of them were overfulfilled. The gross output of producer goods (sector A) rose by 7.8 per cent, compared to a 2.1 per cent planned increase. The output of consumer goods went up by 12 per cent, more than twice the planned increase. Even agriculture did better than had been anticipated with a 5 per cent gain in gross output, nearly 2 per cent above plan. National income produced rose by 9 per cent, or slightly more than according to the plan; but national income available for domestic use was 11 per cent higher than in 1956, thanks to substantial foreign loans granted by the Soviet Union (275 million dollars for 1957–60) and by the United States (93 million dollars).[4] In 1957 the deficit on merchandise trade came to 276 million dollars (compared to 37 million dollars in 1956).[5] The cancellation by the Soviet Union of $525 million dollars of Polish debts—as belated compensation for coal exports sold by Poland to Russia between 1945 to 1953 at prices which barely covered transportation expenses—also released for domestic consumption resources that had originally been earmarked for disposal abroad.

According to estimates prepared by the Chief Statistical Office, the real wages of workers employed in the socialized sector in-

3. Ibid., pp. 3, 7.
4. The planned figures on output and national income are from Secomski, *Z problematyki* . . . Actual results are from the *RS 1959*, pp. 58, 75, 168. A recalculation by an official of the Chief Statistical Office of the industrial production index on the basis of 870 physical-output relatives (aggregated with weights equal to wages plus depreciation in the making of each product) showed that the official index of gross output overstated growth by about 3 percentage points for the period 1956–58 (the index showed a 31 per cent increase over 1955, the recalculation only 27.9 per cent). For the year 1957 the difference was only about 1 per cent. The largest source of overstatement was the textile industry (especially cotton-cloth manufacturing) and machine building. (Interview material.)
5. *RS 1959*, p. 250.

creased by 8.2 per cent in 1957.[6] Polish farmers also benefited from
the economic gains recorded in 1957. Compulsory deliveries of
milk were abolished soon after the October 1956 plenum. Prices
paid by the state for deliveries of grain doubled.[7] According to
estimates published by the Chief Statistical Office the real incomes
of farmers rose by 15 per cent in 1956 and by 6 per cent in 1957.[8]

Besides all these quantitative achievements, the year 1957 was
also marked by a very real, though statistically intractable, improvement in the operation of the socialized sector. The formal
rights granted to industrial enterprises had something to do with
this improvement. But it could also be traced to intangible
changes in the working relationship between the enterprise and
its hierarchy. The pressure applied by ministries and central
boards on producers to deliver output "at any cost" had relented.
Production plans were now set with a margin of reserve; an opportunity was given to enterprises to accumulate a higher level of inventories. The rise in inventories in the entire socialized sector,
including retail trade, amounted to 21.6 billion zlotys in 1957, or
nearly three times as much as had been planned for the year. (The
difference was partly due to the omission in the plans of inventories of imported goods bought with the proceeds of foreign loans
which had not yet been confirmed when the plans were drawn up.)
Total inventories, reckoned in constant prices, were 17.3 per cent
higher than at the end of 1956. A study of industry, excluding
food-processing enterprises showed that inventories had gone up
by 18.7 per cent in 1957, while gross output had risen by only 10.3
per cent. Inventories of raw materials increased more than goods
in process and finished products. A breakdown by quarters suggests that the above-normal accumulation of inventories started in
the second half of 1956 and that it lasted at least until the first
quarter of 1958, when the increases began to taper off.[9] In 1957,
the ratio of investments including inventories and reserves in the

6. *RS 1959*, p. 358.

7. Ibid., pp. 217–19.

8. "Dochody realne ludności chłopskiej z produkcji rolniczej w latach 1956–
1958" (The real income of the peasant population from agricultural production
in the years 1956–1958), supplement to *Biuletyn statystyczny*, no. 2 (1959). It is
worth noting that the value of farmers' investment expenditures, expressed in constant prices, rose by 57 per cent from 1956 to 1957.

9. Bogobowicz and Pruss, "Zapasy przedsiębiorstw uspołecznionych w 1959 r."
WNBP, no. 7 (1960), 315–17, Also *ZG*, no. 9 (1959), 4.

national income rose from 19.5 to 21.5 per cent; but this aggregate proportion concealed a slight decline in the ratio of investments in fixed assets—which was more than made up by the swelling volume of inventories.[10]

During 1958, a year of transition, a number of the trends that had been set in motion by the events of October 1956 continued to prevail; simultaneously, certain retrogressive tendencies, which were to become more noticeable in 1959 and 1960, made their first appearance.

A more ambitious investment program and higher output targets imparted a fresh sense of urgency to the execution of the plans. According to the approved drafts of the Five-Year Plan, investments in fixed assets in 1958 were scheduled to rise by 12.8 per cent, national income by 10.2 per cent, and the gross output of socialized industry by 9.9 per cent. The carrying out of this program did not pan out nearly as well as in the preceding year. Only a little over half the planned increase in national income was realized. Output plans as a whole were fulfilled, but only by virtue of an excess in consumer goods production which just offset the shortfall in producer goods. A part of the above-plan output in consumer goods was stocked up as a contingency reserve to assist the government in managing a contemplated price and wage reform, which actually did not come off; [11] another part was carried over as surplus inventories, which were hard to unload because of the stiffened resistance of consumers to high prices and shoddy quality. (The revival of private trade, the influx of packages from abroad, and increased imports of consumer goods all contributed to this new development.) During the course of 1958, inventories of finished goods held by plants in light industry (including textiles) rose by 56 per cent; inventories of consumer goods in wholesale and retail organizations registered a 28 per cent increase, most of which was due to the piling up of clothing, textiles, and shoes. By way of contrast, output in the producer goods industries tended to outpace the rise in inventories, especially in the second half of the year.[12] The official index of real wages for persons em-

10. M. Kucharski, "Czy zapasy hamują rozwój" (Do inventories hamper growth), ZG, no. 16 (1960), 1, 4.

11. F. P. "Szczególny rok" (An especial year), ZG, no. 21 (1959), 4.

12. Bogobowicz and Pruss, p. 319; and Kucharski, p. 4.

ployed in the socialized sector showed a 3.3 per cent increase for 1958; but this is probably an overstatement if we consider that the real consumption of the farm population rose by about 4 per cent, which would seem to more than account for the 1.5 per cent increase in the nation's personal consumption, as estimated in the national-income accounts.[13]

The inflationary pressures generated by a vigorous investment drive in the second half of 1958 were reinforced by the decentralized outlays of state enterprises, cooperatives, and local peoples' councils. These decentralized outlays came to 15 billion zlotys for the entire year in the state sector and 4.3 billion in the cooperative sector, or a combined total of nearly one-half the volume of centralized outlays.[14] A potential source of monetary disequilibrium was the omission in the wage plan (and hence in the synthetic balances) of labor expenditures by producing enterprises on decentralized projects.

The following figures give an indication of the substantial underestimation of decentralized outlays in the National Economic Plan for 1958. The plan envisaged that the Ministry of Heavy Industry would spend 984 million zlotys on this account; it actually spent 1,431 millions, or 146 per cent of plan; this figure would have risen to 163 per cent if the enterprises of the ministry had been able to secure enough labor and materials to carry out their industrial-technical-financial plans. The financial means accumulated by firms in the ministry from above-plan profits, from the sale of surplus equipment, and from the enterprise fund came to 71 per cent more than the sums that were supposed to remain at their disposal. In addition they received 20 per cent more credits than had been provided for in the plan. In other ministries, similar, if somewhat smaller, discrepancies between planned and actual outlays were discovered.[15]

Another contributing factor to the financial crisis was the breakdown in "wage discipline"; large sums were paid in excess of plan (half a billion zlotys in 1958 alone), which the National Bank could not control because of the unremitting resistance of the

13. *RS 1959*, pp. 60, 258; "Dochody realne ludności chłopskiej. . . ."
14. *RS 1959*, p. 67.
15. Z. Saldak, "Zalety i wady inwestycji zdecentralizowanych" (Advantages and shortcomings of decentralized investments), *ZG*, no. 21 (1959), 5.

associations and of the ministries to the imposition of sanctions on their subordinate enterprises.[16]

These financial strains were not grave in themselves but they were danger signals, which the planners should have heeded when they were preparing their investment program for the forthcoming year. But they ignored these warnings. First they underestimated the pace of investment expenditures in the latter part of 1958. Then they framed a program incorporating the ambitious target scheduled for 1959 in the approved version of the Five-Year Plan (an 11 per cent increase over 1958). Mild weather in the first quarter of 1959 permitted the construction industry to overfulfill its plan. For the first half of the year, investment outlays ran at 14 per cent above the comparable period of 1958, as compared to a planned increase of 11.9 per cent, starting from a lower base. During this period, employment in the construction sector rose by 30,000 persons above plan.[17]

As in the past year, and for similar reasons, the wage plan was overfulfilled. It was forecast in October that the wages paid out above plan would rise to 10 billion zlotys over the entire year, a sum equal to approximately 7 per cent of the planned wage fund. In 1959 decentralized investments in state enterprises actually increased by 4.5 billion zlotys, or by 30 per cent over 1958.[18] This was 18.7 per cent in excess of plan. Most difficult to control from the center were the decentralized investments initiated by local enterprises under the supervision of the peoples' councils of voivodships, counties, and towns, whose relative importance had greatly risen in recent years. In 1959 the voivodships were entrusted with the preparation of investment projects worth 16 billion zlotys, or a fourth of all investment outlays in the socialized sector (the bulk of the voivodship investments were decentralized).[19]

A high level of investments, planned or unplanned, would have been tolerable if the output of food and other consumer goods had kept up with the wages and other incomes from investment

16. Frenkel, "Niedoskonała kontrola," ZG, no. 24 (1959), 6.

17. TL, December 3, 1959, as quoted by Economic Survey of Europe in 1959, p. 23.

18. ZG, no. 40 (1959), 1; ZG, no. 31 (1960), 1.

19. ZG, no. 49 (1958), 8.

projects being injected into the income stream. But, on the contrary, the targeted increases in the output of industrial consumer goods were the smallest in five years. The food situation deteriorated as poor weather conditions brought on an absolute decline in crop output amounting to nearly 2 per cent. Although the size of animal herds stayed at, or slightly below, 1958 levels, production and centralized purchases of meat dropped by close to 5 per cent. This fall in meat deliveries was considered extremely serious in view of the fact that wage earners normally spend about a quarter of any increments in their income on meat alone. Export commitments helped to aggravate the meat shortage: live hogs, weighing a total of 34,453 tons were exported in 1959, in addition to 100,000 tons of meat in raw and processed form; the combined total was nearly 40 per cent greater than in 1957.[20]

During the course of the year, higher incomes from wages, salaries, and pensions converged on reduced stocks of meat. Despite the excess of demand over supply, the government tried to keep a lid on retail prices. Informal rationing and queues formed as consumers competed for their share of a dwindling supply. The situation had become so critical by the end of the summer that the Party was moved to call a special plenum. On October 17, 1959, Gomulka announced that prices of beef, veal, pork, animal fats, and sausage would have to be raised by anywhere from 10 to 38 per cent to re-establish balance in the market.[21] (The average increase came to about 25 per cent.) During the first half of the year the rise in retail prices lagged behind increases in money wages, so that real wages appeared to improve (by an estimated 3.5 per cent), but this was entirely due to the failure of official prices to reflect the growing scarcity of meat products. The effect of the price adjustments of October was to cancel out these earlier gains, such as they may have been.[22]

Gomulka admitted frankly that this economic blow would give the working class something to carp about:

20. RS 1959, p. 255; RS 1960, p. 132.
21. W. Gomulka, "Aktualne trudności i środki niezbędne do ich przezwyciężenia" (The present difficulties and the unavoidable means for overcoming them), ND, no. 12 (1959), 20.
22. Cf. Gomulka's speech, ND, no. 12 (1959), 4 and 32. According to my calculations, real wages must have fallen by 4 to 5 per cent as a consequence of the price increases.

The working class, the toiling people, would not have re-criminations against us if we had not permitted such a great increase in the purchasing power of the population. They object because we are taking back what we gave. It is easy and pleasant to give, but one has to find plenty of excuses to take away. The working class has the right to ask us the bitter question: how do you manage things, that first you give, and then you come to us and say that you gave away too much.[23]

The lesson Gomulka drew from this embarrassing affair was that decentralization had gone too far, that it had led to a breakdown in financial discipline and a falling off in the coordination of plans. This was the remedy he had to offer:

The process of decentralization must be accompanied by the consolidation of central control, especially of financial control . . . This will require an improvement in the functioning of central economic organs so that they may interfere operationally in cases where events occur which may conflict with the assumptions behind the economic plans or with the interests of the socialist economy. In view of the present state of affairs in our economy, the conclusion emerges that the Planning Commission's role in directing the process of execution of the plans should be widened, together with its responsibility for seeing to it that the plans are properly executed.[24]

The resolutions of the plenum echoed the First Secretary's recommendations. They placed special accent on "the reinforcement of inter-ministerial coordination" and on the rights and prerogatives of the Planning Commission to realize this aim. The Commission was to have more opportunity for making changes in approved plans during the course of their execution; it was to acquire wider powers "with respect to material balances, state reserves, foreign trade, the planning and carrying out of investments, the planning of employment, labor productivity, and production costs."[25]

23. Ibid., p. 30.
24. Ibid., p. 28.
25. Resolution of the Third Plenum of the Central Committee of the United Polish Workers' Party, *ND*, no. 12 (1959), 38.

A few kind words on the benefits of decentralization could not conceal the nature of the new Party program. The rod had been spared too long; the infant had become spoiled. Only "administrative measures" could be relied on to eliminate slack in the plans and tighten financial discipline.

2. Recentralization: 1959–60

The October plenum bolstered the partisans of a harder economic line who, ever since mid-1958, had been decrying the excessive deconcentration of power and blaming it for many of the snags that were upsetting the proper functioning of the economy. Bronisław Minc who had been among the first to speak out against overcentralization in 1956 now led the assault against the reform movement. In a truculent article written for *Zycie gospodarcze,* interspersed with dark hints about the class nature of revisionist tendencies in Polish and Hungarian economic thought, Minc argued that the "attempt to reform our economic system, baptized as the 'new model,' had basically ended in failure. This had to be the case . . . since this attempt was built on neomarginalist rather than on Marxist grounds." [26]

About the time of the October plenum an article appeared in the Planning Commission's journal lending concrete evidence to the charge of "soft planning" in the ministries and at lower echelons. The plans submitted by the ministries on the basis of the Planning Commission's directives consistently underestimated the output potential of their branches and overestimated material costs, wage outlays, and other input requirements. The ministries backed up their counterplans with "an arsenal of arguments, then badgered the Commission into setting easy-to-fulfill plans for the year." Afterwards they would proceed to overfulfill these flabby plans; this entitled them to distribute large sums to the staffs of their enterprises in the form of production bonuses, which contributed their bit to the pressure of inflation. This tendency had been manifest in the make-up of the 1960 plans. The ministries had committed themselves in their plan-projects to a total value of output which was 6 billion zlotys less than the directives had provided for; at the same time their employment plans exceeded

26. B. Minc, "W sprawie zmian w zarządzaniu gospodarką narodową," *ZG,* no. 8 (1959).

the directives by 50,000 persons, their aggregate wage fund by about 1.5 billion zlotys, and their requests for investment funds by about 7 billion zlotys. Withal, their targets for labor-productivity increases still averaged out to 2.5 per cent less than the Commission had directed. The report concluded:

> It is inadmissible that the work in this [preparatory] period should consist to such an extent in marshalling arguments to be used in vying for the most favorable plan-indicators, and in elaborating tactics aimed at the defense of positions agreeable to the narrow interests of the sector but frequently conflicting with the interests of the national economy as a whole.[27]

It was not with these admonitions that the Party could expect to restore discipline in the field. What was needed in conjunction with moral suasion was to appoint strong disciplinarians who would impose the will of the Party over the economic system and its participants. It was not hard to find men possessed of such talents. Eugeniusz Szyr, Tadeusz Gede, and Julian Tokarski, who had built up a reputation as reliable and forceful functionaries in the Stalinist period, were elevated to positions of direct command where they could exercise their executive prowess. These personnel changes in the economic sphere were consonant with the struggle against revisionism, with the removal of the more liberal elements in the Party, and with the political comeback of Stalinists, including the notorious General Kazimierz Witaszewski, who was reinstated to a top position in the secretariat of the Central Committee at the end of 1959.

After October 1959 the Economic Committee of the Council of Ministers, headed by Szyr, and the Planning Commission proceeded jointly to check the drift that had led to the meat crisis of the previous summer. Stringent controls were clamped on decentralized investments to prevent a rise in their absolute level in the coming year. Instead of letting enterprises engage in investments if they disposed of sufficient funds from above-plan profits, from the sale of surplus equipment, or from other sources, the

27. S. Hatt, "Pierwsze wnioski z resortowych projektów planów na rok 1960" (The first conclusions drawn from the ministerial projects of plans for 1960), *GP*, no. 10 (1959), 4.

authorities set global limits on these outlays. Along with the limits went all kinds of new restrictions which "practically abolished the idea of decentralized investments." [28] Cooperatives were especially hard hit by the new measures; their decentralized investments for 1960 were slated to drop to 84 per cent of their 1959 volume.

On the whole the restrictive measures were quite successful. If we compare the level of total investments for the first half of the year in 1958, 1959, and 1960, we find that investments rose by 22.5 per cent from 1958 to 1959 but by only 5.9 per cent from 1959 to 1960. Decentralized investments, which had been the chief culprit for above-plan expenditures in 1959, dropped 10 to 15 per cent below the level of 1959 in the second and third quarters of 1960 (as a result of rigorous new regulations on the approval of decentralized projects), then picked up toward the end of the year after additional disbursements had been authorized by the Ministry of Finance.[29]

More severe wage controls were also applied to avert the excesses of the preceding year. Higher piece-rate norms were introduced in a number of plants which had the effect of reducing the earnings of as many as half the workers subjected to the revision. Total wage outlays, which had risen by 10 per cent in the first half of 1959, showed no rise at all from January to July of 1960. For the entire year, they rose by less than 3 per cent. (Owing mainly to increases in food prices early in the year, the population suffered a decline in real wages of about 2 per cent in 1960 compared to 1959.) Sales of consumer goods in state retail shops in the first quarter of 1960 were 5 per cent lower than they had been a year ago.[30] The inflation had been curbed but at the cost of popular hardship and of a curtailment in investment outlays which, according to experts, was likely to prejudice the fulfillment of the long-range plans if the trend was not soon reversed.[31]

28. W. Dudziński, "Inwestycje zdecentralizowane—rozdział zamknięty?" (Decentralized investments—a closed chapter?), ZG, no. 18 (1960), 3.

29. ZG, nos. 31, 32, and 35 (1960); also, Rada Ekonomiczna, "Sytuacja gospodarcza w kraju w roku 1960" (The economic situation in the country in the year 1960), supplement to ZG (February 1961), pp. 20–21.

30. Some of the ground lost in the first three quarters was recovered after the rather favorable results of the 1960 harvest began to be felt on the market. ZG, nos. 32 and 35 (1960); Economic Bulletin for Europe, 12, no. 1 (1960), 16; "Sytuacja gospodarcza . . . ," p. 24.

31. Interview material (1960).

To restore equilibrium in the state retail market was the simplest of the tasks confronting the planners in the fall of 1959. The investment drive begun in the second half of 1958 had fanned the fires of inflation; but it was also responsible for a marked deterioration in the "procurement market" compared to 1957 and 1958. The supply situation of socialized enterprises had improved in 1957 and also, to a lesser extent, in 1958. Over a thousand materials had been crossed off the rationed list. Inventories had risen to fairly comfortable levels. From early 1959 on, however, many of the materials consumed on a large scale by the construction and by the machine-building industries were already in critical supply. Structural steels, nonferrous metals, metal and concrete pipes, cables, and wire were among the scarcest commodities. The deficit spread from one material to the other as consumers tried to get around shortages by ordering substitutes.[32] The level of inventories in industry rose much less than production; the stock of rolled steel products on hand in heavy industry was actually lower at the end of 1959 than at the beginning.[33] Supply conditions do not seem to have improved after the Third Plenum. "There is not a ministry or an enterprise in the course of the first two months of 1960 which received its consignments of materials in the quantities provided for in the plans, even when the latter did not suffice to cover requirements."[34]

New instructions were issued in mid-1960 for preparing the supply plans and the balances that would be incorporated into the National Economic Plan for 1961. Only a few commodities were added to the rationed list, which now included 365 items, but a larger proportion of the total output of each product was earmarked for allocation to specific consuming ministries.[35] The supply plans submitted by ministries and lower organs had to encompass, in addition to rationed materials, any materials used in large quantities, especially where they might be subject to important fluctuations in consumption from one year to the next.

32. The excess pressure on nonferrous alloys, for instance, spilled over to gray iron which soon fell short. See *GM*, no. 10 (1960), 326.

33. Bogobowicz and Pruss, p. 317.

34. W. Dudziński, "Zaopatrzeniowe problemy" (Procurement problems), *ZG*, no. 15 (1960), 1.

35. *GM*, no. 10 (1960), 347; and Komisja Planowania przy Radzie Ministrów, *Załączniki do Instrukcji do opracowania projektu narodowego planu gospodarczego na 1961 r.* (Annexes to the instructions for preparing the project of the national economic plan for 1961), pp. 87–111.

For the last several years, only the physical quantities of materials consumed had been recorded in the supply plan; the new instructions, reverting to the practice of the early 1950s, now required enterprises, associations, and ministries to compute the combined cost of their principal material inputs. The avowed purpose of this regulation was to help forge an elementary link between material allocations and cost plans.[36]

The list of centrally distributed commodities for 1961 is much shorter than it was in 1956, but, since many items are at present informally rationed by the marketing organizations, there will be increasing pressure, as shortages deepen, to transfer responsibility for dividing up scarce supplies from the marketing organizations to the Planning Commission. Once this centralizing process is completed, the system of output planning and materials rationing will be back, for all practical purposes, to what it was before Gomulka took over.

3. Conclusions

The first published data on the results of the first Five-Year Plan should give the regime no cause for alarm. Performance has run close to expectations: targets of gross industrial output have been fulfilled with a good margin to spare; agricultural output fell a few percent short of the mark, but not nearly as short as during the Six-Year Plan. The individual production targets for a number of important industrial materials listed in Table 10:1 were missed, yet the discrepancies were relatively small (in every case listed, less than 5 per cent, the equivalent of a few months delay).

Labor productivity in industry during the Five-Year Plan rose far more than the 27 per cent originally scheduled. (According to a tentative estimate, 92 per cent of the increase in gross industrial output was due to higher productivity.) [37]

The improvement in living standards, though real, was only imperfectly expressed by the index of real wages. For one thing, housing construction, although it developed more or less according to plan,[38] failed to make more than a dent in the enormous

36. See above, Chap. 3, Sect. 6.
37. ZG, nos. 51–52 (1960), 15.
38. A total of nearly fifty thousand rooms were built above plan between 1956 and 1958; but there was a shortfall of 11,000 rooms in 1959 and 33,000 rooms in 1960.

backlog of needs accumulated during earlier years of neglect: altogether 620,000 dwelling units were built from 1956 to 1960, more than half of them by individuals and cooperatives with or without state participation; after subtracting 100,000 units which burnt down, collapsed, or otherwise had to be retired from use, this left a net increase of 520,000 units; there was an estimated addition to the demand for housing (due mainly to newly contracted marriages) of 940,000 units.[39] For another thing, the drop

TABLE 10:1. *First Five-Year Plan (1956–60): Targets and Achievements*

	Final version	Achieved (preliminary estimates)
Index numbers:		
National income (1955 = 100)	146.0	c. 142.0
Gross output (1955 = 100)	149.1	158.0
of which:		
producer goods industries	150.6	159.0
consumer goods industries	147.4	154.0
Gross output of agriculture (1955 = 100)	125.0	120.4
Real wages of employees (official index, 1955 = 100)	130.0	129.0
Production:		
Coal (millions of tons)	105.0	104.6
Crude steel (millions of tons)	7.0	6.7
Rolled steel (millions of tons)	4.6	4.4
Cement (millions of tons)	6.9	6.6
Sulfuric acid (millions of tons)	0.72	0.69
Electric power (billions of kwh)	28.3	29.0

Sources. K. Secomski, "Z problematyki planu 5-letniego," *GP*, no. 9 (1957), 3–5; *ZG*, no. 37 (1960), 5; *ZG*, nos. 51–52 (1960); Rada Ekonomiczna przy Radzie Ministrów, "Sytuacja gospodarcza kraju w roku 1960," Supplement to *ZG*, February, 1961.

in real wages which occurred in 1959 and 1960—after three years of steady improvement—was aggravated by a relative decline in job opportunities outside agriculture and, for those already working in the cities, by the difficulty of finding supplementary employment ("moonlighting").[40]

Prospects for the future are not so bright as the successes chalked up during the Five-Year Plan might presage. Some of these successes were due to the foreign loans extended to the Polish govern-

39. *ZG*, no. 14 (1961), 3.
40. "Sytuacja gospodarcza . . . ," p. 24.

ment during this period—426 million dollars from the United States alone. During the second Five-Year Plan part of the credits must be repaid. This will aggravate an already serious balance-of-payments problem. Moreover, a number of investment projects were completed in recent years which had been started during the Six-Year Plan. This rendered possible large increases in output at little cost. There will be fewer tail-ends of investment projects in the next few years to yield easy increases in output. The next Five-Year Plan will be executed under conditions similar to the early 1950s when many long-gestation projects got under way, which bore fruit only in subsequent periods.[41]

According to the latest version of the plan for 1961–65, approved by the Party in July 1960, investments costing 565 billion zlotys at July 1959 prices will be budgeted for the next five years, or over 50 per cent more than the volume of outlays for 1956–60.[42] Having in mind the high susceptibility of the Polish economy to inflation that was revealed by the events of 1959, one cannot help wonder how the Party hopes to press forward a program of this magnitude without opening a new, wider gap between aggregate demand and the supply of consumer goods. This is directly relevant to the issue of institutional reform: it should by now be clear that the government, in order to combat inflationary tendencies, will not hesitate to curtail the autonomy of producers and of the newly created associations. The only hope the Poles may harbor for a second round of decentralization lies in the ability of the Planning Commission to carry out the second Five-Year Plan without overstraining domestic resources, running a serious deficit in the balance of payments, or unleashing the forces of inflation.

This point is so vital to the entire issue of centralization and decentralization that it may be worthwhile—even at the cost of oversimplifying the issues—to run down the factors that will condition the inflationary potential of the economy in future years.

The main problem facing the government is to supply the retail

41. The problems of the Second Five-Year Plan are discussed along these lines by M. Kalecki in "Podstawowe zagadnienia planu pięcioletniego na lata 1961–1965" (Main problems of the Five-Year Plan for the years 1961–1965), GP, nos. 1–2 (1959), 1–4. On this plan and its relation to the balance of payments see A. Zauberman, "The Polish Economy 1961: II. Policies and Prospects," Soviet Survey, no. 35 (January–March 1961), 54–60.

42. ND, no. 7 (1960), 32.

network with consumer goods, valued at steady prices, in sufficient volume and in a desirable enough assortment to absorb the incomes generated by the production activities and the investment outlays stipulated in the long-range plans. This problem is complicated by the fact that the effective demand of Polish consumers, at prevailing levels of real incomes, is ill-adapted to the structure of supplies in state shops and concords even less with the productive potential of state industry; consumers spend too little on state manufactures, particularly on durables, out of their current incomes and out of additions thereto; they spend too high a proportion of their incomes on foodstuffs, particularly on meat, whose production requires imported feeds and costs the government an excessive amount of foreign exchange.

The problem in recent years has assumed a financial form. Since compulsory deliveries of milk were abolished in 1959 and the prices paid by procurement agencies for other foodstuffs were raised, the tax and profit margins collected by the state on farm products have dwindled. The treasury has had to rely increasingly on turnover taxes levied on the industrial goods sold to the population in order to finance the national economy. But the yield on these taxes is limited by sluggish demand conditions. The production costs of clothing, shoes, and durable goods in state factories are high; choice in retail stores is limited, and quality is generally unsatisfactory. (All this could hardly be otherwise in view of the neglect of these industries during the Six-Year Plan and the failure to renew and to expand their equipment.) In the past, the lack of alternative sources of supply compelled the population, whose stocks of goods had been depleted by the war, to take whatever merchandise retail stores offered. Under conditions of repressed inflation, where almost all consumer goods were priced below their supply-and-demand equilibrium, there was no difficulty finding clients for the available supplies. Nowadays, however, cooperatives and private shops, though still hedged in by government discrimination, have more attractive goods to offer than before; clothing and shoes received in gift packages from abroad are competing with domestic production. State shops are finding it increasingly difficult to clear their inventories. On the other hand, the authorities are reluctant to make deep cuts in the retail prices of industrial goods since they would mainly redound to the benefit of the peasants, who already buy a disproportionate share of these goods. The Ministry of Internal Trade tried to accelerate sales of shoes and textiles in 1959 by making moderate reductions in their prices. More recently it has resorted to advertising campaigns, attractive window displays, and other makeshift devices to keep its goods moving. Up to the end of 1960, these measures had not proved particularly successful.[43]

Another way the state could boost the demand for industrial goods would be to invest more in consumer-goods industries, reduce production costs, and lower the prices of these products (without cutting tax revenue). But this solution would deprive heavy industry of a part of its share of the country's new capital and tend to retard its growth. This would not be politically acceptable.

Why not remedy the demand for industrial goods at present prices by raising industrial wages? This would not be desirable because workers spend such a large part of their income on food. Higher wages would merely tend to aggravate the meat shortage, which was only mitigated by the substantial price increases decreed in the fall of 1959, and perhaps bring on a crisis in other foodstuffs as well. As the extra wages would spill over to the peasant market, the private farmers would be gainers in the end just the same.

It would be possible to raise urban real wages, if the peasants could be induced to sell more food to the state without getting more industrial goods in return. This could be done without recourse to compulsion by raising farm productivity. The second Five-Year Plan has earmarked relatively large sums to this end. The recently created Agricultural Circles are slated to receive

43. Preliminary statistics for the first four months of 1961 did, however, reveal a marked improvement in the structure of demand. While incomes from wages and salaries were 11.5 per cent higher and payments by the state for agricultural purchases 13.1 per cent higher than during the same period of 1960, meat consumption, which usually absorbed a large part of wage increases, had only risen 6.2 per cent. On the other hand, sales of shoes were up 16 per cent over a year ago. Other notable increases took place in sales of clothing (28 per cent), photographic equipment (25 per cent), radios (29 per cent), televisions (30 per cent), and watches (120 per cent). Even the Minister of Internal Trade could not guess whether this favorable shift in the pattern of demand was anything but ephemeral. See M. Lesz, "Na krajowym rynku: Aktualna sytuacja i perspektywy" (On the domestic market: the present situation and perspectives), ZG, no. 24 (1961), 1, 4.

agricultural machinery on an unprecedented scale.[44] Deliveries of fertilizers and insecticides will also be stepped up. But the dwarf size of a majority of private farms [45] places a low ceiling on the effectiveness of these measures. On the other hand, the government is reluctant, for political reasons, to permit the formation, through purchase and inheritance, of efficient large-scale farms, as long at least as they remain under private ownership.

Collectivization of agriculture may be a way out of this dilemma, inasmuch as it might enable the state to collect a larger amount of food from the peasantry without having to give up more industrial goods in return. With this extra food it might be possible to absorb the purchasing power released by the ambitious investments of the next few years. But the Party leadership has no illusions that collectivization could be rammed through in the immediate future without an "intensification of the class struggle in the countryside," that is, without the use of high-handed coercion or terror. In present political circumstances, it is doubtful whether Gomulka and his associates would wish to resort to these means.[46] Even if they did and they managed to lick the inflationary problem, there would no longer be much point afterward to resuming the trend toward decentralization. Once political tensions had been irritated to that extent, only command decisions and centralized means of control could keep the economy on the expansion path laid out by the Communist authorities.[47]

Let us now revert to the economic situation of 1957–58, when fundamental reform was still the talk of the day. What would have happened at that time if the Planning Commission had really abjured direct interference and allowed enterprises, at least within certain aggregate financial limits, to produce, buy, and sell what they pleased at prevailing prices? We should be inclined to

44. See Chap. 5, Sect. 5.

45. In 1958, 47.8 per cent of the land in the possession of private farms belonged to farms of less than seven hectares (41.9 per cent in 1950). These small farms made up 77.8 per cent of the total number of farms above 0.5 hectares in area. Only 13.1 per cent of the farm area was owned by farms of 14 or more hectares. (RS 1960, pp. 207–08.)

46. So far (June 1961), the only concrete measure contemplated by the Party to foist a higher degree of efficiency on the private sector is to confiscate certain privately owned lands, whose cultivation, in the judgment of government officials, has been egregiously neglected.

47. Cf. Kurowski's remarks quoted in Chap. 9, p. 273.

argue that this experiment would have run into very serious difficulties. The price system was so far out of kilter that almost any decisions it might have induced would have been at odds with the planners' priorities—as also with any reasonable considerations of efficiency. Furthermore the failure to gear managers' incentives exclusively to profits would have blunted the influence of prices —for good or for bad—on the decisions of producers.

The price reform of mid-1960, the expanded importance of the Enterprise Fund, and the new bonus system introduced in February 1960 would have mitigated some of the dangers to which decentralization would have exposed the economy two years earlier; but they certainly would not have eliminated them.

Assuming the authorities had been willing to rehaul the incentives system and to set prices on a theoretically justifiable basis, would this have enabled them to carry out an efficient decentralization? Not unless controls on production and on input decisions had simultaneously been dismantled. For enterprises, as long as they are hemmed in by rationing and output orders, will not apply for the same materials and in the same quantities as if they were to base their demand on price considerations alone. Supply and demand decisions must be taken as functions of prices to qualify as indicators of scarcity. Partial decentralization would sever the old lines of direct command before remote controls had been perfected to take their place.

There might be other shortcomings to decentralization from the regime's point of view: Decentralization might hinder the rapid spread among plants of new technologies, which had formerly been diffused from the top down; it could easily cause a falling off in the coordination of investment decisions; it would tend to disperse some of the economic and political power hitherto engrossed by the central authorities.

Once we grant the sovereignty of the political authorities to deploy resources as they see fit—to drive forward their industrialization plans predicated on the development of heavy industry, to direct the bulk of the foreign trade of the country toward the Soviet bloc, to maintain an expensive defense establishment—there is not so much to be said in favor of institutional reforms. Indeed, the ends may have a decisive influence on the choice of means to attain them.

The long-range plans are a case in point. Much has been written in Poland about the disproportions created by the Six-Year Plan and about the need for improved coordination in the second Five-Year Plan. One of the main sources of disproportions in the past, as we have seen, was the rapid expansion of armament industries during the Korean War which went beyond the capacity of the economy to produce the fuels and metallurgical supplies necessary to support the added burden. This increased pressure on the raw-material base of the country compelled the reduction of coal and zinc exports and reinforced incipient balance-of-payments difficulties. Another source of disproportions was the sudden decision taken at the Ninth Party Plenum in the fall of 1953 —in line with Malenkov's New Course—to step up the output of consumer goods and to make drastic cuts in the investment program. The completion of many projects essential to a balanced development of industry was delayed, with obvious consequences. Whether the authorities had resorted to centralized or to decentralized methods in carrying out these sweeping changes in social priority, some dislocation would have ensued. More efficient methods might at best have effected a smoother transition. Michał Kalecki may be correct in arguing that only central controls can make rapid adjustments such as these, the price system being too delicate an instrument to steer the economy during periods of stress.[48] Direct commands, as long as they are reasonably consistent with each other, are sure to bring off at least the main adjustments dictated by changing circumstances.

If we could be sure that the next three five-year plans, whose main lines have already been traced in the long-range program prepared under the direction of Professor Kalecki, would unravel smoothly, that neither tactical reversals nor any other vicissitudes would disrupt the course of their execution, the case for institutional reforms would be much stronger. Judging by the recent past, we have no reason to count on the stability of the planners' premises. The decision made in 1959 to back up the newly formed Agricultural Circles with farm equipment caused important revisions to be made in the second Five-Year Plan. The collectivization of agriculture, if it once got moving, would prompt a great many more changes. Finally, variations in the planners' demand

48. M. Kalecki, "Rady robotnicze a centralne planowanie," *ND*, no. 12 (1956).

may also depend on events in the rest of the Soviet bloc. There
has been a remarkable correlation ever since 1949 in the investment outlays of the Peoples' Democracies, which have been sensitive to political developments in the Soviet Union as well as to
tensions within individual countries in the bloc. It can hardly be
a coincidence that investments in industry rose at a rapid pace
from 1949 to 1952 in Poland and in Bulgaria, Czechoslovakia,
East Germany, Hungary, and Rumania, started declining within
a year after the death of Stalin, rose in 1956, fell in 1957 in the
aftermath of the Polish and Hungarian events of the previous
year, picked up again in 1958, and rose sharply in 1959. The proportion of total industrial investments falling to heavy and light
industry also varied in about the same manner in these various
countries.[49] Poland's long-range plans, it would appear, can no
more be insulated from events in the rest of the Soviet bloc than
from the tribulations of her own political life.

Polish economists, or at least those among them who gravitate
close to the orbit of power, are aware of the political and economic
reasons why decentralization is out of the question at the present
time. The more realistic members of the profession have reconciled themselves to this loss. They hope to mend and improve the
system "from the inside." Many of them are prepared to accept
the basic premises of the Soviet model, including centralized allocation of resources and a price system discharging mainly control
and accounting functions; but they intend to make better use of
it than in the past. Their approach is essentially pragmatic. They
are willing to apply Western economic tools if they can be turned
to account in the solution of concrete problems. The pioneer
studies conducted by the Department for Economic Research of
the Planning Commission in the application of input-output to
the coordination of the material balances are an outstanding example of this more rational attitude toward economics. Other
studies carried out by experts in the Ministry of Foreign Trade
(on the profitability of alternative export opportunities), in the
Ministry of Internal Trade (on income and price elasticities), and

49. Evidence for these parallel trends can be found in the yearly *Economic Survey of Europe* and in the statistical yearbooks of the different countries. A similar
pattern can also be observed in the evolution of employment in the construction
industries of the Peoples' Democracies.

in the economic department of the Academy of Sciences (on investment calculations and regionalization) also testify to the new spirit.

As much as our prejudices would favor more forceful institutional reforms, which would bring the Polish model closer to the ideal archetype of atomistic competition, we are forced to conclude that the "marginal improvements" just mentioned are more likely to satisfy the Party and its leaders—who have preferences for means as well as for ends—than any gingerly measures aimed at decentralization.

Planning by Successive Approximations: Consistency Problems

1. *Inversion by Iteration*

The following is a static model of short-term planning in a growing economy in the absence of foreign trade. The economy is divided into n producing and consuming sectors, each of which produces only one good.[1] All n goods produced are centrally planned and distributed. x_i ($i = 1$ to n) stands for the gross output of the i'th sector and y_i ($i = 1$ to n) for its net output for final demand. (Since this is a static model, final demand includes not only private consumption and armaments but also capital goods and additions to inventories.) Technological coefficients are denoted by a_{ij} (that is, a_{ij} units of good i are needed to produce one unit of good j). There are n^2 such coefficients.

The basic elements of a material balance may be represented as follows:

$$\underset{\text{Resources}}{x_i} \quad = \quad \underset{\text{Disposals}}{\sum_{j=1}^{n} a_{ij} x_j + y_j}$$

Together they form an interlocking set. In matrix form:

$$\bar{x} = \mathbf{A}\bar{x} + \bar{y}$$

where $\bar{x}$ and $\bar{y}$ are respectively vectors of gross output and final demand and $\mathbf{A}$ is the technology matrix.

Let $\bar{y}$ and $\mathbf{A}$ be given, $\bar{x}$ unknown. If computing machines are available, then $\bar{x}$ may be calculated as follows:

1. Joint products are discussed in Appendix B.

1) $\bar{x} - A\,\bar{x} = [I - A]\,\bar{x} = \bar{y}$

and

2) $\bar{x} = [I - A]^{-1}\,\bar{y}$

where $[I - A]^{-1}$ is the inverse of the matrix $[I - A]$. It is assumed for the time being that this inverted matrix exists.[2]

$\bar{x}$ may also be approximated by successive iterations: All that is necessary is that some planning organ in possession of the technological coefficients calculate input requirements for each successive set of estimates of $\bar{x}$ and that these requirements be totaled for each sector and then added to the known final demand for the sector.

This procedure is now described. The first estimate of gross outputs ($\bar{x}^{(1)}$) is computed exclusively from the final-demand vector:

3) $\bar{x}^{(1)} = A\,\bar{y} + \bar{y}$

The second is derived from the first:

$$\bar{x}^{(2)} = A\,\bar{x}^{(1)} + \bar{y} = A\,[A\,\bar{y} + \bar{y}] + \bar{y} = [I + A + A^2]\,\bar{y}$$

The m'th estimate works out to:

4) $\bar{x}^{(m)} = A\,\bar{x}^{(m-1)} + \bar{y} = [I + A + A^2 + \ldots + A^m]\,\bar{y}$

It has been proved [3] that, if enough iterations are carried out, equation 4) will simplify to:

5) $\bar{x}^{(m)} = \bar{x} = [I - A]^{-1}\,\bar{y}$

This expression is identical with 2).

If the iteration process is going to be cut short of ultimate convergence, as will be the case in planning practice, then starting the first iteration with the final-demand vector, whose components may come to only a fraction of total output, may lead to large errors. (It takes many steps to bring out the total gross output of a sector that produces mainly inputs for other sectors.) The planners' task will, in most cases, be simplified if they start the first

2. See below, Sect. 3.

3. F. W. Waugh, "Inversion of the Leontif Matrix by Power Series," *Econometrica*, *18*, no. 2 (1950).

iteration with estimates of gross output ("control figures") derived from a long-term plan or adapted from the previous year's results. Let these initial estimates be called $\bar{x}^0$. Then:

6) $$\bar{x}^{(1)} = \bar{y} + A\bar{x}^0$$
$$\bar{x}^{(2)} = \bar{y} + A\bar{x}^{(1)} = \bar{y} + A\bar{y} + A^2\bar{x}^0 = [I + A]\,\bar{y} + A^2\bar{x}^0$$
$$\bar{x}^{(m)} = [I + A + A^2 + \ldots + A^{m-1}]\,\bar{y} + A^m\bar{x}^0$$

We now note from 4) and 5) that:

$$\bar{x} = [1 + A + A^2 + \ldots + A^{m-1}]\,\bar{y} + [A^m + A^{m+1} + \ldots]\,\bar{y} =$$
$$[I + A + A^2 + \ldots + A^{m-1}]\,\bar{y} + A^m[I + A + A^2 + \ldots]\,\bar{y}$$

If in the above expression we now substitute in the place of the second $\bar{y}$ the vector $\bar{y}^0$ (the net outputs corresponding to the initial trial-set of gross outputs $\bar{x}^0$), the result will be fully equivalent to the right-hand side of the last equation in 6). The closer $\bar{y}^0$ is to $\bar{y}$, the faster will be the convergence to a consistent set of gross outputs $\bar{x}$. Note, in any event, that if the largest characteristic root of A is smaller than unity (which it should be if any net output can be produced by the system), $A^m\bar{x}^0$ will approach zero, and the result of 6) will again be identical in the limit with 2). However, for a small number of iterations, the estimates of $\bar{x}$ will normally be better than those obtained by calculating the first input requirements from the final-demand vector.

Whatever the starting point, the differences between the successive estimates of $\bar{x}$ should eventually begin to fall by a near-constant ratio. This ratio may be averaged for the different sectors. Let this average ratio be k. Then an ultimate approximation to $\bar{x}$ may be obtained by projecting these differences.[4] For example, to extrapolate to an ultimate estimate (x^m) from the fourth iteration:

$$x_i^{(m)} = x_i^{(4)} + (x_i^{(4)} - x_i^{(3)})\frac{k}{1-k}$$

2. Gauss-Seidel Iteration

This method makes more efficient use of the estimates generated at each step in the iteration process. As soon as an estimate of gross output corresponding to a given iteration is available for

4. W. D. Evans, "Input Output Computations," in *The Structural Interdependence of the Economy*, ed. by T. Barna.

the i'th row, it is used to compute the input requirements of all subsequent rows ($i + 1$ to n). Take for example the second iteration in a three-row model. The first row is identical with the normal iteration procedure already described:

$$7) \qquad x_1^{(2)} = a_{11}x_1^{(1)} + a_{12}x_2^{(1)} + a_{13}x_3^{(1)} + y_1$$

But, in making up the second row, advantage is already taken of x_1 estimated above:

$$x_2^{(2)} = a_{21}x_1^{(2)} + a_{22}x_2^{(1)} + a_{23}x_3^{(1)} + y_2$$

Similarly for the third row (using the results $x_1^{(2)}$ and $x_2^{(2)}$):

$$x_3^{(2)} = a_{31}x_1^{(2)} + a_{32}x_2^{(2)} + a_{33}x_3^{(1)} + y_3$$

This process can further be simplified by "netting out" the internal requirements of each sector, viz.:

$$8) \qquad \begin{aligned} (1 - a_{11})x_1^{(2)} &= a_{12}x_2^{(1)} + a_{13}x_3^{(1)} + y_1 \\ (1 - a_{22})x_2^{(2)} &= a_{21}x_1^{(2)} + a_{23}x_3^{(1)} + y_2 \\ (1 - a_{33})x_3^{(2)} &= a_{31}x_1^{(2)} + a_{32}x_2^{(2)} + y_3 \end{aligned}$$

The advantage of Gauss-Seidel is greatest where the technological matrix is most nearly triangular. In the case of a perfectly triangular matrix, one iteration would be sufficient to derive a consistent set of gross outputs from the final demand vector. Let such a matrix be:

$$\begin{bmatrix} a_{11} & 0 & 0 \\ a_{21} & a_{22} & 0 \\ a_{31} & a_{32} & a_{33} \end{bmatrix}$$

Given a final demand vector (y_1, y_2, y_3), we may obtain the corresponding gross outputs as follows:

$$9) \qquad (1 - a_{11})\, x_1^{(1)} = y_1; \text{ hence } x_1 = \frac{y_1}{1 - a_{11}}$$

$$(1 - a_{22})\, x_2^{(1)} = a_{21}x_1 + y_2 = \frac{a_{21}}{1 - a_{11}}\, y_1 + y_2$$

$$\text{and } x_2 = \frac{1}{1 - a_{22}} \left(\frac{a_{21}}{1 - a_{11}}\, y_1 + y_2 \right)$$

$$(1 - a_{33})x_3^{(1)} = \frac{a_{31}}{1 - a_{11}}\, y_1 + \frac{a_{32}}{1 - a_{22}} \left(\frac{a_{21}}{1 - a_{11}}\, y_1 + y_2 \right) + y_3$$

$$\text{and } x_3 = \frac{1}{1 - a_{33}} \left[\frac{a_{31}}{1 - a_{11}}\, y_1 + \frac{a_{32}}{1 - a_{22}} \left(\frac{a_{21}}{1 - a_{11}}\, y_1 + y_2 \right) + y_3 \right]$$

No superscripts are attached to x_1, x_2 and x_3 since they represent final estimates of gross output.

3. *The Technological Matrix and Convergence*

The coefficients computed from the material balances are technological. They may add up to more than unity in any column (e.g. two or three tons of iron ore are required to produce one ton of pig iron). However, if there is a set of measurement units ("prices") for all the x's, which would make all the column sums equal to or smaller than unity, one such sum being actually smaller than unity, the inverse of the $[I - A]$ matrix made up of these technological coefficients must exist. If the set of balances really "interlocks," if it is indecomposable (every industry, directly or indirectly, buys inputs from every other industry), then it is sufficient to observe that these interconnected industries produce *any* surplus over and above their own requirements to conclude that there is an inverse and that iteration would converge.[5] If they did not produce such a surplus for final demand, then the system would "eat itself up." It could only operate for a while by running down stocks and by imports. Normally, every set of balances observed in any working economy fulfills the conditions for convergent iteration. It is conceivable, nevertheless, that *ex ante* the technological coefficients might be such that the system could not produce any net output: *ex post,* there would be changes in the technical processes (e.g. substitution) which would make the economy viable. This situation is unlikely inasmuch as material and labor norms (our coefficients) tend to be extremely tight. If they are on the average *exceeded,* and the economy is still generating goods for final demand, then obviously the *ex ante* coefficients were small enough to permit inversion of the $[I - A]$ matrix. Iteration to reach a consistent plan should have been possible.

4. *Capacity Limitations*

In previous sections, we have been concerned with the problem of achieving mutual consistency in a set of material balances capable of producing a given bill of net outputs. Such calculations presuppose that the physical capacity in each sector is large enough to produce the gross output needed to support the re-

5. Dorfman, Samuelson, and Solow, *Linear Programming and Economic Analysis,* pp. 253–54.

quired bill of net outputs. From experience, or by means of the trial-and-error methods described in Appendix B, the planners should have some definite notions as to which sectors present bottleneck problems and constrain the growth of final demand and which do not. The planners will generally operate the bottleneck sectors at full capacity, if the supply of other exogenous inputs (including foreign exchange) permits. (In cases where these assumptions do not apply, the search for efficiency described in Appendix B would come under consideration.)

In the system about to be described, there are n producing sectors. Of these n sectors, h sectors have a maximum output limited by their productive capacity, while output in the other $(n-h)$ sectors is restricted only by the available materials.

Let the output of the capacity-limited sectors be denoted by x_c $(c = 1, 2, \ldots, h)$ and the output of the unlimited sectors be denoted by x_k $(k = h + 1, h + 2, \ldots, n)$. Final demand in the unlimited sectors is set at y_k $(k = h + 1, h + 2, \ldots, n)$.[6] The direct requirements on the part of capacity-limited sectors for inputs produced by unlimited-capacity sectors may be represented by:

$$\sum_{c=1}^{h} a_{fc} x_c \qquad (f = h + 1, h + 2, \ldots, n)$$

The demand for inputs produced by unlimited-capacity sectors on the part of this same group of unlimited-capacity sectors is:

$$\sum_{k=h+1}^{n} a_{fk} x_k \qquad (f = h + 1, h + 2, \ldots, n)$$

As a first approximation we may introduce net instead of gross outputs in the above expression so that the internal requirements of the unlimited-capacity sectors may be expressed as:

6. It is evident that these y_k cannot be set arbitrarily. If they are too large they may cause the net outputs of the capacity-limited sectors to fall below zero or, more generally, below minimum satisfactory levels. The procedure described below should be repeated until the final-demand requirements in the unlimited sectors have been set in proper relation to the bill of final demand generated in the capacity-limited sectors.

$$\sum_{k=h+1}^{n} a_{fk}\, y_k \qquad (f = h + 1,\ h + 2,\ \ldots,\ n)$$

where the final demands y_k are given.

The first approximation to the gross outputs of the unlimited-capacity sectors may then be set forth as follows:

$$x_{h+1}^{(1)} = y_{h+1} + \sum_{c=1}^{h} a_{h+1,c}\, x_c + \sum_{k=h+1}^{n} a_{h+1,k}\, y_k$$

$$x_{h+2}^{(1)} = y_{h+2} + \sum_{c=1}^{h} a_{h+2,c}\, x_c + \sum_{k=h+1}^{n} a_{h+2,k}\, y_k$$

$$\cdot \quad \cdot \quad \cdot \quad \cdot \quad \cdot \quad \cdot \quad \cdot \quad \cdot \quad \cdot \quad \cdot$$

$$x_{n}^{(1)} = y_{n} \quad + \sum_{c=1}^{h} a_{n,c}\, x_c + \sum_{k=h+1}^{n} a_{n,k}\, y_k$$

Let the column of estimated gross outputs on the left-hand side be represented by vector $\bar{x}^{(1)}$; the first two columns, all made up of known elements, by a single vector $\bar{k}$; and the last column by the product $\bar{A}\,\bar{y}$ (also a vector), where $\bar{A}$ is the reduced technology matrix obtained by omitting all capacity-limited sectors. The set of equations above may be abbreviated in matrix form to the single equation:

$$\bar{x}^{(1)} = \bar{k} + \bar{A}\,\bar{y}$$

We may use this result to obtain a second approximation to the gross outputs of the unlimited-capacity sectors:

$$\bar{x}^{(2)} = \bar{k} + \bar{A}\,\bar{x}^{(1)} = \bar{k} + \bar{A}\,[\bar{k} + \bar{A}\,\bar{y}]$$

Similarly, for the m'th iteration:

$$\bar{x}^{(m)} = \bar{k} + \bar{A}\,\bar{x}^{(m-1)} = \bar{A}^m\,\bar{y} + [\mathbf{I} + \bar{A} + \bar{A}^2 + \ldots \bar{A}^{m-1}]\,\bar{k} =$$
$$\bar{A}^m\,\bar{y} + [\mathbf{I} - \bar{A}]^{-1}\,\bar{k} \cong [\mathbf{I} - \bar{A}]^{-1}\,\bar{k}$$

Whether or not the term $\mathbf{A}^m\,\bar{y}$, which steadily declines toward zero as the number of iterations increases, can be neglected depends on the number of iterations actually carried out and on the desired degree of accuracy in the estimates of the unknown outputs.

Once the gross outputs in $\bar{x}^{(m)}$ have been successfully approximated, they may be used to compute the net outputs of the capacity-limited sectors:

$$y_1 = (1 - a_{11})\, x_1 - \ldots - a_{1h}\, x_h - a_{1,h+1}\, x_{h+1}^{(m)} - \ldots - a_{1n}\, x_n^{(m)}$$

$$\cdots \cdots \cdots \cdots \cdots \cdots \cdots \cdots \cdots \cdots$$

$$y_h = -a_{h1}\, x_1 - \ldots + (1 - a_{hh})\, x_h - a_{h,h+1}\, x_{h+1}^{(m)} - \ldots - a_{hn}\, x_n^{(m)}$$

Suppose h, the number of capacity-limited sectors, equaled one-half the total number of sectors n. Then the maximum number of multiplications required to perform four iterations would be reduced to $1\frac{3}{4}\, n^2$ as compared to $4\, n^2$ in a system where all gross outputs were unlimited.[7] (The presence of zero elements in the technology matrix would of course reduce these numbers.)

If the capacity-limited sectors comprise mainly industries producing raw materials, electric power, and semifabricates—as has generally been the case in the Polish economy—then most of the elements of the reduced matrix $\bar{A}$ are technological coefficients linking industries producing for final demand (e.g. machine-building, consumer goods, armaments, et al.).

In the following example, we shall define a sector producing for final demand as one whose net output amounts to at least 60 per cent of its gross output. In the 95-sector matrix of technological coefficients prepared by the Economic Research Department of the Polish Planning Commission for 1958,[8] 15 sectors (including metals and machinery, textiles, garment-making, shoes, and food-processing industries) qualify as final-demand according to this definition.[9] We assumed that the gross outputs of these sectors were generally limited only by the available supplies of material inputs while all other sectors were capacity-limited (and were scheduled to be operated at capacity levels). We then proceeded to extract from the over-all technological matrix the reduced matrix $\bar{A}$ for the 15 final-demand sectors. Once this was done, it

7. In the limited-capacity case, the maximum number of multiplications equals $2h\,(n - h) + h^2 + m\,(n - h)^2$ where m is the number of iterations carried out. In the usual case, the number of multiplications equals $m\, n^2$.

8. Zakład badań ekonomicznych, "Tablice przepływów materiałów w naturalnych jednostkach miary" (Tables of material flows in physical-measurements units), *Prace i materiały zakładu badań ekonomicznych*, no. 18 (1960).

9. The approximate proportion of net to gross output can be computed from data in Ibid., pp. 24–27.

was found that out of 225 possible entries in the reduced matrix $\overline{A}$, only 12 entries were nonzero, and of the latter all but four lay along the main diagonal.[10] The matrix could be decomposed into several independent submatrices. Only the food-processing industries made up an interconnected whole, but even this submatrix was not "intrinsically positive": neither its square nor its cube contained any more nonzero (positive) elements than the original. The largest characteristic root of $\overline{A}$ turned out to be 0.07.[11] This root is so small that only an insignificant error would be made if the gross output of any sector in $\overline{A}$ were estimated from its final demand plus the direct requirements of the other sectors for its output (ignoring all indirect requirements).[12]

As we have already seen, once the gross outputs of the unlimited sectors are known, the net outputs of the capacity-limited sectors can be obtained in one simple operation, namely, by subtracting the input requirements on the part of *all* sectors from the gross outputs of the capacity-limited sectors. If the net outputs so derived make up an acceptable bill of goods, consistency has been achieved and this phase of the planning process has been successfully completed.

However, if some of the net outputs happen to be negative or too small to satisfy minimum requirements, then final demand in the unlimited sectors may have to be scaled down. This will release scarce material inputs necessary to eliminate the shortfalls in the net outputs of the capacity-limited sectors. It is interesting

10. This input-output table evidently omits many links between sectors. But our main concern is with the use the planners make of the information available to them, not with the over-all efficiency of the system. The table presumably incorporates the bulk of the input-output data in the possession of the Planning Commission.

11. The root was obtained as follows: The $\overline{A}$ matrix was squared and the ratios of identically placed elements in $[\overline{A}]^2$ and $[\overline{A}]$ were computed. The $\overline{A}$ matrix was then cubed and similar ratios were worked out for all elements of $[\overline{A}]^3$ and $[\overline{A}]^2$. These two successive estimates of the characteristic roots were exactly equal. Higher-power estimates for selected elements were also observed to decline by those strictly constant ratios. The largest such ratio, equal to 0.07, was taken to be the dominant root of $\overline{A}$.

12. Each new iteration would add a maximum of $\left(\dfrac{.07}{1-.07}\right)$ or 7.5 per cent to the last increment contributed by the preceding iteration (cf. the last part of Sect. 1). Since the direct requirements are themselves extremely small (of the order of 5 to 70 units of input per 1000 units of output), very little accuracy would be gained by further iterations.

to observe in this connection that, the more sectors are subject to capacity limitations, the greater will be the cutback in the net output of an unlimited sector necessary to bring the residual level of final demand in a capacity-limited sector to the desired level. This follows from a proposition proved by Paul Samuelson [13] to the effect that, the greater the number of capacity-limited sectors, the smaller the change in the gross output of an unlimited sector associated with a given (marginal or discrete) increment in the net output of any unlimited sector.[14] If the curtailment in the gross outputs of unlimited sectors brought about by a retrenchment in one or more of the net outputs of this same group of sectors is small, so will be the reduction in the amount of inputs required from the capacity-limited sectors. This means in turn that there will be less output in the capacity-limited sectors released for end uses.

If our concrete example is at all realistic, it suggests that the planners may, under certain conditions, strike consistent plans without inverting a matrix by iteration. The method of successive approximations would then consist mainly in adapting outputs in final-demand industries to the potential of the capacity-limited sectors.[15]

In the long run, of course, we should expect capacity to be built up in the bottleneck sectors and surplus capacity in the remaining

13. P. A. Samuelson, "An Extension of the LeChatelier Principle," *Econometrica*, 28, no. 2 (1960), 368–79.

14. Let $\overline{\overline{A}}_h$ denote the reduced matrix obtained by omitting h rows and columns, corresponding to capacity-limited sectors, from the original $[I - A]$ matrix and $\overline{\overline{A}}_{h+1}$ denote the matrix obtained from $\overline{\overline{A}}_h$ by omitting one more row and column. The terms $\overline{\overline{A}}_h^{ij}$ and $\overline{\overline{A}}_{h+1}^{ij}$ stand for elements in the i'th row and j'th column of $[I - \overline{\overline{A}}_h]^{-1}$ and $[I - \overline{\overline{A}}_{h+1}]^{-1}$ respectively.
Samuelson has proved that:

$$\overline{\overline{A}}_{h+1}^{ij} < \overline{\overline{A}}_h^{ij} \quad (i, j = h + 2, \ldots, n)$$

In other words, the change in the gross output of the j'th unlimited sector for a given change in the net output of the i'th unlimited sector will be smaller the greater the number of capacity-limited sectors. For the unequal sign to hold in all cases, it must be assumed that the reduced matrices are indecomposable. In practice the reduced matrix may easily turn out to be decomposable even though the original technology matrix was indecomposable.

15. Adjustments are also called for during the planning process by changes in the estimates of feasible outputs for the forthcoming year resulting from the analysis of current plan fulfillment.

sectors to be gradually curtailed. Even if the various capacities remained imperfectly geared to each other, surpluses need not necessarily occur in those industries producing for final demand which happen not to supply each other with inputs.

5. *Organizational Breakdowns of Material Balances*

In Soviet-type economies, scarce materials are rationed out according to a distribution table (or "key") figuring on the outlay side of the material balances. In Poland, this table is drawn up according to individual ministries and "other consumers." Each ministry in turn must divide up its quota among subordinate central boards, which must finally parcel out their ration to ultimate users (generally, producing enterprises). Only the most important products for which the rationed materials will serve as inputs are listed separately in the balance.[16] It will now be shown that it is possible for the planners to frame an internally consistent program without direct knowledge of the technological coefficients (the a_{ij} of earlier sections).[17]

Let us denote by $\bar{v}^s$ the n-dimensional vector of gross outputs v_i^s ($i = 1, 2, \ldots, n$) produced by organization s ($s = 1$, $2, \ldots, o$) (ministries, central boards, or multiplant enterprises). If good i is produced in more than one organization, the total output x_i of this good will equal $\sum\limits_{s=1}^{o} v_i^s$. More generally, the vector of total gross outputs $\bar{x}$ will equal $\sum\limits_{s=1}^{o} \bar{v}^s$. The value of output at fixed prices of organization s is written r_s. The values of the outputs of the different organizations may be adjoined to form the vector $\bar{r}$.

The coefficients b_{is} denoting the input of good i per zloty of output of organization s are known (they can readily be estimated from past deliveries of material inputs to the various organizations

---

16. Chap. 3, Sect. 3.

17. The basic idea for this section is taken from K. Porwit and J. Żurkowski, "Niektóre specjalne przykłady możliwości zastosowania współczynników powiązań międzygałęziowych w planowaniu gospodarczym" (A few special applications of interindustry coefficients in economic planning), *Prace i materiały zakładu badań ekonomicznych*, no. 14 (1958), 1–44.

and from the value of their outputs during corresponding periods). It is also possible to obtain data on the amount of output of good i produced per zloty of output of organization s. These coefficients, written d_{is}, may be arranged for each organization as a column-vector $\bar{d}^s$ made up of n elements. It is assumed that each organization produces its different products in fixed proportions. (Hence it is immaterial what prices are used to weight the outputs of each organization.)

The basic problem is to find the vector $\bar{r}$ capable of sustaining the given bill of net outputs $\bar{y}$.

It is immediately obvious that, if $\bar{y}$ is of dimension n (the number of goods) while $\bar{r}$ is of dimension o (the number of organizations), n being larger than o, as it almost certainly will be, the system is overdetermined and no solution can be found to the problem. (We are in effect dealing with a system of n equations in o unknowns.)

We may circumvent this obstacle by choosing o goods out of the total n and by working exclusively with these goods for the first part of the solution. It is assumed that it is possible to pick out these goods in such a way that none of them will be produced by more than one organization. (This should not be difficult in practice.) The choice should fall mainly on the more important goods, from the viewpoint of their priority standing and from their usual scale of output.

It should be kept in mind that the coefficients b_{ij}, which denote the amount of good i used in making one unit of output of organization j, refer to the entire input required to make not only the o goods selected but also any other goods produced by the various organizations.

For each gross output x_i, we can write down the balance-equation:

$$10) \qquad x_i = \sum_{s=1}^{o} b_{is}\, r_s + y_i \qquad (i = 1, 2, \ldots, o)$$

(The total output of any good must equal the quantities required as inputs by the various organizations plus any net output left over.) [18]

18. If part of the output is exported, it may be allotted to a foreign-trade organization, which is distinguished from the other organizations only in that it contributes no output (its $\bar{v}^s$ vector is empty).

The gross outputs may be computed from the equation:

$$11) \quad v_i^t = x_i = \sum_{s=1}^{o} d_{is}\, r_s = d_{is}\, r_s \quad (i = 1, 2, \ldots , o)$$

This follows from the fact that each x_i is only produced in one organization; since d_{is} expresses the ratio of the output of good i produced in the s'th organization to the total output of this organization, the output of the good itself can be obtained by multiplying this coefficient by the value of output of the organization.

Equations 10) and 11) may be written in matrix form:

$$\bar{x} = \mathbf{B}\,\bar{r} + \bar{y}$$
$$\bar{x} = \mathbf{D}\bar{r}$$

where $\mathbf{D}$ is the matrix of coefficients d_{is} ($i, s = 1, \ldots , o$).

Setting the right-hand sides of these two equations equal to each other, we get:

$$\mathbf{D}\,\bar{r} = \mathbf{B}\,\bar{r} + \bar{y}$$
$$\mathbf{D}\,\bar{r} - \mathbf{B}\,\bar{r} = \bar{y}$$
$$[\mathbf{D} - \mathbf{B}]\,\bar{r} = \bar{y}$$

If $[\mathbf{D} - \mathbf{B}]$ can be inverted, then r can be computed from the relation:

$$\bar{r} = [\mathbf{D} - \mathbf{B}]^{-1}\,\bar{y}$$

The matrix $\mathbf{D}$ is made up of a single element d_{is} per row and per column. By suitable renumbering of rows and columns, every nonzero element can be placed along the diagonal. The matrix obtained by subtracting the matrix $\mathbf{B}$ (with rows and columns similarly renumbered) from the diagonal matrix $\mathbf{D}$ has the appearance of a Leontief matrix, and it should have its properties for the following reason.

If every good x_i can sustain some net output y_i after satisfying the intermediate requirements $\sum_{s=1}^{o} b_{is}\, r_s$, then either the row sums of elements in $[\mathbf{D} - \mathbf{B}]$ are all equal to or smaller than unity (but not all unity) or the matrix can be transformed, without affecting its structural properties, into another matrix with the same characteristic roots and exhibiting the desired property of the row sums.

Once the value of each organization's output in the vector $\bar{r}$ is known, the gross outputs $(i = 1, 2, \ldots, o, \ldots, n)$ for all goods produced by the system may be computed from equation 11), generalized by including all n goods in matrix **D**. [By adjoining $(n - o)$ rows to the matrix **D**, its dimensions are raised to $n \times o$. The vector obtained by multiplying this $n \times o$ matrix by an o-dimensional vector must be of dimension n.]

The net output y_i of a good i not originally included in the set of o goods may be calculated by subtracting $\sum\limits_{s=1}^{o} b_{is} r_s$ $(i = o + 1, \ldots, n)$ from the corresponding x_i.

If, in a given case, the resulting bill of net outputs y_{o+1} to y_n were not satisfactory, then net outputs y_1 to y_o would have to be adjusted in order to release resources for the remaining sectors. The procedure would have to be repeated until the net-output proportions in vector $\bar{y}$ for all n goods were deemed satisfactory.

APPENDIX B

The Efficiency Problem

1. *Unique Production Processes*

a. *Definitions.* The coefficients used in the basic model of this section are tabulated below:

There are n goods and f exogenous factors in the model. The first n columns, or activities, in the table represent the unique processes for making a unit of gross output of each of the n goods. The coefficients in the gross output processes are denoted by a_{ij} where the index i refers to the row (any of the n goods or f factors) and the index j to one of the n gross-output columns. The square matrix of n^2 coefficients (first n rows, first n columns) is identical with the technology matrix $[I - A]$ described in Appendix A.[1] All the factor supplies available for the plan period are assumed to be exogenously given. (Endogenously produced factors are considered in Sections 1e and 3 below).

The second set of n columns in the table are the net output activities. The level of activity in these columns shows the amount of a good available for final demand after satisfying input requirements on the part of all sectors for that particular good. If a minimum level of final demand has been prescribed for a good in the last column of the table, which corresponds to the right-hand constants in the system of equations underlying the table, then the

---

1. The matrix $[I - A]$ may be decomposable (i.e., some sectors may not receive inputs, either directly or indirectly, from some other sectors), but it must be invertible. The a_{ij} coefficients stand for numbers that may be positive or negative If positive, they represent inputs, if negative, jointly produced outputs. Since all coefficients are preceded by a minus sign (the matrix A being subtracted from the identity matrix), the sign of the numerical coefficients in $[I - A]$ will be negative if a_{ij} is an input, positive if it is an output. The coefficients of the last f rows, however, must all be negative.

TABLE B:1. *Table of Detached Coefficients for General Model*

Good or factor	Activity	Gross outputs							Net outputs							Surplus factors			Restraints
		1	$\cdots$	$-a_{1d}$	$\cdots$	$-a_{1,d+1}$	$\cdots$	$-a_{1n}$											
Good	1	$1-a_{11}$	$\cdots$	$-a_{1d}$	$\cdots$	$-a_{1,d+1}$	$\cdots$	$-a_{1n}$	-1	$\cdots$	0	0	0	$\cdots$	0	0	$\cdots$	0	b_1
$\cdot$																			
Good	d	$-a_{d1}$	$\cdots$	$1-a_{dd}$	$\cdots$	$-a_{d,d+1}$	$\cdots$	$-a_{dn}$	0	$\cdots$	-1	0	0	$\cdots$	0	0	$\cdots$	0	b_d
Good	$d+1$	$-a_{d+1,1}$	$\cdots$	$-a_{d+1,d}$	$1-a_{d+1,d+1}$	$\cdots$	$-a_{d+1,n}$		0	$\cdots$	0	-1	0	$\cdots$	0	0	$\cdots$	0	0
$\cdot$																			
Good	n	$-a_{n1}$	$\cdots$	$-a_{nd}$	$\cdots$	$-a_{n,d+1}$	$\cdots$	$1-a_{nn}$	0	$\cdots$	0	0	$\cdots$	-1		0	$\cdots$	0	0
Factor	1	$-a_{n+1,1}$	$\cdots$	$-a_{n+1,d}$	$\cdots$	$-a_{n+1,d+1}$	$\cdots$	$-a_{n+1,n}$	0	$\cdots$	0	0	$\cdots$	0	-1	$\cdots$	-1	$-b_{n+1}$
$\cdot$																			
Factor	f	$-a_{n+f,1}$	$\cdots$	$-a_{n+f,d}$	$\cdots$	$-a_{n+f,d+1}$	$\cdots$	$-a_{n+f,n}$	0	$\cdots$	0	0	$\cdots$	0	0	$\cdots$	-1	$-b_{n+f}$

net output activities for that good show the amount left for final demand after meeting this minimum demand. The goods for which such a minimum net output has been prescribed are listed in the first d rows.

The last set of f columns are slack activities for the disposal of exogenous factors. An activity in this set will be operated at positive level wherever the sum of the allotments of the factor corresponding to this activity among the n gross output sectors fails to exhaust the factor's initial supply shown in the column of restraints.

Every process is perfectly divisible. Constant returns to scale prevail throughout.

In the representative equations below, the coefficients are taken from the table; the levels at which the activities are operated are denoted by x_j $(j = 1, \ldots, n+1, \ldots, 2n+1, \ldots, 2n+f)$.

All x_j must be non-negative. For the n goods, we have:

1) $$x_h - \sum_{j=1}^{n} a_{hj}\, x_j - x_{n+h} = b_h \qquad (h = 1, \ldots, d)$$

2) $$x_i - \sum_{j=1}^{n} a_{ij}\, x_j - x_{n+i} = 0 \qquad (i = d+1, \ldots, n)$$

For the f factors:

3) $$-\sum_{j=1}^{n} a_{n+g,j}\, x_j - x_{2n+g} = -b_{n+g} \qquad (g = 1, \ldots, f)$$

For the time being we postulate only that the preference function of the planners is a monotonically increasing function of the net outputs:

$$U = U\,(x_{n+1}, \ldots, x_{n+n})$$

The problem is to maximize U.

Each feasible bundle of net outputs may be conceived as an n-dimensional vector, a point with n coordinates in the net output space. If all the feasible points were connected, they would form a polyhedron, which would represent a production-possibilities surface in the net output space. Under the given conditions (constant returns to scale and perfect divisibility of processes), the polyhedron would be convex: all its interior points and all the points on the lines connecting its vertices could be represented as combinations of the coordinates of its vertices, or extremal points. (To make such a combination, each of the vectors to be totaled is multiplied by a positive fraction, chosen in such a way that the fractions add up to unity.)

b. *Efficient Points.* A program is represented by a vector $\bar{p}$ of $2n + f$ activity levels $(x_1, \ldots, x_{n+1}, \ldots, x_{2n+1}, \ldots, x_{2n+f})$. This vector will be partitioned into three subvectors of smaller order: vector $\bar{x}$ $(x_1, \ldots, x_n)$, a vector of gross outputs; vector $\bar{y}$ $(x_{n+1}, \ldots, x_{2n})$, a vector of net outputs; and vector $\bar{f}$ $(x_{2n+1}, \ldots, x_{2n+f})$, a vector of unutilized factor supplies.

A feasible program $\bar{p}$ will be termed efficient if no other program $\bar{p}'$ $(x'_1, \ldots, x'_{2n+f})$, with subvector of net outputs $\bar{y}'$, can be found such that $\bar{y}' \geqq \bar{y}$ (no element in $\bar{y}'$ is smaller than in $\bar{y}$ and at least one element in $\bar{y}'$ is larger than its corresponding element in $\bar{y}$). The number of independent variables equals the number of activities minus the number of restraints, or $(2n + f) - (n + f) = n$. Out of $2n + f$ elements in the solution vector only n can be chosen independently. Once the n elements of vector $\bar{x}$ are set, this fixes the level of all elements in $\bar{y}$ and $\bar{f}$. If the solution is basic, there will be a total of at most f nonzero elements in $\bar{y}$ and $\bar{f}$, where f is equal to the number of exogenous factors.[2]

We first assume that the technology matrix contains no joint-product coefficients.

· We may now prove the general theorem for this appendix:

If a program $\bar{p}$ uses up the entire supply of at least one factor, some positive amount of which is needed to make every producible good, it must be efficient.

Let the k'th exogenous factor be fully employed in making the set of feasible gross outputs $\bar{x}$ in $\bar{p}$. Its equation may be written:

4) $$\sum_{j=1}^{n} a_{kj} x_j = b_k$$

2. See Chap. 1, Sect. 2b. The independence of variables in programming is discussed in the mathematical appendix to Oskar Lange's *Ekonomia polityczna* (Political economy), *1*, 188–93.

In equation 4), subscript k is an integer between $n + 1$ and $n + f$. Both sides of equation 3) have been multiplied by -1; x_k is zero by virtue of the fact that the entire supply b_k is exhausted among the n gross output sectors.

Try any other feasible solution $\bar{x}'$ in $\bar{p}'$ with coordinates $x'_j (j = 1, \ldots, n)$, one or more of which differ from the coordinates of $\bar{x}$. This new solution must also satisfy 4), but it need not exhaust the supply of the exogenous factor k.

5) $$\sum_{j=1}^{n} a_{kj} x'_j \leq b_k$$

Subtracting 4) from 5) we get:

$$\sum_{j=1}^{n} a_{kj} (x'_j - x_j) \leq 0$$

Since all the a_{kj} coefficients are strictly positive (factor k is used in making every one of the x_j), it is not possible for all elements x'_j to be equal to or larger than their corresponding elements x_j, unless all elements are identical in the two solution vectors. If any of the elements differ, one or more elements in $\bar{x}'$ must be smaller than in $\bar{x}$.

Let the difference $\bar{x}' - \bar{x}$ between the two vectors be denoted by the vector $\Delta\bar{x}$, some of whose elements must be negative (others may be positive or zero). If $\bar{x}'$ is to yield a program $\bar{p}'$ which is more efficient than $\bar{p}$, all the elements of $\bar{y}'$ (net outputs) must be equal to or larger than the elements of $\bar{y}$ generated by the initial program $\bar{p}$. If at least one element is to be absolutely greater, the elements of the vector $\Delta\bar{y}$ obtained by subtracting $\bar{y}$ from $\bar{y}'$ must all be positive or zero, with at least one element in $\Delta\bar{y}$ larger than zero.

The relation between the gross and net outputs for the two solution vectors is represented by the following equations:

6) $$[I - A]\,\bar{x} = \bar{y} + \bar{b}; \quad [I - A]\,\bar{x}' = \bar{y}' + \bar{b}$$

where $\bar{b}$ is the vector of minimum net outputs in the last column of Table B:1.

Subtracting the first of these two equations from the second, we obtain:

7) $[I - A] \Delta \bar{x} = \Delta \bar{y}$

Pre-multiplying both sides of 7) by $[I - A]^{-1}$:

8) $[I - A]^{-1} [I - A] \Delta \bar{x} = \Delta \bar{x} = [I - A]^{-1} \Delta \bar{y}$

It has been proven by S. B. Noble [3] that all the elements of $[I - A]^{-1}$ must be nonnegative (strictly positive if A is indecomposable) as long as all the elements of the technology matrix A are positive. This is true by definition in the absence of joint products.

All the elements of $\Delta \bar{x}$ must be nonnegative since this vector is equal to the product of a matrix with a vector, neither of which contains negative elements. But we have found that for $\bar{x}'$ to differ from $\bar{x}$, the vector $\Delta \bar{x}$ must contain one or more negative elements. Clearly then there exists no vector $\bar{x}'$ differing from $\bar{x}$ capable of generating a point $\bar{y}'$, one or more of whose elements are larger than corresponding elements in $\bar{y}$ and none smaller. Program $\bar{p}$, containing $\bar{x}$ and $\bar{y}$, must therefore be efficient.

The assumption that the fully employed exogenous factor is needed as an input in every one of the n gross output processes may now be relaxed. Let the first e coefficients in row k equal zero. There is then no direct restraint on the part of the bottleneck factor k to an expansion of the first e gross outputs. If these first e outputs can be expanded without causing a reduction in the remaining group of $(n - e)$ outputs, an initial program fully employing factor k may be improvable. But if the matrix $[I - A]$ is indecomposable, any increase in the gross output of one of the first e elements will require, directly or indirectly, material inputs from the remaining $(n - e)$ gross outputs. This means that some of the net outputs of these remaining sectors will have to be curtailed as a result of the expansion in the first e sectors. The initial $\bar{p}$ must be efficient and the general theorem holds. But if the matrix A of $[I - A]^{-1}$ is decomposable (and there is at least one column of zeros in rows $e + 1$ to n of the inverse), the initial solution $\bar{p}$ may be inefficient.

Suppose now that more than one factor has been fully committed in the initial solution. For every such fully employed fac-

3. S. B. Noble, "Measures of the Structure of Some Static Linear Economic Models, Serial T-90/58." The George Washington University Logistics Research Project, 1958 (mimeograph).

tor, we can repeat the above analysis. Wherever any nonzero coefficients appear among the first e columns (where only zero's were
found in the k'th row when only one factor was fully employed)
the levels for those columns will no longer be free to vary without
affecting the other elements in $\bar{x}$. When as many of the x_j as possible have been "locked" in this manner, the only gross outputs
that will still be free to vary without reducing any other outputs
will be those whose production processes have zero coefficients in
all rows except in those corresponding to underemployed factors.

The only rule that has to be appended to fit the case where the
matrix is decomposable and one or more gross outputs are produced with only inputs from factors available in excess supply is
that the activity levels for these processes must be raised until
such "free supplies" have been eliminated.[4]

c. *Joint Products.* We shall distinguish two general types of programs involving joint products: (1) programs where each good
is produced by only one process, but with the same process able
to produce more than one good; (2) programs where goods produced jointly in one process may also appear as an output of some
other process.

The first type offers no problem. Solutions to such programs
will be efficient if they satisfy the conditions stated in the previous
section for programs involving a single product per process. If this
proposition is not self-evident, it may be proved as follows.

Consider a program with d different processes producing g
goods. Since more than one good may be produced by each process,
but no good is made by more than one process, g is larger than d.
The coefficients in this program may be arranged in a rectangular
matrix with g rows and d columns. Out of the g rows, d can always
be selected in such a way as to form, together with the columns, a
$d \times d$ square matrix where no joint-product coefficients will appear (a good will be produced in a separate process only if it does
not figure as a joint product in any other process). Call this matrix
D. If $[I - D]$ has an inverse, all its elements will be positive. Now
suppose an initial feasible solution—i.e. a set of activity levels for

---

4. It is not possible for a good to be made without either material inputs or
exogenous factors. Endogenously produced factors, such as foreign exchange and
productive capacity, are not considered until Sections 1e and 3.

all production processes, net outputs, and excess factor supplies—has been worked out which fully employs one or more of the exogenous factors. (If **D** is decomposable, it is assumed that the solution fully employs enough factors to eliminate all productive slack in the system.) Then any reallocation designed to yield a more efficient solution must reduce one or more of the activity levels for production processes. Since all the elements of $[I - D]^{-1}$ are positive, this reduction, for the same reasons as were set forth in the previous section, must cause a drop in one or more of the net outputs in the d rows selected. The initial solution must therefore have been efficient.

We examine now the second case, where a good produced by one of the gross output processes may also appear as a joint product in other processes. Again we form a square matrix **A** with as many rows of coefficients as there are gross output processes (each row must of course correspond to a separate, endogenously produced good). In the **A** matrix all input coefficients are positive, while output, or joint-product, coefficients are negative.

The general theorem of Section 2b must hold true as long as every element in $[I - A]^{-1}$ is positive, for $\Delta \bar{x}$ of 8) will then be nonnegative as long as $\Delta \bar{y}$ is nonnegative. Whether or not this condition obtains will depend on the size of the negative joint-product coefficient(s) in the **A** matrix. Let such a negative coefficient be located in the i'th row and j'th column $(i \neq j)$. Then the identically located element in $[I - A]^{-1}$, denoted by A_{ij}, will equal the sum of a convergent series, whose first three elements are:

$$a_{ij} + \sum_{k=1}^{n} a_{ik} a_{kj} + \sum_{k=1}^{n} \sum_{h=1}^{n} a_{ik} a_{kh} a_{hj} + \ldots$$

Since a_{ij} is negative, A_{ij} may be negative. On the other hand, if a_{ij} is small and the elements $a_{ik} a_{kj}$ $(k \neq i, j)$ are large, the sum of the series may turn out positive.

In case one or more negative elements do occur in $[I - A]^{-1}$, then it is possible, using equation 8), to construct a solution vector satisfying the conditions of the general theorem but generating an inefficient $\bar{y}$.

d. *Synthetic Balances.* In addition to the material and factor balances, the planners in Soviet-type economies must prepare aggregate balances, expressed in value terms, to equilibrate money incomes and outlays, foreign payments and receipts, etc.[5] Supposing these balances were struck simultaneously with the other balances already considered, would the efficiency conditions of the general theorem still apply? We shall show that they would apply, unless the synthetic balances were the only "factors" fully employed.

TABLE B:2. *A Program Including a Balance of Income and Outlays*

| | Gross outputs | | Net outputs | | Surplus factors | | |
	Good 1	Good 2	Good 1	Good 2	Labor	Factor 2	Restraints
Good 1	1	$-a_{12}$	-1	0	0	0	b_1
Good 2	$-a_{21}$	1	0	-1	0	0	b_2
Synthetic balance	$-a_{41}W_1$	$-a_{42}W_2$	p_3	p_4	0	0	$-p_3 b_1 -$ $p_4 b_2 - b_3$
Labor	$-a_{41}$	$-a_{42}$	0	0	-1	0	$-b_4$
Factor 2	$-a_{51}$	$-a_{52}$	0	0	0	-1	$-b_5$

The simple model illustrated in Table B:2 may serve as the starting point of our analysis. This table differs essentially only in its third row from Table B:1. The coefficients $a_{41} W_1$ and $a_{42} W_2$ are the wage costs per unit of output of the first and second good respectively. W_1 and W_2 are wages per year (assuming all the flows in the table relate to the entire plan-year), while a_{41} and a_{42} are the labor inputs per unit of output, which also appear in the following row. The coefficients p_3 and p_4 are the fixed retail prices at which the net outputs of the two goods are sold to the population. (It is assumed for convenience that only consumer goods are produced by the system, but this in no way restricts the generality of the example.) The constant on the right-hand side of the equation consists of the value at retail prices of the minimum net outputs ($b_1 p_3 + b_2 p_4$), together with a constant b_3 which stands for the planned increase in the cash balances of the population plus the budgeted value of direct taxes levied on wages. After multiplying all the coefficients in the third row of the table by -1 and transposing some of the terms, we may write the synthetic balance as follows:

$$a_{41} W_1 x_1 + a_{42} W_2 x_2 - b_3 = p_3 x_3 + p_3 b_1 + p_4 x_4 + p_4 b_2$$

The total wage fund (or $a_{41} W_1 x_1 + a_{42} W_2 x_2$) minus the planned increase in cash balances and direct taxes must equal the

5. See Chap. 4.

retail value of consumer goods sold to the population, the expression on the right-hand side.

If labor or the second factor is fully employed, we can form the same equation as 4) and show that any alternative solution must reduce the gross output of either good 1 or good 2. This in turn, for the same reasons as were spelled out in Section 2b, must cause a decline in the net output of one of these goods.

However, if a program commits fully neither the available labor supply nor the other factor but exactly satisfies the synthetic balance, this program may be, in fact must be, inefficient. It is clear that both gross outputs may increase—as long as factor capacities hold out—with a concomitant rise in the net outputs. There are enough degrees of freedom to allow a new synthetic balance to be struck at a higher level of activity fully employing at least one factor.[6] The balance of incomes and outlays of the original program would correspond to an underemployment equilibrium. In a Soviet-type economy where productive resources are usually strained to the utmost to achieve rapid development, such a situation is not likely to arise.

While the superimposition of a synthetic restraint on an already efficient program cannot cause it to become inefficient, it does narrow down the choice of programs open to the planners, particularly if retail prices and wages are fixed. A program which is optimal from the viewpoint of the bill of net outputs that it is capable of sustaining may so disturb financial equilibrium as to be unacceptable to the planners. The source of this imbalance may be an excessive level of investments (a concentration on net outputs capitalized for use in subsequent periods), but it may also be due to a bias in the program toward labor-intensive consumer goods whose production may release an excessive volume of personal incomes.

e. *Foreign Trade.* Linear-programming models involving unique processes for domestically produced goods but admitting alterna-

6. A basic feasible solution to the program of Table B:2 must include five activities, since there are five restraints to the program. Hence if both labor and factor 2 are in surplus and both goods are produced, six, instead of five, activities will be operated at positive levels. If one surplus factor is eliminated, the levels of the remaining five activities can be raised. If there were a second synthetic balance (e.g. built up from factor 2), then a basic solution might exist which involved surpluses of both factors.

tive import and export activities have been investigated by Hollis Chenery.[7] To show that solutions to such programs may be inefficient, a simple two-commodity version of a model embracing import and export activities is laid out below.

Each good may be involved in one of three processes. (1) It may be produced domestically with inputs a_{i1} ($i = 2, 3, 4$) for good 1 and a_{k4} ($k = 1, 3, 4$) for good 2; (2) it may be imported, in which case the foreign-exchange cost per unit of the first good will be a_{42} and per unit of the second good a_{45}; (3) finally, it may be exported, at a price per unit in foreign exchange of a_{43} for the first good and a_{46} for the second. (a_{42} may differ from a_{43} and a_{45} from a_{46}, since foreign-trade markets may be imperfect; but inasmuch as it is assumed that quantities traded do not affect foreign prices, these coefficients are not likely to diverge by more than transportation costs.)

As in the previous models, above-minimum net outputs and surplus-factor supplies are tabulated in the last two pairs of activity columns.

Consider a basic feasible solution employing the entire supply (b_3) of the exogenous factor and the initial stock of foreign exchange (b_4). In this solution both goods are produced in above-minimum outputs. The question before us is whether it is possible, by means of foreign trade, to increase the net output (or net availability, including imported quantities) of one good without reducing that of the other. First, it may be noted that the foreign-exchange proceeds from exporting good 1 may be used in any one of three ways: (1) to increase the output of good 1 by importing the materials needed in making this good domestically; (2) to increase the output of good 2 by importing the material inputs required for its production; (3) to import good 2 directly.

The export of good 1, if it is not going to reduce the net output of this good available for domestic consumption, will necessitate an increase in its gross output. Since the exogenous factor is fully employed, this increase in production can only be achieved by cutting back the domestic output of the other good, whose net output, unless it is compensated by imports, must fall. If the foreign exchange is used exclusively to buy inputs for the production of the first good, the new bill of net outputs may be prefer-

7. H. B. Chenery, "The Interdependence of Investment Decisions," in *The Allocation of Economic Resources*, pp. 87–90.

TABLE B:3. *Table of Detached Coefficients for a Foreign-Trade Model*

	Good 1			Good 2			Net outputs		Excess factors		Restraints
	Domestic production	Import	Export	Domestic production	Imports	Exports					
Good 1	1	1	-1	$-a_{14}$	0	0	-1	0	0	0	b_1
Good 2	$-a_{21}$	0	0	1	1	-1	0	-1	0	0	b_2
Exogenous factor	$-a_{31}$	0	0	$-a_{34}$	0	0	0	0	-1	0	$-b_3$
Foreign exchange	$-a_{41}$	$-a_{42}$	a_{43}	$-a_{44}$	$-a_{45}$	a_{46}	0	0	0	-1	$-b_4$

able to the old, but it will not be more efficient, considering that the net output of the second good has fallen. The strategy of purchasing imported inputs for the second good with the exchange obtained by exporting the first makes no sense in this case, since the output of the second good must fall (to release scarce factors for use by the first good) and its foreign-exchange requirements must diminish *pari passu*.

The only way to contrive a more efficient solution is to export one good and use the foreign exchange to import the other. If this transaction is to render possible an increase in the net availability of both goods, then the foreign-exchange earned from the exports of the first good must not only suffice to compensate through imports the drop in the net output of the second good (caused by the increase in the output of the first), but also to finance the higher requirements for imported inputs consumed by the first good (unless there is enough foreign exchange released by the curtailment of the second good's output to finance these imports).

These conditions may well be satisfied if the country exports the good in which it has a comparative advantage. But there is no signal by which the planners would normally be apprised of this opportunity. Even if one or more exogenous factors were initially in surplus, this would not be a reliable indication that one good should be exported and the other imported; [8] whether or not such a transaction was worthwhile would depend on a comparison of import and export prices together with an estimate of the relative costs of increasing the output of one commodity at the expense of the other.

A more important consideration, perhaps, is that the planners, though they may be alert to the opportunity itself, have no simple way of ascertaining the optimal volume of foreign-trade transactions. The only thing they can do is to try out a number of variants and, for each variant, laboriously compute the bill of net outputs that it may yield, taking into account the various import and export combinations open to the economy.

8. If foreign exchange was in short supply, however, a surplus in one or more exogenous factors might reveal the possibility of increasing domestic output by using a part of the increment in output to purchase imported inputs. If the input-output matrix was decomposable and there were no other factor in short supply, the net output for domestic consumption of the exported good could be increased without reducing the output of the second good.

2. *Alternative Processes*

As in the example described in the text (p. 25) and for the reasons stated there, the analysis of alternative processes in this section will be confined to a choice of processes involving only two goods and two factors (capital and labor). It will be assumed here that the two goods consume positive amounts of each other's outputs. This is of course the more general case. The table of detached coefficients for the initial program is shown below (p. 363).

The coefficients of the last two rows, normally preceded by a negative sign, have been multiplied by -1 to make them all positive.

The initial program, we shall assume, included activities 1, 2, 3, and 6: only the first, or priority, good was produced in above-minimum net output. Capital was a bottleneck in production; labor was in surplus. The above-minimum net output of good 1 can be computed by solving the above system of four simultaneous equations. Using Kramer's rule, we find that x_3 equals:

$$\frac{b_3 (1 - a_{12} a_{21}) - b_2 (a_{12} a_{31} + a_{32}) - b_1 (a_{21} a_{32} + a_{31})}{a_{21} a_{32} + a_{31}}$$

An alternative process (reproduced as the last column of Table B:4) is now introduced for producing the priority good. The elements of the new column vector are $[1, -a'_{21}, a'_{31}, a'_{41}]$. It is known that the process makes less intensive use of the scarce factor, so that $a'_{31} < a_{31}$. The new coefficient for the second factor a'_{41} may be larger than a_{41}. Nothing is presumed about the relative magnitudes of a'_{21} and a_{21}. If the new process is going to make it possible to produce more efficiently than before, the introduction of the new process must cause the net output of the first good to rise.

The net effect on any of the included variables of introducing the new process can be computed from the equations below:

$$\Delta x_1 - a_{12}\, \Delta x_2 - \Delta x_3 \qquad\qquad = -1$$
$$-a_{21}\, \Delta x_1 + \quad \Delta x_2 \qquad\qquad = +a'_{21}$$
$$a_{31}\, \Delta x_1 + a_{32}\, \Delta x_2 \qquad\qquad = -a'_{31}$$
$$a_{41}\, \Delta x_1 + a_{42}\, \Delta x_2 \qquad\quad + \Delta x_6 = -a'_{41}$$

In the above system of equations, Δx_j ($j = 1, 2, 3, 6$) stands for the change in the activity levels of the initially included activities

TABLE B:4. *Table of Detached Coefficients for a Model Involving Alternative Processes*

	Gross outputs		Net outputs		Surplus factors		Restraints	Alternative process for making good 1
Good 1	1	$-a_{12}$	-1	0	0	0	b_1	1
Good 2	$-a_{21}$	1	0	-1	0	0	b_2	$-a'_{21}$
Capital	a_{31}	a_{32}	0	0	1	0	b_3	a'_{31}
Labor	a_{41}	a_{42}	0	0	0	1	b_4	a'_{41}

brought about by the introduction of the new process operated at unit level. The elements in the alternative-process column have been transposed from the left to the right-hand side with a change in sign.

Solving for Δx_3:

$$\Delta x_3 = \frac{\begin{vmatrix} 1 & -a_{12} & -1 & 0 \\ -a_{21} & 1 & a'_{21} & 0 \\ a_{31} & a_{32} & -a'_{31} & 0 \\ a_{41} & a_{42} & -a'_{41} & 1 \end{vmatrix}}{\begin{vmatrix} 1 & -a_{12} & -1 & 0 \\ -a_{21} & 1 & 0 & 0 \\ a_{31} & a_{32} & 0 & 0 \\ a_{41} & a_{42} & 0 & 1 \end{vmatrix}} = \frac{-a'_{31}(1-a_{12}a_{21}) + a_{31}(1-a_{12}a'_{21}) - a_{32}(a'_{21}-a_{21})}{a_{21}a_{32}+a_{31}}$$

Normally this ratio should be positive if a'_{31} is appreciably smaller than a_{31}. In other words, it should be advantageous to introduce the new process either in conjunction with the first process, or by itself. On the other hand, if the difference between a'_{31} and a_{31} is small, if a'_{21} is larger than a_{21}, and if a_{32} is not zero, the above ratio may be negative. In that event, of course, it would not be worthwhile to introduce the new process, as long, at least, as the first good was greatly preferred to the second. (The reader will note that if a'_{21} is zero, Δx_3 must be positive, as we should expect.)

Essentially the profitability of introducing an alternative process depends on the direct versus the indirect demand for the bottleneck factor. The direct demand equals a_{31} in one case, a'_{31} in the other; the indirect demand depends on the chains $a_{32} a'_{21}$ and $a_{31} a_{12} a'_{21}$. If the sum of these two chains exceeds the indirect requirements through a_{21}, or $a_{12} a_{21} a'_{31}$ plus $a_{32} a_{21}$, the introduction of the new process may reduce the net output of the first good that can be made with the available amount of the scarce factor.

If the indirect claims on the bottleneck factor(s) are large enough to more than offset the difference in the direct requirements, the planners should notice on recalculating their feasible bill of net outputs that the introduction of the new process has reduced the net output of at least one desirable good. We should expect them to keep looking for some other process for making one of the two goods which would permit them to produce more net output, economize on the scarce factor(s), and absorb some or all of the excess labor.

If Δx_3 turns out to be positive, then it will pay to combine the two processes, unless every element in the new process (including the input coefficient corresponding to the factor in excess) is smaller than its counterpart in the initial process, in which case the new process will totally replace the old. To maintain a basic solution, which will be optimal if the preference function is linear in the appropriate range, the excess labor must disappear.

Once all factors are fully employed, there is no longer any reliable way to proceed toward more efficient solutions. From here on, experience and intuition take over: no simple rules will apply.

3. Long-Range Plans

One theoretical result pertinent to multiperiod planning is already established in the economic literature. Dorfman, Samuelson, and Solow have proved that any feasible program which fully employs the entire capital stock in the initial period and all endogenously produced factors subsequently must be efficient.[9] This efficient path of capital accumulation, termed "Leontief trajectory," is only one of several possible dynamic cases warranting systematic investigation.

We shall now study the efficiency of a three-period model involving two goods and two factors, one exogenous and one endogenous. It will be shown that if a program fully utilizes the exogenous factor in every period—more generally, if the conditions for static efficiency are satisfied in every period—this program must be efficient dynamically.

A program will be termed "efficient dynamically" if no alternative program can be contrived in which the net output of one or more goods with a positive valuation in the preference function of the planners would be made available during any period in larger amount than in the solution to be tested and in which none of the desirable outputs available during any period would be smaller than in the initial solution.

This definition implies that net outputs of the same good made

9. (*Linear Programming and Economic Analysis*, pp. 341–42.) Capital goods are the only factors of production in the version of Leontief's dynamic model studied by Dorfman, Samuelson, and Solow. However, the introduction of other exogenous factors, such as labor or foreign exchange, would not invalidate their results.

available during different periods are fundamentally incommensurable. There is no rate of discount that would permit a comparison of the benefits yielded by goods delivered during different periods. A solution may be efficient if it produces any more of a desirable net output in the first period than alternative solutions, no matter how much more of this same net output the alternative solutions could deliver in subsequent periods.

In Table B:5, illustrating this simplified model, two goods potentially produced in three different periods at levels x_1^t and x_2^t ($t = 1$, 2, 3) are produced with two factors initially available in quantities b_3^1 and b_4^1 (superscripts refer to the time period, subscripts to the row-equation for a good or factor). The first factor (endogenously produced) is a capital asset which is generated as net output by the first good. The second factor, which may represent labor, is totally exogenous, i.e. its availability grows from b_4^1 to b_4^2 to b_4^3 according to its own (demographic) laws. Good 1, besides being used as a capital good, is also consumed as a current input by both sectors. The second good, also used as an input by both sectors, yields net output for final demand that must be consumed during the course of the year. The minimum desired net outputs of good 2 may change from one period to the next ($b_2^1 \gtrless b_2^2 \gtrless b_2^3$).

The capital good used as the first factor does not depreciate. Its total supply available for any period equals its initial supply b_3^1 plus any quantities produced in preceding periods. Capital goods produced in one period can only be put to work in the next. Their gestation period is shorter than one period.

The input coefficients a_{ij}^t ($i = 1, 2$, 3, 4; $j = 1$, 2; $t = 1$, 2, 3) may—and normally will—vary from one period to the next as a result of technical progress. All a_{ij}^t are strictly positive: the submatrices for each time period are indecomposable and there are no joint products.

There are altogether eighteen activities, operated at levels x_1 to x_{18}. They include six gross output processes (x_1, x_2, x_7, x_8, x_{13} and x_{14}), six net output activities (x_3, x_4, x_9, x_{10}, x_{15} and x_{16}), and six disposal activities for factors in surplus (x_5, x_6, x_{11}, x_{12}, x_{17}, and x_{18}).

Finally, it should be noted that the preference function to be maximized includes, in addition to the net output of good 2 at

TABLE B:5. Table of Detached Coefficients for Dynamic Model

Good or factor	Activity	First Period Gross outputs (1)	(2)	Net outputs (3)	(4)	Surplus factors (5)	(6)	Second Period Gross outputs (7)	(8)	Net outputs (9)	(10)	Surplus factors (11)	(12)	Third period Gross outputs (13)	(14)	Net outputs (15)	(16)	Surplus factors (17)	(18)	Re-straints
Good 1	1)	$1-a_{11}^1$	$-a_{12}^1$	-1	0	0	0	0	0	0	0	0	0	0	0	0	0	0	0	b_1^1
Good 2	2)	$-a_{21}^1$	$1-a_{22}^1$	0	-1	0	0	0	0	0	0	0	0	0	0	0	0	0	0	b_2^1
Factor 1	3)	$-a_{31}^1$	$-a_{32}^1$	0	0	-1	0	0	0	0	0	0	0	0	0	0	0	0	0	$-b_3^1$
Factor 2	4)	$-a_{41}^1$	$-a_{42}^1$	0	0	0	-1	0	0	0	0	0	0	0	0	0	0	0	0	$-b_4^1$
Good 1	5)	0	0	0	0	0	0	$1-a_{11}^2$	$-a_{12}^2$	-1	0	0	0	0	0	0	0	0	0	b_1^2
Good 2	6)	0	0	0	0	0	0	$-a_{21}^2$	$1-a_{22}^2$	0	-1	0	0	0	0	0	0	0	0	b_2^2
Factor 1	7)	0	0	0	0	0	0	$-a_{31}^2$	$-a_{32}^2$	0	0	-1	0	0	0	0	0	0	0	$-b_3^2$
Factor 2	8)	0	0	0	0	0	0	$-a_{41}^2$	$-a_{42}^2$	0	0	0	-1	0	0	0	0	0	0	$-b_4^2$
Good 1	9)	0	0	0	0	0	0	0	0	0	0	0	0	$1-a_{11}^3$	$-a_{12}^3$	-1	0	0	0	b_1^3
Good 2	10)	0	0	0	0	0	0	0	0	0	0	0	0	$-a_{21}^3$	$1-a_{22}^3$	0	-1	0	0	b_2^3
Factor 1	11)	0	0	0	0	0	0	0	0	0	0	0	0	$-a_{31}^3$	$-a_{32}^3$	0	0	-1	0	$-b_3^3$
Factor 2	12)	0	0	0	0	0	0	0	0	0	0	0	0	$-a_{41}^3$	$-a_{42}^3$	0	0	0	-1	$-b_4^3$

periods 1, 2, and 3, the total stock of factor 1 available at the end of period 3. The objective of the problem may thus be expressed as:

$$\max f\,(x_4,\ x_{10},\ x_{16},\ S^3)$$

where S^3 stands for the terminal stock of the endogenous factor 1 equal to the sum of x_3, x_9 and x_{15}, the net outputs of the capital good produced in periods 1, 2, and 3 respectively.

Consider a program fully employing factor 2 in every period. Since no endogenously produced factors are consumed in the first period, conditions in this period must be identical with the static case: Any reshuffling of resources must entail a drop either in the net output of the first or of the second good. Any sacrifice of the second good, which directly enters the maximand function, is ruled out (at least for the purpose of constructing a more efficient solution).

To compensate for a decline in the terminal stock due to the drop in the capacity produced in the first period, the net output of good 1 in the second period must be raised. If the exogenous factor is fully employed in the second period, this can only be done at the expense of the net output of good 2, again with adverse effect on the maximand.

Similar arguments apply to reallocations in the second and third periods. Any drop in the net output of good 1 in period 2 must be offset by a rise in the net output of this same good in period 1, which must reduce the net output of good 2 in this period. It is even more obvious that no reorganization is possible in period 3 without affecting some desirable net output.

The assumption made about the indestructibility of the endogenously produced factor cannot be relaxed without making some other assumption. For if all endogenously produced capacity had a service life equal to one period only, then a solution that failed to fully employ newly made capacity in every period might easily be inefficient. The net output of good 1 in periods 1 and 2 could be cut without effect on the terminal stock (equal in this case solely to the net output of good 1 in period 3); inputs would then be released which would make it possible to step up the net output of good 2 in some period. To ensure the efficiency of solutions meeting the usual requirements, the (not unreasonable) assumption would have to be made that every endogenously produced capacity should be fully utilized during its one-period existence.

The number of goods used for current consumption and the number of exogenous factors may be arbitrarily increased without affecting any point of the above analysis. But a new problem arises where more than one good may be capitalized to serve as an endogenously produced factor. The new degree of freedom in the system opens the way to inefficient solutions. For, now, an alternative program may exist which, compared to the original solution, would generate more net output of one capital good at the expense of some other capital good(s) in the first period and, to make up for the loss in terminal capacity, would provide for a larger net output in the second period of the capital good(s) sacrificed in the first period. If this reallocation made it possible to increase desirable net output in some period without loss either of current consumption in any period or of terminal stock for any capital good, the new solution would be more efficient than the old.

For example, let there be two capital goods (goods 1 and 2, called factors 1 and 2 in their productive capacity) and one current-consumption good (good 3). A program $\bar{p}'$ is found which produces in period 1 more net outputs of goods 2 and 3 and less of good 1 than program $\bar{p}$. Suppose that factor 1 was not fully utilized in period 2. So far $\bar{p}'$ is superior to $\bar{p}$ in every respect except that its period 1 contribution to the terminal stock of first-factor capacity is lower than the initial solution's. The increased supply of factor 2 capacity in period 2 may, in conjunction with a reallocation of the exogenous factor, (1) increase both the net output of the consumption good in period 2 and of the first capital good, compared to the initial program, and (2), as its only negative effect, reduce the net and gross outputs of good 2. The increase in the net output of the first good in period 2 may more than offset the loss in period 1. At the same time, the gain in the net output of the second good *achieved in period 1* may be more than enough to sustain the loss of this good in period 2. The net impact of the introduction of the new program may be to leave the terminal stock of both factor capacities unchanged (or even to augment it) and to raise the net output of good 3 in periods 1 or 2.

This case might occur if the input coefficients were such that the relative difficulty of producing the two types of capital goods differed appreciably in periods 1 and 2. A solution which called for too large a net output of a capital good that would become relatively easier to produce in the next period (and too small a net output of some other capital good) and which did not fully commit in the second period the capacity initially generated by the first capital good would, in all likelihood, be inefficient.

The following rule would seem to guarantee the efficiency of solutions in multiperiod models: no endogenously produced capacity should be left unemployed in a given period unless the opportunity cost of producing this capacity (in terms of other endogenous capacities foregone) was expected to rise from this period on (as compared to the relative costs that prevailed during the period when the excess capacity was originally produced). On common sense grounds, we should expect that this rule would normally be observed in planning practice.

APPENDIX C

TABLE C:1. (Form B-1) Balance for Material M—For 1955

(1)	(2)	(3)	(4)	(5)	(6) (7) (8) (9)	(10)	(11)
	1953	1954		1955		Index	Index
						(10)	(11)
Item	Actual	Plan	Anticipated fulfillment	Plan	By quarters I II III IV	Percentage ratio of columns 5 and 3	Percentage ratio of columns 5 and 4
Sources							
1. Output							
a) by ministry							
2. Other domestic sources							
3. Imports							
4. Change in suppliers' inventories							
Total							
Disposals							
I. Total nonmarket supply:							
1. Ministry A:							
Allocation							
Consumption							
2. Ministry B:							
Allocation							
Consumption							
....							
Miscellaneous ministries							
Allocation							
Other consumers							
Allocation							

TABLE C:1 (cont.)

II. Market supply				
Allocations				
Total				
Sales				
1. Direct sales by producing plants [a]				
2. Sales through commercial organizations				
III. State reserves				
IV. Planning Commission reserves				
V. Exports				
VI. Losses				
VII. Increases in inventories				
Total disposals				
Suppliers' inventories at end of year:				
quantity				
days				
By ministry				
In trade network				
Consumers' inventories at end of year:				
quantity				
days				
By ministry				

[a] Sales to individual consumers, canteens, plant cafeterias, etc.

Source. Krygier, ed., *System zaopatrzenia w gospodarce planowej*, pp. 72–73.

TABLE C:2. *(Form B-2) Consumption and Deliveries for 1955 Material M Ministry X*

Consumption

	Actual consumption 1953	1954			1955	
		Plan (first six months)	Actual	Anticipated fulfillment	Plan	By quarters
A. Consumption for production needs:						
1. For industrial production:						
For production of good X etc.						
Consumption per unit of output						
2. For construction and machine-assembly:						
a. Centrally assigned investments						
b. Centrally assigned capital repairs						
3. Other productive activity:						
B. Consumption for non-production uses:						
1. Decentralized investments						
2. Decentralized capital repairs						
For sanitation and safety:						
C. Procurement needs of budget organizations:						

TABLE C:2 (cont.)

	Quantity	Days
I. Total consumption		
II. Losses		
III. Increases in inventories		
IV. Decreases in inventories		
Total deliveries		
Inventories at end of period		

Source. Krygier, p. 74.

Bibliography

Polish Periodicals

Budownictwo przemysłowe (Industrial construction).
Chemik (The chemist).
Dziennik urzędowy Ministerstwa Aprowizacji i Handlu (Daily official gazette of the Ministry of Procurement and Trade).
Dziennik urzędowy Ministerstwa Przemysłu (Daily official gazette of the Ministry of Industry).
Dziennik Ustaw Rzeczypospolitej Polskiej (The official gazette of the Polish Republic).
Ekonomika i organizacja pracy (Management and work organization).
Ekonomista (The economist).
Finanse (Finances).
Głos pracy (The voice of labor).
Gospodarka górnictwa (Mining economy).
Gospodarka materiałowa (Material economy).
Gospodarka planowa (Planned economy).
Gospodarka węglem (Coal economy).
Handel wewnętrzny (Internal trade).
Inwestycje i budownictwo (Investments and construction).
Materiały i budownictwo (Materials and construction).
Monitor Polski (Polish monitor).
Nowe drogi (New paths).
Prace i materiały zakładu badań ekonomicznych P.K.P.G. (Papers and materials of the economic research section of the State Commission for Economic Planning).
Problemy projektowe hutnictwa (Project-making problems in metallurgy).
Przegląd kolejowy (Railroad survey).
Przegląd statystyczny (Statistical survey).
Przegląd ustawodawstwa gospodarczego (Survey of economic legislation).
Przemysł chemiczny (Chemical industry).
Rachunkowość (Accounting).
Trybuna Ludu (Peoples' tribune).
Wiadomości Narodowego Banku Polskiego (News of the National Bank of Poland).

Wiadomości statystyczne (Statistical news).
Zycie gospodarcze (Economic life).

Books and Articles

Alton, T. P., *Polish Postwar Economy*, New York, Columbia University Press, 1955.

Augustowski, Z., "Zmniejszenie kosztów własnych a obniźka cen" (The compression of costs and the reduction of prices), *Gospodarka planowa*, no. 1, 1951.

——— "Ceny środków produkcji" (Prices of means of production), *Gospodarka planowa*, no. 1, 1953.

Bąbiński, C., "O błędach w metodologii planowania inwestycji przemysłowych i budownictwa" (On errors in the methodology for planning industrial investments and construction), *Inwestycje i budownictwo*, no. 2, 1955.

Balassa, B., *The Hungarian Experience in Economic Planning*, New Haven, Yale University Press, 1959.

Bartnicki, M. and Rakowski, M., "O aktualnych problemach efektywności inwestycji" (On actual problems in investment efficiency), *Inwestycje i budownictwo*, no. 5, 1959.

Basztoń, R., "Problemy zaopatrzenia" (Procurement problems), *Gospodarka materiałowa*, no. 14, 1956.

Berliner, J. S., *Factory and Manager in the U.S.S.R.*, Cambridge, Mass., Harvard University Press, 1957.

Blass, B., "Nowy system finansowy" (The new financial system), *Gospodarka planowa*, no. 21, 1947.

——— "Plan finansowy w naszej praktyce planowania" (The financial plan in our planning practice), *Gospodarka planowa*, no. 3, 1949.

Bobrowski, C., "Stopień swobody wyboru: Uwagi na marginesie wytycznych rozwoju gospodarczego na lata 1961–1965" (The scope of the freedom of choice: remarks on the directives for economic development for 1961–1965), *Gospodarka planowa*, nos. 1–2, 1959.

Bogobowicz, L. and Pruss, W., "Zapasy przedsiębiorstw uspołecznionych w 1959 r." (The inventories of socialized enterprises in 1959), *Wiadomości Narodowego Banku Polskiego*, no. 7, 1960.

Borejdo, I., "Plan techniczny w hutnictwie" (The technical plan in metallurgy), *Zycie gospodarcze*, no. 8, 1948.

Borysiewicz, J., *System cen środków produkcji w przemyśle na przykładzie hutnictwa* (The system of producer goods prices in industry with special reference to metallurgy), Warsaw, Polskie Wydawnictwa Gospodarcze, 1955.

───── and Jakubowski, B., "Usamodzielnienie przedsiębiorstw a problematyka cen" (The autonomy of enterprises and the price problem), *Zycie gospodarcze,* no. 22, 1956.

Boyarski, A., "Sebestoimost' i stoimost' " (Cost and value), in *Voprosy ekonomiki planirovania i statistiki* (Problems of economics, planning, and statistics), Moscow, Akademiia Nauk S.S.S.R., 1957.

Brus, W., "Oddziaływanie prawa wartości a bodźce ekonomiczne" (The influence of the law of value and economic incentives), *Ekonomista,* no. 3, 1955.

───── "W sprawie bodźców zainteresowania materialnego" (On material incentives), *Nowe drogi,* no. 12, 1955.

───── "Spór o rolę planu centralnego" (Controversy on the role of the central plan), *Zycie gospodarcze,* no. 12, 1957.

───── "Październik, model Październikowy" (October, the October model), *Zycie gospodarcze,* no. 42, 1957.

Brzezinski, Z., *The Soviet Bloc: Unity and conflict,* Cambridge, Mass., Harvard University Press, 1960.

Buch, W., "Kierunki rozwoju przemysłu w planie perspektywicznym 1961–1975" (Growth trends for industry in the perspective plan 1961–1975), *Gospodarka planowa,* no. 8, 1958.

Carr, E. H., *A History of Soviet Russia, Socialism in One Country, 1924–1926, 1,* New York, Macmillan, 1951–58.

Cennik robót budowlanych i instalacyjnych na rok 1950 (Price catalogue for construction and installation works for the year 1950), 6 vols. Warsaw, Wydawnictwo Ministerstwa Budownictwa, 1950.

Charłap. Z. and Szturm de Sztrem, E., "Statystyka karteli w Polsce" (Statistics of cartels in Poland), *Statystyka Polski,* Warsaw, 1935.

Chęcinski, T., "Rynek chemiczny w 1948 roku" (The chemical market in the year 1948), *Przemysł chemiczny,* no. 1, 1949.

Chenery, H. B., "The Interdependence of Investment Decisions," in *The Allocation of Economic Resources,* Stanford, Stanford University Press, 1959.

Czarkowski, J. and Oyrzanowski, B., *Bilans pieniężnych dochodów i wydatków ludności* (The balance of money incomes and outlays of the population), Warsaw, Polskie Wydawnictwa Gospodarcze, 1957.

Dąbczak, B., "Zagadnienie sortymentów w węglu energetycznym na tle produkcji w latach 1950 do 1955" (The problem of the size and quality of steam coals in the light of output in the years 1950 to 1955), *Gospodarka weglem,* no. 1, 1957.

Dąbrowski, E., "Kontrola funduszu płac w walce o obniżenie kosztów własnych" (Control of the wage fund in the struggle for the compression of costs), *Wiadomości Narodowego Banku Polskiego,* no. 9, 1956.

Deutschman, Z., "Z zagadnień zaopatrzenia materiałowo-technicznego" (Selected problems in material-technical procurement), *Gospodarka planowa*, no. 7, 1955.

—— and Witkowski, H., "Zagadnienia oszczędności zużycia materiałów w gospodarce Polski Ludowej" (Problems in economizing the use of materials in the economy of Peoples' Poland), *Ekonomista*, no. 4, 1955.

Dobrowolski, J., "O nowe zasady finansowania" (For new principles of financing), *Gospodarka materiałowa*, no. 5, 1957.

Dochód Narodowy Polski 1954 i 1955 (National income of Poland 1954 and 1955), Warsaw, Główny Urząd Statystyczny, 1957.

"Dochody realne ludności chłopskiej z produkcji rolniczej w latach 1956–1958" (The real income of the peasant population from agricultural production in the years 1956–1958), supplement to *Biuletyn statystyczny* (Główny Urząd Statystyczny), no. 2, 1959.

Domar, E. D., "A Soviet Model of Growth," in *Essays in the Theory of Economic Growth*, New York, Oxford University Press, 1957.

Dorfman, R., Samuelson, P. A., and Solow, R. M., *Linear Programming and Economic Analysis*, New York, McGraw-Hill, 1958.

Druto, J., "Zagadnienie bilansów materiałowych" (The problem of material balances), *Gospodarka planowa*, nos. 1–2, 1947.

Dudziński, W., "Zaopatrzeniowe problemy" (Procurement problems), *Zycie gospodarcze*, no. 15, 1960.

—— "Inwestycje zdecentralizowane—rozdział zamknięty?" (Decentralized investments—a closed chapter?), *Zycie gospodarcze*, no. 18, 1960.

Dziewanowski, M. K., *The Communist Party of Poland. An Outline of History*, Cambridge, Mass., Harvard University Press, 1959.

Erlich, A., "The Polish Economy after October 1956: Background and Outlook," *American Economic Review*, 49, no. 2, 1959.

—— "Comment," in *Value and Plan*, ed. by Gregory Grossman, Berkeley, University of California Press, 1960.

Ernst, M. C., "Measurement of Polish Industrial Growth 1937, 1946–1955," unpublished Ph.D. dissertation, Columbia University, 1958.

Evans, D. W., "Input Output Computations," in *The Structural Interdependence of the Economy*, ed. by T. Barna, New York, John Wiley, 1956.

Fedak, Z., "Cena grupowa" (The group price), *Zycie gospodarcze*, no. 5, 1949.

Ficowski, S., "Zmiana cen środków produkcji" (The reform of producer goods prices), *Wiadomości Narodowego Banku Polskiego*, no. 6, 1956.

———— "Struktura zapasów w gospodarce narodowej w latach 1950–1955" (The structure of inventories in the national economy in the years 1950–1955), *Wiadomości Narodowego Banku Polskiego*, no. 1, 1957.

Fiszel, H., *Czynniki i rezerwy przyspieszenia krążenia środków obrotowych w gospodarce Polski Ludowej (na przykładzie hutnictwa żelaza)* [Factors and reserves in the acceleration of the circulation of turnover funds in the economy of Peoples' Poland (with special reference to ferrous metallurgy)], Warsaw, Książka i Wiedza, 1954.

———— "Środki obrotowe przemysłu i ich struktura jako wyraz wyższości socjalistycznych stosunków produkcji nad kapitalistycznymi" (Turnover funds and their structure as an expression of the superiority of socialist over capitalist production relations), *Materiały i studia*, Warsaw, Książka i Wiedza, 1954.

———— "O oddziaływaniu prawa wartości na produkcję socjalistyczną" (On the influence of the law of value on socialist production), *Ekonomista*, nos. 1–2, 1954.

———— "W sprawie systemu cen zbytu w gospodarce Polski Ludowej" (On the system of transfer prices in the economy of Peoples' Poland), *Ekonomista*, no. 4, 1954.

———— "Jednakowe wyroby muszą posiadać jednolite ceny" (Identical goods must have identical prices), *Trybuna Ludu*, No. 115, April 27, 1955.

———— "O prawdziwy rachunek ekonomiczny" (For a correct economic calculation), *Nowe Drogi*, no. 5, 1956.

———— *Prawo wartości a problematyka cen w przemyśle socjalistycznym* (The law of value and the price problem in socialist industry), Warsaw, Panstwowe Wydawnictwo Naukowe, 1956.

———— "Ceny surowców podstawowych" (Prices of basic raw materials), *Ekonomista*, no. 6, 1957.

Frenkel, S., "Niedoskonała kontrola" (Imperfect control), *Zycie gospodarcze*, no. 34, 1959.

———— "Mimo wszystko dobre wyniki" (Good results in spite of all), *Zycie gospodarcze*, no. 12, 1958.

Gass, S. I., *Linear Programming: Methods and Applications*, New York, McGraw-Hill, 1958.

Gliński, B., "W rok po reorganizacji systemu zarzadzenia" (A year after the reorganization of the administrative system), *Gospodarka planowa*, no. 10, 1959.

————, Nowicki, A., and Marzantowicz, T., "W sprawie bodźców zainteresowania materialnego: Możliwości premiowania przedsiębiorstw socjalistycznych z zysku" (On Material Incentives: Possibilities of rewarding socialist enterprises from profits), *Gospodarka planowa,* no. 4, 1956.

Gomułka, W., Speech before the Eighth Party Plenum of the Polish United Workers' Party, *Nowe drogi,* no. 10, 1956.

—————— "Aktualne trudności i środki niezbędne do ich przezwyciężenia" The present difficulties and the unavoidable means for overcoming them), *Nowe drogi,* no. 12, 1959.

Gradowski, T. and Kiernożycki, A., "Wskaźniki dyrektywne planu a samodzielność przedsiębiorstwa" (Plan directives and enterprise autonomy), *Gospodarka planowa,* no. 10, 1959.

Granick, D., "Polish Interviews, July 1958" (mimeographed notes).

—————— "An Organizational Model of Soviet Industrial Planning," *Journal of Political Economy, 47,* no. 2, 1959.

Guz, L., "Centralne zarządy czy departamenty branżowe" (Central boards or branch departments), *Trybuna Ludu,* May 31, 1956.

Gwiaździński, J., "Perspektywy rozwoju hutnictwa żelaza w Polsce" (Perspectives for the development of ferrous metallurgy in Poland), *Problemy projektowe hutnictwa,* no. 1, 1957.

Halecki, O., ed., *Poland,* New York, Praeger, 1957.

Hatt, S., "Pierwsze wnioski z resortowych projektów planów na rok 1960" (The first conclusions drawn from the ministerial projects of plans for 1960), *Gospodarka planowa,* no. 10, 1959.

Hatt, S. and Karpinski, A., "Palące problemy planowania" (Urgent planning problems), *Zycie gospodarcze,* no. 6, 1957.

Himmel, B., "W sprawie produkcji pozaplanowej i ponadplanowej" (On unplanned and above-plan production), *Zycie gospodarcze,* no. 16, 1955.

Hładyj, M., "Nowe ceny i nowe warunki sprzedaży metali nieżelaznych" (New prices and new sales conditions for nonferrous metals), *Gospodarka materiałowa,* no. 15, 1960.

Hodoły, A., "Analiza podaży" (The analysis of supply), *Handel wewnętrzny,* no. 6, 1956.

Holzer, A., "Bilans maszyn w planowaniu gospodarczym" (The balance for machines in economic planning), *Gospodarka planowa,* no. 4, 1952.

Hortyński, S., "Gospodarka materiałowa w Bielskim przemyśle włókienniczym" (Material economy in the Bielsko textile industry), *Zycie gospodarcze,* no. 7, 1955.

Ilecki, W. and Machoń, Z., "Zagadnienie zaopatrzenia w Centralnym Związku Spółdzielczości Pracy" (The procurement problem in the

Central Union of Work Cooperatives), *Gospodarka materiałowa,* no. 11, 1956.

Iwański, T., "Próba ekonomicznej oceny realizacji Planu C.Z.P.H. w r. 1952" (An attempt at an economic appraisal of the execution of the plan for the Central Board of the Metallurgical Industry), *Gospodarka planowa,* no. 2, 1953.

Jampel, W., "Kierunki zmian w handlu polskim na tle oceny jego działalności" (Trends in Polish trade and the appraisal of its operation), *Handel wewnętrzny,* no. 3, 1957.

Jarno, J., "Wyroby metalowe" (Metal goods), *Gospodarka materiałowa,* no. 7, 1957.

Jasny, N., "A Note on Rationality and Efficiency in the Soviet Economy," I and II, *Soviet Studies, 12,* no. 4, 1961, and *13,* no. 1, 1961.

Jaworski, W., "Bank a przedsiębiorstwa eksperymentujące" (The bank and experimenting enterprises), *Finanse,* no. 2, 1957.

Kaczorowski, M., "Główne problemy ekonomiczne produkcji i gospodarki materiałami budowlanymi" (The main economic problems in the production and economy of building materials), *Inwestycje i budownictwo,* no. 9, 1954.

Kalecki, M., "Dynamika inwestycji i dochodu narodowego w gospodarce socjalistycznej" (The dynamics of investments and national income in a socialist economy), *Ekonomista,* no. 5, 1956.

——— "Rady robotnicze a centralne planowanie" (Workers' councils and central planning), *Nowe drogi,* nos. 11–12, 1956.

——— "Wpływ czasu budowy na współzależność inwestycji i dochodu narodowego a 'współczynnik zamrożenia'" (The influence of construction time on the relation between investment and national income), *Ekonomista,* no. 1, 1957.

——— "O cenach surowców podstawowych" (On the prices of basic raw materials), *Ekonomista,* no. 3, 1958.

——— "Czynniki określające tempo wzrostu dochodu narodowego w gospodarce socjalistycznej" (Factors determining the rate of increase of national income in a socialist economy), *Gospodarka planowa,* no. 8, 1958.

——— "Plan perspektywiczny na lata 1961–1975" (The perspective plan for the years 1961–1975), *Nowe drogi,* no. 8, 1958.

——— "Podstawowe zagadnienia planu pięcioletniego na lata 1961–1965" (Main problems of the Five-Year Plan for the years 1961–1965), *Gospodarka planowa,* nos. 1–2, 1959.

Karczmar, M., "Problemy reformy systemu kredytowego" (Problems in the reform of the credit system), *Finanse,* no. 3, 1957.

Karpiński, A., *Plan techniczno-przemysłowo-finansowy* (The technical-industrial-financial plan), Warsaw, Panstwowe Wydawnictwa Gospodarcze, 1954.

——— *Zagadnienia socjalistycznej industrializacji Polski* (Problems in the socialist industrialization of Poland), Warsaw, Polskie Wydawnictwa Gospodarcze, 1958.

Karpiński, Z., *Obieg pieniężny w gospodarce socjalistycznej* (Monetary circulation in the socialist economy), Warsaw, Panstwowe Wydawnictwa Gospodarcze, 1951.

Karski, R., "Planowanie produkcji a organizacja zaopatrzenia i zbytu" (Production planning and the organization of procurement and marketing), *Gospodarka planowa*, no. 9, 1956.

Kawalec, W., "Realny wynik decentralizacji" (The real outcome of decentralization), *Zycie gospodarcze*, no. 49, 1958.

Kawecki. A., "Rozszerzyć kompetencję C.Z." (Widen the competence of the central boards), *Trybuna Ludu*, May 31, 1956.

Kazalski, L., "Podstawy eksperymentów płacowych" (Principles of the wage experiments), *Zycie gospodarcze,* no. 10, 1959.

Kołudzki, L., "Jakość i cena materiałów a postęp techniczny" (The quality and price of materials versus technical progress), *Budownictwo przemysłowe,* no. 1, 1956.

Korytkowski, J., "Efektywność ekonomiczna nakładów inwestycyjnych w przemyśle chemicznym" (The economic efficiency of investment outlays in the chemical industry), *Przemysł chemiczny,* no. 1, 1956.

Kowalski, F., "System cen fabrycznych w przemyśle środków spożycia" (The system of factory prices in the consumer-goods industry), *Gospodarka planowa,* no. 6, 1954.

Krajewski, T., "O zmianach cen środków produkcji i towarowej taryfy kolejowej" (On changes in producer goods prices and in railway shipping rates for merchandise), *Przegląd kolejowy,* no. 1, 1956.

Kreisberg, J., "Drewno jest za tanie" (Lumber is too cheap), *Zycie gospodarcze,* no. 14, 1956.

Król, H., "Zagadnienie zainteresowania obniżką kosztów własnych w przedsiębiorstwie—nadal aktualne" (The problem of cost-reduction incentives in industry is still in order), *Gospodarka planowa,* no. 9, 1958.

Krygier, K., ed., *System zaopatrzenia w gospodarce planowej* (The procurement system in the planned economy), Warsaw, Polskie Wydawnictwa Gospodarcze, 1955.

———, Tafet, A., and Witkowski, H., "Podstawowe tezy do programu Ogólnej Konferencji Zbytu-Zaopatrzenia" (Basic theses for the program of the General Conference on Marketing and Procurement), *Gospodarka materiałowa*, no. 9, 1956.

Krzeczkowska, E., "Walka o regulującą rolę państwa na rynku w latach 1947–1949" (The struggle for the regulating role of the state on the market in the years 1947–1949), *Materiały i studia, 2*, Warsaw, Książka i Wiedza, 1955.

Kucharski, M., "Ekonomiczne znaczenie nadwyżki budżetowej" (The economic significance of the budget surplus), *Finanse*, no. 6, 1956.

——— "Czy zapasy hamują rozwój" (Do inventories hamper growth), *Życie gospodarcze*, no. 16, 1960.

Kuczyński, M., "Rozwój systemów premiowania personelu inżyniero-technicznego i administracyjnego w przemyśle polskim" (The development of bonus systems for engineering-technical and administrative personnel), *Ekonomika i organizacja pracy*, no. 4, 1955.

Kurowski, L. ed., *Prawo finansowe* (Financial law), Warsaw, Panstwowe Wydawnictwa Naukowe, 1955.

Kurowski, S., "Model a cele gospodarki narodowej" (The model and the ends of the national economy), *Życie gospodarcze*, no. 7, 1957.

Kuziński, S., "Niektóre dysproporcje sześciolatki w naszym przemyśle" (A few disproportions of the Six-Year Plan in our industry), *Nowe drogi*, no. 9, 1956.

——— *Główne proporcje rozwoju gospodarczego Polski Ludowej* (Chief proportions in the economic development of Peoples' Poland), Warsaw, Książka i Wiedza, 1960.

Kwejt, J., *Analiza działalności gospodarczej przedsiębiorstw przemysłowych* (Analysis of the economic activity of industrial enterprises), Warsaw, Oddział Wydawniczy Z.S.E., 1956.

Lange, O., "Aktualne problemy nauk ekonomicznych w Polsce" (Actual problems of the economic sciences in Poland), *Ekonomista*, no. 5, 1956.

——— "Końcowe przemówienie" (Final speech), *Ekonomista*, no. 5, 1956.

——— "The Role of Planning in Socialist Economy," *Indian Economic Review*, August 1958.

——— *Ekonomia polityczna* (Political economy), *1*, Warsaw, Państwowe Wydawnictwo Naukowe, 1959.

Lesz, M., "W rok po reformie handlu" (A year after the reform of trade), *Nowe drogi*, no. 3, 1959.

——— "Na krajowym rynku: Aktualna sytuacja i perspektywy" (On the domestic market: the present situation and perspectives), *Życie gospodarcze*, no. 24, 1961.

Leszek T., and Pudlik, S., "Płace" (Wages), in *Zarys rozwoju metodo-*

logii planowania w Polsce Ludowej 1944–1954, ed. by B. Minc et al., Warsaw, Polskie Wydawnictwa Gospodarcze, 1956.

Lipczyński, H., "Nowe zadania handlu zagranicznego" (The new tasks of foreign trade), *Gospodarka planowa,* no. 1, 1957.

Lipiński, E., "O przedmiocie ekonomii i prawach ekonomicznych" (On the subject of economics and on economic laws), *Ekonomista,* no. 5, 1956.

Lissowski, W., "Metody rachunku ekonomicznego w perspektywicznym planowaniu regionalnym" (Methods of economic calculation in the regional long-range plan), *Gospodarka planowa,* no. 1, 1958.

Liwowski, J., "Normalizacja w przemyśle włókien sztucznych" (Standardization in the artificial-fibers industry), *Przemysł chemiczny,* no. 6, 1954.

Łoś, J., "Zmiany w spożyciu robotników przemysłowych w związku ze zmianami zamożności" (Changes in the consumption of industrial workers in relation to changes in their income), *Handel wewnętrzny,* no. 6, 1957.

Madej, Z., "Ceny i rentowność w państwowych przedsiębiorstwach przemysłowych" (Prices and profitability in state industrial enterprises), *Gospodarka planowa,* no. 12, 1957.

——— "Bodźce ekonomiczne oparte na zysku" (Economic incentives based on profit), *Finanse,* no. 8, 1960.

Magiera, W. and Dowgiallo, A., "Ekonomiczna efektywność inwestycji wodnych" (The economic efficiency of water investments), in *Zagadnienia ekonomicznej efektywności inwestycji,* Warsaw, Polskie Wydawnictwa Gospodarcze, 1956.

Majewski, S., "Po wprowadzeniu reformy cen artykułów zaopatrzenionych i inwestycyjnych" (After the introduction of the reform of prices for procurement and investment goods), *Finanse,* no. 9, 1960.

Malicki, M., "Hierarchia trudności" (A hierarchy of difficulties), *Zycie gospodarcze,* no. 49, 1958.

Marczewski, J., *Planification et croissance économique des démocraties populaires,* 2 vols. Paris, Presses Universitaires de France, 1956.

Materialy i oborudowanie primeniaemye v ugol'noi promyshlennosti (Materials and equipment used in the coal industry), Moscow, 1955.

Materiały i studia (Materials and studies), Instytut Nauk Społecznych przy KC PZPR (Institute of Social Sciences of the Central Committee of the Polish United Workers' Party), 2 vols. Warsaw, Książka i Wiedza, 1954–55.

Metrycka, W., "Głos w dyskusji o cenach" (An opinion in the discussion about prices), *Gospodarka planowa,* no. 6, 1954.

Michotek, S., "Uwagi w sprawie kosztów budowy mostów kablo-betonowych" (Remarks on the construction costs of cable-concrete bridges), *Inwestycje i budownictwo,* no. 8, 1957.

Mieszczańkowski, M., "Koncepcja Kurowskiego a rzeczywistość" (Kurowski's concept and reality), *Zycie gospodarcze,* no. 12, 1957.

Minc, B., "Ceny niezmienne" (Fixed prices), *Gospodarka planowa,* nos. 6–7, 1949.

——— "Zmiany w metodologii planowania na rok 1952" (Changes in the methodology of planning for the year 1952), *Gospodarka planowa,* no. 7, 1951.

——— "Planowanie kosztów własnych i cen" (The planning of costs and prices), *Gospodarka planowa,* no. 6, 1952.

——— "W sprawie bodźców zainteresowania materialnego w gospodarce socjalistycznej" (On material incentives in a socialist economy), *Gospodarka planowa,* no. 3, 1956.

——— "W sprawie metod planowania" (On the subject of planning methods), *Trybuna Ludu,* March 20, 1956.

——— "W sprawie zmian w zarządzaniu gospodarką narodową" (On changes in the management of the national economy), *Zycie gospodarcze,* no. 8, 1959.

Minc, H., "O właściwą metodę planowania w Polsce" (For a correct method of planning in Poland), *Nowe drogi,* no. 8, 1948.

Ministerstwo Hutnictwa, *Instrukcja branżowa Ministerstwa Hutnictwa o zasadach sporządzania i zatwierdzania dokumentacji projektowo-kosztorysowej dla inwestycji* (Branch instructions of the Ministry of Metallurgy on the principles for preparing and confirming the technical and cost documentation for an investment), no. 2, Warsaw, Centralne Wydawnictwa Druków, 1955.

Ministerstwo Kolei, *Taryfa Polskich Kolei Państwowych 1954, 1956* (Polish State Railways tariff), Kraków, Wydawnictwo Komunikacyjne, 1953, 1954.

Misiak, M., "Samodzielność przedsiębiorstwa w uchwałach i praktyce" (The autonomy of the enterprise in decrees and practice), *Zycie gospodarcze,* no. 10, 1959.

——— "Bodźce napiętego planowania?" (Incentives for taut planning?), *Zycie gospodarcze,* no. 1, 1961.

Montias, J. M., "Price-setting Problems in the Polish Economy," *Journal of Political Economy, 45,* December 1957.

——— "Producers' Prices in a Centralized Economy: The Polish Experience," unpublished Ph.D. dissertation, Columbia University, 1958.

——— "Planning with Material-Balances in Soviet-Type Economies," *American Economic Review, 49,* December 1959.

———— "Economic Reform and Retreat in Yugoslavia," *Foreign Affairs,* January 1959.

———— "Producers' Prices in a Centrally Planned Economy: The Polish Discussion," in *Value and Plan* ed. by G. Grossman, Berkeley, University of California Press, 1960.

Mościcka, W., Niemira, H., and Gajda, G., "O niektórych zagadnieniach funkcjonowania systemu premiowego w przemyśle" (Problems in the functioning of the bonus system in industry), *Finanse,* no. 2, 1956.

Noble, S. B., "Measures of the Structure of Some Static Linear Economic Models, Serial T-90/58," George Washington University Logistics Research Project, 1958 (mimeograph).

Nowak, J., "Odkówki i odlewy staliwne" (Steel forgings and castings), *Gospodarka materiałowa,* no. 3, 1957.

Olczakowski, W., ed., *Gospodarka węglem w przemyśle* (Coal economy in industry), Warsaw, Panstwowe Wydawnictwa Techniczne, 1957.

Oldakowski, Z., "Bodźce antyprodukcyjne" (Counterproduction bonuses), *Głos pracy,* June 18, 1956.

O zasadach sporządzania i zatwierdzania dokumentacji projektowo-kosztorysowej dla inwestycji (Principles for preparing and confirming the technical and cost documentation for an investment), Warsaw, P.K.P.G., 1953.

Pajestka, J., "Wprowadzenie do metod badań efektywności inwestycji produkcyjnych" (Introduction to the methods for studying the efficiency of productive investments), in *Zagadnienia ekonomicznej efektywności inwestycji,* Warsaw, Polskie Wydawnictwa Gospodarcze, 1956.

Piklikiewicz, H., "Metodologia i organizacja bilansowania maszyn i urządzeń" (The methodology and organization for balancing machines and equipment), *Gospodarka materiałowa,* no. 21, 1954.

Pirożynski, Z., *System budżetowy Polski Ludowej* (The budgetary system of Peoples' Poland), Warsaw, Panstwowe Wydawnictwa Gospodarcze, 1952.

———— "Budżet Państwa podstawowym planem finansowym Polskiej Rzeczypospolitej Ludowej" (The State Budget is the basic financial plan of the Polish Peoples' Republic), *Finanse,* no. 4, 1954.

Polaczek, S., "Spór o ceny surowców podstawowych" (The controversy over the prices of basic raw materials), *Zycie gospodarcze,* no. 15, 1958.

Polish Institute of International Affairs, "System of Planning and Administration of the Polish National Economy 1956–1958," *Legislation of Poland,* Warsaw, no. 6, 1959.

Pomorski, J., "Problem cen" (The price problem), (mimeograph). Warsaw, November 1945.

Popkiewicz, J., "Prawdziwa rentowność" (True profitability), *Trybuna Ludu,* January 6, 1957.

Porwit, K., "Międzygałęziowa koordynacja planu zaopatrzenia" (Interbranch coordination of the supply plan), *Gospodarka materiałowa,* no. 10, 1958.

———— et al., "Uwagi o metodach centralnej koordynacji planu gospodarczego" (Remarks on the methods for the central coordination of the economic plan), *Prace i materiały zakładu badań ekonomicznych,* no. 11, 1958.

———— and Żurkowski, J., "Niektóre specjalne przykłady możliwości zastosowania współczynników powiązań międzygałęziowych w planowaniu gospodarczym" (A few special applications of interindustry coefficients in economic planning), *Prace i materiały zakładu badań ekonomicznych,* no. 14, 1958.

Pospiech, A., "Z doświadczeń nad badaniami efektywności w 'Biprohucie'" (Some of the experiences in studying the efficiency of investments in "Biprohuta"), in *Zagadnienia ekonomicznej efektywności inwestycji,* Warsaw, Polskie Wydawnictwa Gospodarcze, 1956.

Powell, R., "Soviet Monetary Policy," unpublished Ph.D. dissertation, University of California, 1953.

Pryor, F., "Foreign Trade in the Communist Bloc," unpublished Ph.D. dissertation, Yale University, 1961.

Przedpełski, J., "Efektywność inwestycji w przemyśle węgla brunatnego" (The efficiency of investments in the brown-coal industry), *Gospodarka górnictwa,* no. 11, 1956.

Rajewski, Z., "Powiązanie N.P.G. z systemem finansowym Państwa" (The link between the National Economic Plan and the state financial system), *Gospodarka planowa,* no. 7, 1958.

Rajkiewicz, A., "Zatrudnienie" (Employment), in *Zarys rozwoju metodologii planowania w Polsce Ludowej 1944–1954,* Warsaw, Polskie Wydawnictwa Gospodarcze, 1956.

Rakowski, M., *Zagadnienia planowania wieloletniego w Polsce Ludowej* (Problems of long-range planning in Peoples' Poland), Warsaw, Polskie Wydawnictwa Gospodarcze, 1955.

———— "Tablice efektywności inwestycji eksportowych" (Tables of efficiency of export investments), *Prace i materialy zakładu badań ekonomicznych,* no. 1, 1957.

Ramowe wytyczne badań ekonomicznej efektywności inwestycji (Branch rules for the study of the economic efficiency of investments), Warsaw, P.K.P.G., 1956.

Rocznik polityczny i gospodarczy 1958, 1960 (Political and economic yearbook 1958, 1960), Warsaw, Polskie Wydawnictwa Gospodarcze, 1958, 1960.

Rocznik statystyczny 1947, 1948, 1949, 1956–60 (Statistical yearbook 1947, 1948, 1949, 1956–60). Warsaw, Główny Urzad Statystyczny.

Róg, S., "Ceny niezmienne" (Fixed prices), *Zycie gospodarcze*, nos. 13–14, 1949.

———— "Przemysł" (Industry), in *Zarys rozwoju metodologii planowania w Polsce Ludowej 1944–1954*, ed. by B. Minc et al., Warsaw, Polskie Wydawnictwa Gospodarcze, 1956.

Rolow, A., "Ulepszyć współpracę przy planowaniu i realizacji zadań eksportowych" (Improve collaboration in planning and in carrying out export tasks), *Gospodarka planowa*, no. 7, 1956.

Rose, E., "Problem dwoistych cen w Polsce" (The problem of two-level prices in Poland), *Zycie gospodarcze*, no. 19, 1946.

Rotsztejn, B., "O organach i podstawowych zasadach oraz trybie ustalania cen środków produkcji" (On the organs and on the basic principles for setting the prices of means of production), *Przegląd ustawodawstwa gospodarczego*, no. 4, 1955.

———— "Ustalanie cen środków produkcji w przemyśle drobnym" (Price-setting for means of production in small-scale industry), in *Z zagadnien cen środków produkcji*, Warsaw, Panstwowe Wydawnictwa Gospodarcze, 1956.

Rzędowski, I., "Czy zrównać ceny krajowe ze światowymi?" (Should domestic prices be equalized with world prices?), *Zycie gospodarcze*, no. 38, 1957.

Sałdak, Z., "Zalety i wady inwestycji zdecentralizowanych" (Advantages and shortcomings of decentralized investments), *Zycie gospodarcze*, no. 21, 1959.

Samuelson, P. A., "An Extension of the LeChatelier Principle," *Econometrica, 28,* no. 2, 1960.

Secomski, K., "Na marginesie planu inwestycyjnego" (Remarks on the investment plan), *Zycie gospodarcze*, no. 16, 1946.

———— "Zagadnienia inwestycyjne i budowlane w świetle uchwał II-go Zjazdu P.Z.P.R." (Investment and construction problems in the light of the resolutions of the Second Congress of the United Polish Workers' Party), *Inwestycje i budownictwo*, no. 5, 1954.

———— *Planowanie inwestycji* (Investment planning), Warsaw, Panstwowe Wydawnictwa Naukowe, 1954.

———— "Uzasadnienie celowości zamierzonej inwestycji" (The justification of the purpose of a contemplated investment), in *Zagadnienia ekonomicznej efektywności inwestrycji,* Warsaw, Polskie Wydawnictwa Gospodarcze, 1956.

―――― "O zasadzie planowania centralnego i o roli nowej Komisji Planowania" (On the foundation of central planning and on the role of the new Planning Commission), *Gospodarka planowa,* no. 1, 1957.

―――― "Z problematyki planu 5-letniego" (Selected problems of the Five-Year Plan), *Gospodarka planowa,* no. 9, 1957.

Siemiątkowski, L., "Reforma cen artykułów zaopatrzeniowych" (The price reform for procurement items), *Wiadomości Narodowego Banku Polskiego,* no. 6, 1960.

Sławin, W. et al., "Tablice przepływów materiałów w naturalnych jednostkach miary" (Tables of materials-flows in natural-measurement units), *Prace i materiały zakładu badań ekonomicznych,* no. 18, 1960.

Spór o ceny (The price controversy), Warsaw, Książka i Wiedza, 1958.

Sprawozdanie Komisji Planu Gospodarczego i Budżetu 1950 (Report of the Commission on the Economic Plan and on the 1950 budget). Warsaw, P.K.P.G., 1950.

Spulber, N., *The Economics of Communist Eastern Europe,* Cambridge, Mass., The Technology Press of Massachusetts Institute of Technology, 1957.

Stalin, J., *Ekonomicheskie problemy sotsializma v S.S.S.R.* (Economic problems of socialism in the U.S.S.R.), Moscow, Gosudarstvennoe izdatelstvo politicheskoy literatury, 1952.

Stankiewicz, W. J., and Montias, J. M., *Institutional Changes in the Postwar Economy of Poland,* New York, Mid-European Studies Center, 1955.

Stasikowski, S., "Podstawy urzeczywistnienia rentowności hut polskich" (Principles for putting the profitability of Polish steel mills on a realistic basis), *Zycie gospodarcze,* no. 5, 1946.

Stępinski, J., "Ceny porównywalne i ceny niezmienne w budownictwie" (Comparable and fixed prices in construction), *Gospodarka planowa,* no. 5, 1955.

―――― "Możliwości badania kosztów budownictwa a dotychczasowa praktyka" (The possibilities of investigating building costs, and practice up to date), *Inwestycje i budownictwo,* no. 3, 1956.

Strzemiński, A., "Efektywnośc inwestycji w przemyśle węgla brunatnego" (The efficiency of investments in the brown-coal industry), *Gospodarka górnictwa,* no. 2, 1957.

Styś, W., "Zagadnienie intensyfikacji i opłacalności produkcji rolnej"

(The problem of the intensification and profitability of agricultural production), *Ekonomista*, no. 4, 1957.

Sytuacja gospodarcza w kraju w roku 1960 (The economic situation in the country in the year 1960), supplement to *Zycie gospodarcze*, February 1961.

Szerwentke, A., "Wykonanie 6-letniego planu inwestycji" (Fulfillment of the Six-Year Investment Plan), *Gospodarka planowa*, no. 1, 1957.

Szonert, K., "System cen w materiałach budowlanych" (The price system for building materials), *Materiały i budownictwo*, no. 4, 1954.

———— "System cen fabrycznych a obowiązki aparatu zbytu" (The system of factory prices and the obligations of the marketing network), *Gospodarka planowa*, no. 5, 1954.

Szymańczyk, J., "Progresywne normy zużycia—to waźne zadanie dla przedsiębiorstwa" (Progressive consumption norms are an important assignment for the enterprise), *Gospodarka materiałowa*, no. 18, 1960.

"Tezy Rady Ekonomicznej w sprawie niektórych kierunków zmian modelu gospodarczego" (Theses of the Economic Council concerning some changes in the economic model), *Zycie gospodarcze*, no. 22, 1957.

Toeplitz, J. L., "KSR po roku" (Conferences of workers' self-management after a year), *Zycie gospodarcze*, no. 28, 1959.

Tomanek, K., "Ceny, rozliczenia i finansowanie" (Prices, settlements of accounts, and financing), *Gospodarka materiałowa*, no. 15, 1956.

United Nations, Economic Commission for Europe, "The Polish Economy since 1950," *Economic Bulletin for Europe*, 9, no. 3, 1957.

———— *Economic Survey of Europe in 1956*, Geneva, 1957; *in 1959*, Geneva, 1960; *in 1960*, Geneva, 1961.

Wajs, M., "Przyczyny i skutki pewnej reformy płac" (Causes and results of a certain price reform), *Zycie gospodarcze*, no. 36, 1959.

Wakar, A., "Wskaźniki efektywności ekonomicznej inwestycji" (Coefficients of investment efficiency), *Ekonomista*, no. 1, 1957.

Wang, A., "Co zmienić w systemie cen" (What should be changed in the price system), *Trybuna Ludu*, no. 348, 1956.

Warzecha, B., "Reforma cen bez wstrząsów" (A price reform without shocks), *Zycie gospodarcze*, no. 30, 1957.

———— and Tyc, W., "Bilansowanie materiałów nie bilansowanych centralnie" (The balancing of materials not balanced centrally), *Gospodarka materiałowa*, no. 18, 1955.

Waugh, F. W., "Inversion of the Leontief Matrix by Power Series," *Econometrica*, *18*, no. 2, 1950.

Welfe, W., "Obliczanie indeksu fizycznych rozmiarów produktu globalnego" (The calculation of the physical index of gross output), *Przegląd statystyczny*, nos. 1–2, 1955.

Wełpa, B., "Kierunki zmian w rozmieszczeniu sił wytwórczych w latach 1961–1975" (Trends in changes in the allocation of productive forces in the years 1961–1975), *Gospodarka planowa*, no. 9, 1958.

Winter, E., "Niektóre zagadnienia systemu rozliczeń zysków i strat oraz środków obrotowych" (On the system for settling profits and losses and turnover funds), *Finanse*, no. 6, 1954.

―――― "Zreformować system finansowania strat przedsiębiorstw państwowych" (The system for financing the losses of state enterprises should be reformed), *Finanse*, no. 2, 1956.

Witkowski, H. and Krygier, K., "Z zagadnień organizacji zaopatrzenia materiałowego w przemyśle" (Selected problems in the organization of material procurement in industry), *Życie gospodarcze*, no. 1, 1951.

Wścieklica, B., "Hierarchia potrzeb inwestycyjnych" (The hierarchy of investment needs), State Commission for Economic Planning, 1945 (mimeograph).

Ząbkowicz, L., "Organizacja prac nad zmianą cen artykułów inwestycyjnych i zaopatrzeniowych w przemyśle maszynowym" (The organization of the work on price changes for investment and procurement goods in the machine-building industry), *Gospodarka planowa*, no. 11, 1954.

Zachariasz, J., "O właściwą politykę cen surowców" (For a correct price policy for raw materials), *Finanse*, no. 6, 1956.

―――― "Niektóre zagadnienia rewizji cen zaopatrzeniowych" (A few problems in the revision of procurement prices), *Gospodarka planowa*, no. 6, 1960.

Zagadnienia ekonomicznej efektywności inwestycji (Problems in the economic efficiency of investments), Warsaw, Polskie Wydawnictwa Gospodarcze, 1956.

Zakład badań ekonomicznych, "Tablice przepływów materiałów w naturalnych jednostkach miary" (Tables of material flows in physical-measurements units), *Prace i materiały zakładu badań ekonomicznych*, no. 18, 1960.

Załączniki do Instrukcji do opracowania projektu narodowego planu gospodarczego na 1961 r. (Annexes to the instructions for preparing the project of the National Economic Plan for 1961). Warsaw, Komisja planowania gospodarczego, 1960.

Zalewski, J., "Analiza ekonomiczna" (Economic analysis), *Rachunkowość*, no. 8, 1956.

Zalewski, R., "Uwagi o sposobie opracowania narodowego planu gospodarczego w przemyśle" (Remarks on the method for elaborating the national economic plan in industry), *Gospodarka planowa,* no. 4, 1953.

Zarys rozwoju metodologii planowania w Polsce Ludowej 1944–1954 (Outline of the development of planning methodology in Peoples' Poland 1944–1954), ed. by B. Minc et al., Warsaw, Polskie Wydawnictwa Gospodarcze, 1956.

Zauberman, A., *Industrial Development in Czechoslovakia, East Germany, and Poland, 1937–1956,* Royal Institute of International Affairs, London, Oxford University Press, 1958.

———— "The Polish Economy 1961: II. Policies and Prospects," *Soviet Survey,* no. 35, 1961.

Zawadzki, A. W., "Niektóre zagadnienia finansowe w gospodarce Rad Narodowych" (A few financial questions in the economy of the Peoples' Councils), *Gospodarka planowa,* no. 9, 1959.

Zdziech, J., "Co dała Pafawagowi konferencja partyjno-ekonomiczna" (What Pafawag got out of the party-economic conference), *Zycie gospodarcze,* no. 22, 1954.

Zieńkowski, L., *Jak oblicza się dochód narodowy* (How national Income is computed), Warsaw, Polskie Wydawnictwa Gospodarcze, 1959.

Zwass, A., "Szybkość obiegu pieniądza gotówkowego w Polsce, N.R.D. i Jugosławii" (The velocity of monetary circulation in Poland, the German Democratic Republic, and Yugoslavia), *Finanse,* no. 9, 1960.

Zweig, F., *Poland Between Two Wars,* London, Secker and Warburg, 1944.

Z zagadnień cen środków produkcji (Selected problems on producer goods prices), Warsaw, 1956.

Index of Names Cited

Aleksander, C., 98 n.
Alton, T., 53 n., 78 n.
Augustowski, Z., 222 n., 224 n., 226, 242–44, 286

Bąbiński, C., 216 n.
Balassa, B., 172 n.
Barna, T., 337 n.
Bartnicki, M., 162 n.
Basztoń, R., 111 n.
Berliner, J., 172 n.
Berman, J., 52, 54, 271
Bierut, B., 52, 56, 76, 77, 263
Blass, B., 148 n., 198 n.
Bobrowski, C., 52–55, 171 n., 272 n.
Bogobowicz, L., 143, 314 n., 323 n.
Borejdo, I., 147 n.
Borysiewicz, J., 241 n., 245–49, 279, 286
Boyarski, A., 253 n.
Brus, B., 176, 177 n., 267–68, 272 n., 274–75, 285
Brzezinski, Z., 274 n., 278 n.
Buch, W., 157 n.

Carr, E. H., 55
Charłap, Z., 50 n.
Chęcinski, T., 197 n.
Chenery, H. B., 359
Cyrankiewicz, J., 54
Czarkowski, J., 124, 131, 134

Dąbczak, B., 239
Daniszewski, T., 270 n.
Deutschman, Z., 83 n., 103 n.
Dietrich, T., 55
Dobrowolski, J., 183 n.
Domar, E., 63 n.
Dorfman, R., 34 n., 339 n., 365
Dowgiallo, A., 152 n.
Drewnowski, J., 272 n.
Druto, J., 147 n.
Dudziński, W., 322 n., 323 n.
Dziewanowski, M. K., 52 n., 56 n., 268 n.

Engels, F., 56
Erlich, A., 57 n., 63 n., 284 n.
Ernst, M. C., 53 n., 59–60
Evans, D. W., 337 n.

Fedak, Z., 197 n.
Ficowski, S., 138 n., 186 n.
Fiszel, H., 109 n., 151 n., 184, 202, 208, 212 n., 213, 215, 248, 264, 281–82

Frenkel, S., 121 n., 181 n.

Gajda, G., 175 n.
Gass, S. I., 17 n., 22 n.
Gede, T., 321
Gliński, B., 177 n., 181 n., 186 n., 209, 306 n.
Gomulka, W., 48, 52 n., 63, 76, 77, 271, 311, 318–19, 324, 329
Gradowski, T., 305 n.
Granick, D., 30 n., 79 n., 98 n., 104 n., 105 n., 111 n.
Grossman, G., 245 n.
Gwiaździński, J., 158 n.
Guz, L., 265 n.

Haendel, I., 187 n., 233
Hatt, S., 275 n., 321 n.
Hayek, F. von, 273
Himmel, B., 111 n.
Hładyj, M., 290
Hodoły, A., 207 n.
Holzer, A., 87 n.
Horowitz, L., 272 n.
Hortyński, S., 111 n.

Ilecki, W., 101 n.
Issa, A., 89 n.
Iwański, T., 226 n.

Jakubowski, B., 279
Jampel, W., 207 n.
Jarno, J., 108 n.
Jaworski, W., 178 n.
Jędrychowski, S., 78, 158
Jesionowski, J., 266 n.

Kaczorowski, M., 188 n.
Kalecki, M., 66 n., 154–59, 178 n., 272 n., 275–76, 282 n., 326 n., 331
Karczmar, M., 183 n.
Karpiński, A., 58 n., 59 n., 179 n., 275 n.
Karpiński, Z., 203 n.
Karski, R., 107 n.
Kazalski, L., 122 n.
Khrushchev, N., 271
Kiernożycki, A., 305 n.
Kłosiewicz, W., 270 n.
Kołudzki, L., 188 n.
Kowalski, F., 201 n., 206 n.
Kozdra, W., 308 n.
Krajewski, T., 235 n.
Kreisberg, J., 280 n.

Król, H., 175 n.
Krygier, K., 83 n., 87 n., 107 n.
Krzeczkowska, E., 195
Kucharski, M., 140 n., 315 n.
Kuczyński, M., 174 n.
Kurowski, L., 194 n.
Kurowski, S., 267, 273–74, 307, 329 n.
Kuziński, S., 38 n., 57 n., 64, 67 n.
Kwejt, J., 180 n.

Lange, O., 53, 78, 160 n., 266–68, 272 n., 274, 285
Lenin, V. I., 56
Leontief, W., 365 n.
Lesz, M., 126, 328 n.
Leszek, T., 121 n.
Lipczyński, H., 99 n.
Lipiński, E., 267, 272 n.
Lipiński, J., 282, 285–86
Lisikiewicz, J., 285 n.
Lissowski, W., 67 n., 155 n.
Liwowski, J., 111 n.
Łoś, 127 n.

Machoń, Z., 101 n.
Madej, Z., 238 n., 239 n., 302 n.
Magiera, W., 152 n.
Majewski, S., 291 n.
Malenkov, Iu., 331
Malicki, M., 112 n.
Marczewski, J., 58
Marx, K., 44, 56, 276
Marzantowicz, T., 177 n., 181 n., 186 n., 209
Marzec, J., 237
Metrycka, W., 206 n.
Michotek, S., 280
Mieszczańkowski, M., 274 n.
Minc, B., 90, 174, 178 n., 198 n., 199 n., 202 n., 263, 264 n., 267, 285–88, 320
Minc, H., 2 n., 52, 54–57, 64, 66 n., 78, 102, 263, 271
Misiak, M., 303 n., 305 n.
Montias, J. M., 54 n., 121 n., 193 n., 245 n., 274 n., 280 n.
Mościcka, W., 175 n.

Niemira, H., 175 n.
Noble, S., 354
Nowak, J., 98 n.
Nowicki, A., 177 n., 181 n., 186 n., 209

Ochab, E., 76, 263, 269
Olczakowski, W., 241 n.
Oldakowski, Z., 177 n.
Oyrzanowski, B., 124, 131, 134, 139 n.

Pajestka, J., 149 n., 272 n.
Piklikiewicz, H., 90

Pirożyński, Z., 182 n., 206
Polaczek, S., 282
Pomorski, J., 146 n., 192 n., 193 n.
Popkiewicz, J., 273 n.
Porwit, K., 91, 93 n., 136, 345 n.
Pospiech, A., 150 n.
Powell, R., 138 n.
Pruss, W., 143, 314 n., 323 n.
Przedpełski, J., 169 n.
Pudlik, S., 121 n.

Rajewski, Z., 135 n.
Rajkiewicz, A., 119 n.
Rakowski, M., 154 n., 162 n., 164, 166 n., 167
Róg, S., 86 n., 199 n.
Rolow, A., 99 n.
Röpke, W., 273
Rose, E., 191 n.
Rotsztejn, B., 212 n., 214 n., 215
Rumiński, B., 57 n.
Rzędowski, I., 280–82

Saldak, Z., 316 n.
Samuelson, P. A., 34 n., 339 n., 344, 365
Secomski, K., 69 n., 146 n., 149 n., 151, 297, 312, 313 n., 325
Siemiątkowski, L., 292 n.
Sławin, W., 91, 93, 94 n.
Solow, R. M., 34 n., 339 n., 365
Stalin, J., 20, 37, 52 n., 56, 57 n., 65, 204, 231 n., 267, 274, 332
Stankiewicz, W., 54 n., 121 n.
Stasikowski, S., 195 n.
Stępinski, J., 216 n., 217 n.
Strzemiński, A., 169 n.
Styś, W., 73 n.
Szerwentke, A., 62 n.
Szonert, K., 198 n., 211 n.
Szturm de Sztrem, E., 50 n.
Szymańczyk, J., 294 n.
Szyr, E., 158–59, 265, 321

Tafet, A., 107 n.
Tito, J., 58
Toeplitz, J., 310 n.
Tokarski, J., 321
Tomanek, K., 109 n.
Tyc, W., 107 n.

Wajs, M., 122 n.
Wakar, A., 160–62
Wang, A., 275
Warzecha, B., 107 n., 275 n.
Waugh, F., 336 n.
Welfe, W., 199 n.
Wełpa, B., 120 n.
Winter, E., 182 n.
Witaszewski, K., 321

Witkowski, H., 83 n., 103, 107 n.
Wścieklica, B., 146 n.
Wyrozembski, Z., 286–87

Ząbkowicz, L., 225 n.
Zachariasz, J., 279, 288–89, 291 n., 292
Zagórski, J., 286
Zalewski, J., 174 n.

Zalewski, R., 87 n.
Zauberman, A., 326 n.
Zawadzki, A. W., 299 n.
Zdziech, J., 225 n.
Zieńkowski, L., 124, 126 n.
Żurkowski, J., 345 n.
Zwass, A., 143
Zweig, F., 50 n.

Subject Index

Above-plan losses of enterprises, 140, 182–84, 205. *See also* Deficits, financial

Above-plan output: and allocations, 31, 107, 110–12; and bonuses, 174–75, 181 n.; and subsidies to enterprises, 205; and the wage fund, 120–21, 315

Above-plan profits, 141, 182, 197, 316

Academy of Sciences, economic research in, 333

Accountants, role in enterprises, 174

Accounting prices, 83, 196–98, 204–05, 278–79, 284

Accounting rubles, 165–67

"Accounting transit," 83

Accounts of price differences. *See* National Bank of Poland

"Accumulation," 128, 152, 185, 208–09. *See also* Saving; "Surplus value"

Administration of the economy: during Six-Year Plan, 3, 30, 76–83; organizational changes since *1956*, 263–66, 294–307

Aggregation: of norms and processes, 7, 11–12, 94 n., 97–81, 104; in planning industrial outputs, 6, 29, 91, 201, 298

Agricultural Bank, 117, 130

Agricultural Circles (*Kółka rolnicze*), 159, 328

Agricultural output, 58, 60, 72, 156 n., 159, 313, 318

Agriculture: allocation of resources to, 5, 62, 64; mechanization of, 159, 329, 331; planning of, 90–91; in prewar Poland, 50

Allocation of materials: to low-priority sectors, 66, 100–01; to ministries, 87, 101–02, 104; to private sector, 55, 101; and powers of bureaucracy, 307

Amortization. *See* Depreciation allowances

"Annual Plan Indices," 295. *See also* Directives

Applications for materials, 98, 111–12, 294, 323. *See also* Materials, requirements of enterprises

Armaments industry, 57 n., 58, 64, 72, 74, 269, 273, 330–31

Associations (*zjednoczenia*), 299–300, 306

Assortment (product-mix), of enterprises, 84, 110, 172, 181, 186 n., 200; and prices, 245–46

Assortment plan, 174, 177–78, 180, 186, 187 n., 190, 208, 246, 277

Austro-Hungary, 49

Autarky, tendencies toward, 65, 274, 281–82, 293

Average-cost pricing, 44, 197, 241, 243, 260–62, 279, 282, 284, 287–88; deviations from, 240–50, 254–62; methodology of, 204, 214, 222, 225, 231–35, 245–46, 250–54; and opportunity cost, 170, 245

Balance of incomes and outlays: of population, 85, 116–18, 122–27, 142 n.; of ministries, 118, 130, 132

Balance of the national economy, 85

Balance of national income, 118

Balance of payments: planning of, 16, 85; problems, 155, 311, 326, 331. *See also* Foreign exchange, shortages of

Balanced growth, 55

Balances, methodology of, 84–90, 93. *See also* Machinery balances; Material balances

Bank controls, on enterprises, 138–39, 179, 184, 203

Bank credits: long-term, 130, 146–47, 295; short-term, 117–18, 124, 130, 135, 137–40, 179, 184–85, 203, 316

Bank loans, overdue, 137 n.

Bank transfers, 203–04

Bargaining, between higher and lower administrative organs, 5, 102, 104

Basic solutions, in planning models, 20–22, 36, 358–59, 362, 365

Black market, 125, 144

Bonuses: to managing staff of enterprises, 105, 174–78, 186–87, 200, 254, 303–04, 306; for cost-reduction, 175–78, 186, 188 n.; labor productivity, 174; and price-setting theory, 254–55, 330; production, 174–75, 187, 256, 320; to personnel of administrative organs, 174, 176; to workers, 181, 307–08

Bottlenecks: in planning model, 6, 8,

15, 20, 24; and planning practice, 5, 7, 25, 99, 114, 146; in Poland's economic development, 155–57, 160 n.; and the price system, 44, 170

"Bourgeois Economics," official attitudes toward, 56, 332

Bribing, as means of obtaining scarce materials, 108

Budget, state: deficits, 146; expenditures, 72; fulfillment of, 141; planning of, 116–18, 130, 135; relation to enterprises, 81, 182–83; revenue breakdown, 132, 206; and settlement of financial surpluses and deficits of central boards, 204, 229; surpluses, 69, 118, 129, 132, 139–40, 144; surpluses, planned and realized, 141

Budget differences, positive and negative, 132, 229

Budget enterprises, 196

Budget grants: for investment outlays, 1, 117, 130, 132, 146 n., 220, 277, 295; to local peoples' councils, 299; to replenish working capital of enterprises, 132, 137, 183

Budget line, 41, 44–46, 257

Budgetary organizations, 81, 121, 133, 204, 211

Budgets, of peoples' councils, revenues and expenditures, 118, 132 n., 299, 316

Buffer sectors, 4, 5, 8, 100–01

Building contractors, 215–16

Building materials, prices of, 210–11, 217, 222, 280

Building-materials industry, 9, 12, 60–61, 63, 79, 85; deficits in, 226 n., 240

Bulgaria, 332

Bureaucratization of planning methods, 84, 86, 87, 185

Bureaucrats, attitude toward decentralization, 274 n., 278, 304, 307, 311

Capacity balances, 53, 57, 87, 148, 153, 157

Capacity limitations, 3–4, 99; in planning model, 6, 13, 18, 20–21, 339–45

Capital accumulation, model of, 365

Capital charges, 162, 287. See also Interest

Capital (input) coefficients, 33–34, 37, 62

Capital-output ratios, aggregated, 154–56

Cartels, in prewar Poland, 50, 199, 200

Catalogue prices, 225, 239, 241, 248

Catching up with the West, efforts aimed at, 157, 159

Cement, 58, 167–68, 226 n., 325; prices of, 211 n., 237

Central Board: of the Inorganic Industry, 31, 238, 293; of Machine Economy, 90, 265; of the Tool Industry, 237

Central Boards of Industry (centralny zarząd przemysłu): abolition of, 299; administrative powers of, 294; deficits in, 230, 237, 293; personnel of, 265 n.; in planning process, 5, 7, 79–81, 84–88, 104, 105, 119, 121, 168–69, 172–73, 177, 265; role in financial system, 182–83, 185, 188, 197–98, 205; role in price-setting, 199, 225 n., 235

Central Committee of Polish United Workers' Party: commission of, 299 n.; secretariat of, 64, 76–77, 321; Ninth Plenum (after First Congress), September 1953, 65, 331; Seventh Plenum (after Second Congress), July 1956, 268–71, 312; Eighth Plenum (after Second Congress), October 1956, 57 n., 270–72, 294, 312; Twelfth Plenum (after Second Congress), October 1958, 158–59; Second Plenum (after Third Congress), June 1959, 160 n.; Third Plenum (after Third Congress), October 1959, 319–20, 323

Central Marketing Board (Centralny zarząd zbytu), 80–81, 83, 90, 188 n., 300. See also Marketing organizations

Central Planning Office (Centralny urząd planowania), 52, 54–56, 146, 193, 195

Centralization: and development goals, 273; extreme, 6, 79, 83–84, 86, 90, 173, 190, 241, 263, 269; new trends toward (1959–60), 294, 319

Chemical industry, 60, 64, 94, 109, 155 n., 180; financial deficits in, 238; organization of, 79–81

Chemicals, transfer prices of, 229, 233, 236–38

Chief Statistical Office, 11, 126, 239, 313, 314

Class structure, and financial planning, 125

Coal (bituminous): consumption of, 103; costs of, 238; export prices of, 106, 291; grades of, 103, 110, 200, 239, 241, 260–61; production and exports, 50, 68, 312, 325, 331; supply and stocks of, 100, 109–10; transfer prices of, 238–39, 241–42, 289, 291

Coal mining: accounting prices in, 205 n.; development of, 155 n.; efficiency

Coal mining (*continued*)
of investments in, 168–70; financial deficits, 222, 224, 226, 228, 232, 238, 240; priority status of, 146 n.; relation to other industries, 10, 94, 164

Coefficients of foreign-exchange efficiency, 166–68

Coefficients of investment efficiency. *See* Investment efficiency, calculations of

Coke, prices of, 249

Coking coals, deficit in, and prices of, 242

Collective farms: dissolution of in *1956*, 272; funds allotted to, 65; money incomes of, 123–24

Collectivization of agriculture, 53, 58, 65, 72–73, 159 n., 329, 331

Commercial centrals, 192, 196–98, 203–04. *See also* Marketing organizations

Commissions on the Assessment of Investment Projects, 154 n.

Communal services, 72

Communists, in Poland, 52. *See also* Polish United Workers' Party

"Comparable prices" (*ceny porówny-walne*), 202

Comparative advantage in foreign trade, 23, 167–68, 281, 361

Competition, in prewar Poland, 50

"Compound relation," as basis for price-setting, 246–47, 249–50

Compulsory deliveries, farm products, 52, 59, 314, 327

Congresses of Trade Unions, 270, 309

Construction: of new housing, 63, 65, 171, 324; of new plants, 62

Construction sector, 85, 94, 188; allocations of materials and funds to, 66, 96; costs in, 5, 216–17; employment in, 61, 71, 317

Consumer goods: allocations to retail market, 96; quality of, 3, 63 n., 73, 209, 315, 327; planning of, 29, 85, 116, 126; profitability of, 149, 208–09; sales and supplies of, 69, 72–73, 120, 322, 327; sector, growth of, 60, 63, 64, 74, 313; sector, in priority scale, 4, 8, 64, 100–01, 109–10; sold by producer-goods industries, 229–30. *See also* Retail market

Consumers, industrial, relations with suppliers, 108, 111

Consumers' preferences, 273

Contracts, between socialized enterprises, 83

"Control by the zloty," 203. *See also* Bank controls

Control figures. *See* Directives, planning

Control of plan fulfillment, 87

Convex linear combinations, 15 n., 19

Convexity of production surfaces, 22 n., 44–46, 352

Cooperation between socialized enterprises, 83, 173, 177

Cooperatives, producers', nonagricultural, 4, 53, 82, 112, 211, 292, 296; allocations of materials to, 101, 211; prices charged by, 215; prices paid by, 211

Cooperatives, service, 211

Coordination: between various administrative organizations, 31, 88, 92, 135–36, 142, 154, 157–58, 164 n., 227, 319; of central plans, 84–89, 319. *See also* Material balances, consistency of

Copper mining, government policy on, 292–93

Cost-accounting: enterprises on, 81, 194, 196, 203; in construction sector, 191, 215, 217, 219; of investment projects, 150, 215–17; methods, 176–77, 195, 197, 203, 212–13, 241

Cost limits, 240, 254–56. *See also* Costs planning

Cost-of-living index, 70

Costs planning: relation to procurement plans, 86, 135–36, 324; and financial plans, 133, 135–36, 137, 215. *See also* Planned costs

"Cost-plus" prices, 198, 212

Cost-reduction plans, of enterprises, 83, 135, 140, 175–76, 180, 185, 202, 205, 215

Cost savings, due to investment outlays, 160–62

Costs, total, of enterprises, aggregated by ministry, 133, 141

Costs, average unit, of enterprises: and allocation of materials, 110, 249–50; comparable, 177; of least efficient plants, 168, 283–84, 286, 288; and their product-mix, 178, 186 n.; range of in different industries, 287–88. *See also* Marginal-cost pricing

Council of Ministers: composition of, 77–78; ordinances and directives of, 199, 299, 302; role in planning system, 7, 77, 84, 87, 104, 121, 296–97; role in price-setting, 221, 224 n.

Council on Mutual Economic Aid (Comecon), 158 n.

Currency holdings: of enterprises and other socialized organizations, 133; of the population, 116–17, 124. *See also* Monetary circulation

Current planning. *See* Planning, short-term

Credit plan, 118, 130–31, 142. *See also* Bank credits

Credit reform, 178, 184–86. *See also* Bank credits

Czechoslovakia, 3, 50, 332

Debts, of enterprises, 184–85

Decapitalization, of low-priority sectors, 61

Decentralization, 5, 6, 31, 48, 78 n., 111, 190, 265, 268, 274–75, 278, 294–304, 319, 326, 330, 332–33; and democratization, 268, 273, 275. *See also* Delegation of planning functions

Decentralized funds of enterprises, 134, 302, 304, 321

Decreasing returns to scale, in planning model, 13

Deficit enterprises, 204, 239–40, 278

Deficits, financial, 194–95, 204, 230, 239–40. *See also* Subsidies

Delegation of planning functions, 31, 84, 87–89, 92–93, 106, 294, 297

Deliveries, of materials ordered, 111, 184; payment for, 184, 204

Demand, nonmarket, estimation of, 88, 158 n.

Department of Costs and Price Policy, of Planning Commission, 79, 225–26, 237, 239–40, 242, 244, 279, 288

Department for Economic Research, of Planning Commission, 91, 332, 342

Department of Perspective Planning, of Planning Commission, 79, 154 n.

Deposits, of enterprises with National Bank of Poland, 118, 130–31, 133, 137–38

Depreciation allowances, 134, 162, 164 n., 195, 225, 238, 251 n., 264, 277, 287, 289, 301

Depression in the *1930s*, 49

Development. *See* Economic development; Industrialization

Development Fund of enterprises, 302

Development of water resources, planning of, 152–53

Directives, planning, 7, 29, 84, 86, 157, 186, 188, 253, 297, 320, 337; received by enterprises, 172–73, 188, 264, 295,

303–06. *See also* Priority of central directives

Directors, of enterprises, 264, 271, 307–09. *See also* Managing staff of enterprises

Disaggregation: of balances, 29–30; in price-setting, 236. *See also* Nomenclature

Disproportions, in long-term development of Polish economy, 37–38, 64, 67, 113, 151, 170–71, 331

Draft-plans ("projects"): long-term, 155–57; short-term, 84, 88–89, 95, 147, 296–97

"Dynamic efficiency," in long-term planning model, 365–66

East Germany, 3, 332

Economic calculation, 38, 46, 152–54, 161–62, 231 n., 267, 284; relation to physical balances, 43, 145, 149, 168–70. *See also* Investment efficiency; Foreign trade, economic calculations in

Economic Commission for Europe, 63 n., 70

Economic Committee of the Council of Ministers (K.E.R.M.), 78, 192, 321

Economic Council (*Rada Ekonomiczna*), 78, 111, 272, 276–78, 282–83, 288; Theses on Price Formation, 282–85. *See also* "Polish Economic Model"

Economic development, and planning problems, 2–5, 10, 144, 274–76, 344–45

"Economic instruments," versus administrative orders, 276–77

Economies of scale, in construction industry, 66

"Effective prices," 197, 205

Effective rates (*kursy wynikowe*), in foreign-trade calculations, 165–66, 290–91

Efficiency: definition of, in planning models, 10–11, 34, 352, 368; marginal conditions for, 40; in long-term plans, 34–36, 169; in short-term plans, 10–33

Efficiency locus, 41

Efficient solutions, in planning model, 21–23

Elasticity of demand, price, income, 127 n., 187, 332

Elasticity of substitution, 259

Electric power, output, 312, 325

Electronic computers (as aid in planning), 10, 11, 15, 32, 38–39, 335

Embargo, allied, on trade with Soviet bloc, 64, 291

Employment: by enterprises, 121, 138, 304–05; growth and structure of, 61, 71; planning of, 120–21, 320–21; of women, 61, 74, 115. See also Labor balances

Endogenously produced factors, in long-term planning, 34–35, 365–70

Enterprise Fund, 133, 178–82, 269, 295, 301–02, 307, 316, 330

Enterprises, socialized: administrative autonomy of, 203, 285, 294–96, 301, 304–07, 314; relation to banks, 81, 203, 305 (see also Bank controls); role in planning system, 7, 79–81, 84, 86–89, 172–74 (see also Planning "from the bottom up"); sales of surplus capital goods and stocks, 196, 307, 316. See also Cost-accounting, enterprises on

Equalizing Fund, 192

Equipment, condition of, 103–04. See also Service life of equipment; Obsolete equipment

"Equivalent relation" as basis for price-setting, 246–47, 250

Ersatz materials, prices of, 221, 244

Exchange rate: of U.S. dollar, 165 n., 168, 290–91; on imported materials, 195, 206

"Exogenous barriers" to development, 155–56

Exogenous factors: full employment of, 14–15, 24, 32, 34–35; in long-term planning, 34–35, 365–66, 368–69; in short-term planning, 13–15, 18, 19, 22, 25–27, 100, 340, 349; unemployment of, 18–20

Expeditors, 108

Experimenting enterprises, 178 n.

Exportable goods, 23–24, 282

Export capacity, 166–67, 171

Exports, 68, 106; of aluminum, 166; of cement, 167–68; of coal, at prices below world market, 313; of cotton cloth, 167–68; directives on, 305; of individual goods, value of, 167; of meat, 318; planning of, 98–99, 293, 346; prices paid to domestic producers, 132, 206 n.; of raw materials, profitability of, 281. See also Coal, production and exports

External economies, 274

Extremal points, in net-output surface, 17–19, 20

Factory prices (ceny fabryczne), 206, 278

Factory-accounting price, 196–97, 204–05

Farm marketings, 59, 72, 328. See also Government purchases, of farm products

Fats industry, 60

Feasible solutions, in planning model, 20–22, 24, 353, 355–56, 359, 364

"Feedback," 154, 254. See also Interdependencies, circular

Final demand: in long-term planning, 33, 113; in short-term planning, 7–8, 13, 21 n., 22, 24, 94, 113, 335, 339, 349–51

Financial assets of enterprises, redistribution of by higher authorities, 183, 300

Financial discipline, 319–20

Financial plans, 1, 17, 115–18, 121–37, 140–41

Financial program, 130–34

Financial system: 1947 reform, 196–98; 1949–50 reforms, 198, 202–05, 218–19

Five-Year Plan—
first, 1956–60, 20, 38, 120, 153–54, 161–62, 311–12; fulfillment, 313, 315, 324–25; preliminary drafts of, 312–13, 315
second, 1961–65, 38, 158–59, 161, 326, 331

Fixed capital: assigned to enterprises, 196; inventory and valuation of, 289. See also Interest, on fixed assets

Fixed prices, of 1937–38, 39, 59 n., 178, 191, 199–202

Food, consumed on farms, 125 n.

Food expenditures, in budgets of peasants and workers, 125 n., 327

Food-processing industry, 64, 73, 79, 90, 118

Food supplies, 71, 318, 327–28

Foreign exchange: allocation of, 4, 115; in planning model, 16, 359–61; shortages of, 65, 156, 169, 171, 210, 327. See also Balance-of-payment problems

Foreign investment, in national income analysis, 128, 134

Foreign loans, to Poland, 157, 313, 325–26. See also Soviet aid; United States, loans to Poland

Foreign markets of Poland, 49

Foreign trade: economic calculations in, 157, 165–68, 171, 200, 264; in planning model, 23–24, 33, 359–61; prices in, 165–66. See also Imports; Exports

Foreign-trade centrals. *See* Import-export enterprises

Formula, for calculating the efficiency of investments, 162–64, 166

Garment industry, 60, 71, 209
Gauss-Seidel iterative procedure, 94 n., 337–39
General Gouvernement, 191–92
"Genetic" planning, 55
German occupation, during World War II, 50, 147, 191, 196
Germany, relations with Poland, 49–51
Gestation period of investments, in long-term planning, 34, 155, 161–62, 326, 366
Glavk (Soviet), equivalent to central board of industry, 79
Gomulka reforms, 47, 173, 294–310
Gomulka regime, 3, 171, 271–72, 318–20
Government borrowing, 117
Government purchases of farm products, 123, 132, 141, 318, 327, 328 n.
Government saving, in national income analysis, 128–29
Great Britain, wartime planning in, 31
Gross output, value of, 3–5, 59, 172, 178, 201–02, 277, 295
Gross outputs, in planning model, 8, 14–15, 17–18, 253, 335–37
Group prices, 197

Handicrafts, 50, 53 n., 59, 71, 82, 124, 126, 180, 298
Harrod-Domar model, relation to Kalecki's model, 155 n.
Harvests: information on and planning of, 100, 106, 141; size of and state of economy, 69–70, 322 n.
Heavy industry: financial deficits in, 118, 149, 177, 228, 231; priority development of, 31, 37 n., 57, 62, 273, 330
Hoarding, of materials, by enterprises, 107, 138
Household budgets: breakdown of, 125; foreign exchange content of, 166, 327
Housing: availability of and labor supply, 4, 119–20, 171; rural, 63, 157; urban, 63, 157, 217, 325
Hungary, 320, 332

Imported raw materials, 68, 327
Import-export enterprises, 81, 206, 346 n.
Imports: directives on, 305; planning of, 24, 96, 98

Incentives: of higher organizations, 277, 299; of managers in socialized enterprises, 47, 82, 84, 174–82, 274–75, 277, 294, 303–04; workers', 116, 119–20, 180, 275, 301. *See also* Profit incentives
Incomes, personal, 122, 128, 142–43, 318, 328, 357–58. *See also* Balance of incomes and outlays
Index-number problem, 59 n.
Indices of price changes, 225, 227, 233–39
Indivisibilities, 13, 67
Industrial administration, structure of, 80–81
Industrial output: Ernst index, 53, 59–60; independent estimates of, 59–60; official index of, 59, 313, 325; in old plants, 62; relation to prewar, 53. *See also* Gross output, value of
Industrialization, 3, 49, 60, 274, 281, 330
Industry: large-scale (key), 4, 53, 194, 213–15; small-scale, local, 4, 77 n., 82, 180, 213–14, 298–99
Infant industries, protection of, 281–82
Inflation: and economic calculation, 146; and financial planning, 116, 135, 137–44; and the price system, 69, 218, 250, 253
Inflationary pressures, 48, 49, 52, 68–74, 147, 195, 311, 316, 318–22
Informal pressures and interventions, on higher echelons by enterprises, 102, 107–08, 112
Information available to central planners: on production processes and performance of the economy, 3, 10–12, 22, 31 n., 32–33, 37, 40, 46, 85, 87, 95–97, 136, 249–50, 343; on technological progress abroad, 57; on ultimate destination of resources allotted, 33, 97, 323
Input-output analysis, formal methods of, 10, 91, 113, 164, 332
Input-output coefficients, 6, 9, 12, 13, 93–94, 96–97, 251, 297–98, 335, 339. *See also* Norms, material-consumption
Instructions: on preparing investment projects, 151–52, 160–63; of planners, and reforms, 278
"Instruments of production," prices of, 242–43. *See also* Price-setting for investment goods
Insurance payments, 123
Interdependencies: circular, and the consistency of balances, 10, 29, 94–95, 342–

Interdependencies (*continued*)
43, and price-setting, 225, 232–33, 239, 250, 254, 288–89; in construction sector, 66; in industrial structure, 8–9, 29, 67, 93–95, 342–43

Interest: on fixed assets of enterprises, 44, 266, 277, 283; in foreign-trade calculations, 166–67; in long-term planning model, 366; on overdue accounts, 184; on short-term credits, 138; used in selecting investment projects, 162–65; on working capital of enterprises, 283

Interfirm crediting, 184–85, 196

Intermediate goods, planning of, 24, 25

Internal cost-accounting of enterprises, 81

Intertemporal comparisons, in planning model, 36, 366

Inventories: above-norm, 138, 185, 314; of consumer goods, 116, 131, 142–44, 315; of enterprises, seasonal, 137–38; of enterprises, financing of, 130, 135, 137–38, 142; levels of, 109, 112, 143, 270, 311, 314–15, 323; in national income analysis, 128, 315; in planning process, 85, 96, 107, 142, 270; valuation of, 139 n.

Investment costs, 69, 72. See also Cost estimates

Investment efficiency, calculations of, 149, 153, 157, 160–65, 168–71, 200, 274–75, 280, 284, 293

Investment funds: allocations of to different sectors, 4, 37, 57, 58, 61–62, 64–65, 74, 118, 146, 313, 332; applications for by ministries and other organizations, 154, 321; and capacity of construction sector and of capital-goods industries, 147–48, 153; planning and distribution of, 16, 37, 57, 82–83, 85, 129, 140, 144, 148, 153–54, 157

Investment limits, 67 n., 157–58, 295, 322

Investment projects: blueprints of, 147, 150; capital-intensive, 31 n., 164; choice of variants, 152–53, 161–64; delays in completion of, 66, 107; documentation for and justification of, 151–53; planning of, 37, 79, 148, 150–52, 285

Investments in national economy: ancillary, 163–64; burden on economy, 61, 158, 326; decentralized, 121, 259, 264, 295, 301–03, 316–17, 321–22; levels of, 65, 68, 69, 72, 85, 311–12, 316–17, 322, 326; in national-income analysis, 128–

29; private, 62, 68, 146 n.; "programming" of, 148–49; share in national income, 61, 62, 66, 72, 154–56, 312–15

Investments in Soviet bloc, 332

Isoquants, production, 27–28, 40–43, 255–56

Iterative procedures: convergence of, 9, 93–94, 252–54, 337, 339; number of computations involved, 342–43. See also Planning by successive approximations; Gauss-Seidel iterative procedure

Joint products: in planning model, 13, 15–16, 22, 32, 354–56; prices of, 241, 244

Kalecki's growth model, 154–55

Korean War, 37, 64, 74, 331

Kramer's rule, 362, 364

Labor: abundance of and planning methods, 2–5, 37, 44 n.; allocation of, 3, 16, 43, 61, 71; decentralized allocation of, 31, 115, 220, 256; migration of, 4, 60, 74, 115, 119–20; recruitment, 119–20; shortages, 119; skilled, 115, 119, 176; supply of, 3, 16, 43, 61, 71, 74

Labor (manpower) balances, 82, 118–20, 147; regional, 119–20

Labor costs, direct and indirect ("congealed"), 43–44, 287

Labor exchanges, 120

Labor-intensive goods, and financial equilibrium, 358. See also Substitution, of labor for capital

Labor norms. See Norms, labor

Labor productivity: in agriculture, 328–29; planning of, 3, 37, 62, 75, 85, 89, 121–22, 153, 293, 321; in transformation industries, in Poland and abroad, 281–82; trends in industry, 60, 75, 284, 289, 324

Labor theory of value, 44

Labor turnover, 179

Land reform, 52

Launching of new capacity, delays in, 107, 151

"Law of value," 190, 204, 231 n., 267

Leading links, 6

Leather industry, 60, 94

Leontief matrix, 15 n., 252, 347

Leontief trajectory, 365

Light industry, bonus system in, 174–75

Lignite, efficiency of investments in, 168–70, 260–61

Linear programming, 32 n., 47 n., 358–59

Linearity of preference function, 17, 19, 365

Liquidity, in financial system, 138–39, 141

Local authorities, autonomy of, 269. *See also* Peoples' councils

Location, of industry, 171, 298

Long-term planning: in planning model, 33–39, 365–70; in planning practice, 20, 66, 79, 147–60, 264, 332; relation to yearly plans, 33, 38, 85. *See also* Perspective balances; Perspective plan (*1961–75*)

Lublin Committee, 51

Machinery, prices of, 212, 225–27, 235, 291–92

Machinery balances, 6, 87 n., 89–90

Machine-building industry, 61, 64, 67, 71, 79, 94, 104 n., 229; profits and losses in, 227, 229–30, 240

Macroeconomic equilibrium, 16–17, 85. *See also* Synthetic balances

"Main proportions" of economy, planning of, 25, 29, 86

Major repairs, 61, 173; financial planning of, 133–34, 277, 295

Managing staff of enterprises, autonomy of, 81, 141, 172–73, 175 n., 187–88, 202–03, 264, 269, 275, 285, 294–96, 301

Marginal-cost pricing, Polish views on, 283–88

Marginal costs: of goods exported, 168; in planning model, 44, 46

Marginal productivity, 28, 40, 45, 110, 254, 259 n.

Market demand, analysis of, 126–27, 131, 328

Market economy, and Soviet-type system, 38 n., 76, 280, 333

Marketed output of enterprises, 172, 201–02, 276

Marketing offices (*biura zbytu*), 81, 98, 109

Marketing organizations: role in distributive system, 31, 80–81, 84, 89, 105 n., 107, 192, 214, 260, 324; role in price-setting, 225 n., 241 n., 261. *See also* Marketing offices; Sales offices

Markets, role of in socialist economy, 1, 47, 267–68, 273–75, 278

Marshall Plan, 54

Marxist doctrine, 54, 56, 127, 133, 241, 266–68, 274, 320

Marx's reproduction scheme, 267

Material balances: consistency of, 6–10, 18, 29, 85–89, 91–95, 101–02, 113, 253–54, 297, 335–39; and foreign-trade decisions, 99, 167–71; goods balanced by lower organs, 90, 97, 157 n.; mechanical closure of, 101–02, 136; planning and makeup of, 29, 79, 95–100, 147, 335, 345; relation to synthetic balances, 16–17, 31. *See also* Delegation of planning functions; Perspective (long-term) balances

Material-intensive goods, and production bonuses, 178

Materials: centrally allocated, 84, 87, 297–98, 323–24; exchanges of among enterprises, 108; informally rationed by lower organizations, 107, 324; quality of deliveries, 103–04, 111 n.; requirements of enterprises, 7, 82–84, 86, 95–97, 98, 112. *See also* Allocations of materials; Applications for materials; Rationing of producer goods

Matrix inversion, 252–53, 336, 339. *See also* Technology matrix

Meat: prices of, 126, 318; supplies, crisis in (*1959*), 318–19, 321, 327

Metallurgical industry: coordination of branches within, 150–51; costs estimation in, 236–37; deficits in, 184, 195, 222–24, 226, 229–30; growth of, 58, 60, 155 n.; long-term plans of, 150–51, 158 n.; planning of, 9, 12, 50, 79, 94, 104 n., 109, 146 n., 157 n., 186–87; priority status of, 146 n., 150; wages and other earnings in, 73, 180

Metallurgical products, prices of, 195, 200–02, 222–30, 245–50, 287

Metal-processing industries, 9, 60, 71, 121 n., 160 n., 186, 224–25, 229–30; branches of, 230

Metal products, prices of, 227, 232, 236

Mining (extractive) industries, 64, 94, 180. *See also* Coal mining; Ministry of Mining

Ministries, industrial: in financial system, 185, 205, 229; goods planned by, 90; and labor norms, 264; organization of, 79–81, 265; in planning system, 5, 7, 77–78, 84–89, 92, 96–97, 104, 119, 121, 157 n., 163, 297, 320–21; relation to associations, 306; role in preparing investment projects, 150–53; role in price-setting, 221–22

Ministry—
of Agriculture, 78
of Construction and Building Materials, 181
of Construction of Towns and Settlements, 216
of Finance, 78, 137, 140, 142, 144, 179–81, 184, 188, 198, 204, 220, 229, 260, 322
of Foreign Trade, 78, 81, 265, 332
of Heavy Industry, 78 n., 180, 316
of Industrial Construction, 216–17
of Industry and Trade, 52, 56, 192–93, 195–97
of Internal Trade, 126–27, 164 n., 328, 332
of Light Industry, 77 n., 306
of Machine-building, 212, 213 n., 225
of Metallurgy, 152, 177 n., 179, 265; price-setting in, 232, 235–36. See also Metallurgical industry
of Mining, 77 n., 81, 179, 181, 221–22, 238
of National Defense, 221
of Procurement and Trade, 192. See also Ministry of Internal Trade
of Small-Scale Industry and Handicrafts, 82, 211, 213 n., 214, 231 n.
of State Control, 77, 181
Modernization of plants, planning of, 153, 161
Monetary circulation: levels of, 52, 70, 124–25, 130–31, 142–43; planning of, 16, 17 n., 116–17, 125, 142, 357
Monetary controls, effectiveness of, 141–44. See also "Control by the zloty"
Monetary reform, 17 n., 69–70
Monopoly management (gestia), 300
Moral-political appeals, in planning system, 55, 266–67, 321

National Bank of Poland: accounts of price differences, 198, 214; assets of, 130, 140; bookkeeping transfers between enterprises, 203; capital of, 118 n.; 130; cash plan of, 125, 130–31; liabilities of, 130, 140 n.; role in financial system, 117–18, 138, 179, 182, 185, 196–98, 203; short-term credits. See Bank credits
National defense, in budget, 132. See also Armaments
National Economic Plan, 54, 84–87, 92, 104, 121, 135, 140, 323
National income: budget expenditures as share of, 132, 206; computation of

and price system, 278; levels and growth rates of, 50, 59, 156, 159, 313; methodology of, 54–55, 118, 127–30; planning of, 85, 118, 154–56; services in, 59 n., 118; turnover taxes as share of, 207
Nationalization, 1, 51, 148; decree of January 1946, 52–53
Negative price differences, 132, 192. See also Price differences; Subsidies
Net output, as value added, 127
Net outputs: in planning model, 8, 13, 14, 15–21, 34, 337–39, 358; relation to gross outputs, 342. See also Final demand
New Course (1953–54), 2, 37, 65–66, 74, 331
New products: costs of, 177, 200; prices of, 201, 208, 222 n., 243
Nomenclature: of prices, 191, 200, 226, 236; of supply plans and of orders, 105–06, 157 n., 236, 298
Nonferrous metals: prices of, 200, 248–49, 261, 290–91; shortages of, 67
Nontypical products: importance of, 212; prices of, 198, 212–16
Norms: construction, 3–5, 57, 217; depreciation, 289; labor, 264, 268–70, 301, 308, 322, 339; labor, and planning of wage fund, 121–22; material-consumption, 3–5, 12, 32, 88–89, 91–93, 97–98, 101–04, 107, 172, 294, 339; of natural increase, 90; progressive, 103–04, 269; working capital, 137, 182, 295
Nowa Huta (steel mill), 54, 217

"Objects of production," prices of, 242–44. See also Prices of producer goods
Obsolete equipment, 74, 110, 112; retirement of, 153, 155
Opportunity cost: and foreign trade alternatives, 165; of investment outlays, 162 n.; in planning model, 22, 38; relation to accounting costs, 147, 170
Optimal program, 21–23, 27, 32 n.
Orders: for materials on the part of enterprises, 105, 109; and prerogatives of suppliers, 264, 305. See also Applications for materials
Organizational breakdowns, and consistency of balances, 96–97, 345–48
"Organized transit," 83
Output targets, 7, 11, 47, 58, 86–87, 96, 102, 105, 140, 276, 295, 297–98, 305; and investment plans, 152–53; primacy of, 173–74, 176, 178, 186, 269

Packages from abroad, 123–24, 315, 327

"Paper cycles," 239. *See also* Interdependencies, circular

"Pax," discrimination in favor of, 211 n.

Peasant markets (*targowiska*), 116, 126, 144, 328

Peasant population, incomes and expenditures, 124–26. *See also* Population, agricultural

Pensions, 123

Peoples' Councils (*Rady narodowe*), role in economic system, 82, 118, 214, 221, 265, 297–99. *See also* Planning commissions of voivodships and counties; Voivodships

Personnel policy, in administration of the economy, 52, 55–56, 321

Perspective (long-term) balances: consistency of, 1, 33, 37–38, 53, 66, 148, 150–51, 159, 169, 344–45; for fuels, 169; makeup of, 154 n., 157; and price system, 144, 169–71

Perspective plan (*1961–75*), 145, 154–59, 331

Piece-rates. *See* Norms, labor

Pig iron, 150–51

Plan failures, in low-priority sectors, 60, 63–64

Plan fulfillment: in agriculture, 311, 324; of allocations, 111, 113, 323; of assortment, 187 n.; construction of housing, 324; financial, 140–43, 147; of investment outlays, 147, 317; output, 186 n., 202, 208. *See also* Bonuses, production; Six-Year Plan, fulfillment

Planned costs, 196, 205, 214, 219, 255–56

Planners, skill and experience of, 2–3, 28, 52, 114

Planners' "freedom of choice," 171

Planners' preferences, 13, 15, 17–19, 110, 178, 186 n., 274, 330; function of, 13, 14, 22, 36, 351, 365–66, 368

Planning: bureaucratic limitations of, 17, 25, 30, 32, 86, 136, 191, 227; capacity-limitations and, 9–10, 94–95; in Communist China, 2 n.; errors in, 106, 110; "from above" (*od góry*), 88–89, 112–13; "from the bottom up," 87, 136; optimal sequence in, 94–95; parallel method of, 88–89; short-term, in Polish practice, 76–104, 112–14, 119–22, 297–99, 323–24; short-term, models of, 6–33, 335–65; stages of, 1–6, 8, 55; subjective elements in, 2, 30, 55, 102. *See also* Financial plans

Planning by successive approximations

(iterative): and consistency of material balances, 9, 46, 48, 91–98, 158, 336–37; and price-setting, 234–36

Planning Commission (State Commission for Economic Planning until 1956; later, Planning Commission of Council of Ministers), 7, 9, 11–12, 16, 30, 43, 48, 66, 163, 171, 188; balancing departments of, 79, 87; organization of, 78–79, 142, 158, 263, 265, 296; reforms of *1956*, 296–97; role in planning process, 84–89, 90, 93, 96–101, 113, 142, 151, 153, 157, 203, 294, 319–21; role in price-setting, 207, 220–22, 231–39, 241; suggested reforms in, 266

Planning commissions of voivodships and counties, 82, 265. *See also* Voivodships

Planning methods, changes in, 87–89, 135–36, 296–99, 323–24

Planning schedule, 86–89

Plans: execution of, 55, 101, 104–12, 140; monthly, 305; quarterly, 105, 120, 142, 173, 305; relation to reality, 11, 30, 75; tautness of, 2, 30, 33, 102, 108; versions of, 23, 39, 87–88, 92, 95, 105. *See also* Cost planning; Financial plans; Five-Year Plans; Long-term planning; National Economic Plan; Perspective plan; Six-Year Plan

Plant (factory) councils (*rady zakładowe*), 270, 308–09

Plants (*zakłady*), as parts of enterprises, 81, 203

Plastics, prices of, 261, 290

Poland, historical and political background, 49–51

"Polish Economic Model," 48, 270, 272, 274, 311, 320; Theses of Commission on, 276–79, 288

Polish economic writings, 56, 266–68, 320

Polish Economists, Second Congress of, 266–68

Polish United Workers' Party—
Congresses: First (*1948*), 57; Second (*1954*), 65, 67, 311; Third (*1959*), 308
First Secretaries, 76 n., 263, 269, 271
organization of, 76–77
policies of, 6, 48, 52, 56, 58, 65, 74, 78, 148–49, 270, 278, 288, 321, 329, 333
publications of, 265–66
role of Party organizations in enterprises, 77, 270, 308–09
statutes of, 309 n.
See also Central Committee . . . ; Politbureau

Polish Workers' Party, 51, 54, 56

Politbureau, of Polish United Workers' Party, 76, 159, 271

Political parties (in Poland), 51–52. *See also* Polish United Workers' Party; Socialist Party

Political repression, 52, 56, 74, 273

Population of Poland, 51; agricultural, 50, 60, 159 n.; urban, 63, 72, 125

"Positive price differences," 205–06

Power industry, 60, 64

Poznan riots, 68, 268–69, 312

Pressures (administrative), of higher on lower organs, 6, 275, 314

Price differences: account of, 194, 204; in foreign trade, 206. *See also* "Positive price differences"

Price reforms—
and coordination of plans, 275
of building materials, of *January 1957*, 280
of producer goods, *1948–50*, 139, 187, 222–24, 241; of *1953*, 224–28, 242–43; of *1956*, 188, 217, 231–40, 246 n.; of *July 1960*, 278–79, 288–93, 330

Prices—
of close substitutes, 244, 248–49, 260–61
"commercial," 192–93, 195, 210
of consumer goods, in planning model, 16, 17. *See also* Price-setting for consumer goods; Retail prices
"controlled," 192
of construction works, 215–18, 280
delivered, 204, 213
domestic, of imports, 206
during German Occupation, 191–92
of fabricated products, 225, 229, 236, 292
on free markets, 69–70, 73, 193, 260, 284
of housing, 212, 217
implicit or "shadow," 28, 47 n.
negative, 259 n.
in Poland, and world-market prices, 248–49, 260–61, 278–83, 288, 290–91
in private trade, 54, 116, 126
of producer goods: fixed for number of years, 135, 220, 283–84; and investment calculations, 145, 169–70, 280; relation to fixed prices, 200–02; relation to prices of consumer goods, 40, 232–33, 278, 292; and relative scarcities, 245, 247–48, 279, 284, 293; "rigid," 147

and quality of materials, 241, 243
of raw materials and semifabricates, 195–96, 228–30, 279, 283, 289
reflecting future scarcities, 191, 261, 284, 286
relation to prewar, 192, 194
relation to variable costs, 283–84
of services, 209–10
"stable," 192–94
uniformity of, 83, 196, 204–06, 213–15, 218

Price-setting—
administrative responsibility for, 221–22
for consumer goods, 1, 39–40, 191, 205–10, 284, 292
for investment goods, to encourage investments, 194, 220, 224 n., 229, 292
for producer goods, 1, 5, 166 n., 204–05, 220–50; and administrative convenience, 219, 223–24, 229, 260, 284; demand-oriented, 241, 245; to insulate consumers' costs from quality of deliveries, 247, 249–50; to stimulate output of products in demand, 242; to induce substitution, 194, 221, 242, 244, 254–61, 279–80, 290; organization of work on, 224–25; supply-and-demand elements in, 284. *See also* Prices of producer goods
theory of, 41–47, 241–62, 282–89

Price stability, and convenience of planners, 191, 220–21, 283

Price system: accounting and control functions of, 48, 190–91, 249–50, 273, 283, 287; aggregation function of, 48, 190–91, 201, 218, 287; "automatism" of, 46–47, 275–76, 278; and bonuses, 178; guidance function of, 5, 39–48, 69, 146–47, 191, 198, 240, 243, 250, 268, 275–76, 330–31; and incentives, 181, 205, 268; influence on producers' decisions, 188, 190, 240, 279; and operative rules of enterprises, 39; relation to efficient outputs, 40–43, 46, 47 n., 220, 250, 261, 286, 330; role of in planned economy, 11, 47, 190, 268. *See also* Economic calculation

Price trends, of consumer goods, 49, 69, 73, 207

Priority of central directives, 82, 142, 173

Priority scale: of economic sectors, 2–4, 6, 8, 18, 20–21, 37, 75, 91, 98–101, 109–10, 113; and investment planning, 61, 66, 73, 146–47, 152–53

Private agriculture, 59, 82, 91, 159 n., 328–29; size and productivity of farms in, 329

Private industry, 4, 53, 54, 82, 211

Private sector: government discrimination against, 53–54; links with socialized sector, 101, 193–94, 218, 296; in planning system, 1, 53, 122, 124, 216

Private trade: retail, 54, 123–24, 126, 315, 327; wholesale, 53–54. See also Peasant market

Processing costs, foreign-exchange content of, 167

Procurement centrals, 83, 90, 203–04, 265 n.

Procurement prices (ceny zaopatrzeniowe), 210–11

Procurement (supply) problems, of enterprises, 83, 109–13, 269–70, 323. See also Production breakdowns; Shortages of materials

Procurement-technical plan: long-term, 157 n.; short-term, 86–89, 92, 135, 323–24

Producer goods sector, growth of, 55, 60, 74, 313, 325. See also Heavy industry

Production—
breakdowns, due to materials shortages, 99, 269–70, 276
costs, structure of, 69
function, of consumers of materials, 46, 249–50
possibilities surface, 11, 19, 22, 43–45, 254–55, 351–52
processes: alternative, 9, 11, 12, 14 n., 23–33, 38, 99–100, 113–14, 163–64, 170, 242, 285; combination of, 27–28, 32; rays to represent, 26–28; unique, in planning model, 12–22, 25–27, 34–35, 349–58

Productive sectors, in Marxist terminology, 118, 127

Productivity, average, of producer goods, and their relative prices, 242, 245–48

"Profitability coefficient," 162. See also Interest rate on investment projects; Return, internal rates of

Profit incentives, 178–81, 186, 243, 275, 277, 303–04, 306

Profit maximization, 39, 45, 47

Profits of enterprises: planned, 179–82, 184, 197, 204–05, 295, 303; left at disposal of enterprises, 128–29, 154, 178, 182, 197; taxes and levies on, 117–18, 128–29, 137, 140, 182–83, 197, 295

Profits: of individual ministries, 230; and losses, and volume of output, 205

"Prohibition by use," 101, 188

Projections of steel requirements, 158 n.

Project-making, 150–52, 154, 161

Project-making organizations (biura projektowe), 30, 57, 150–53, 154 n., 163, 169, 215, 300

Provinces. See Voivodships

Purchasing power of population, planning of, 17, 115–16. See also Balance of incomes and outlays; Personal incomes

Purchasing-power parity of zloty and U.S. dollar, 166

Quality controls, 174–75

Railroads, state ownership of, 50. See also Transportation system

Railroad tariffs, 233–34, 238, 291

Rationing—
of credit, 138
of consumer goods: abolition of, 69–71, 207, 218, 226–27; formal, 2, 39, 52, 116, 193; informal (queuing, etc.), 63 n., 116, 139, 208
of housing, 209
of producer goods, 76, 101, 107, 112, 277, 297, 323–24; and price-setting theory, 5, 47, 250, 254–60, 293, 330; and powers of the bureaucracy, 305, 307; and the selection of material inputs, 188–89, 224. See also Allocations of materials

Raw-material industries, lags in expansion of, 67, 171, 331

Real incomes of farm population, 314, 316

Real wages, 63, 68, 74, 75, 269, 311–16, 318, 322, 324–25. See also Standard of living

Reconstruction of wartime destruction, 1, 51, 53, 55, 146–47

Recoupment period, 160–62

Recovered Territories (post-German), 51–52, 119

Regional planning, 79, 82, 333

"Relationing" of producers' prices, 242, 244–49, 290

Rents, controls on, 209

Requests for materials, inflated, 5, 108, 294

Research institutes, 300

"Reserves" (slack): in draft-plans of organizations, 88, 95, 98, 177, 320–21; in

"Reserves" (continued)
  planning production capacity, 151,
  314; in production, 275
Reserves, unallocated supplies, 96, 104,
  108
Resolution of shortages in draft-balances,
  98–101
Resource endowment, adaptation of
  plans to, 38
Restrictive regulation, 101
Retail market (state and cooperative
  shops), 125, 327–28; sales in, 123, 125,
  131, 323, 327; as source of supplies for
  socialized enterprises, 108; structure
  of demand in, 327–28
Retail prices, 206, 208, 211–12, 292–93,
  318; general reductions in, 137, 140,
  328. See also Prices of consumer goods;
  Price-setting, consumer goods
Return on investment projects, internal
  rate of, 146, 161. See also "Profitability
  coefficient"
Return, net, in foreign currency, 166
Revisionism, struggle against, 320–21
Revisions in yearly plans, 95, 105. See
  also Plans, versions of
Rubber industry, 60
Rumania, 332
Rural markets, 126 n.

Salaries of managing personnel, 176
Sales centrals. See Commercial centrals
Sales of enterprises, consolidated by min-
  istry, 117–18, 133
Sales offices (biura sprzedaży), 81, 90, 109,
  178, 197–98
Saving, personal, 70, 117–18, 128
Saving and investment, aggregate, 127–29
Savings banks (P.K.O.), 117–18
Scarcity indicators in physical planning,
  11, 23, 28, 361
"Secondary distribution of incomes," as
  tool of national income analysis, 129
Security Police (U.B.), 268, 271–72
Sejm (Polish Parliament), 53, 77, 135,
  144, 265, 296
Sellers' market, for producer goods, 111,
  215
Semifabricates, in balancing process, 95
Service life of equipment in investment
  calculations, 162–63
Services, in national income, 127–30
Shortages: of component parts, 107, 113;
  of materials, 4, 66–68, 107–08, 110–12,
  113, 146–47, 169, 323–24. See also Pro-
  duction breakdowns

Silesia, 49, 51, 81, 119, 235
"Simple relation," as basis for price-
  setting, 246
Simultaneous equations and the coordination of material balances, 9, 335, 346,
  362, 364
Six-Year Plan, 37–38, 56–68, 69, 84, 139,
  187, 201–02, 266, 327; fulfillment of,
  58, 60, 63–64, 67–68, 71, 120, 312; initial
  and final targets, 58; preparation of,
  150–51; revisions in, 57–58, 150, 170–
  71, 269; statistical results of, 59–62
Social and cultural outlays in state
  budget, 132, 135. See also Budget
Social security payments, 117, 122–23
Socialist Party, in Poland, 51, 54, 56, 76
Socialized sector, 54, 61. See also Nationalization
Soviet aid to Poland, 54, 313
Soviet bloc: coordination of development plans in, 158, 332; Poland's trade
  with, 291, 330; prices in trade within,
  165 n., 291
Soviet development and Polish planning, 267, 274
Soviet licenses for producing Polish
  equipment, 65 n.
Soviet model, influence on Polish plan-
  ning, 1, 48, 55–56, 95, 103, 138 n., 202,
  222 n., 263, 274
Soviet prices, and Polish price-setting,
  248–49, 291
Soviet science, Polish attitude toward, 267
Soviet Union: planning in, 11, 23, 31, 55,
  67, 116; political events in, and Poland, 5, 65, 263, 331; and Poland's Recovered Territories, 51–52; relations
  with Poland, 51–52, 271; role in Polish
  Six-Year Plan, 57
Soviet War Communism, 52
Specialized banks, 117, 203
Stalinists, 270 n., 271
Standard of living, in Poland, 51, 53, 312;
  comparisons with Western Europe,
  157; of peasants, 53, 73. See also Real
  wages
Standard project, in investment calcula-
  tions, 160–61
Standardization, 3, 243
State Commission for Economic Plan-
  ning. See Planning Commission
State controls, in prewar Poland, 50
State Council (Rada Państwa), 77
State farms (P.G.R.), 73
State Price Commission, 207, 221, 292
Statistics, available to planners. See In-

formation available to central planners

Steel: output, 58, 312, 325; supply and stocks of, 67, 98, 106 n., 108 n., 109–10, 323. *See also* Metallurgical industry; Metallurgical products

Steel mills, 150–51, 202, 229

Stochastic factors, in planning, 35 n., 106–07

Subsidies: of consumer goods, 292; to individual industries, 230, 237–38; in financial system, 182–84, 213; to national economy, 72, 118, 132, 165, 183, 205, 213, 219, 221, 226, 229. *See also* Budget grants; Building materials; Coal mining; Metallurgy

Substitution: in the course of carrying out plans, 30, 31, 32, 174, 187; of labor for capital, 62, 75, 281, 362–64; to mitigate material shortages, 98–100, 114, 165, 323, 339; in planning models, 25–27, 31, 37, 62–63; prompted by price changes, 187–89, 240, 257, 280; in short- and long-run, 285–86; technological possibilities of, 242. *See also* Ersatz materials; Price-setting for producer goods, to stimulate substitution

Sulfuric acid, output, 312, 325

Supply. *See* Procurement

Surplus capacities, in planning, 13, 18, 24–28, 31, 32

"Surplus value," 133, 222 n.

Surpluses: of undesired items, 110–11, 138, 178; and deficits, as scarcity indicators, 11, 17, 25–29, 32, 361

Sweden, 55 n., 280

Synthetic balances: in planning model, 16, 357–58; in planning practice, 85, 116–18, 127, 136, 142, 159

"Synthetic indices," and calculations, 7, 154 n., 160–61

Taxes: on households, 116, 118, 123, 128–29, 132; on private enterprise, 54, 132; on producer goods, 139, 197, 204. *See also* "Positive price differences"; Turnover taxes

Technical-industrial-financial plan, of enterprises, 173, 264, 303, 306, 316

"Technical-organizational ceilings," as obstacles to growth, 155, 156 n.

Technical personnel, supply and planning of, 115, 119

Technological coefficients. *See* Input-output coefficients; Norms, material-technical

Technological progress: in long-term

planning model, 366; planning of, 172–73; in Poland, 6, 36–37, 122, 155–56, 246, 286, 330

Technology, in Polish economy: obsolete elements in, 57, 65; up-to-date and cost of investments, 146

Technology matrix, 9, 15 n., 93–94, 252, 335, 338, 349, 352, 354; characteristic roots of, 253, 337, 339, 343; decomposability of, 18, 21, 36 n., 253, 339, 343, 344 n., 349 n., 354–55, 366; existence of matrix inverses derived from, 339, 347, 355; of sectors not limited by capacity, 341–41

"Teleologists," in Soviet and Polish planning, 55

Terminal stock of capital goods, in long-term planning model, 34–36, 368–69

Terms of trade (rural-urban), 73

Textile industry, 48, 60, 71, 79, 94, 109, 118

Three-sector model, 53

Three-Year Plan of Reconstruction (*1947–49*), 53, 56, 69, 147

Tied sales, 111

Trade bills, financing of, 137

Trade unions, 211, 270, 308–09

Transfer prices (*ceny zbytu*), 38 n., 178, 204, 208, 210. *See also* Prices of producer goods

Transportation: planning of, 96; costs, 213; system, capacity of, 85, 100, 119, 146

Treasury deposits, with National Bank of Poland, 117, 130, 132, 142

Trial-balances, of Planning Commission, 85, 87, 95

Triangularity, of technology matrix, 93, 338, 343

Trust (*zjednoczenie*), 81, 197, 203. *See also* Associations

Trybuna Ludu, and thaw of *1956*, 265–66

Turnover taxes, 39, 61 n., 72, 137, 202, 221; in financial system, 117, 132, 194, 206–07; margins of, 208–09, 292, 327; paid by individual ministries, 230; and the price system, 197, 202, 204–05, 210, 218

Underemployment, in agriculture, 3, 159

Unemployment of labor: in planning model, 13–14, 358, 362–65; before World War II, 49–50; since World War II, 61, 119, 325

United States, loans to Poland, 313, 326
United Workers' Party. *See* Polish United Workers' Party
"Use value" (*wartość użytkowa*), 247–48. *See also* Productivity (average) of producer goods

Value added, 251. *See also* "Accumulation"
"Value-men" (*Wartościowscy*), proposals for reform, 48, 272–74, 284–85
Vertical disintegration, and official index of industrial output, 3, 59 n.
Village Machine Centers (G.O.M.), 272
Voivodships (*województwa*): investment outlays of, 317; Party authorities in, 77, 271; peoples' councils of, 298–99; role of provincial authorities in economic system, 77, 82, 213 n., 269, 298–99. *See also* Peoples' councils, planning commissions

Wage fund: of enterprises, 120–21, 135, 138, 179–80, 264, 295, 304; planning and control of, 16, 85, 115, 120, 137, 140, 277, 293, 321–22; in planning model, 357; total, of socialized sector, 122–23, 317; unplanned excesses in, 122, 138, 316–17
Wage policy, and movement of labor, 1, 115

Wages: categories, in enterprises, 121; increases in, and price-setting, 226–27, 232–33, 237, 293; levels and trends of, 68–69, 70–72, 122, 139, 207, 222, 226–28, 237, 322; paid in kind, 194–95; of skilled workers, 73; structure of, in industry, 73–74
Warehouses, 83, 109, 111, 203, 210
Warsaw Party Committee, 77
Warsaw Subway, lags in construction of, 66 n.
Wartime destruction in Poland, 49–51, 63. *See also* Reconstruction
Waste and efficiency, criticism of, 68, 263, 268–69, 280
Workers' councils, 270–71, 275, 307–10
Workers' self-management, conferences of, 309–10
Wholesale network, 96, 108, 204, 210
Wholesale prices (*ceny hurtowe*), 210. *See also* Prices of producer goods; Transfer prices
Working capital, of enterprises, 72, 130, 132, 137, 179, 182–85, 196–97, 204, 302

Yugoslav model, influence on Poland, 270, 274

Zeran works, 65 n., 270 n.

Yale Studies in Economics

1. RICHARD B. TENNANT. The American Cigarette Industry. A Study in Economic Analysis and Public Policy
2. KENNETH D. ROOSE. The Economics of Recession and Revival. An Interpretation of 1937–38
3. ALLAN M. CARTTER. The Redistribution of Income in Postwar Britain. A Study of the Effects of the Central Government Fiscal Program in 1948–49
4. MORTON S. BARATZ. The Union and the Coal Industry
5. HENRY C. WALLICH. Mainsprings of the German Revival
6. LLOYD G. REYNOLDS AND CYNTHIA H. TAFT. The Evolution of Wage Structure
7. ROBERT TRIFFIN. Europe and the Money Muddle
8. MARK BLAUG. Ricardian Economics. A Historical Study
9. THOMAS F. DERNBURG, RICHARD N. ROSETT, AND HAROLD W. WATTS. Studies in Household Economic Behavior
10. ALBERT O. HIRSCHMAN. The Strategy of Economic Development
11. BELA A. BALASSA. The Hungarian Experience in Economic Planning
12. WALTER C. NEALE. Economic Change in Rural India: Land Tenure and Reform in Uttar Pradesh, 1800–1955
13. JOHN M. MONTIAS. Central Planning in Poland
14. PAUL W. MACAVOY. Price Formation in Natural Gas Fields: A Study of Competition, Monopsony, and Regulation
15. HARRY A. MISKIMIN. Money, Prices, and Foreign Exchange in Fourteenth-Century France
16. HENRY W. BROUDE. Steel Decisions and the National Economy
17. ROBERT M. MACDONALD. Collective Bargaining in the Automobile Industry: A Study of Wage Structure and Competitive Relations